International Trade, Competitive Advantage and Developing Economies

Available research suggests that less developed countries have significant competitive advantage over developed countries in three major areas of international trade: agriculture, textiles and clothing (T&C), and cross-border labor mobility. Incidentally, these are also the trade sectors which experienced widespread protectionist measures, especially in the developed world, for decade after decade. Under the World Trade Organization (WTO), which replaced the General Agreement on Tariff and Trade (GATT) in 1995, many of the restrictions in T&C trade have been phased out, but this sector continues to face much higher tariff and non-tariff barriers than any other manufacturing sector in world economy. The agricultural sector also experienced significant dismantling of deeply entrenched trade barriers under the WTO over the course of the past two decades, but the sector still remains plagued by quite extensive domestic supports, export subsidies, and tariff barriers. At the same time, despite both theoretical expositions and empirical trends pointing to significant potential gains from cross-border labor mobility, the sector remains mired in a complex quagmire of economic and political restrictions around the world. Thus, all three sectors in which less developed countries have exports interests still remain less liberalized than the sectors in which developed countries have exports interests.

This book provides an in-depth and up-to-date scholarly analysis of all three trade sectors—agriculture, T&C and cross-border labor mobility—with a penetrating scrutiny of historical backgrounds and developments, cross-currents of interests and perspectives of both developed and developing countries, and evolving trade patterns and potentials in a more liberalized and globalized world economy. The book also identifies critical economic issues and options for less developed countries in the WTO negotiations for further liberalization of agriculture, T&C, and cross-border labor mobility. This volume will be an important point of reference for students, scholars, and practitioners of international trade, economic development, development economics, and WTO-related issues.

Caf Dowlah is Professor of Economics at the City University of New York, USA.

Routledge studies in the modern world economy

1 **Interest Rates and Budget Deficits**
A study of the advanced economies
Kanhaya L. Gupta and Bakhtiar Moazzami

2 **World Trade after the Uruguay Round**
Prospects and policy options for the twenty-first century
Edited by Harald Sander and András Inotai

3 **The Flow Analysis of Labour Markets**
Edited by Ronald Schettkat

4 **Inflation and Unemployment**
Contributions to a new macroeconomic approach
Edited by Alvaro Cencini and Mauro Baranzini

5 **Macroeconomic Dimensions of Public Finance**
Essays in honour of Vito Tanzi
Edited by Mario I. Blejer and Teresa M. Ter-Minassian

6 **Fiscal Policy and Economic Reforms**
Essays in honour of Vito Tanzi
Edited by Mario I. Blejer and Teresa M. Ter-Minassian

7 **Competition Policy in the Global Economy**
Modalities for co-operation
Edited by Leonard Waverman, William S. Comanor and Akira Goto

8 **Working in the Macro Economy**
A study of the US labor market
Martin F. J. Prachowny

9 **How Does Privatization Work?**
Edited by Anthony Bennett

10 **The Economics and Politics of International Trade**
Freedom and trade: volume II
Edited by Gary Cook

11 **The Legal and Moral Aspects of International Trade**
Freedom and trade: volume III
Edited by Asif Qureshi, Hillel Steiner and Geraint Parry

12 **Capital Markets and Corporate Governance in Japan, Germany and the United States**
Organizational response to market inefficiencies
Helmut M. Dietl

13 **Competition and Trade Policies**
Coherence or conflict
Edited by Einar Hope

14 **Rice**
The primary commodity
A. J. H. Latham

15 **Trade, Theory and Econometrics**
Essays in honour of John S. Chipman
Edited by James C. Moore, Raymond Riezman and James R. Melvin

16 **Who benefits from Privatisation?**
Edited by Moazzem Hossain and Justin Malbon

17 **Towards a Fair Global Labour Market**
Avoiding the new slave trade
Ozay Mehmet, Errol Mendes and Robert Sinding

18 **Models of Futures Markets**
Edited by Barry Goss

19 **Venture Capital Investment**
An agency analysis of UK practice
Gavin C. Reid

20 **Macroeconomic Forecasting**
A sociological appraisal
Robert Evans

21 **Multimedia and Regional Economic Restructuring**
Edited by Hans-Joachim Braczyk, Gerhard Fuchs and Hans-Georg Wolf

22 **The New Industrial Geography**
Regions, regulation and institutions
Edited by Trevor J. Barnes and Meric S. Gertler

23 **The Employment Impact of Innovation**
Evidence and policy
Edited by Marco Vivarelli and Mario Pianta

24 **International Health Care Reform**
A legal, economic and political analysis
Colleen Flood

25 **Competition Policy Analysis**
Edited by Einar Hope

26 **Culture and Enterprise**
The development, representation and morality of business
Don Lavoie and Emily Chamlee-Wright

27 **Global Financial Crises and Reforms**
Cases and caveats
B. N. Ghosh

28 **Geography of Production and Economic Integration**
Miroslav N. Jovanović

29 **Technology, Trade and Growth in OECD Countries**
Does specialisation matter?
Valentina Meliciani

30 **Post-Industrial Labour Markets**
Profiles of North America and Scandinavia
Edited by Thomas P. Boje and Bengt Furaker

31 **Capital Flows without Crisis**
Reconciling capital mobility and economic stability
Edited by Dipak Dasgupta, Marc Uzan and Dominic Wilson

32 **International Trade and National Welfare**
Murray C. Kemp

33 **Global Trading Systems at Crossroads**
A post-Seattle perspective
Dilip K. Das

34 **The Economics and Management of Technological Diversification**
Edited by John Cantwell, Alfonso Gambardella and Ove Granstrand

35 **Before and Beyond EMU**
Historical lessons and future prospects
Edited by Patrick Crowley

36 **Fiscal Decentralization**
Ehtisham Ahmad and Vito Tanzi

37 **Regionalisation of Globalised Innovation**
Locations for advanced industrial development and disparities in participation
Edited by Ulrich Hilpert

38 **Gold and the Modern World Economy**
Edited by MoonJoong Tcha

39 **Global Economic Institutions**
Willem Molle

40 **Global Governance and Financial Crises**
Edited by Meghnad Desai and Yahia Said

41 **Linking Local and Global Economies**
The ties that bind
Edited by Carlo Pietrobelli and Arni Sverrisson

42 **Tax Systems and Tax Reforms in Europe**
Edited by Luigi Bernardi and Paola Profeta

43 **Trade Liberalization and APEC**
Edited by Jiro Okamoto

44 **Fiscal Deficits in the Pacific Region**
Edited by Akira Kohsaka

45 **Financial Globalization and the Emerging Market Economies**
Dilip K. Das

46 **International Labor Mobility**
Unemployment and increasing returns to scale
Bharati Basu

47 **Good Governance in the Era of Global Neoliberalism**
Conflict and depolitization in Latin America, Eastern Europe, Asia and Africa
Edited by Jolle Demmers, Alex E. Fernández Jilberto and Barbara Hogenboom

48 **The International Trade System**
Alice Landau

49 International Perspectives on Temporary Work and Workers
Edited by John Burgess and Julia Connell

50 Working Time and Workers' Preferences in Industrialized Countries
Finding the balance
Edited by Jon C. Messenger

51 Tax Systems and Tax Reforms in New EU Members
Edited by Luigi Bernardi, Mark Chandler and Luca Gandullia

52 Globalization and the Nation State
The impact of the IMF and the World Bank
Edited by Gustav Ranis, James Vreeland and Stephen Kosak

53 Macroeconomic Policies and Poverty Reduction
Edited by Ashoka Mody and Catherine Pattillo

54 Regional Monetary Policy
Carlos J. Rodríguez-Fuentez

55 Trade and Migration in the Modern World
Carl Mosk

56 Globalisation and the Labour Market
Trade, technology and less-skilled workers in Europe and the United States
Edited by Robert Anderton, Paul Brenton and John Whalley

57 Financial Crises
Socio-economic causes and institutional context
Brenda Spotton Visano

58 Globalization and Self Determination
Is the nation-state under siege?
Edited by David R. Cameron, Gustav Ranis and Annalisa Zinn

59 Developing Countries and the Doha Development Round of the WTO
Edited by Pitou van Dijck and Gerrit Faber

60 Immigrant Enterprise in Europe and the USA
Prodromos Panayiotopoulos

61 Solving the Riddle of Globalization and Development
Edited by Manuel Agosín, David Bloom, George Chapelier and Jagdish Saigal

62 Foreign Direct Investment and the World Economy
Ashoka Mody

63 The World Economy
A global analysis
Horst Siebert

64 Production Organizations in Japanese Economic Development
Edited by Tetsuji Okazaki

65 The Economics of Language
International analyses
Edited by Barry R. Chiswick and Paul W. Miller

66 **Street Entrepreneurs**
People, place and politics in local and global perspective
Edited by John Cross and Alfonso Morales

67 **Global Challenges and Local Responses**
The East Asian experience
Edited by Jang-Sup Shin

68 **Globalization and Regional Integration**
The origins, development and impact of the single European aviation market
Alan Dobson

69 **Russia Moves into the Global Economy**
Breaking out
John M. Letiche

70 **The European Economy in an American Mirror**
Barry Eichengreen, Michael Landesmann and Dieter Stiefel

71 **Working Time Around the World**
Trends in working hours, laws, and policies in a global comparative perspective
Jon C. Messenger, Sangheon Lee and Deidre McCann

72 **International Water Treaties**
Negotiation and cooperation along transboundary rivers
Shlomi Dinar

73 **Economic Integration in the Americas**
Edited by Joseph A. McKinney and H. Stephen Gardner

74 **Expanding Frontiers of Global Trade Rules**
The political economy dynamics of the international trading system
Nitya Nanda

75 **The Macroeconomics of Global Imbalances**
European and Asian perspectives
Edited by Marc Uzan

76 **China and Asia**
Economic and financial interactions
Edited by Yin-Wong Cheung and Kar-Yiu Wong

77 **Regional Inequality in China**
Trends, explanations and policy responses
Edited by Shenggen Fan, Ravi Kanbur and Xiaobo Zhang

78 **Governing Rapid Growth in China**
Equity and institutions
Edited by Ravi Kanbur and Xiaobo Zhang

79 **The Indonesian Labour Market**
Shafiq Dhanani, Iyanatul Islam and Anis Chowdhury

80 **Cost–Benefit Analysis in Multi-level Government in Europe and the USA**
The case of EU cohesion policy and of US federal investment policies
Alessandro Ferrara

81 **The Economic Geography of Air Transportation**
Space, time, and the freedom of the sky
John Bowen

82 **Cartelization, Antitrust and Globalization in the US and Europe**
Mark LeClair

83 **The Political Economy of Integration**
Jeffrey Cason

84 **Critical Issues in Air Transport Economics and Business**
Rosario Macario and Eddy Van de Voorde

85 **Financial Liberalisation and Economic Performance**
Luiz Fernando de Paula

86 **A General Theory of Institutional Change**
Shiping Tang

87 **The Dynamics of Asian Financial Integration**
Edited by Michael Devereux, Philip Lane, Park Cyn-young and Wei Shang-jin

88 **Innovative Fiscal Policy and Economic Development in Transition Economies**
Aleksandr Gevorkyan

89 **Foreign Direct Investments in Asia**
Edited by Chalongphob Sussangkarn, Yung Chul Park and Sung Jin Kang

90 **Time Zones, Communications Networks, and International Trade**
Toru Kikuchi

91 **Miraculous Growth and Stagnation in Post-War Japan**
Edited by Koichi Hamada, Keijiro Otsuka, Gustav Ranis and Ken Togo

92 **Multilateralism and Regionalism in Global Economic Governance**
Trade, investment and finance
Edited by Junji Nakagawa

93 **Economic Growth and Income Inequality in China, India and Singapore**
Trends and policy implications
Pundarik Mukhopadhaya, G. Shantakumar and Bhanoji Rao

94 **Foreign Direct Investment in China**
Spillover effects on domestic enterprises
Deng Ziliang

95 **Enterprise Forms and Economic Efficiency**
Capitalist, cooperative and government firms
Kazuhiko Mikami

96 **Diversity and Transformations of Asian Capitalism**
Edited by Boyer, Uemura and Isogai

97 **Knowledge Transfer in the Automobile Industry**
Global–local production networks
Dessy Irawati

98 **Exchange Rates and Foreign Direct Investment in Emerging Asia**
Selected issues and policy options
Ramkishen S. Rajan

99 **Singapore, the Energy Economy**
From the first refinery to the end of cheap oil, 1960–2010
Ng Weng Hoong

100 **China–India Economics**
Challenges, competition and collaboration
Amitendu Palit

101 **Case Studies on Chinese Enterprises**
Edited by Donglin Xia

102 **Argentina's Economic Growth and Recovery**
Michael Cohen

103 **The Korean Labour Market After the 1997 Economic Crisis**
Edited by Joonmo Cho, Richard B. Freeman, Jaeho Keum and Sunwoong Kim

104 **China and India**
The quest for energy resources in the 21st century
Zhao Hong

105 **Beyond the Global Crisis**
Structural adjustments and regional integration in Europe and Latin America
Edited by Lionello Punzo, Carmen Aparecida Feio and Martin Putchet Anyui

106 **The Global Economic Crisis in Latin America**
Impacts and responses
Edited by Michael Cohen

107 **The Processes and Practices of Fair Trade**
Trust, ethics and governance
Edited by Brigitte Granville and Janet Dine

108 **Regional Development through Ecological Business**
Unique cases in Japanese rural regions
Makoto Hirano

109 **Aging and Economic Growth Potentials in the Pacific Region**
Edited by Akira Kohsaka

110 **Crises of Global Economy and the Future of Capitalism**
An insight into the Marx's crisis theory
Edited by Kiichiro Yagi, Nobuharu Yokokawa, Shinjiro Hagiwara and Gary A. Dymski

111 **The Financial History of the Bank for International Settlements**
Kazuhiko Yago

112 **Freight Transport and the Modern Economy**
Michel Savy and June Burnham

113 **Thoughts on Economic Development in China**
Edited by Ma Ying and Hans-Michael Trautwein

114 **China's Ethnic Minorities**
Social and economic indicators
Rongxing Guo

115 **Globalization, Outsourcing and Labour Development in ASEAN**
Shandre Thangavelu and Aekapol Chongvilaivan

116 **The Role of Informal Economies in the Post-Soviet World**
The end of transition?
Colin C Williams, John Round and Peter Rodgers

117 **Demystifying the Chinese Economy Miracle**
The rise and future of relational capitalism
Yongqin Wang

118 **Globalism and Regional Economy**
Edited by Susumu Egashira

119 **Russia's Changing Economic and Political Regimes**
The Putin years and afterwards
Andrey Makarychev and André Mommen

120 **Innovation and Regional Development in China**
Edited by Ingo Liefner and Yehua Dennis Wei

121 **International Trade Negotiations and Domestic Politics**
The intermestic politics of trade liberalization
Edited by Oluf Langhelle

122 **Emerging Knowledge Economies in Asia**
Current trends in ASEAN 5
Edited by Dessy Irawati and Roel Rutten

123 **The Internationalization of the Renminbi**
International Monetary Institute, Renmin University of China

124 **Financial Globalization and Regionalism in East Asia**
Edited by Takuji Kinkyo, Yoichi Matsubayashi and Shigeyuki Hamori

125 **Successful Business Dealings and Management with China Oil, Gas and Chemical Giants**
EurIng. Henry K. H. Wang

126 **State Building and Development**
Edited by Keijiro Otsuka and Takashi Shiraishi

127 **International Economic Development**
Leading issues and challenges
Edited by Fu Lai Tony Yu, Wai Kee Yuen and Diana S. Kwan

128 **Innovation, Globalization and Firm Dynamics**
Lessons for enterprise policy
Edited by Anna Ferragina, Erol Taymoz and Kamil Yilmaz

129 **International Remittance Payments and the Global Economy**
Bharati Basu with James T. Bang

130 **The Open Society and its Enemies in East Asia**
The relevance of the Popperian framework
Edited by Gregory C. G. Moore

131 **The Economics of Knowledge Generation and Distribution**
The role of interactions in the system dynamics of innovation and growth
Edited by Pier Paolo Patrucco

132 **Japan's Aid**
Lessons for economic growth, development and political economy
Edward M. Feasel

133 **The Geographical Transformation of China**
Edited by Michael Dunford and Weidong Lui

134 **The Economics of Cooperative Education**
A practitioners' guide to the theoretical framework and empirical assessment of cooperative education
Yasushi Tanaka

135 **Comparing Post War Japanese and Finnish Economies and Societies**
Edited by Yasushi Tanaka, Toshiaki Tamaki, Jari Ojala and Jari Eloranta

136 **Measuring National Income in the Centrally Planned Economies**
Why the West underestimated the transition to capitalism
William Jefferies

137 **Crises in Europe in the Transatlantic Context**
Economic and political appraisals
Edited by Bruno Dallago and John McGowan

138 **The International Monetary System, Energy and Sustainable Development**
Edited by Sung Jin Kang and Yung Chul Park

139 **Capitalism and the World Economy**
The light and shadow of globalization
Edited by Toshiaki Hirai

140 **Irish Economic Development**
High-performing EU state or serial under-achiever?
Eoin O'Leary

141 **Banking on Equality**
Women, work and employment in the banking sector in India
Supriti Bezbaruah

142 **Poverty, Inequality and Growth in Developing Countries**
Theoretical and empirical approaches
Edited by Atsushi Maki

143 **Decentralization and Infrastructure in the Global Economy**
From gaps to solutions
Edited by Jonas Frank and Jorge Martínez-Vázquez

144 **The Global Commercial Aviation Industry**
Edited by Sören Eriksson and Harm-jan Steenhuis

145 **International Trade, Competitive Advantage and Developing Economies**
How less developed countries are capturing global markets
Caf Dowlah

International Trade, Competitive Advantage and Developing Economies

How less developed countries are capturing global markets

Caf Dowlah

Routledge
Taylor & Francis Group
LONDON AND NEW YORK

First published 2016 by Routledge

2 Park Square, Milton Park, Abingdon, Oxfordshire OX14 4RN
52 Vanderbilt Avenue, New York, NY 10017

Routledge is an imprint of the Taylor & Francis Group, an informa business

First issued in paperback 2020

British Library Cataloguing in Publication Data
A catalogue record for this book is available from the British Library

Library of Congress Cataloging-in-Publication Data
Dowlah, C. A. F.
International trade, competitive advantage and developing economies : how less developed countries are capturing global markets / Caf Dowlah.
pages cm
1. Developing countries–Commerce. 2. Competition–Developing countries. 3. International trade. 4. Competition, International. I. Title.
HF1413.D69 2015
382.09172'4–dc23 2015005691

ISBN: 978-1-138-90357-9 (hbk)
ISBN: 978-0-367-66873-0 (pbk)

Typeset in Times New Roman
by Wearset Ltd, Boldon, Tyne and Wear

Contents

Figures

Tables

Boxes

Preface

This book is a kind of sequel to my last book on WTO-related issues entitled *Backwaters of Global Prosperity* (2004), in which I argued that lack of liberalization of two crucial sectors of exports interests of less developed countries—agriculture and textiles and clothing (T&C)—contributed significantly to marginalization of these countries in the global economy during the period of GATT (1947–1994). This book, in sharp contrast, strikes a more optimistic chord.

Thanks to the Uruguay Round Agreements on these sectors and their faithful implementation under the WTO, agriculture is now more liberalized than ever before, and the T&C sector is currently as liberalized as any other manufacturing sector. As a result, tides seem to be shifting—evidently less developed countries have been making great inroads in global production, exports, and employment in these sectors. This book also focuses on another very important sector of exports interest to less developed countries: global labor mobility. Thus, a single volume provides in-depth coverage to all three crucial sectors—agriculture, T&C and cross-border labor mobility—in which less developed countries enjoy a competitive advantage in the contemporary world economy.

I have been working on these sectors for more than two decades, and many colleagues around the world advised me over the years to prepare such a comprehensive volume for university students, policy makers and transnational business executives to help them understand international trade, trade policies, and WTO-related issues from the perspectives of less developed countries. This is my earnest harvest of such an effort, and I thank them all for their ideas and encouragement.

The project took several years for me to complete, and, in the course of it, I received assistance from numerous sources. While I am grateful to all, I owe very special thanks to the US Fulbright Commission for granting me a Fulbright Visiting Scholar award, and to my employer—the City University of New York—for granting me a research grant to work on the project.

I am also grateful to many prominent scholars around the world who kept breaking new frontiers in the area of international trade policies and WTO-related issues. The book borrows lavishly from many of their theoretical and empirical works, of course, with due acknowledgment. I am, however, profoundly grateful to Professors Bernard Hoekman of the European University Institute, David Sumner of University of California-Davis, Gary Hufbauer of the Petersen Institute of International Economics, and Nicholas Hope of Stanford University for very graciously reviewing draft chapters of the book, and for their extremely constructive suggestions which significantly contributed in improving the content, analysis, and message of the book.

I am also grateful to the publisher of the book—Routledge—and its commissioning editor Emily Kindleysides for taking a keen interest in the project and guiding me through the publication process. I owe very special thanks to Laura Johnson for her friendly editorial assistance, to Ann King for her excellent copy-editing of the manuscript, and to Hannah Riley for her skillful production of the book.

Finally, none of the above is responsible for the contents of this treatise or for any inaccuracies it may contain. The responsibility is mine alone. The time and toil dedicated to the project will be worthwhile if the book helps readers to develop a compassionate understanding of international trade issues and policies for improving the shares of less developed nations in global prosperity in the twenty-first century. After all, if it is possible to make the whole world better off, why settle for less?

Caf Dowlah
Forest Hills, New York
February 7, 2015

Acronyms and abbreviations

AAP	Agreement on Anti-Dumping Procedures
ACP	African, Caribbean and Pacific countries
ACRE	Average Crop Revenue Election
AGOA	Africa Growth and Opportunity Act
AMP	Adverse Market Payments
AMS	Aggregate Measure of Support
APEC	Association of Asia-Pacific Economic Cooperation
ARC	Agricultural Risk Coverage
ASCM	Agreement on Subsidies and Countervailing Measures
ASEAN	Association of South-East Asian Nations
ATC	Agreement on Textiles and Clothing
CAFTA	US-Central America Free Trade Agreement
CAP	Common Agricultural Policy
CBD	Convention of Biodiversity
CCPs	Counter-Cyclical Programs
CIG	Conservation Innovation Grants
CRP	Conservation Reserve Program
CSE	Consumer Support Estimate
CSFP	Commodity Supplemental Food Program
CSP	Conservation Stewardship Program
DDR	Doha Development Round
DMSP	Dairy Market Stabilization Program
DPPSP	Dairy Product Price Support System
DSB	Dispute Settlement Body
DSU	Dispute Settlement Understanding
EBA	Everything but Arms
EC	European Community
ECOSOC	Economic and Social Council
EEC	European Economic Community
EPZ	Export Processing Zone
EQIP	Environmental Quality Incentive Program
EU	European Union
EUROSTAT	Statistical Office of the European Communities

FAO	Food and Agriculture Organization
FAOSTAT	GAO Statistical Database
FDI	Foreign Direct Investment
FMDP	Foreign Market Development Program
FTAA	Free Trade Agreement of the Americas
G7	Canada, France, Germany, Italy, Japan, United States, United Kingdom
G8	G7 plus Russian Federation
GATS	General Agreement on Trade in Services
GATT	General Agreement on Tariff and Trade
GDP	Gross Domestic Product
GSM	Export Credit Guarantee Program
GSP	Generalized System of Preferences
HS	Harmonized System
IDA	International Development Association
ILO	International Labor Organization
IMF	International Monetary Fund
IPR	Intellectual Property Rights
ITC	International Trade Center
ITCB	International Textiles and Clothing Bureau
ITO	International Trade Organization
LAC	Latin America and Caribbean
LDC	Least Developed Countries
MAI	Multilateral Agreement on Investment
MEA	Multilateral Environmental Agreement
MENA	Middle East and North Africa
Mercosur	Argentina, Brazil, Paraguay and Uruguay
MFA	Multi-Fiber Arrangement
MFN	Most Favored Nation
MILC	Milk Income Loss Contract Program
MPS	Market Price Support
MTO	Multilateral Trade Organization
MVA	Manufacturing Value Added
NAC	Nominal Assistance Coefficient
NAFTA	North American Free Trade Agreement
NAMA	Non-Agricultural Market Access
NFIDC	Net Food-Importing Developing Country
NPC	Nominal Protection Coefficient
NTBs	Non-Tariff Barriers
NTMs	Non-Tariff Measures
OBM	Own Brand Manufacture
ODI	Overseas Development Institute
ODM	Own Design Manufacture
OECD	Organization of Economic Cooperation and Development
OEM	Original Equipment Manufacture

PPMs	Processes and Production methods
PSA	Pre-Shipment Inspection
PSE	Producer Support Estimates
QRS	Quantitative Restrictions
QUAD	Canada, EU, Japan and the US
R&D	Research and Development
S&D	Special and Differential Treatment
SCM	Subsidies and Countervailing Measures
SITC	Standard International Trade Classification
SPSS	Sanitary and Phyto-Sanitary Measures
SSA	Sub-Saharan Africa
SURE	Supplemental Revenue Assistance Payments
T&C	Textiles and Clothing
TBT	Technical Barriers to Trade
TF	Trade Facilitation
TFP	Total Factor Productivity
TNC	Trade Negotiations Committee
TPRB	Trade Policy Review Body
TRI	Trade Restrictive Index
TRIM	Trade-Related Investment Measures
TRIPS	Trade-Related Aspects of Intellectual Property Rights
TRQ	Tariff Rate Quotas
TSE	Total Support Estimate
UN	United Nations
UNCED	United Nations Conference on Environment and Development
UNCTAD	United Nations Conference for Trade and Development
UNDESA	United Nations Department of Economic and Social Affairs
UNDP	United Nations Development Program
UNEP	United Nations Environment Program
UNIDO	United Nations Industrial Development Organization
UR	Uruguay Round
URAA	Uruguay Round Agreement on Agriculture
US	United States
USAID	United States Agency for International Development
USDA	United States Department of Agriculture
WHO	World Health Organization
WMO	World Migration Organization
WTO	World Trade Organization

1 Introduction

An overview of the international trading system

Introduction

International trade did exist since time immemorial, but it may safely be argued that it had never been more liberalized, less discriminatory, and more globalized than it is today. If history is any guide, even up until the eighteenth century international trade regimes were driven by imperial, colonial, and mercantilist forces. Moreover, such trade regimes, by and large, were coercive, restrictive, and discriminatory in character, and, more often than not, driven by beggar-thy-neighbor policies. It was in the nineteenth century that the world began to witness a discernible move toward bilateral trade treaties that embraced greater openness and liberalization (WTO, 2011, 48–51). Such moves were, however, either halted or reversed by the powerful protectionist developments in the 1870s and during the interregnum between the two World Wars. It is only since World War II that the world has been witnessing a sustained development toward a more liberalized international trading system, which incessantly propels greater integration and interdependence of economies and nations around the world.

Much of the credit for the thrust for such a powerful and far-reaching development may be attributed to the Bretton Woods Conference of 1944,[1] in which the victorious world leaders envisaged a new world economic order with three key pillars: the International Monetary Fund (IMF), which would provide global exchange rate stability, the International Bank for Reconstruction and Development (the World Bank), which would provide reconstruction capital for war-ravaged countries, and the International Trade Organization (ITO), which would oversee the administration of a more liberalized multilateral trading order. While the first two of the proposed institutions of the new global governance structure came into being, the ITO could not be realized—thanks to vigorous opposition from US Congress.[2]

With the collapse of the ITO initiative, the General Agreement on Tariffs and Trade (GATT) emerged as a temporary platform for governing international trade. The origin of the GATT may be traced to the ongoing deliberations among the US and some of its allies since 1945 to boost international trade by reversing the devastating legacy of protectionist measures of the 1930s (Hoekman, 2002; Eichengreen and Irwin, 2010). These countries signed the original GATT agreement on October 30, 1947 in Geneva, with the objectives of raising living standards across the world by ensuring full utilization of global resources, increasing volumes of real income and effective demand, and expanding the production and exchange of goods and services under a more liberalized trade regime (GATT, 1972).[3]

The GATT was founded on the twin principles of reciprocity and non-discrimination. While the principle of reciprocity envisaged mutually advantageous arrangements among contracting parties for reciprocal reductions in tariff bindings, the principle of non-discrimination envisaged uniform rights and obligations of all contracting parties. In operational terms, the latter meant the Most-Favored Nation (MFN) treatment of all contracting parties of GATT; in other words, multilateralization of reciprocal tariff reductions that contracting parties might negotiate bilaterally (Bagwell and Staiger, 2004, 54–58). Although 11 of the 23 signatories were developing countries, the original GATT agreement contained no special provision for them.[4] The temporary GATT, thus established to reduce trade barriers through bilateral agreements, survived for almost five decades, before it was absorbed into the World Trade Organization in 1995.

Multilateral negotiations under the GATT

Over the course of its existence, the GATT (1947–1994) provided a global platform for rule-based trade regimes, settled scores of international trade disputes, and achieved a total of eight rounds of multilateral trade negotiations (see Table 1.1). The first GATT round established the GATT itself—it guaranteed MFN status to all contracting parties on a reciprocal basis and agreed on concessions to some 45,000 tariff lines worth $10 billion, one-fifth of global trade at that time. In all, the first five GATT rounds of trade negotiations between 1948 and 1963 succeeded in reducing weighted tariffs by 36 percent. The next three rounds—the Kennedy Round (1964–1967), the Tokyo Round (1973–1979), and the Uruguay Round (1986–1994) brought down tariffs further by another 37 percent, 33 percent, and 38 percent, respectively.

The GATT rounds of trade negotiations also addressed non-tariff barriers (NTBs). The Kennedy Round, for example, hammered out agreements on customs valuation and anti-dumping issues, and the Tokyo Round further widened the GATT coverage on NTBs by reaching agreements on subsidies and countervailing measures, technical barriers to trade (TBT), import licensing procedures, anti-dumping laws, and government procurement. Another lasting contribution of the Tokyo Round was the 'Enabling Clause,' which allowed GATT contracting parties to grant favorable tariff and non-tariff treatments to the developing countries under what came to be known as the Special and Differential Treatment (SDT) measures. With each round of trade negotiations, up until the Uruguay Round, the GATT contributed to the further liberalization of the international trading system, but many countries still continued to use bilateral agreements to impose voluntary export restraints (VERs), quota restrictions (QRS), and other such trade-distorting measures.

Table 1.1 The GATT negotiating rounds, 1947 to 1994, and major achievements

GATT rounds	*Year*	*No. of member countries*	*Value of trade (US$ billion)*	*No. of tariff concessions*	*Weighted tariff reduction*
Geneva	1947	23	10	45,000	
Annecy	1949	33	–	5,000	
Torquay	1950	34	–	8,700	
Geneva	1956	22	2.5	–	
Dillon	1960–1961	45	4.9	4,400	–36 (1948–1963)
Kennedy	1962–1967	48	40	–	–37
Tokyo	1973–1979	99	300	–	–33
Uruguay	1986–1993	118	–	–	–38

Source: Author's compilation from WTO website.

GATT discrimination against the exports interests of developing countries

Multilateral trade negotiations of the first seven rounds of the GATT, prior to the Uruguay Round (1986–1994), however, concentrated primarily on the reduction of tariffs and NTBs to manufactures only. Moreover, these negotiations were participated in mainly by industrialized developed countries. Although some developing countries took part in these negotiations, they merely served as onlookers—since only a few of them were manufacturing exporters. Many developing countries were not even members of the GATT at that time—37 of them joined GATT in 1987, following the launch of the Uruguay Round. Moreover, most of the developing countries, prior to the Uruguay Round, swam against trade liberalization—being early in the industrialization process, they were more interested in seeking legitimacies for sheltering domestic production under import substitution, infant industry protection, and such other protectionist agendas.[5]

Second, up until the Kennedy Round, all tariff negotiations were bilateral—they were based on reciprocal, product-by-product exchange of concessions of manufactures. Developing countries, being primarily agricultural commodity exporters, had little to gain from such negotiations or concessions. The Kennedy Round, for example, brought down tariffs by 50 percent for manufacturing goods, but that affected 26 percent of goods of exports interest to developing countries, compared to 36 percent of goods of exports interest to industrialized countries. Similarly, the Tokyo Round's tariff reductions affected 26 percent of goods of export interests to developing countries, compared with 33 percent for the developed countries (Hudec, 1987).

Third, while most of the manufacturing tariffs, in which developed countries had exports interests, crumbled with successive rounds of GATT negotiations, tariffs and NTBs to trade in textiles and clothing (T&C), a manufacturing sector in which developing countries had exports interests, moved in the opposite direction. The GATT Agreement left the T&C out of its jurisdiction by designating it as a 'special case,'[6] apparently with the consideration that developing countries, being principally primary good producers, would be unable to reciprocate in manufacturing trade. As explained in Chapter 3, the underlying motivation for designating the T&C as a 'special case' actually lay with the implications of 'low-cost' imports from less developed countries for employment and economic growth in developed countries. The MFN principle also did not bode well for many developed countries: many chose not to comply with this principle, considering injurious effects of T&C imports on their domestic industries. As a result, and as explained in Chapter 3, highly discriminatory and restrictive trade regimes proliferated in the T&C sector throughout the GATT period, seriously impeding industrialization and economic growth of less developed countries for several decades.

Fourth, agriculture, another area in which developing countries enjoyed competitive advantage, remained almost completely outside the rule-based multilateral trading system throughout the GATT period. As explained in Chapter 2, in the absence of any trade discipline, developed countries faced no difficulty in adopting widespread protectionist measures to insulate domestic agriculture from international competition. A wide variety of instruments were used for such protections, which included market price supports—under which farmers were paid the difference between domestic and international prices; direct supports—under which governments provided product-specific subsidies to domestic producers or consumers; and general agricultural supports—under which governments provided support for agricultural research, training, marketing, and infrastructure. Some developed counties even acquired a competitive advantage in agriculture through massive domestic supports, and exported such subsidized products by depressing international prices. In the absence of any restraints, such protective and trade-distortive measures in agriculture went unchecked for several decades, reaching a peak in the late 1980s.

The Uruguay Round as a watershed event in the multilateral trading system

The Uruguay Round, the final round of multilateral trade negotiations under the GATT, came as a watershed event in the entire history of the global governance of multilateral trade. The seven-year-long negotiations of the Round came to an end in 1994 with the Marrakesh Ministerial Declaration which replaced the GATT itself with a new multilateral trading watchdog called the World Trade Organization (WTO).[7] The WTO Agreement, 'The Final Act Embodying the Results of the Uruguay Round,' brought all trading sectors—agriculture, manufacturing, and services—under the strengthened multilateral trade rules and disciplines of GATT. In scope and magnitude, it far exceeded that of the botched ITO proposal envisaged by the Havana Charter in 1947, and the provisional GATT agreement it replaced. The WTO Agreement incorporated over a dozen agreements in the goods area, in addition to scores of agreements in services, investment, and intellectual property areas, including the General Agreement on Trade in Services (GATS), the Trade-Related Intellectual Property Rights (TRIPs), the Trade-Related Investment Measures (TRIMs), and the Dispute Settlement Understanding (DSU).[8]

Coming in the immediate aftermath of the Cold War, the WTO Agreement symbolized the universal triumph of capitalism—as a knock-out victory of free market and free trade over autarchic, nationalistic, or protectionist policies of the past. It also came at a point when scores of developing countries developed greater stakes in global manufacturing trade. Several developing countries, especially the East Asian Tigers, graduated from primary commodities to export-oriented manufactures, and some developing countries, such as Bangladesh, China, Malaysia, Mexico, and Turkey, broke into labor-intensive manufactures. A vibrant, rule-based multilateral trading system thus became more relevant to their exports interests than ever before.

The WTO emerged as a powerful watchdog of multilateral trade

Compared with its predecessor, the WTO also came with a much stronger institutional framework for the monitoring and enforcement of multilateral agreements. While the GATT was a provisional intergovernmental treaty in which signatories were 'contracting parties,' in the WTO the signatories are 'members' who have empowered the WTO to serve as a "regulator of regulatory actions taken by governments that affect trade and the conditions of competition facing imported products on domestic markets" (Hoekman and Kostecki 2001, 37).[9] Unlike the GATT, as Higgott and Weber (2005, 434–455) point out, the WTO advances and consolidates commercial law (*lex mercantoria*), which defines global governance increasingly in terms of the logic of market access. Under this evolving framework, the WTO aims at achieving the progressive commercialization of many public services, which were previously subject to regulation premised on the notion of the public goods provision to all.[10] Moreover, unlike the Breton Woods institutions such as the World Bank and the IMF, in which voting rights of members depend on their financial contributions to these institutions, the WTO Agreement grants equal voting rights to all members,[11] and, due to what is called the 'single undertaking' approach, the WTO's decisions are equally binding for all its members.

The new architecture of the global trading system, as envisaged by the WTO, also provides stronger frameworks for the negotiation and implementation of multinational trade agreements, the settlement of international trade disputes, the monitoring of trade policies of member countries, and cooperation with sister organizations, such as the World Bank and the IMF, for greater coherence in global economic policy making. Moreover, unlike its predecessor the GATT, which was under no obligation to hold annual meetings, the WTO is officially responsible for holding a biannual meeting of its top decision-making body, known as the WTO Ministerial. The WTO agreements also commit the institution to greater transparency and accountability in all its deliberations and negotiations. On top of all that, all decisions of the WTO must be reached through a consensus.[12]

The Uruguay Round integrated the textiles and clothing sector into the GATT discipline

The Uruguay Round Agreements also succeeded in sounding a death-knell to the long-standing protectionist regimes in T&C trade that prevailed, even thrived, during the GATT period. As Chapter 3 explains, under what came to be known as the Multi-Fiber Arrangements (MFAs), an elaborate mechanism of quota and non-quota restrictions reigned in the T&C trade up until December 1994. The MFA protocols, put in place for the first time in 1973 on a short-term basis, had been extended five times by 1993, and, each time, quota restraints were further intensified, country and product coverage further enlarged, and additional trade restrictive measures added. By the mid-1980s, more than 70 percent of T&C

products imported to developed countries were subject to quota and non-quota restrictions (UNCTAD, 1986).

The Uruguay Round Agreement on Textiles and Clothing (ATC) called for the progressive phasing out of all MFA restrictions and other discriminatory measures within a period of 10 years, so that at the end of the transitional period, by January 1, 2005, the era of discriminatory and bilateral quota measures could be eliminated completely, and the T&C trade in its entirety would be brought under strengthened GATT rules and discipline. As Chapter 3 explains, the full implementation of the agreement, and thus full integration of the sector into the multilateral discipline, however, did not occur until 2009. The T&C trade is now as free as any other manufacturing trade under the WTO.

The Uruguay Round integrated agriculture into the GATT discipline

Similarly, while successive GATT rounds of multilateral trade negotiations brought down both tariff and non-tariff barriers in manufacturing trade, agricultural trade faced movements in the opposite direction. Farm subsidies and import restrictions proliferated in many developed countries to such an extent that they hugely depressed international farm prices relative to non-farm products, worsening terms of trade for many developing countries (Tyers and Anderson, 1986, 1992). Over time, such restrictions to market access in agricultural products became so widespread that "even the semblance of conformity with GATT obligations was dropped" (Hoda and Gulati, 2007, 15). As Chapter 2 explains, the Uruguay Round Agreement on Agriculture (URAA) brought the agricultural sector under the strengthened GATT discipline for the first time in history. The URAA required WTO members to submit quantitative commitments on a commodity-by-commodity basis for the liberalization of market access, to eliminate or reduce domestic support and export subsidies in agriculture, and granted developed countries up until 2000 and developing countries up until 2004 to implement liberalization commitments. Although the URAA now stands implemented, as Chapter 2 explains, the sector is still not free from many of the protectionist measures which historically plagued international trade in this sector.

The WTO Agreement also brought the services sector, which currently contributes over 50 percent to global GDP and over 75 percent to the GDPs of high-income countries, into the strengthened GATT discipline for the first time under the General Agreement on Trade in Services (GATS). The WTO acknowledges four modes of supply of services under the GATS: Mode-1: supply of service from the territory of one member to another member, such as international telephone calls; Mode-2: consumption abroad, such as foreign travelers involved in tourism; Mode-3: commercial presence, such as opening a bank branch in another country; and Mode-4: temporary cross-border movement of natural persons in an individual capacity, such as temporary movements of healthcare professionals to deliver services across borders. So far, however, no tangible progress has been made in the WTO negotiations in respect of Mode-4. Instead, as Chapter 4 explains, trade in this sector rather remains mired in complex political, economic, and legal quagmires, although available theoretical expositions as well as empirical evidence suggest that despite growing anti-immigration sentiments across the world, GATS Mode-4 holds the promise of actually opening up a large window of opportunity for the liberalization of temporary cross-border labor mobility by mitigating against controversial effects of permanent or other forms of labor migration (Dowlah, 2012; Winters and Mattoo, 2011; UNCTAD, 2009).

The Doha Development Round

The Doha Development Round—the ninth round of multilateral trade negotiations—was launched in November 2001 at the fourth WTO Ministerial meeting held in Doha (Qatar).[13] The Round came in the immediate aftermath of the September 11 attack on the World Trade Center when the threat to global security propelled the need for a united effort to build a more secure and peaceful world, and to push forward Millennium Development Goals set by the United Nations Millennium Summit in 2000 to halve world poverty by 2015 (Ismail, 2009). The Round was also set against the backdrop of the fiasco of the Seattle Ministerial of the WTO in 1999. The Seattle debacle, among other things, brought to the surface a more assertive role of the developing countries in the WTO negotiations. Most of the developing country members of the WTO were unhappy with the lack of transparency in the WTO negotiations, as unelected and unaccountable international bureaucrats formulated policies and made decisions infringing the sovereignty of national governments. They also resented the so-called Green Room process of negotiations through which powerful countries often passed off their own decisions and priorities as those of the whole WTO. They also vehemently opposed any new round of negotiations, as proposed by the United States and the United Kingdom, before the implementation of the earlier agreements (Dowlah, 2004, 29–50).

Largely responding to evolving developments, the Doha Round promised to focus more closely on the needs and interests of developing countries, something that had been grossly compromised in previous rounds when developing countries arguably played passive and defensive roles. The mandate of the Doha Round included a wide range of subjects including the further liberalization of agriculture, improving market access to industrial goods, services trade facilitation, strengthening of the WTO rules relating to trade remedies, and mushrooming proliferations of the regional trade agreements. Agricultural liberalization was billed as the cornerstone of the DDR—as the Uruguay Round mandated further negotiations on the long-term objective of substantial reductions in agricultural support and protection by 2000, one year before the end of the implementation period of URAA for developed countries. The primary focus of DDR, however, remained broad-based development—reducing trade barriers in order to expand global economic growth, development, and opportunity, especially poverty reduction in less developed countries.

The Doha Round, now in its thirteenth year, still continues, however, making it the longest round of multilateral negotiations under the GATT–WTO. Over

Table 1.2 The WTO ministerial conferences and major achievements

Ministerials	*Key achievements*
First Ministerial: Singapore, December 9–13, 1996	Participated in by more than 120 WTO members, the Ministerial, among others, reviewed the first two years of WTO activities and the implementation of the Uruguay Round Agreements. The Ministerial called for: (1) full implementation of the Agreement on Textiles and Clothing (ATC) and use of safeguard measures as sparingly as possible; (2) improved market access in services trade—in financial services, movement of natural persons, maritime transport services, and basic telecommunications; (3) completing negotiations on financial services, maritime transport services, and professional services in accountancy by 1997; and (4) undertaking more analytical work on emergency safeguards measures, and government procurement in services and subsidies. The Ministerial rejected the use of labor standards for protectionist purposes and expressed commitment to the observance of internationally recognized core labor standards as provided by the International Labor Organization (ILO), and committed to address the problem of marginalization of the LDCs and greater coordination with other multilateral agencies in providing technical assistance to the LDCs.
Second Ministerial: Geneva (Switzerland), May 19–20, 1998	The Ministerial commemorated the fiftieth anniversary of the multilateral trading system under the GATT-WTO, and recalled its contribution toward economic growth, employment, and stability through the liberalization and expansion of trade. The Ministerial also adopted a declaration on global electronic commerce.
Third Ministerial: Seattle (Washington), November 30 to December 3, 1999	Ended in fiasco.
Fourth Ministerial: Doha (Qatar), November 9–14, 2001	The Ministerial committed to long-term objective to establish a fair and market-oriented trading system in agriculture by correcting and preventing restrictions and distortions in world agricultural markets, and launched the Doha Development Round (DDR) for comprehensive negotiations aimed at substantial improvements in agricultural market access, reductions, and phasing out of all forms of export subsidies, and reduction in trade-distorting domestic supports. It also committed to continue special and differential treatment (SDT) for the developing countries and enable them to take care of their development needs, including food security and rural development, and non-trade concerns. The Ministerial also took note of the progress made by the negotiators in respect of Article XIX of the General Agreement on Trade in Services (GATS). More on the DDR in the main text.

continued

Table 1.2 Continued

Ministerials	*Key achievements*
Fifth Ministerial: Cancun (Mexico), September 10–14, 2003	The Ministerial reaffirmed its commitment to the mandate on agriculture of the Doha Declaration, and asked for a Special Session of the Committee on Agriculture to intensify work to translate the Doha objectives into reform modalities on market access, export competition, and domestic support. The Ministerial also instructed the Trade Negotiations Committee (TNC) to consult with the Negotiating Groups on Agriculture and Non-Agricultural Market Access (NAMA) to address the impact of the distortions that existed in the trade of cotton, man-made fibers, and textiles and clothing to ensure comprehensive consideration of the sector. The Director-General of the WTO was instructed to consult with the other international organizations to effectively direct existing programs and resources toward diversification of the economies where cotton accounts for the major share of their GDP. The Ministerial also asked for a Special Session of the Council for Trade in Services to conclude negotiations on rule-making under GATS Articles VI:4, X, XIII, and XV.
Sixth Ministerial: Hong Kong-China, December 13–18, 2005	The Ministerial reaffirmed its commitment to the mandate on agriculture as set out in the Doha Declaration and welcomed the progress made by the Special Session of the Committee on Agriculture since 2004. The Ministerial also reviewed three bands for reductions in Final Bound Total Aggregate Measure of Support (AMS) and in the overall cut in trade-distorting domestic support as well as in product-specific and non-product-specific *de minimis* limits, and pledged to review Green box criteria to ensure that programs of developing country members that caused no more than minimal trade distortion were effectively covered. The Ministerial also emphasized the progressive and parallel elimination of all forms of export subsidies and disciplines on all export measures by 2013, market consistency in respect of export credits and export credit guarantees or insurance programs, and elimination of trade-distorting practices of state-trading enterprises (STEs). In respect of market access, the Ministerial noted the progress made on *ad valorem* equivalents and adopted four bands for structuring tariff cuts, and recognized the treatment of sensitive products, taking into account the criteria of food security, livelihood security, and rural development, and granted developing countries recourse to a special safeguard mechanism based on import quantity and price triggers. The Ministerial also made a commitment to eliminate all forms of export subsidies for cotton in developed countries by 2006, and called upon the developed countries to grant duty- and quota free access for cotton exports from the LDCs. The Ministerial also reaffirmed all elements of the NAMA Framework adopted by the WTO General Council in August 2004 and adopted the Swiss Formula with coefficients to reduce or as appropriate eliminate tariffs, tariff peaks, high tariffs, and tariff escalation, in particular on products of export interests to the developing countries. The Ministerial also committed itself to take into account the special needs and interests of developing countries. With regard to the services trade, the Ministerial reaffirmed the objectives and principles stipulated in the GATS, the Doha Declaration, the Guidelines and Procedures for the Negotiations on Trade in Services adopted by the Special Session of the Council for Trade in Services in March 2001, and the Modalities for the Special Treatment for LDC members in the Negotiations on Trade in Services adopted in September 2003 and August 2004.

Seventh Ministerial: Geneva (Switzerland), December 2009	The conference was not designed for any negotiations, but members stressed the importance of concluding the Doha Round by 2010. The Ministerial also agreed on a moratorium not to charge import duties on electronic commerce, and not to bring 'non-violation' cases to the WTO dispute settlement process until the next Ministerial, to be held in 2011.
Eighth Ministerial: Geneva (Switzerland), December 2011	The Ministerial adopted a waiver to enable developing and developed country members to provide preferential treatment to services and service suppliers of LDCs in order to promote their trade in those sectors and modes of supply that are of particular interest to them. The concessions came in accordance with Article XIX:3 of the GATS, and in furtherance of the modalities established in September 2003 and the Hong Kong Ministerial Declaration of 2005. This waiver, scheduled to last for 15 years, releases developing and developed country members from their legal obligation to provide non-discriminatory treatment to all trading partners so that they can grant preferential treatment to the LDCs. In addition, the Ministerial called for new approaches to revive the Doha Round negotiations, especially in line with the 'Revised Draft Modalities for Agriculture.'
Ninth Ministerial: Bali (Indonesia), December 2013	The Ministerial adopted what is called the 'Bali Package.' Salient features of the package are explained in the text.

Source: Author's compilation from WTO website.

the years it has experienced sporadic periods of progress, stalemates and setbacks, and has even often been declared clinically dead.[14] At the Eighth WTO Ministerial, held in Geneva in 2011, acknowledging an impasse in the DDR negotiations, WTO members emphasized new approaches to revive the negotiations.[15] In 2012, the revived negotiation process centered on a limited agenda to pick what was called 'low-hanging fruit,' which eventually led to an agreement at the Ninth WTO Ministerial, held in Bali (Indonesia) in December 2013.

Achievements of the Bali Ministerial (2013)

The Bali Package encompassed tangible progress in respect of several contentious issues, including trade facilitation, LDC issues, agriculture, and lingering disputes over cotton subsidies.[16] A binding agreement on trade facilitation (TF) has been one of the key achievements of the Package, which appears to have galvanized expectations for a successful completion of the Doha Round. The TF agreement, which seeks to harmonize customs procedures and rules across the world, requires WTO members to promptly publish information in a non-discriminatory and easily accessible manner in order to enable all interested parties to be acquainted with their importation, exportation, and transit procedures.[17] The Bali Ministerial also established a Preparatory Committee on TF to receive notification of commitments from member countries and to draw up a Protocol of Amendment to insert the Agreement into Annex 1A of the WTO Agreement. The TF agreement also offers developing countries and LDCs significant technical and financial assistance to streamline their customs procedures and rules.

In respect of agriculture, the Bali Package provides that land reform, rural livelihood security, and poverty alleviation programs—such as land rehabilitation, soil conservation and resource management, drought management, flood control, and rural employment programs—will be considered to fall within the scope of the non-exhaustive list of general services programs in Annex 2, paragraph 2 of the URAA. In operational terms this means that government spending in such general services can be included in the Green Box—the category of domestic support considered not to distort trade. Such expenditures, thus, can be made without limits. Responding to the demands of some of the leading developing countries, the Bali Package also provided that, as an interim measure until a permanent solution is found, WTO members should refrain from challenging through the WTO dispute settlement mechanism any supports provided by developing countries for traditional staple food crops in pursuance of public stockholding programs for food security purposes.

The Bali Ministerial, however, failed to reach an agreement on export competition issues, such as export subsidies, export credits, and other such advantages associated with increasing exports, but agreed to ask WTO members to exercise the utmost restraint in using any forms of export subsidy. The Ministerial, however, succeeded in making some progress in respect of streamlining tariff rate quota (TRQs) administration and phasing out trade-distorting cotton subsidies of the United States which allegedly discriminate against the exports interest of cotton-producing African countries—the so-called ‘Cotton-4’: Benin, Burkina Faso, Chad, and Mali.

In respect of the LDC issues, the Bali Ministerial provided for the operationalization of a waiver on preferential treatment to services and service suppliers, duty-free and quota-free market access, and for a monitoring mechanism for special and differential treatment flexibilities.

The Ministerial asked WTO members to provide preferential rules of origin to imports from LDCs, and to make such preferential rules of origin as transparent, simple, and objective as possible. The WTO members were also asked to extend preferences to LDCs’ services and service suppliers, consistent with the waiver decision under Article XVI of GATS, by granting improved market access, for example, through eliminating the economic needs tests and other quantitative limitations. The Ministerial also asked WTO members to provide enhanced technical assistance and capacity building to help LDCs benefit from the operationalization of the waiver, delivery of targeted and coordinated technical assistance aimed at strengthening the domestic and export services capacity of LDCs, and making optimal use of existing aid-for-trade channels.[18]

Finally, the Bali Ministerial asked WTO members to prepare a clearly defined work program on the remaining Doha Round issues so that the Round could be successfully completed by the end of 2014.[19] This work program is expected to build on the decisions taken at the Ninth Ministerial, particularly on agriculture, development, and LDC issues, as well as other central issues of the Doha mandate. The current Director General of the WTO, Roberto Azevêdo, deemed the Bali Package a success “precisely because it delivered for everyone—it received strong support from least-developed, developing and developed Members alike.”[20] Apparently, the Bali Package seems to have succeeded in doing so. It has delivered for some vocal developing countries, such as India and Brazil, who were demanding the rights to public stockholding for food security purposes. It also delivered for the LDCs by granting preferential rules-of-origin requirements, preferential treatment to LDCs’ service providers, and duty-free and quota-free access to developed country markets. It also delivered for developed countries—presumably the TF agreement would open up the global market for developed country business conglomerates through the harmonization and streamlining of customs rules and procedures in developing countries. According to Azevêdo, the Bali Package is expected to boost the global economy by $1 trillion per year and to generate up to 21 million jobs across the world.[21]

Problems with the WTO negotiating processes

One of the central issues for the new global architecture of trade governance, as provided by the WTO, centers on its decision-making process, which basically continues the age-old GATT practices. Officially, the WTO’s decision-making process underpins three key principles: non-discrimination, transparency, and consensus. In order to reach a consensus decision, the WTO depends on something called 'concentric circles,' which envisages that members with different viewpoints meet in small groups to iron out differences among themselves before they bring the matter to progressively larger groups of members, eventually placing a decision before the entire WTO membership for approval. Each group is headed by a coordinator, and the coordinators of all such groups take part in the Green Room consultation to reach an informal consensus under the chairmanship of the WTO Director General. The Green Room consultation thus "ensures that all positions, countries and regions, are represented in the negotiations," the WTO website claims.[22]

The 'concentric circles' model of the decision-making process encourages WTO members to belong to some groups on the basis of geographic links, or common positions, or both, and the groups may include WTO members, non-WTO members, as well as observers. In recent years there have been proliferations of such groups with wide-ranging agendas. Some groups promote general interests, some stand for regional representations, while others press for specific products, sectors, or issues. Groups that represent regional interests include the African Group (comprising 42 African countries) and the EU group (comprising 29 EU members). The general interest groups include the LDC group (comprising 34 WTO members),[23] and the G-90 group (comprising the African Group, African, Caribbean and Pacific (ACP), and the LDCs).

Some groups that represent specific positions in respect of negotiation in an area include the G-20, a coalition of developing countries, which envisages ambitious reforms of agriculture in developed countries with some flexibility for developing countries;[24] the G-33 group, one of the largest coalitions of developing countries, which envisages flexibility for developing countries to undertake limited market opening in agriculture issues;[25] and the Cotton-4 group, a coalition of West African cotton-exporting countries, which seeks cuts in cotton subsidies and tariffs. Other important groups, especially in the context of the Doha Round, include the Small, Vulnerable Economies (SVEs) group—conmprising 15 WTO members—which presses for reforms in agricultural issues; and the NAMA-11 group—comprising 12 WTO members—which seeks tariff reductions and greater liberalization in respect of non-agricultural market access.[26]

The emergence of such groups—especially the G-20, the NAMA-11, the G-33, the SVEs, the LDCs, the Africa Group, the ACP, and the Cotton-4—have literally changed the landscape of WTO negotiations. In sharp contrast to the GATT period—when most of the developing countries were arguably mere onlookers, lacking interests in manufacturing tariff reductions or being incapable of articulating and presenting their cases—now "these coalitions are capable of providing a strong countervailing force to the power and influence" of the most powerful WTO members, such as the EU and the US (Ismail, 2009, 59).[27] The failures of several of the WTO Ministerials, including the Seattle fiasco of 1999, Cancun Ministerial 2003, and the Doha Round's many failures in reaching agreements in modalities and making tangible progress may be attributed to the more assertive role of such developing country groups. As a result, the days of reaching agreements by swapping concessions between the biggest players—

namely the EU and the US—seem to have come to an end.[28] The WTO's decision-making process therefore needs a sweeping overhaul to accommodate the interests and voices of less developed countries.

This book focuses on the interests of the less developed countries, comprising both developing countries and the group of countries known as the LDCs. There is, however, no universally accepted taxonomy of countries. International organizations like the World Bank, the UN, and the IMF—whose taxonomies are widely used—use very different classification systems, and often such taxonomies lack clarity with regard to their underlying rationale.[29] The World Bank, for example, divides countries into four categories on the basis of per capita gross national income (GNI): low-income, lower middle-income, upper middle-income, and high-income countries.[30] Generally, low- and middle-income economies are referred to as developing economies. This study follows the same interpretation. The study also uses the LDC category as defined by the UN Economic and Social Council, which identifies the LDCs on the basis of three criteria: per capita GNI, human assets, and economic vulnerability to external shocks.[31]

Conclusions

The world has been witnessing a sustained development toward a more liberalized and more globalized international trading system since the end of World War II, and it may be safely concluded that the world trading system has never been more liberal or more globalized than it is today. Much of the credit for the scale, depth, and magnitude of this liberalization and globalization may be attributed to the multilateral trading system that evolved under the auspices of the GATT and its successor, the WTO. While the GATT focused mainly on the manufacturing sector and thus on the exports interests of developed countries, the WTO that replaced it in the mid-1990s embraces all international trade sectors—agriculture, manufacturing, as well as services—and is more geared to raising boats all around the world. On top of that, the WTO also further strengthens the GATT disciplines and principles of international trade, and equips itself with far-reaching regulatory and watchdog powers unparalleled in world history. Such a comprehensive and all-encompassing mandate and scope of the WTO raises the stakes for all countries in multilateral trade negotiations and agreements, but it does so more in respect of the less developed countries, as many of them are becoming increasingly dependent on international trade for economic growth and development. It is still more so because of the fact that the WTO does not guarantee unfettered free trade—it rather provides a global platform for multilateral trade negotiations, where the bargaining and negotiation outcome largely depends on member countries' global market power.

In recent years, however, in sharp contrast with the past, developing countries have been demonstrating a more organized, more vocal, and more articulate stance in WTO negotiations, often posing powerful challenges to the age-old Green Room processes of consensus building which worked well during the period of the GATT. Such challenges were reflected in the failures of several of the WTO Ministerials, and occasional setbacks with the progress of the Doha Round of negotiations. Although the last WTO Ministerial—the Bali Conference—has apparently succeeded in putting the Doha Round back on track for a successful completion, many of the contentious issues in the agriculture and services sectors still remain unresolved. The successful liberalization of these sectors in future WTO rounds would hinge on nothing less than fundamental reforms in the WTO decision-making processes, greater accommodation of the interests of developing countries, and more transparent and participatory multilateral trade negotiations.

Notes

1 The conference, dubbed the United Nations Monetary and Financial Conference, was held in a little-known village called Bretton Woods in New Hampshire. It was attended by leaders of 44 allied nations, including the US President Franklin Roosevelt and the UK Prime Minister Winston Churchill.

2 Although over 50 countries at the United Nations Havana Conference in 1947 agreed to create such a specialized UN agency, US Congress expressed concern that the Havana Charter envisaged an ITO with scopes far beyond trade disciplines to encompass such other issues as rules on employment, commodity agreements, restrictive business practices, international investment, and services, and so on. Facing such formidable Congressional opposition, President Harry Truman preferred to withdraw the bill from the consideration of Congress rather than having it voted down. For more details see Hoekman and Kostecki (2001), and Trebilcock and Howse (1995).

3 Eleven of the GATT signatories were developing countries—Brazil, Burma (Myanmar), Ceylon (Sri Lanka), Chile, China, Cuba, India, Lebanon, Pakistan, Rhodesia, and Syria. Developed country signatories were: Australia, Belgium, Luxembourg, the Netherlands, New Zealand, Norway, the United Kingdom, the United States, France, Canada, and Czechoslovakia. Germany and Japan, countries which lost World War II, were not among the signatories. Germany became a member of the GATT in 1951, and Japan followed suit in 1955. In 1950, however, three original signatories to the GATT agreement—China, Lebanon, and Syria—withdrew their membership. For more details see Dowlah (2004, 29–50).

4 In the 1960s, however, the GATT relaxed its twin principles in respect of less developed countries. A GATT declaration in 1961—the Promotion of Trade of Less Developed Countries—called for preferential market access for developing countries, and in 1964 the GATT adopted a specific legal framework granting developing countries less than full reciprocity in trades inconsistent with their level of development. Next, the Enabling Clause, adopted by the Tokyo Round of the GATT, granted developing countries preferential market access to developed country markets on a non-reciprocal and non-discriminatory basis. The Enabling Clause also granted favorable treatment for developing countries in other GATT rules dealing with non-tariff barriers (such as technical barriers to trade, subsidies, and countervailing duties), and special and differential treatment (SDT) to the LDCs. For more details see GATT (1979), Dowlah (2011), and Michalopoulas (2000).

5 Such protectionist policies often resulted in dysfunctional and counterproductive consequences for many developing countries. For more details see Sutherland (2005), World Bank (2003), Dowlah (2003), and Michalopoulas (2000).

6 See Articles XII and XIX of GATT—'Restrictions to Safeguard the Balance of Payments,' and 'Emergency Action on Imports of Particular Products.' See GATT (1972) for greater details.

7 A total of 125 countries formally participated in the Marrakesh Ministerial Meeting held in April 1994 in Morocco to ratify the 'Final Act Embodying the Results of the Uruguay Round of the Multilateral Trade Negotiations.' Of these, 104 signed the WTO Agreement, and seven countries—Australia, Botswana, Burundi, India, Japan, the Republic of Korea, and the US—deferred the signing because of legislative procedures back home.
8 For more details see www.wto.org/english/res_e/booksp_e/analytic_index_e/wto_agree_01_e.htm#p.
9 Apparently, the idea of establishing a global trade watchdog, equipped with a permanent and solid institutional status to play a greater role in global economic policy making in cooperation with the Bretton Woods institutions, surfaced in the early 1990s with a Canadian proposal, which was subsequently backed by the European Union. The Canadian proposal, however, sought to call it the Multilateral Trade Organization (MTO). Eventually the acronym WTO was chosen, as there is another UN organization with the same acronym—the World Tourism Organization.
10 Such a conflict between the trade of tangible goods under strengthened GATT discipline and the trade of services under GATS also raises conflicts among WTO member countries' rights to "maintain restriction under the GATS and the right to liberalize under the GATT 1994" (Matsushita, 2004, 87).
11 Although all WTO members are responsible for the WTO's budgetary expenditures, the share is based on a formula that takes into account each member's share in international trade. As a result, members with the largest shares in global trade bear most of the financial burden of the WTO. In 2010, for example, more than 45 percent of the share of the WTO's budget was borne by six members—the US (13 percent), China including Hong Kong–China (9.2 percent), Germany (8.9 percent), Japan (5.1 percent), the UK (5.1 percent), and France (4.6 percent).
12 The consensus under the WTO, however, implies the absence of a negative consensus. This means that all participating members must oppose a decision in order to turn it down. The opinions of non-participating members are ignored. Moreover, whether the negative opinions of participating member countries will be counted or not depends on the concerned member country's share in global trade as well as how fundamental the objection is.
13 For other WTO Ministerial conferences and their key achievements, see Table 1.2.
14 *The Economist* magazine, in its September 8, 2012 issue, for example, declared, "The Doha trade talks are dead. Replace them with a rapid new deal, called the Global Recovery Round."
15 One of the serious issues that contributed to such stalemates or failures was the sharply different position of WTO members in respect of agricultural modalities proposed by the document entitled 'Revised Draft Modalities for Agriculture.' This document addressed some of the most vexing issues in the sector, such as tariffs, tariff peaks, tariff rate quotas (TRQs), tariff escalations, producer supports, export subsidies, export credits, and so on. For more details, see WTO document: TN/AG/W/4/Rev.4, December 2008.
16 For more details on the achievements of the Bali Ministerial Conference, see www.wto.org/english/thewto_e/minist_e/mc9_e/desci36_e.htm.
17 Such requirements are, however, extremely comprehensive, and may well be economically costly for many developing countries. The Agreement, for example, requires all WTO members to make easily accessible information on their ports, airports, and other entry points; applied rates of duties and taxes of any kind imposed on or in connection with importation or exportation; fees and charges imposed by or for governmental agencies; rules for the classification or valuation of products for customs purposes; laws, regulations, and administrative rulings of general application relating to rules of origin; import, export, or transit restrictions or prohibitions; penalty provisions against breaches of import, export or transit formalities; appeal procedures; and

procedures relating to the administration of tariff quotas. For more details see WTO document: WT/MIN(13)/36•WT/L/911.

18 For more details see www.wto.org/english/thewto_e/minist_e/mc9_e/desci36_e.htm–Trade.

19 Like many deadlines set in the past, the WTO missed this deadline as well. The latest deadline for the work program on the remaining issues of the Doha Round was set for July 2015, but as of May 2015 the program is yet to be completed. Even in late April 2015, WTO Director General Roberto Azevêdo told the WTO Trade Negotiations Committee, "We still have a long way to go" to conclude a work program on the remaining Doha Round issues by July (see "Statement by Roberto Azevêdo to the TNC," www.wto.org/english/news_e/news_e.htm, last accessed May 8, 2015).

20 Roberto Azevêdo took office as the sixth Director General of the WTO in September 2013 for a four-year term.

21 For more details see www.wto.org/english/thewto_e/dg_e/dg_e.htm.

22 For more details see www.wto.org/english/tratop_e/dda_e/negotiating_groups_e.htm.

23 The least developed countries (LDCs), a general interest group, currently comprises 34 WTO members, eight WTO observers, and six non-WTO members or observers. The WTO members are: Angola, Bangladesh, Benin, Burkina Faso, Burundi, Cambodia, the Central African Republic, Chad, the Democratic Republic of the Congo, Djibouti, Gambia, Guinea, Guinea-Bissau, Haiti, the Lao People's Democratic Republic, Lesotho, Madagascar, Malawi, Mali, Mauritania, Mozambique, Myanmar, Nepal, Niger, Rwanda, Senegal, Sierra Leone, the Solomon Islands, Tanzania, Togo, Uganda, Vanuatu, Yemen, and Zambia. The WTO observers are: Afghanistan, Bhutan, Comoros, Equatorial Guinea, Ethiopia, Liberia, Sao Tomé and Principe, and Sudan, and non-WTO members or observers are: Eritrea, Kiribati, Somalia, South Sudan, Timor-Leste, and Tuvalu.

24 Currently the G-20 group comprises 23 WTO members: Argentina, Bolivia, Brazil, Chile, China, Cuba, Ecuador, Egypt, Guatemala, India, Indonesia, Mexico, Nigeria, Pakistan, Paraguay, Peru, the Philippines, South Africa, Tanzania, Thailand, Uruguay, Venezuela, the Bolivarian Republic, and Zimbabwe.

25 The G-33 group currently comprises 46 WTO members: Antigua and Barbuda, Barbados, Belize, Benin, Bolivia, Botswana, Côte d'Ivoire, China, Congo, Cuba, the Dominican Republic, El Salvador, Grenada, Guatemala, Guyana, Haiti, Honduras, India, Indonesia, Jamaica, Kenya, Korea, Madagascar, Mauritius, Mongolia, Mozambique, Nicaragua, Nigeria, Pakistan, Panama, Peru, Philippines, St. Kitts and Nevis, St. Lucia, St. Vincent and the Grenadines, Senegal, Sri Lanka, Suriname, Tanzania, Trinidad and Tobago, Turkey, Uganda, Venezuela, the Bolivarian Republic, Zambia, and Zimbabwe.

26 Currently the SVE (agriculture) group comprises 15 WTO members: Barbados, Bolivia, Cuba, the Dominican Republic, El Salvador, Fiji, Guatemala, Honduras, the Maldives, Mauritius, Mongolia, Nicaragua, Papua New Guinea, Paraguay, and Trinidad and Tobago. The NAMA group comprises 12 WTO members: Côte d'Ivoire, Cameroon, Congo, Cuba, Ghana, Kenya, Macao, China, Mauritius, Nigeria, Sri Lanka, Suriname, and Zimbabwe. There is another NAMA group called Friends of Ambition (NAMA), which comprises 35 WTO members.

27 Ismail (2009, 59), however, cautions that the bias or incorrect weighting of the power of important committee chairs, who are in most cases from the EU and the US, could still undermine the efforts of developing country coalitions to sustain their attempts to achieve a more balanced, fair, and development-friendly outcome in the WTO negotiations.

28 An impressive literature has emerged in recent years on the WTO negotiation processes, the roles played by different groups, the reasons for the failures of several WTO Ministerials, and the obstacles faced by the Doha Round. This study, however, is not about negotiating the processes or stances of different groups or countries. For more details on WTO negotiations see Odell (2006), Wilkinson (2006), Matsushita (2004), Ismael (2009), and Conceiçao-Heldt (2011). See also Dowlah (2004, ch. 2),

which provides a detailed account of the failure of WTO Ministerials held in Seattle and Cancun.

29 See Nielsen (2011) for a detailed analysis of diverse taxonomies used by these institutions. The author also presents an alternative system based on transparent data-driven methodology.

30 The World Bank revises its classification of countries each year in July on the basis of estimated GNI per capita of the previous year. The July 2013 classification of the World Bank categorized countries as follows: Low income: up to $1,035; Lower middle income: $1,036 to $4,085; Upper middle income: $4,086 to $12,615, and high income: $12,616 or more. For more details see http://data.worldbank.org/news/new-country-classifications?print.

31 The UN reviews the LDC category every three years on the basis of the human assets index and economic vulnerability index. The latest round of LDC review, held in 2012, determined GNI per capita under $992 for inclusion, and above $1,190 for graduation. For more details see http://unohrlls.org/about-ldcs/criteria-for-ldcs.

References

Anderson, K. and Winters, A. (2008). The challenge of reducing international trade and migration barriers. Policy Research Working Paper No. 4598. Washington, DC: World Bank.

Bagwell, K. and Staiger, R. (2004). *The Economics of the World Trading System.* Boston, MA: MIT Press.

Conceiçao-Heldt, E. (2011). *Negotiating Trade Liberalization at the WTO: Domestic politics and bargaining dynamics.* New York: Palgrave Macmillan.

Dowlah, C. (2003). Agriculture and the new trade agenda in the WTO negotiations: Economic analysis of interests and options for Bangladesh. In M. Ingco (ed.), *Direction in Development: Agriculture, trade, and the WTO in South Asia* (pp. 38–95). Washington, DC: World Bank.

Dowlah, C. (2004). *Backwaters of Global Prosperity: How globalization and the GATT/WTO trade regimes marginalize the world's poorest nations.* New York: Praeger.

Dowlah, C. (2011). Trade preferences and economic growth: An assessment of the US GSP schemes in the context of least developed countries. In L. YongShik *et al.* (eds), *Law and Development Perspective on International Trade Law* (pp. 334–355). New York: Cambridge University Press.

Dowlah, C. (2012). Mode 4 of WTO's General Agreement on Trade in Services: Can it spur cross-border labor mobility from developing countries? *The Law and Development Review*, 5(2), 56–82.

Dowlah, C. (2014). Cross-border labor mobility—A critical assessment of WTO's GATS mode 4 vis-à-vis regional trade agreements. *Journal of International Trade Law and Policy*, 13(1), 2–18.

Eichengreen, B. and Irwin, D. (2010). The slide to protectionism in the great depression: Who succumbed and why? *Journal of Economic History*, 70(4), 871–897.

GATT (General Agreement on Tariff and Trade). (1972). Basic agreements and selected documents. Eighteenth supplement. Geneva: GATT.

GATT (General Agreement on Tariff and Trade). (1979). *Differential and More Favorable Treatment, Reciprocity and Fuller Participation of Developing Countries (Enabling Clause). Decision of 28 November, 1979.* Geneva: GATT.

Higgott, R. and Weber, H. (2005). GATS in context: Development, an evolving lax mercatoria and the Doha agenda. *Review of International Political Economy*, 12(3), 434–455.

Hoda, A. and Gulati, A. (2007). *WTO Negotiations on Agriculture and Developing Countries*. Baltimore, MD: Johns Hopkins University Press.

Hoekman, B. (2002). The WTO: Functions and basic principles. In B. Hoekman, A. Mattoo, and O. English (eds), *Development, Trade and the WTO—A handbook* (pp. 41–49). Washington, DC: World Bank.

Hoekman, B. and Kostecki, M. (2001). *The Political Economy of the World Trading System: From GATT to WTO.* New York: Oxford University Press.

Hoekman, B. and Mattoo, A. (2011). Services trade liberalization and regulatory reform: Reinvigorating international cooperation. World Bank Policy Research Working Paper No. 5517. Washington, DC: World Bank.

Hudec, R. (1987). *Developing Countries in the GATT Legal System.* New York: Cambridge University Press.

Ismail, F. (2009). *Reforming the World Trade Organization: Developing countries in the Doha Round.* Geneva: CUTS International and Freiderich Ebert Stiftung.

Matoo, A. and Carzaniga, A. (eds). (2003). *Moving People to Deliver Services*. Washington, DC: World Bank.

Matsushita, M. (2004). Governance of international trade under World Trade Organization agreements—Relationships between World Trade Organizations agreements and other Agreements. *Journal of World Trade*, 38(2), 185–200.

Michalopoulos, C. (2000). Trade and development in the GATT and WTO: The role of special and differential treatment for developing countries. World Bank Policy Research Working Paper. Washington, DC: World Bank.

Moses, J. and Latnes, B. (2004). The economic costs to international labor restrictions: Revisiting the empirical discussion. *World Development*, 32(10), 1609–1626.

Nielsen, L. (2011). Classifications of countries based on their level of development: How it is done and how it could be done. IMF Working Paper No. WP/11/31. Washington, DC: IMF.

Odell, J. (2006). Chairing A WTO negotiation. *Journal of International Economic Law*, 8(2), 425–448.

Sutherland, P. (2005). The Doha Development Agenda: Political challenges to the world trading system—a cosmopolitan perspective. *Journal of International Economic Law*, 8(2), 363–375.

Trebilcock, M. and Howse, T. (1995). *The Regulation of International Trade*. London: Routledge.

Tyers, R. and Anderson, K. (1986). Distortions in world food markets. Background Paper No. 22 for the World Development Report 1996. Washington, DC: World Bank.

Tyers, R. and Anderson, K. (1992). *Disarray in World Food Markets: A Quantitative Assessment.* New York: Cambridge University Press.

UNCTAD (United Nations Conference on Trade and Development). (1997). *Trade and Development Report 1997.* Geneva: United Nations.

UNCTAD (United Nations Conference on Trade and Development). (2009). Contribution of migrants to development: Trade, investment and development linkages. Geneva: UNCTAD/DITC/TNCD/2009/2.

Wilkinson, R. (2006). *The WTO: Crisis and the governance of global trade.* London: Routledge.

Winters, M. and Mattoo, A. (2011). *Unfinished Business? The WTO's Doha Agenda.* Washington, DC: World Bank.

World Bank. (2003). *Global Economic Prospects: Realizing the development promises of the Doha Round.* Washington, DC: World Bank.

WTO (World Trade Organization). (2011). *World Trade Report 2011*. Geneva: WTO.

2 Liberalization of the agricultural sector

Introduction

Agricultural trade has long been subject to protracted protections and widespread distortions throughout the world. Such protections, often attributed to the sensitive character of agriculture for its implications for national food security and other such expediencies, were extensively practiced by both developed and developing countries, although the former evidently excelled in the race. Many developed countries, especially those belonging to the European Union, not only acquired a short-lived competitive advantage in agriculture through massive domestic subsidies and export supports, but also often contributed to global market instability by trading such subsidized agricultural products at uncompetitively low prices. Developing countries, for their part, also adopted various protectionist measures but those evidently resulted in lowering of domestic output, higher food prices, negative taxation of agriculture, and prolonged dependence on food aid.[1]

Worse still, while successive rounds of the General Agreement on Tariff and Trade (GATT) negotiations brought down tariffs and non-tariff barriers for manufactures, in which developed countries had greater comparative advantage and thus greater export interests, agricultural trade, in which developing countries had natural comparative advantage and thus exports interests, faced movement in the opposite direction. Eventually, however, agricultural trade was brought to the negotiation table by the GATT Ministerial Conference held in Punta del Este (Uruguay) in 1986. The successful conclusion of the Uruguay Round negotiations ultimately paved the way for the integration of the sector into the strengthened GATT discipline in 1994 under what is known as the Uruguay Round Agreement on Agriculture (URAA). Despite full implementation of the agreement under the auspices of the World Trade Organization (WTO) which replaced the GATT, international trade in agriculture still remains largely distorted, and unquestionably far less liberalized than trade in the manufacturing sector. Moreover, any further liberalization of the sector largely depends on the success of ongoing or future negotiations under the WTO.

The chapter has been organized as follows. The following section sheds light on the processes that led to the eventual integration of the agricultural sector into the GATT discipline. The third section explains the major features of the URAA and the fourth section provides a critical evaluation of the implementation of the agreement. The fifth section provides an analysis of the consequences of the URAA implementation. The sixth section explores post-URAA issues and WTO negotiations in the context of developing countries. The seventh section concludes the chapter.

Integration of agriculture into the GATT discipline

The original GATT, being primarily concerned with manufacturing trade, left agricultural trade largely outside its jurisdiction, while allowing the contracting parties to impose quantitative restrictions (QRS) in the trade.[2] Over the course of time, such exceptions emerged into an elaborate scheme of trade protections, which were rather aggressively implemented in both developed and developing countries. Developed countries traditionally used three major protectionist instruments: (1) market price supports geared to make up the difference between domestic and international prices caused by border barriers such as tariffs and quantitative restrictions: such instruments often accounted for about 70 percent of total protection in OECD countries; (2) direct support—product-specific subsidies to domestic producers or consumers—which played a rather limited role, as they came from the state exchequers but often prevailed for a long period of time; and finally (3) general supports—government supports provided through research, training, marketing, and infrastructure projects (Anderson *et al.*, 2006; OECD, 2005).

With agricultural trade left to the discretion of GATT contracting parties, developed countries also provided export subsidies to promote exports of agricultural products, and introduced variable levies to ensure that imported agricultural products were priced at a level higher than that of domestically produced products. Many developed countries also restricted imports by imposing quotas and QRS, voluntary export restraints (VER), state-trading enterprises (STEs), and so on. In many developed countries such restrictions proliferated to such an extent that they hugely depressed international farm prices relative to non-farm products (Tyers and Anderson, 1986). Time series data for the developed and newly industrializing countries up until the 1970s showed a clear tendency for national governments to subsidize agricultural relative to industrial production in the course of their economic development (Anderson and Hayami, 1986; Lindert, 1991).

Developing countries, on the other hand, pursued trade and foreign exchange rate policies which further depressed the incentives of their farmers (Krueger *et al.*, 1988; Balassa and Associates, 1971). Artificially orchestrated low prices of agricultural commodities in developing countries created downward pressure on domestic prices threatening the livelihoods of those people whose incomes depended on agriculture (World Bank, 1996). Moreover, agricultural protection policies in developing countries also resulted in high implicit taxes for farmers, as public sector support for farmers was either absent or negative (Valdes and McCalla, 1996).

Such protectionist policies proliferated for decades, as international trade in agriculture remained largely outside the GATT negotiations. The original GATT agreement, however, contained general provisions in respect of all subsidies, which applied to agricultural products as well. Article XVI of the GATT mandated notification and consultation requirements for the contracting parties granting or maintaining any measures of subsidies or supports aimed at increasing exports or reducing imports. Such provisions, however, had little effect on restraining farm subsidies and import restrictions in developed countries. Over time, restrictions on market access to agricultural products became so widespread that "even the semblance of conformity with GATT obligations was dropped" (Hoda and Gulati, 2007, 15). Obviously, developing countries, having a natural competitive advantage in agriculture, were worse off due to such protectionist measures adopted by developed countries.

A major impetus to bring agriculture before the GATT negotiating table, however, came from the US in the early 1980s, when American agricultural exports came under threat from highly subsidized agricultural exports of the European Community (EC). The US sought to utilize the GATT dispute settlement mechanism to challenge the EC's agricultural subsidy practices pursued under a program known as the Common Agricultural Policy (CAP). Established by the Treaty of Rome in 1957, the CAP program sought to achieve food self-sufficiency in the then net food-importing EC countries by providing massive domestic supports, price interventions, and trade protections. By the mid-1980s, the remarkable success of the program transformed the EC into a net exporter of agricultural products, when its subsidized exports began to depress global agricultural prices.

At the GATT negotiation table, the EU, however, insisted on managed international trade in agriculture in order to keep its CAP scheme beyond the scope of GATT negotiations, while the US, which enjoyed a competitive advantage in many agricultural products but also protected some of the products, advocated for the greater liberalization of agriculture. The resulting deadlock hindered progress toward agricultural liberalization for many years. In the early 1980s, however, a GATT Committee on Agriculture was established to look into domestic and export subsidies as well as government procurement procedures in agriculture. Despite the trade in agriculture remaining plagued with a complex mosaic of tariff and non-tariff barriers, including quantitative restrictions, variable import levies, minimum import prices, discretionary import licensing, VERs, and so on, the GATT Committee on Agriculture failed to make any progress (Dowlah, 2004, 107–136).

In the mid-1980s, agricultural liberalization received greater momentum at the GATT Ministerial Conference in Punta del Este. Several powerful developments contributed to this momentum. First, with President Ronald Reagan and Prime Minister Margaret Thatcher, the ideological balance around the world "swung towards greater reliance on markets, competition and deregulation" (Hoekman and Kostecki, 2001, 215). Second, by the mid-1980s major agricultural exporting countries faced growing surplus stocks, as global supplies increased faster than both domestic and international demand. This occurred because while major industrialized countries, such as the US and the EU, reinforced subsidized exports of agriculture, major food-importing countries strived hard to attain food self-sufficiency.[3] Third, at the same time there had been a rich harvest of studies that brought to surface how: (1) government interventions distorted agricultural production resulting in economically costly inefficient policies in many developed countries; (2) non-tariff barriers, such as variable import levies, insulated domestic producers from exposure to international prices, and thereby artificially debased global demand and supply conditions in agricultural commodities (FAO, 1998); (3) a small number of powerful farm producers pressured governments to provide increasing export subsidies and domestic supports in developed countries (Johnson, 1991; Tangermann *et al.*, 1994); and (4) artificially determined low prices of agricultural commodities resulted in high implicit taxes on farmers in developing countries (World Bank, 1996; Valdes and McCalla, 1996).

While obviously evolving developments as well as diverse interests and objectives of negotiating parties made multilateral negotiations in agriculture quite strenuous, the conflict between the US and the EU—the largest agricultural producers in the world who jointly controlled 40 percent of international trade in agriculture—proved to be the hardest of all. While the US demanded what is called a zero-zero option (namely phasing out all agricultural subsidies and quantitative restrictions over a period of 10 years while harmonizing world health and safety measures), the EU resisted such liberalization by seeking short-term measures that would leave the existing levels of protection undisturbed.[4] Traditional agricultural exporters, the Cairns Group,[5] sided with the US but demanded binding commitments for eliminating domestic supports and export subsidies. Net food importing developing countries, on the other hand, sought further liberalization of the sector, hoping to lower their food import bills. Japan and South Korea, which had highly protected rice markets and strong domestic opposition to reforms and no appreciable export activity in agriculture, supported the prohibition of export subsidies, but vigorously opposed proposals for the abolition of quantitative import controls and reduction of tariffs (Dowlah, 2004, 110–111).

With negotiating groups sharply divided in their positions, the GATT agricultural negotiations progressed sluggishly. As a result, at the Midterm Review in Montreal in 1988, the GATT Agricultural Group failed to produce a text for discussion. Although negotiations resumed in April 1989, acrimonious issues prolonged agricultural negotiations for three further years. Eventually, in November 1992, the so-called Blair House Accord was reached, when the US dropped its demand for a zero-zero option and agreed to adopt a series of short-term measures to freeze domestic support, export subsidies, and border protection at the existing levels, while requiring commitments from the GATT contracting parties to the long-term objectives of reducing government intervention in these areas. The Blair House Accord eventually paved the way for the adoption of what came to be known as the Uruguay Round Agreement in Agriculture (URAA).

Major features of the Uruguay Round Agreement in Agriculture (URAA)

With the objective of bringing the entire agricultural sector under the strengthened GATT discipline in a systematic and timely manner, the URAA required all WTO members to submit Country Schedules[6] of quantitative commitments of liberalization on a commodity-by-commodity basis. The Schedules covered three major aspects of agricultural trade: (1) liberalization of market access (applicable to both tariffs and non-tariff barriers); (2) elimination or reduction of domestic support to agricultural production; and (3) export subsidies—reduction or elimination of support to agricultural exports. Developed countries were granted six years—up until 2000—to implement the commitments, while developing countries were given 10 years—up until 2004—to accomplish the same objective.

Market access commitments

The market access measures mandated by the URAA encompassed four major areas: tariffication, tariff reduction, maintenance of current access levels, and

Table 2.1 Main measures of the Uruguay Round Agreement on Agriculture

Measures	*Developed countries*	*Developing countries (LDCs exempted)*
Market access reduction in tariffs	36%	24%
Minimum reduction per tariff line	(15%)	(10%)
Transition period (base period 1986–1988)	6 years	10 years
Market access opportunity	5%	4%
Deadline	2000	2005
Domestic support reduction commitments (in AMS)	20%	13.3%
Transition period (base period 1986–1988)	6 years	10 years
de minimis rule (% of value of production)	5%	10%
Exceptions	Blue and Green boxes	Blue and Green boxes and S&D
Reduction in value of export subsidies (per product)	36%	24%
Reduction in volume of subsidized exports	21%	14%
Transition period (base period 1986–1988)	6 years	10 years
Exceptions	–	Support for marketing and domestic and international transport

Source: Author's compilation from WTO website.

special treatment and special safeguards. The tariffication scheme required WTO members to convert non-tariff barriers of the base period (1986–1988) into tariff equivalents and to establish a base rate of duty for each product covered by the URAA. No tariffs could be increased without negotiations with other members.[7] Developed countries were required to reduce the unweighted average tariff by 36 percent, with a minimum of 15 percent in each tariff line, over a six-year period. Developing countries were required to reduce the unweighted average tariff by 24 percent, with a minimum of 10 percent in each tariff line, by the end of the 10-year transition period (see Table 2.1). At the end, all tariffs would be bound at the final level, and no tariff rates could be raised above these levels in the future, except under specific circumstances. The least developed countries (LDCs) were exempted from such reduction commitments.

The agreement required WTO members to maintain current access levels for each individual product, as determined by the volume of imports in the base period (1986–1988). In case the current level was negligible, a minimum access had to be established at not less than 3 to 5 percent of domestic consumption of the base period.[8] This implied that a proportion of imports of a commodity that had previously been subject to NTBs would be allowed into the importing country at a reduced tariff rate. Special treatment provisions allowed members to claim exemptions from tariffication commitments for certain sensitive products, while special safeguard provisions enabled members to apply additional tariffs to specified commodities where import prices were particularly low or in cases of a sudden surge in imports. In both cases normal tariffs could be supplemented by additional duties.[9] The agreement also allowed what is called tariff rate quotas (TRQs)—a minimal tariff rate for a limited volume of imports—to address situations where tariffs replaced NTBs. The initial TRQ was the quota of imports permitted to enter the country at below the normal tariff rate, and the final TRQ reflected any changes in the initial quota due to increased quota size or reduced tariff.[10]

Domestic support commitments

The URAA introduced what is called the Aggregate Measure of Support (AMS) to quantify trade-distorting domestic supports, and required a 20 percent cut in the base-total AMS (value of total AMS between 1986 and 1988) by developed countries and a 13.3 percent cut by developing countries (see Table 2.1) in respect of: (1) product-specific AMS—support provided to a specific agricultural product; (2) non-product-specific AMS—support directed at the agricultural sector as a whole; (3) the equivalent measure of AMS—alternative means of support not measurable by AMS methodology; and (4) total AMS—the total value of all non-exempted domestic support provided to agricultural producers.

To facilitate the AMS calculation, agricultural policies were placed in three boxes: (1) the Amber Box, which included policies that substantially impacted trade patterns and flows; (2) the Green Box, which included policies that did not affect agricultural production and trade substantially, such as direct payment schemes that subsidize farmers' incomes, certain types of investment aid, research, training and extension, marketing information, and decoupled income support, which had no influence on production decisions; and (3) the Blue Box, which included policies that fitted neither the Amber nor the Green Boxes but fell in between. These policies largely relate to compensatory payments and land-set-aside programs of the EU and deficiency payments programs of the US. Such direct payments under production-limiting programs were exempt from AMS reduction if such payments were based on fixed area and yields. The AMS calculation, however, was conditioned by what is called *de minimis* exemption, which allowed support of no greater than 5 percent for developed countries and up to 10 percent for developing countries, of the total value of production of a particular product.

Export subsidies commitments

In order to eliminate trade-distortive export subsidies, the URAA required developed countries to reduce the volume of subsidized exports by 21 percent and the expenditures on subsidies by 36 percent over a six-year period (see Table 2.1). Developing countries were required to reduce the volume of subsidized exports by 14 percent and the expenditure on subsidies by 24 percent over a 10-year period. Export subsidy reduction commitments were, however, 'front loaded,' which enabled member countries to locate the level of subsidies prevailing in 1991 to 1992, provided that the level of subsidies during this period exceeded that in the base period. No new export subsidies were allowed, and the allowed subsidies had to be applied in a way that would not undermine the cuts in export subsidies. The agreement covered a wide range of subsidies, such as payments in kind, subsidized stock exports, producer-financed export subsidies, export marketing, cost subsidies, export-specific transportation subsidies, and subsidies on goods incorporated into exports. The LDCs were exempted from such reduction commitments.

Projected benefits of the URAA

The integration of the agricultural sector into the GATT discipline was underpinned by sweeping promises and great expectations, and showed an annual global economic welfare benefit of $165 billion from the liberalization of agriculture and food processing, $43 billion of which would accrue to low-income countries and $121 billion to high-income countries (see Table 2.2). Anderson and colleagues (1999) showed $260 billion annual global economic welfare benefit from removing trade distortions, 32 percent of which would result from the liberalization of agriculture and food processing in OECD countries alone.[11] More recent studies show even larger benefits from agricultural liberalization. Martin and Anderson (2006), for example, showed a potential global benefit of $287 billion, of which $159 billion (55 percent) would accrue to high-income countries, and $128 billion (45 percent) would accrue to developing countries.

Table 2.2 Economic welfare of removing post-Uruguay Round Trade distortions in agriculture (in US$ billions)

Liberalizing region	*Benefiting region*	*Agriculture and food processing*
High income		
	High income	110.5
	Low income	11.6
	Total	122.1
Low income		
	High income	11.2
	Low income	31.4
	Total	42.6
All countries		
	High income	121.7
	Low income	43.0
	Total	164.7

Source: Author's compilation from Anderson (2004).

The liberalization of agriculture was also expected to lead to major cutbacks in agricultural production in the OECD countries, a significant rise in agricultural production in developing countries, and a substantial rise in world prices of agricultural goods. Agricultural liberalization is expected to result in major cutbacks in the EU's agricultural production, a significant increase in the share of the US in wheat and food grains trade, some gains for Australia, and noteworthy benefits for the former Soviet Republics. Higher grain prices projected to help exporters and offset the policy bias against agriculture exist in many developing countries. In other words, benefits of developing countries from a liberalized agricultural trade would depend on potential efficiency gains from domestic policy reforms as well as improved market access.[12]

Agricultural liberalization was also expected to lead to structural changes in world agricultural production and consumption. Production was projected to shift from highly subsidized regions to low-subsidized or non-subsidized regions. That is, in the absence of subsidies, agricultural production would decline in the developed world, while greater opportunities and market access would lead to higher production in countries with real comparative advantage; that is, the developing areas of the world (Mathews, 2001, 23). At the same time, consumption in the developed world was expected to rise as prices fell, while consumption in developing countries would fall because prices would rise. Import prices of wheat, maize, beef, and dairy products, which many developing countries import, were projected to increase, while prices of coffee, cocoa, and cotton, which many developing countries export, were projected to fall.[13] Net food importing countries—mostly LDCs—stood to lose as world prices of many basic foodstuffs they imported would increase. Overall, such structural shifts in production and consumption were expected to generate greater advantages for developing countries compared with developed countries (Valdes and McCalla, 1996, 420).

Implementation of the URAA

Although the URAA has brought the agricultural sector into the GATT discipline for the first time, it did not envisage full integration of the sector into a rule-based, market-controlled GATT discipline—even after the end of the 10-year transition period. On the contrary, the agreement left much of the reforms needed for liberalizing agricultural trade to diverse interpretations, country discretions, and future negotiations (Dowlah, 2004, 116). The progress made thus far in respect of the implementation of the URAA has been evaluated below on the basis of three major pillars of the agreement: market access, domestic supports, and export subsidy.

Market access commitments

Tariffication

One of the landmark achievements of the URAA has been what is called tariffication—a process by which import bans, quotas, and other restrictive import measures were converted into more transparent and easily measurable quantified tariffs. The agreement has already succeeded in converting non-tariff border measures in agriculture into tariffs—as a result, all agricultural tariffs are now bound tariffs. This means that any increase in agricultural tariffs beyond bound tariffs would require negotiation with other members. The URAA has also succeeded in achieving the goal of reducing tariffs on average by 36 percent in developed countries (a minimum of 15 percent per individual tariff lines) and by 24 percent in developing countries. In addition, rules are now in place for the application of additional (safeguard) duties up to one-third of normal duties in case of imports surges, or when world prices fall below preset trigger prices for goods subject to tariffication. The agreement has also provided for a minimum access commitment as a share of domestic consumption for products subject to tariffication.

The success of the URAA in respect of tariffication, however, has not been entirely unblemished. At the initial stages of implementation, many WTO members resorted to what is called 'dirty tariffication.' Many countries fixed bound tariffs at higher levels than applied tariffs, and often targeted such dirty tariffication to key agricultural product groups, such as cereals, oilseeds, meat, and dairy products. The URAA required developed countries to cut tariffs by 36 percent but at the same time allowed them to do so on the basis of an unweighted average of all tariffs. As individual tariff lines needed to be cut by only 15 percent, many developed countries met the goal by cutting tariffs sharply on least sensitive products while applying maximum tariffs to important and sensitive products. Many developing countries also hesitated in making larger cuts in agricultural bound tariffs, as higher bound tariffs allowed them not to alter tariff rates in order to stabilize domestic farm prices in case of low world prices (Dowlah, 2004, 127–131).

Table 2.3 Average MFN applied tariffs and bound rates by major sectors in recent years (simple averages in %)

Country groups	*Year*	*Applied rate (%)*			*Bound rate (%)*			*Bound coverage (%)*		
		All goods	*Agricultural goods*	*Industrial goods*	*All goods*	*Agricultural goods*	*Industrial goods*	*All goods*	*Agricultural goods*	*Industrial goods*
Low income (32)	2006/2010	10.6	13.6	10.3	50.9	63.1	38.2	69.2	100.0	64.5
Middle income (94)	2007/2010	8.7	12.8	8.4	36.1	53.1	29.4	84.0	99.9	81.5
High-income non-OECDs (17)	2008/2010	5.2	11.3	4.6	18.0	32.4	13.4	90.5	99.8	89.1
High-income OECDs (11)	2009/2010	6.4	11.9	5.8	24.2	39.2	18.3	87.5	99.9	85.6
World, all above countries (154)	2006/2010	8.8	12.8	8.4	36.8	52.4	29.1	81.6	99.9	78.8

Sources: Author's compilation from UNCTAD TRAINS database and *World Tariff Profile* (WTO, 2008, 2010).

Note

Based on simple average of MFN applied tariffs available in the latest year. Product categories are defined by HS classifications as all goods (HS 01–97), agricultural goods (HS 01–24), and industrial goods (HS 25–97).

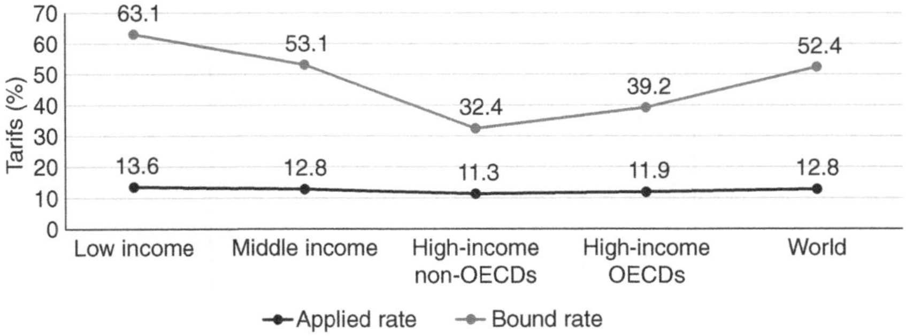

Figure 2.1 Dirty tariffication in agricultural goods.

As a result, although the tariffication goals of the URAA stand satisfied, there are still 'waters in the tariff' in many countries, meaning that domestic prices in these countries are below their import prices plus the tariff. As Table 2.3 shows, in 2010, the average applied rate of tariffs in agriculture was 12.8 percent in the world, against average bound tariffs of 52.4 percent. In low-income countries the gap was the highest—the average applied tariff in agriculture stood at 13.6 percent against the average bound tariff rate of 63.1 percent, followed by middle-income developing countries, for whom the average MFN applied tariff was 12.8 percent against the bound rate of 53.1 percent. In the high-income countries, the gap was smaller for non-OECD countries than in OECD countries—while the former had an average applied MFN tariff in agriculture of 11.3 percent against an average bound tariff of 32.4 percent, the latter had an average applied tariff of 11.9 percent against a bound tariff of 39.2 percent. Thus, the gap between the average applied MFN tariff and average bound tariffs in agriculture was the highest in low-income countries and the lowest in high-income non-OECD countries (see Figure 2.1).

Such 'waters in the tariff' indicate that those WTO members with very high bound tariffs can facilitate market access by applying tariffs below bound rates or through preferential access as a result of reciprocal trade arrangements, in addition to impeding market access by applying high tariffs and tariff peaks. Pointing to such waters in the tariffs, the US accused Brazil, Chile, India, Indonesia, and Mexico in 2014 of applying less than one-third of their average bound tariffs in agricultural trade (WTO, 2014). As Table 2.4 indicates, average bound tariffs in these countries in 2011 to 2012 were 35.4 percent, 26 percent, 113 percent, 47 percent, and 44.5 percent, respectively, while their average applied tariffs were 10 percent, 6 percent, 33.5 percent, 7.9 percent, and 21 percent, respectively. Table 2.4 also shows large differences between applied and bound tariffs in several countries belonging to the G-20 (developing countries group) and the Cairns group (see Figure 2.2).[14] The US had both average bound tariffs and applied tariffs at the same rate—4.7 percent. China's rates were very close—

Table 2.4 Average bound, applied, and effective agricultural tariffs in selected countries (in %), 2011 to 2012

Country	*Average bound rate*	*Average applied rate (2012)*	*Trade weighted average tariff (2011)*	*Country*	*Average bound rate*	*Average applied rate (2012)*	*Trade weighted average tariff (2011)*
Argentina	32.6	10.5	11.8	Israel	73.4	17.0	16.7
Brazil	35.4	10.1	12.0	Japan	22.1	16.6	13.9
European Union	13.7	13.2	8.6	Mexico	44.5	21.2	27.6
Canada	17.5	16.2	13.6	Paraguay	33.1	10.0	12.7
Chile	26.0	6.0	6.0	Philippines	35.1	9.8	9.5
China (2011)	15.8	15.6	9.2	Romania	–	–	–
Colombia	91.5	14.9	15.4	South Africa	39.6	8.4	10.1
Costa Rica	42.7	11.3	9.8	Thailand	39.0	21.8	12.3
Cypress	–	–	–	Turkey	61.0	41.2	23.4
Guatemala	51.0	9.6	9.7	United States	4.7	4.7	3.9
India	113.1	33.5	48.4	Uruguay	33.9	9.8	11.3
Indonesia	47.0	7.9	4.3	Venezuela	55.8	16.8	15.9

Source: Author's compilation from WTO database and *World Tariff Profile* (WTO, 2013).

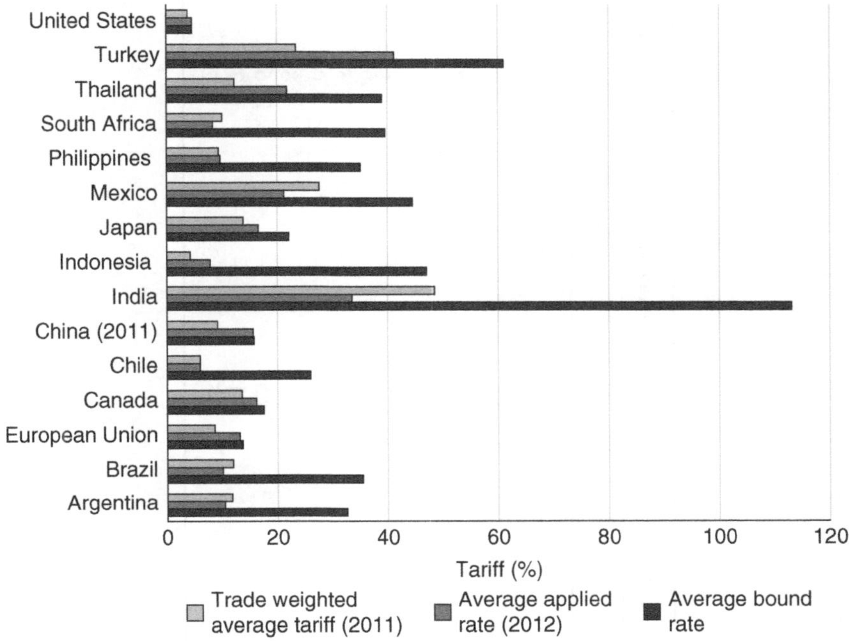

Figure 2.2 Average bound, applied, and trade-weighted agricultural tariffs in selected countries, 2011 to 2012 (in %).

average bound tariffs at 15.8 percent, and the average applied tariff rate at 15.6 percent, but Chinese tariff rates were more than three times that of the US rate.

Historically, applied MFN tariffs for agriculture and food had been significantly higher than those on manufactures—signifying higher protection in the sector. As Table 2.5 indicates, in 2001, the average import-weighted applied tariff in agriculture in the world was 16.7 percent, compared with 3.5 percent in manufacturing (excluding textiles and clothing), signifying 4.7 times higher protection afforded to agriculture compared with manufacturing. In 2005, import-weighted average applied tariffs for agricultural processed food in the world was 15.2 percent, compared with 3.1 percent in manufacturing (excluding textiles and clothing), signifying five-times higher protection in agriculture compared with manufacturing. Between 2001 and 2005, the import-weighted average applied agricultural tariff in the high-income developed world barely moved—it fell from 16.0 percent in 2001 to 15.9 percent in 2005. On the other hand, during the same period the import-weighted average applied agricultural tariffs fell from 17.7 percent to 14.2 percent in the developing countries. Most of this reduction occurred in the middle-income countries, as import-weighted average applied tariffs did not change much in low-income countries (see Figure 2.3).

The trend in average unweighted MFN applied tariff rates, however, shows a continuous and steady decline since 1990 (see Table 2.6). For the world as a

Table 2.5 Import-weighted average applied tariffs by sector and region, 2001 and 2005 (in %)

Importing region	*Agriculture, processed goods*		*Textiles and clothing*		*Other manufacturing*		*All goods*
	2001	*2005*	*2001*	*2005*	*2001*	*2005*	*2001*
High-income countries	16.0%	15.9	7.5%	7.3	1.3%	1.2	2.9%
Developing countries	17.7	14.2	17.0	14.3	8.3	7.1	9.9
Middle-income countries	16.5	12.1	16.8	13.6	7.3	6.0	8.9
Low-income countries	22.2	22.0	17.9	17.9	14.5	14.1	15.9
Developing countries by region							
East Asia and the Pacific	26.3	–	17.8	–	8.6	–	10.5
China	37.6	10.3	19.4	9.6	11.3	5.5	13.6
South Asia	33.9	–	20.1	–	22.2	–	23.5
Europe and Central Asia	14.8	–	10.7	–	4.1	–	6.0
Middle East and North Africa	14.1	13.1	27.1	23.9	7.2	7.2	9.8
Sub-Saharan Africa	18.2	–	23.7	–	10.5	–	12.6
Latin America and the Caribbean	10.3	–	11.3	–	7.1	–	7.7
World total	16.7	15.2	10.2	9.3	3.5	3.1	5.2

Source: Author's compilation from Anderson *et al.* (2006a).

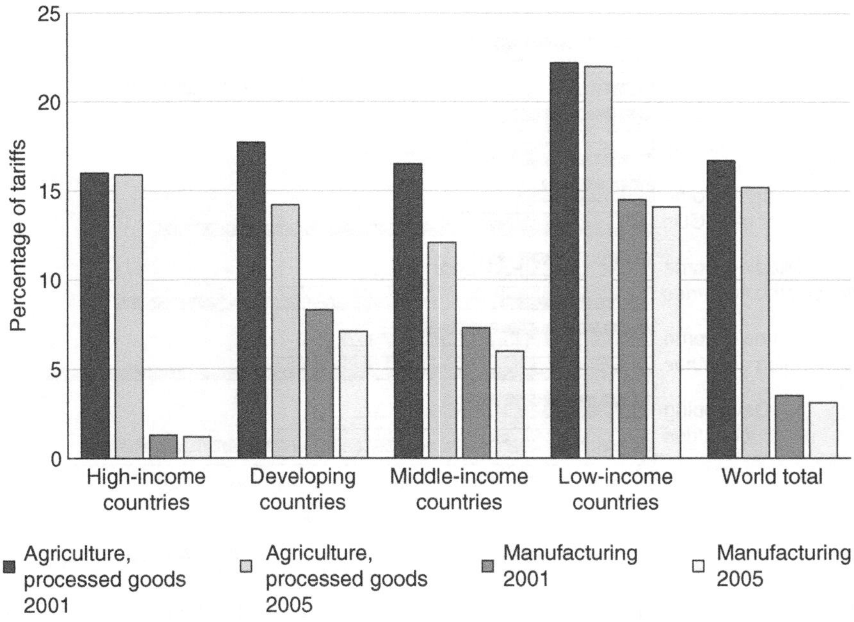

Figure 2.3 Import-weighted average applied tariffs in agriculture and manufacturing, 2001 to 2005 (in %).

Table 2.6 Trends in average unweighted MFN applied tariff rates in developing and industrial countries, 1990 to 2010 (in %)

Country/group	*1990*	*1995*	*2000*	*2005*	*2010*
Developing countries (134)	22.8	15.9	13.4	9.8	8.1
Low-income (34)	25.1	15.6	13.6	11.9	9.9
Middle-income (100)	22.3	15.9	13.3	9.0	7.5
High-income non-OECDs (19)	20.4	8.6	5.7	5.5	4.6
High-income OECDs (11)	12.9	9.9	7.9	6.2	6.2
World, all above countries (164)	21.9	14.5	12.4	9.3	7.6

Sources: Author's compilation from UNCTAD TRAINS database and *WTO Tariff Profile* (WTO, 2008).

whole, average applied tariff rates declined by 65 percent between 1990 and 2010—they fell from 22 percent in 1990 to 14.5 percent in 1995, then to 12.4 percent in 2000, to 9.3 percent in 2005, and to 7.6 percent in 2010. During the same period, average applied MFN tariffs came down from 22.8 percent to 8.1 percent in developing countries, from 25.1 percent to 9.9 percent in low-income countries, from 22.3 percent to 7.5 percent in middle-income countries, from 20.4 percent to 4.6 percent in high-income non-OECD countries, and from 12.9

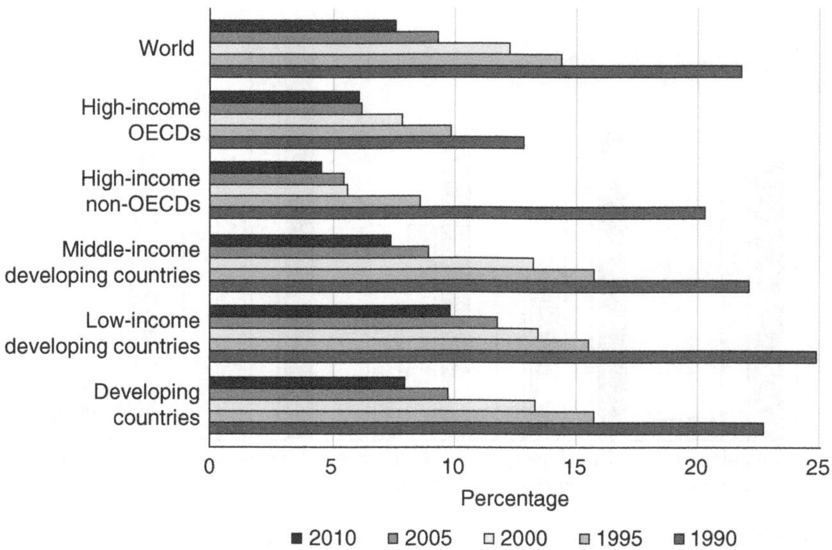

Figure 2.4 Average unweighted MFN applied tariff rates in developing and advanced countries, 1990 to 2010 (in %).

percent to 6.2 percent in high-income OECD countries.[15] In 2010, low-income developing economies had the highest applied MFN tariff rate (9.9 percent), followed by middle-income developing countries (7.5 percent), and high-income non-OECD countries had the lowest applied MFN tariff rate (4.6 percent), while the global average was 7.6 percent (see Figure 2.4).

As the discussion above indicates, although average unweighted MFN applied tariff rates in agriculture have steadily declined, the average import-weighted applied tariff in agriculture has not declined at all—it fell from 16 percent in 2001 to 15.9 percent in 2005. That is because agricultural trade is still inundated with numerous tariff peaks, *ad valorem* tariffs, tariff rate quotas (TRQs), tariff escalations, opaque tariffs, and other, similar protections.

Tariff peaks

Tariff peaks, usually defined as a tariff above 15 to 20 percent of its *ad valorem* equivalent,[16] have been a particular problem in agricultural trade, especially because they are often geared to protect arbitrarily determined 'sensitive products' from international competition. The URAA's tariffication process allowed the conversion of previously protected NTBs into tariffs without specifically defining it numerically. As a result, many countries converted their NTBs into very high or extremely high tariffs, known as tariff peaks.[17] Some countries have fixed tariffs for so-called nationally sensitive products exceeding even 1,000 percent, and as a result, overall, over 65 percent of all agricultural tariff lines may be considered as sensitive products.[18] Iceland, for example, has more than 430 tariff lines above 20 percent, and 5,000 percent tariffs on Christmas trees and foliage. Norway has 307 tariff lines above 100 percent, and 5,000 percent tariffs on flour meal (ICTSD, 2009).

Moreover, wide dispersions exist between average tariffs and tariff peaks in many countries. As Table 2.7 indicates, the Republic of Korea shows the highest tariff peak of 917 percent with a very high variance across its tariff lines, while among the Quad countries—the EU, the US, Canada, and Japan—the EU showed the highest peak at 506 percent, followed by the US (350 percent), Canada (238 percent), and Japan (50 percent). With an average tariff rate of 11 percent and a maximum *ad valorem* tariff of 50 percent, Japan maintains an average tariff rate of 34.6 percent for grain, 54.6 percent for milk, and 32.5 percent for meat (Aksoy, 2005, 47–48). Due to such a wide difference between average tariff rates and the tariff peaks, average tariff rates barely reflect the actual protection of domestic products in many countries.

Existing agricultural tariff peaks also indicate that some countries impose such tariffs across the entire sensitive sector of their economies. For example, Canada maintains average applied tariffs of 114 percent on dairy (average bound tariff 314 percent), 88 percent on poultry (average bound tariff 598 percent), and 19 percent on processed foods (average bound tariff 275 percent). Similarly, Japan maintains 560 percent average applied tariffs on rice (bound tariff 778 percent), 118 percent on peanuts (bound tariff 737 percent), 180 percent on dairy (bound tariff 661 percent), 188 percent on wheat (bound tariff 306 percent), 50 percent on processed food (bound tariff 445 percent), and 30 percent on corn (bound tariff 218 percent). India, which has over 54 percent of its agricultural

Table 2.7 Tariff peaks and variance in selected countries (in %)

Country/group	*Average tariff*	*Maximum tariff*	*Standard deviation*	*Share of lines covered*
Canada	4.1	238.0	13.5	74.2
Japan	10.9	50.0	10.1	84.8
United States	9.9	350.0	26.5	99.5
European Union	19.0	506.3	27.3	85.9
Republic of Korea	39.9	917.0	107.9	97.9
Brazil	13.2	55.0	5.6	100.0
Costa Rica	14.2	154.0.0	18.0	100.0
Morocco	67.4	376.5	70.6	100.0
Indonesia	8.9	170	25.6	100.0
Malawi	16.5	25.0	8.5	100.0
Togo	15.6	20.0	6.1	99.9
Uganda	13.6	15.0	3.2	100.0

Source: Aksoy (2005, 48), attributed to the WTO integrated database.

Note

Most-favored nation, out-of-quota, applied tariffs.

tariff lines at 51 to 100 percent bound tariffs, and approximately 35 percent at 100 and 300 percent bound tariffs, maintains over 100 percent applied tariffs on corn, peanuts, and cotton (against bound tariffs of 300 percent), and on beef, pork, poultry, rice, wheat, and tobacco (against bound tariffs of 150 percent).

China, which has a bound rate and applied rate of tariff at around 16 percent, on the other hand, maintains a few tariff peaks. It has about 45 percent average applied bound tariffs on wheat (average bound tariff of 50 percent), 30 percent on tobacco (average bound tariff of 35 percent), and 25 percent applied tariffs on corn (bound tariff of 30 percent). The US also has some tariff peaks—43 percent on peanuts (bound rate 164 percent), 70 percent on tobacco (bound rate 440 percent), and 26 percent on dairy (bound rate 139 percent). The EU, which has only about 5 percent of tariff lines at 51 to 100 percent tariffs, maintains tariff peaks of 82 percent on beef (bound tariff 408 percent), 24 percent on dairy (bound tariff 264 percent), 30 percent on corn (bound tariff 175 percent), 61 percent on wheat (bound tariff 148 percent), 24 percent on poultry (bound tariff 94 percent), and 24 percent on pork (bound tariff 65 percent) (WTO, 2014).

The food-processing sector is another major area where tariff protection remains frequent and high in many developed country markets. The EU food industry accounts for about 30 percent of all tariff peaks—rates ranging between

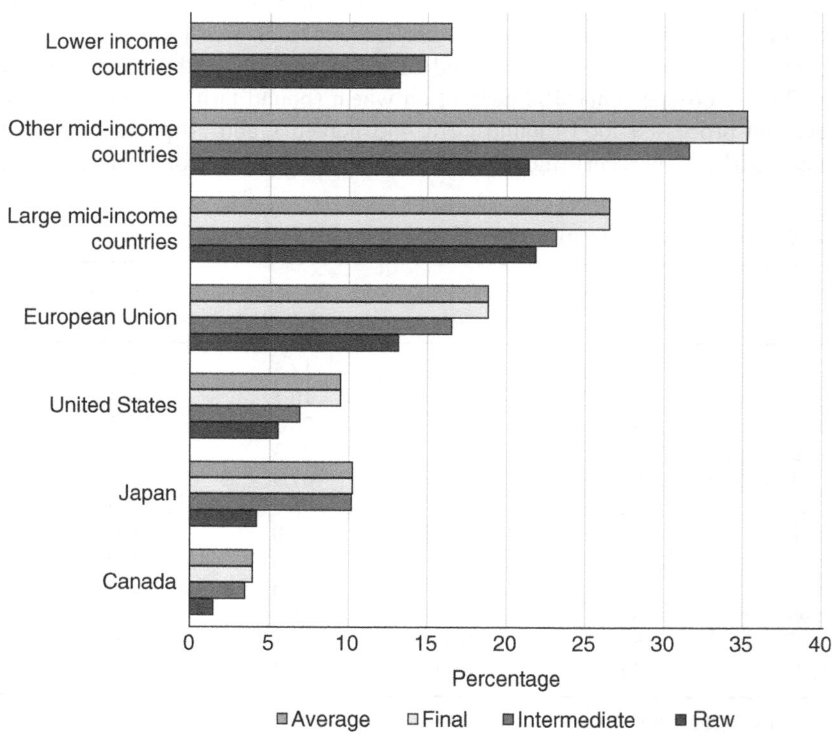

Figure 2.5 Tariff rate escalation in agriculture in selected countries (in %).

12 and 100 percent beyond the stages of immediate processing industries. Additional duties are also imposed to compensate processing industries for higher prices of agricultural inputs. Products subject to particularly high rates include cereals and sugar-based products, fruit preparations, canned fruit juices, and so on. In the US, the food industry accounts for one-sixth of all tariff peaks, falling into the same range as the EU (12 to 100 percent). Examples of such tariff peaks in the US include orange juice (31 percent), peanut butter (132 percent), and tobacco products (350 percent).[19] In Japan, the food industry accounts for 40 percent of all tariff peaks, and major protected products include margarine, canned meat, sugar confectionary, cereal products, preserved fruit, and vegetables.

As the discussion above indicates, both developed and developing countries have been using wide-ranging tariff peaks in both primary and processed agricultural products, but tariff peaks seem to be predominant in a few product groups, such as meat, dairy, cereals, and vegetables.[20] There are, however, certain tariff peaks that are very specific to certain countries, such as rice in Japan and South Korea, foliage in Iceland, flour in Norway, livestock in Switzerland, tobacco and cotton in the US and Japan, and beef, dairy, and corn in the EU.

Tariff rate quotas (TRQs)

One of the offshoots of the URAA's tariffication process is known as TRQs, which allow WTO members to apply lower tariff rates for specified quantities and higher tariff rates for quantities that exceed the quota. While complying with the tariffication process, many WTO members began to utilize this instrument to provide limited market access for sensitive commodities, fearing that tariffication might lead to extremely high tariffs. In an extensive study, Gibson and colleagues (2001, 16–20) found TRQs prevalent mostly in a few sensitive products, such as meat, dairy, and cereals. The study also found that the average over-quota tariff (tariff applied on imports in excess of the quota volume) for 25 of the countries was higher than the 62 percent average for all tariffs, and in 14 countries the average tariff for the TRQ lines was at least twice that for all lines.

The pattern of TRQ utilization also reveals that developed countries have been using TRQs more aggressively than developing countries. In the OECD countries almost 28 percent of domestic agricultural production is protected by TRQs. The rates however varied from country to country—from 68 percent in Hungary, 38 percent in the EU, 26 percent in the US, and 13 percent in Japan, while Australia and New Zealand had no TRQs at all (Aksoy, 2005, 49). Of the 1,371 individual tariff commitments reported to the WTO by 37 members, the top 10 countries in terms of number of TRQs were: Norway (232), Poland (109), Iceland (90), EC-15 (87), Bulgaria (73), Colombia (67), Korea (67), Venezuela (61), the US (54), and South Africa (53). Most of the TRQs were concentrated in four product groups—fruit and vegetables (355), meat products (247), cereals (217), and dairy products (181) (WTO, 2000). Developing countries, on the other hand, applied TRQs as simple tariffs (no higher tariff is levied on over-quota imports), which made TRQs ineffective in those countries (Abbott and Morse, 2000).

A basic problem with the existing pattern of TRQs is that they defeat the very purpose for which they were introduced by the architects of the URAA in the first place. As Josling (2004, 26–27) points out, across all WTO members the average over-quota tariff is 123 percent, five countries have average over-quota tariffs of at least 150 percent, and, in certain cases, over-quota tariffs exceed even 1,000 percent. Such over-quota tariffs have led to lower quota filling rates, often falling below 65 percent. Thus over-quota tariffs have been frustrating the very objective of the TRQs which was expected to increase market access for commodities that previously faced quantitative barriers. The existing pattern of TRQs also indicates that they are mainly directed to traditional partners, or are made accessible under preferential arrangements, which may be pre-empting trading opportunities for newcomers by leaving little room for imports from such countries.

Tariff escalations

Tariff escalations raise tariffs with levels of processing of products, and thus trade protection escalates with the increased levels of processing. In agriculture, tariff escalations have important bearings, especially in respect of processed foods. As Table 2.8 indicates, although tariff escalations in agricultural processed food take place all over the world, levels of escalation vary among developed and developing regions. Table 2.8 also indicates that even for raw materials, tariff rates are very high in low-income and mid-income countries compared with advanced industrialized economies. At the intermediate level of processed agricultural foods, tariff rates increase significantly for all countries,

Table 2.8 Tariff rate escalation in agriculture in selected countries and groups of countries (in %)

Country/group	*Raw*	*Intermediate*	*Final*	*Average*	*Share of lines covered*
Quad countries	6.1	9.3	14.8	10.7	86.7
Canada	1.4	3.4	3.8	3.8	76.0
Japan	4.2	10.2	10.3	10.3	85.5
United States	5.5	7.1	9.5	9.5	99.3
European Union	13.2	16.6	19.0	19.0	85.9
Large middle-income countries	21.9	23.3	26.6	26.6	91.3
Other middle-income countries	21.6	31.7	35.4	35.4	97.7
Lower-income countries	13.2	14.8	16.6	16.6	99.8

Source: Aksoy (2005, 48, Table 3.8).

Notes

Most-favored nation applied, *ad valorem*, out-of-quota duties. Data refer to 1999 to 2001 period.

but more so for low-income and mid-income countries. In the end, tariffs on final products are much lower in advanced countries compared with developing countries. For example, tariffs on final products were 9.5 percent in the US, 3.8 percent in Canada, and 19 percent in the EU (see Figure 2.5). In developing countries, on the other hand, final tariffs ranged between 16.6 percent in low-income countries (such as Bangladesh, Guatemala, Indonesia, and Zimbabwe) and 26.6 percent in middle-income countries (such as Bulgaria, Costa Rica, Malaysia, and the Philippines), and 35.4 percent in high-income developing countries (such as India, Brazil, China, and South Africa). The prevalence of relatively low tariffs on raw materials, then higher tariffs on intermediate products, and highest on consumer-ready items indicates that the first-stage processors of raw materials do not gain much benefit from protection (Josling, 2004, 26).

Gibson *et al.* (2001, 22–23) note that tariff escalation was most evident in the country schedules of Eastern Europe and the Middle East, followed by North America, South Asia, and the EU. In Eastern Europe, tariffs tended to escalate by at least 10 percent in all but three processing chains. The largest example of escalation, however, was found in sweeteners in North Africa, where the mean tariff increased by over 100 percent over those on sugar beet and sugar cane. Among the processed agricultural products tariff escalation was most pronounced for meat, sweeteners, and vegetable oil. In 2002, average tariff escalations in developed countries for some agricultural processed goods (final products) were as follows: (1) coffee—12.1 percent in the EU, 10.1 percent in the US, and 19.8 percent in Japan; (2) cocoa—30.6 percent in the EU, 15.3 percent in the US, and 21.7 percent in Japan; and (3) fruit—22. 5 percent in the EU, 10.2 percent in the US, and 16.7 percent in Japan.[21] These averages, however, mask very high peaks on individual products. For example, many agricultural products, such as live, fresh, chilled, or frozen crustaceans, faced tariff escalations of more than 100 percent in Japan and the US (Bacchetta and Bora, 2001).[22]

Effects of tariff escalations on developing countries

The available literature indicates that global trade in processed agricultural products grew faster than in primary agricultural products over recent decades. During the 1981 to 2000 period, exports of processed agricultural products grew at 6 percent annually, compared with 3.3 percent for primary products, raising developing countries' share in agricultural trade from 60 percent in 1981 to 1990 to 66 percent in 1991 to 2000. On the other hand, during the 1995 to 2008 period, trade in processed agricultural products more than doubled, from $211 billion to almost $500 billion—and grew much faster than overall agricultural goods. Moreover, annual growth rates had been exceptionally high for the processed forms of cereals, fruit, vegetables, pulses, tropical beverages, and poultry products. Much of the benefits of such higher growth accrued to high-income developed countries (Liapis, 2011, 16–17).

Table 2.9 shows tariff escalation rates (unweighted averages) in food and beverage products for different groups of economies as well as certain selected countries. As Table 2.9 indicates, tariff escalations are very high for low-income and middle-income developing countries (15.2 percent and 14 percent respectively), compared with those of high income OECD or non-OECD countries (9.8 percent and 8.4 percent, respectively). Higher rates of tariff escalations pose higher barriers to exports from developing countries as higher tariff escalation translates into higher effective rates of protection. As effective rates of protection depend on the fractions of value added after deducting intermediate inputs from the product value, with tariffs escalating with additional processing, the effective rate of protection also increases. Thus, increasing effective rates of protection for value added also means fewer opportunities for economically viable food and beverage processing in primary products producing countries. Higher tariff escalation may thus inhibit the growth of processed agricultural goods in developing countries in particular and global trade growth in general (Josling, 2004, 26).

As the discussion above suggests, tariff escalation prevails in a large number of agricultural commodity sectors such as meat, sugar, fruit, coffee, cocoa, and hides and skins. Although most of these products are of export interest to low-income developing countries, it is the food-processing industries in developed countries that are the primary beneficiaries of escalated tariffs in these products. Such a scenario also leads to the conclusion that tariff escalation in agricultural products has the potential to depress the growth of agricultural value addition and that of processed products in developing countries. The reason is simple: high tariff escalation reduces demand for processed imports from developing countries, and thus retards expansion of their processing industries, which in turn reduces opportunities for developing countries to accumulate modern skills, capital, and export diversification. Moreover, excessive reliance on primary product exports may also lead to the depletion of natural resources and disturb the ecological balance in developing countries (Cheng, 2007). Greater concentration on exports of less processed commodities in developing countries may also result in increased exposure to the risk of commodity price volatility, which, in turn, may significantly impede market access for these countries in global agricultural trade (FAO, 2004).[23]

Domestic support commitments

Domestic production support remains a great concern for global agricultural trade. The URAA grants exclusion of certain expenditures, such as those for public stockholding for food security purposes or for domestic food aid to vulnerable sections, from the AMS calculations, provided that the volume and accumulation of such stocks correspond to predetermined targets related solely to food security, and that the process of accumulation and disposal is financially transparent. It is precisely this exemption which allows WTO members to continue with some of the most retrenched support structures for subsidizing agriculture without failing to

Table 2.9 Tariff escalations in food and beverage products, 2005 to 2010 (unweighted average, in %)

Country code	*Country/group*	*Year*	*Food and beverage products*		
			Final goods	*Food primary*	*Food processing*
2	China	2010	13.6	10.7	14.6
4	Canada	2010	2.7	1.1	3.9
4	European Union	2010	3.8	2.3	5.0
4	Japan	2010	8.9	4.4	11.2
4	Korea, Republic of	2010	40.9	71.0	29.2
4	United States	2010	2.2	1.1	2.8
1	Low-income group (31)	2006/2010	15.2	13.4	15.9
2	Middle-income group (95)	2005/2010	14.0	12.0	14.9
3	High-income non-OECDs (17)	2007/2010	8.4	9.0	8.3
4	High-income OECDs (11)	2009/2010	9.8	9.5	10.0
1 to 4	World, all above countries (154)	2005/2010	13.6	11.9	14.3

Source: Author's compilation from UNCTAD TRAINS database.

Notes

Country codes are based on the classifications by income per capita in WDI 2011, where 1 = low income, 2 = middle income, 3 = high-income non-OECDs, and 4 = high-income OECD countries. Product categories are based on broad economic classification (BEC) under world integrated trade solution (WITS) of UNCTAD. European Union (27) counts as one.

meet their support reduction commitments under the URAA. As a result, many developed countries still continue to provide significant domestic supports to major agricultural commodities, such as sugar, rice, vegetables, wheat, beef, coarse grain, and dairy products.

Developed countries' agricultural subsidy structures are examined below in terms of Producers Support Estimates (PSE) and Total Support Estimates (TSE)—some of the central measurement instruments used by the OECD countries for this purpose. The PSE shows the annual monetary transfers (market price supports) to farmers from policy measures aimed at maintaining domestic prices for farm goods at levels higher (and occasionally lower) than those at the country's border, and providing payments to farmers (budgetary payments) on the basis of the quantity of a commodity produced, the amount of inputs used, the number of animals kept, the area farmed, or the revenue or income received by farmers, and so on. The TSE shows the share of GDP invested in total agricultural support in a given year.

The PSE comes close to the AMS calculation, but they are not same. The purpose of the PSE is to monitor and evaluate progress in agricultural policy reform, whereas the AMS is used as the basis for a legal commitment to reduce domestic support in the URAA. Moreover, the PSE covers all transfers to farmers from agricultural policies, whereas the AMS covers only domestic policies deemed to have the greatest production and trade effects (Amber box), and excludes trade policies that are covered under the WTO market access and export subsidy disciplines. The AMS also excludes production-limiting policies (Blue box) that are considered to be non- or least trade distorting (Green box) and certain trade distorting policies (e.g., input subsidies) when the level of domestic support is smaller than a specified *de minimis* level. Moreover, market price support in the PSE is measured at the farm gate level using actual producer and reference (border) prices for commodities in a given year, whereas market price support for the AMS is calculated by taking into consideration the difference between annual prices fixed by policy makers (administered prices) and world prices in the base period (1986–1988). Domestic supports to agriculture in the leading OECD and non-OECD countries have been analyzed below in terms of the PSE and the TSE, and are examined from the perspectives of the WTO mandated AMS.

Total agricultural support

In nominal terms, total agricultural support in the OECD countries, measured in TSE,[24] has increased from $296 billion in the base year (1986–1988) to $383.6 billion on average between 2006 and 2010: approximately 30 percent. As Table 2.10 indicates, among major OECD countries, the largest increase took place in the US (125 percent) followed by Canada (37 percent), Japan (9 percent), and the EU (6 percent). Smaller percentage increases in the EU, Japan, and Canada, compared with the US, however, should be understood in the context that the actual amounts spent for TSE in these countries in the base period were significantly higher than in the US (see Figure 2.6).[25]

Table 2.10 Total agricultural supports (TSE) in major OECD countries, 1986 to 2010 (in US$ billions)

Countries/ groups	*Indicators*	*Average 1986–1988*	*Average 1991–1995*	*Average 1996–2000*	*Average 2001–2005*	*2006*	*2007*	*2008*	*2009*	*2010*	*Average 2006–2010*
OECD	TSE	296.32	354.53	334.46	336.23	357.02	351.02	373.91	377.14	383.61	368.54
	TSE as % of GDP	2.97	2.10	1.38	1.05	0.96	0.89	0.93	0.96	0.93	0.93
Canada	TSE	7.52	6.63	4.91	7.05	8.98	9.05	8.37	9.66	10.30	9.27
	TSE as % of GDP	1.78	1.14	0.75	0.79	0.70	0.64	0.56	0.72	0.65	0.65
European Union	TSE	111.55	130.70	120.71	124.57	142.38	142.98	153.53	135.50	118.33	138.54
	TSE as % of GDP	2.56	1.82	1.40	1.15	0.98	0.84	0.84	0.83	0.73	0.84
Japan	TSE	58.42	77.27	66.58	56.60	47.72	45.25	53.59	57.26	63.64	53.49
	TSE as % of GDP	2.38	1.77	1.53	1.33	1.09	1.03	1.10	1.14	1.16	1.10
United States	TSE	60.18	70.86	84.10	93.82	94.92	97.17	104.71	123.63	135.49	111.18
	TSE as % of GDP	1.28	1.08	0.96	0.84	0.71	0.69	0.73	0.88	0.93	0.79

Source: Author's compilation from OECD-Stat.

Note
TSE = Total Producer Support Estimates.

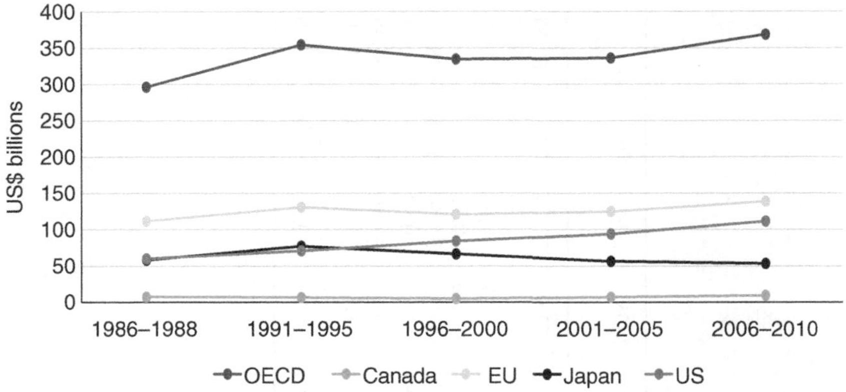

Figure 2.6 Total agricultural supports (TSE) in major OECD countries, 1986 to 2010 (in US$ billions).

In terms of its share in GDP, TSE came down sharply in the OECD countries during this period—falling from 3 percent in the base year to under 1 percent in 2010. This decline in the share of GDP had been gradual but steady. It fell to 2.1 percent on average between 1991 and 1995, then to 1.4 percent between 1996 and 2000, to 1.1 percent between 2001 and 2005, and finally to 0.9 percent between 2006 and 2010. Such a decline has been underpinned by a similar decline in the shares of agricultural support in GDPs of major OECD countries. For example, in the base year (1986–1988), the EU's share of agricultural support was 2.6 percent of its GDP, which declined to 0.8 percent during the 2006 to 2010 period. Similarly, Canada's share declined from 1.8 percent to 0.6 percent, Japan's share dropped from 2.4 percent to 1.1 percent, and the US's share dropped from 1.3 percent to 0.8 percent during the same period.

Agricultural producer support

As with the TSE, producer support to agriculture (PSE), which is a part of TSE, also fell consistently throughout the 1986 to 2010 period. In the base year (1986–1988), producer supports (measured as PSE) in OECD countries stood at 37 percent of gross farm receipts, which fell to 31.4 percent during the 1996 to 2000 period, then to 29.4 percent between 2001 and 2005, and to 22.4 percent between 2006 and 2010 (see Table 2.11).[26] Overall, producer supports in OECD, in terms of shares of GDP, thus declined significantly, by about 65 percent during the 1986 to 2010 period. In nominal terms, however, agricultural producer support showed an increase—from \$239.4 billion on average in 1986 to 1988 to \$250.4 billion on average between 2006 and 2010—of about 4 percent.

During the same period, average producer support in the EU, in nominal terms, increased from \$97.3 billion to \$120.3 billion—registering an increase of

Table 2.11 Agricultural producer supports (PSE) in OECD countries, 1996 to 2010 (in US$ billions)

	Average 1986–1988	*Average 1991–1996*	*Average 1996–2000*	*Average 2001–2005*	*2006*	*2007*	*2008*	*2009*	*2010*	*Average 2006–2010*
OECD	239.40	268.24	251.58	248.17	255.34	248.12	257.88	249.52	241.26	250.43
PSE (%)	37.0	33.4	31.5	29.4	26.4	22.0	21.0	22.7	19.9	22.4
EU	97.32	113.23	106.26	108.52	123.91	124.34	131.87	118.99	102.40	120.30
PSE (%)	39.2	36.0	34.4	32.1	29.0	23.5	22.0	23.3	19.8	23.5
Japan	49.75	60.23	51.11	45.49	39.41	35.24	42.62	46.47	55.22	43.79
PSE (%)	64.0	58.2	58.0	56.2	51.6	46.7	48.3	48.9	53.3	49.8
US	36.41	29.48	42.79	42.28	30.50	33.18	30.74	33.02	27.59	31.00
PSE (%)	21.9	15.3	19.5	17.4	11.2	10.0	8.8	10.6	7.7	9.7
Canada	6.02	4.91	3.54	5.23	6.60	6.29	5.68	6.76	7.16	6.50
PSE (%)	35.7	25.0	16.4	20.4	20.9	16.4	13.3	17.4	16.7	16.9

Source: Author's compilation from OECD-Stat.

Note
PSE = Producer's Support Estimates.

over 20 percent. Canada also experienced an increase in average annual producer support during this period, from $6 billion in 1986 to 1988 to $6.5 billion in 2006 to 2010 (see Figure 2.7). For the US and Japan, however, agricultural producer supports declined during the same period. In the US, producer supports, in nominal terms, fell from $36.4 billion in 1986 to 1988 to $31 billion in 2006 to 2010, and in Japan, from $49.7 billion to $43.8 billion.

Table 2.12 shows agricultural producer supports among selected OECD and non-OECD countries during the period 1986 to 2012. In 2012, producer support in terms of percentage of gross farm receipts among OECD members was the lowest in New Zealand (0.8 percent), followed by Australia (2.7 percent), Chile (3.3 percent), and the US (7.1 percent).[27] In the same year the highest percentage of producer support, in terms of gross farm receipts, went to the farmers of Norway (63.1 percent), followed by Switzerland (56.6 percent), Japan (60 percent), South Korea (53.8 percent), and Iceland (47.3 percent). Obviously producer supports in these latter countries have not changed much as a percentage of total farm support over the years. Back in 1986, the benchmark year for agricultural liberalization, such supports stood at 70 percent in Norway, 76 percent in Switzerland, 65 percent in Japan, 64.5 percent in Korea, and 75.6 percent in Iceland. Even in 2005, at the end of the 10-year transition period, agricultural producers' supports remained almost the same in these countries—65.8 percent in Norway, 66.7 percent in Switzerland, 53.8 percent in Japan, 59.7 percent in Korea, and 66.9 percent in Iceland. Clearly, overall producers' supports in terms of percentage of gross farm receipts in many OECD countries have not changed much, even after the full implementation of the URAA.

In the US, however, producers' supports to farmers fell drastically over the years. While in 1986 24.1 percent of gross farm receipts came from the state exchequer, the share fell to 23.3 percent in 2000, then to 15.3 percent in 2005, and to 7.1 percent in 2012. In the EU-27 also, producers' supports fell significantly

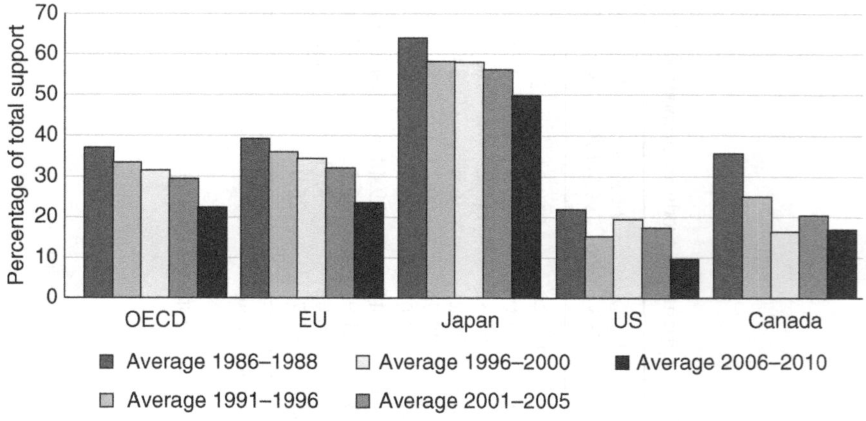

Figure 2.7 Producers' supports in major OECD countries as a percentage of total agricultural supports, 1986 to 2010 (in %).

during the same period—from 38.6 percent in 1986, the share fell to 32.7 percent in 2000, then to 30.8 percent in 2005, and to 19 percent in 2012. While the US cut down producers' supports to farmers by more than half, the EU-27 did so by one-third between 2005 and 2012.[28] Remarkably, New Zealand, a major agricultural country, reduced its producers' support, from 19.7 percent in 1968 to under 1 percent in 2012.

Among major non-OECD agricultural producers, China has clearly been demonstrating an upward trend in its supports to farmers. The country's share in producer supports in total farm support more than doubled between 1995 and 2012—an increase from 5.5 percent in 1995 to 16.8 percent in 2012. Indonesia has also increased its producers' supports threefold during the period—from 6 percent in 1995 to 21 percent in 2012. In the Russian Federation, agricultural producers' support increased from 14.2 percent in 1995 to 21.5 percent in 2010, but then fell to 13.5 percent in 2012. Brazil, a major agricultural country, has been demonstrating a downward trend in producers' support to farmers—from 5.7 percent in 2000, its share fell to 4.6 percent in 2012. In South Africa, producers' support to farmers fell more drastically during the period—from 14.9 percent in 1995 to 3.2 percent in 2012.[29] Overall, developing countries had a smaller share in agricultural producers' supports than developed countries throughout the period, indicating that producers' support to farmers is basically a problem with the developed countries.

Aggregate Measure of Support (AMS)

As discussed above, the URAA separates domestic agricultural supports into three categories—the Green box, the Blue box, and the Amber box[30]—and restricts only subsidies that fall into the Amber box. Price supports interventions, input subsidies, income transfers, and other such subsidies that affect production and trade brought under the Amber box—no matter whether they were product specific, non-product specific, or applied to agricultural production as a whole. Developed countries were allowed to maintain *de minimis* Amber box supports up to 5 percent of the value of agricultural production, and the limit was set at 10 percent for developing countries. All WTO members with subsidies larger than *de minimis* levels had to make reduction commitments expressed in terms of an Aggregate Measure of Support (AMS)—a quantified measure of trade-distorting domestic supports. Developed countries were given six years (up until 2000) to cut 20 percent of their AMS, and developing countries were given 10 years (up until 2004) to cut their AMS by 13.3 percent (see Table 2.13).

All 32 developed country members which provided domestic supports to agriculture submitted their concession commitments to the WTO by 2000. Surprisingly, the commitments showed that reducing the Amber box supports was not much of a problem for most of them. Even the top three agricultural subsidy providers in the world—the US, the EU, and Japan, which together accounted for more than 85 percent of agricultural supports in 1995—significantly exceeded their WTO commitments. As Table 2.13 shows, the US made a commitment to

Table 2.12 Agricultural producer supports in selected OECD and non-OECD countries, 1986 to 2012 (producer PSE in %, producer NPC in ratio, PSE amount in US$ billions, unless otherwise indicated)

Countries/groups		*1986*	*1990*	*1995*	*2000*	*2005*	*2010*	*2012*
OECD	PSE estimates	222.79	251.09	269.17	244.78	268.59	241.77	258.64
	PSE	37.6	31.8	31.2	32.3	27.7	19.2	18.6
	NPC	1.5	1.4	1.3	1.3	1.2	1.1	1.1
Australia	PSE estimates	1.50	1.33	1.37	0.68	1.11	1.26	1.36
	PSE	12.9	7.9	6.4	3.3	3.6	2.8	2.7
	NPC	1.1	1.1	1.0	1.0	1.0	1.0	1.0
Canada	PSE estimates	6.0	6.25	4.07	4.3	6.32	7.15	7.59
	PSE	37.4	31.9	19.1	19.3	21.3	16.7	14.3
	NPC	1.4	1.4	1.1	1.1	1.1	1.1	1.1
Chile	PSE estimates	...	...	436.2	577.3	319.7	285.6	387.9
	PSE	...	...	8.7	11.2	5.0	2.6	3.3
	NPC	...	...	1.1	1.1	1.0	1.0	1.0
European Union	PSE estimates	84.99	105.11	123.42	86.23	125.52	102.56	106.98
	PSE	38.6	32.9	34.8	32.7	30.8	19.8	19.0
	NPC	1.7	1.5	1.4	1.3	1.2	1.0	1.0
Iceland	PSE estimates (US$ millions)	158.8	177.0	134.5	153.0	254.2	126.6	151.4
	PSE	75.6	72.1	59.8	69.6	66.9	44.3	47.3
	NPC	3.9	3.4	2.5	3.0	2.7	1.6	1.7
Japan	PSE estimates	46.07	42.68	72.79	54.06	44.41	56.84	64.76
	PSE	65.1	51.5	62.2	59.7	53.8	54.9	55.9
	NPC	2.7	2.0	2.5	2.4	2.1	2.0	2.1
South Korea	PSE estimates	9.3	19.15	25.37	19.25	22.04	15.28	20.48
	PSE	64.5	74.3	72.8	66.1	59.7	40.1	53.8
	NPC	2.8	3.8	3.5	2.9	2.3	1.6	2.0
Mexico	PSE estimates (US$ millions)	549.8	4303.1	–1059.5	7411.6	4979.9	6272.1	7070.6
	PSE	3.6	15.8	–4.7	23.4	12.9	12.4	12.3
	NPC	0.9	1.1	0.9	1.2	1.1	1.0	1.1
New Zealand	PSE estimates (US$ millions)	791.0	97.8	77.7	20.1	128.7	100.9	122.6
	PSE	19.7	2.2	1.3	0.3	1.3	0.7	0.8
	NPC	1.0	1.0	1.0	1.0	1.0	1.0	1.0

Norway	PSE estimates	2.41	3.52	2.90	2.15	3.35	3.63	4.27
	PSE	69.6	71.2	64.3	66.5	65.8	60.4	63.1
	NPC	4.2	4.1	2.5	2.5	2.4	2.0	2.0
Switzerland	PSE estimates	4.48	5.93	6.04	4.43	5.51	5.0	5.94
	PSE	75.9	72.8	65.3	70.7	66.7	52.4	56.6
	NPC	4.1	3.8	2.7	2.7	2.2	1.5	1.5
Turkey	PSE estimates (US$ millions)	3.16	7.62	7.32	8.50	16.5	21.56	16.69
	PSE	17.3	24.4	25.2	30.5	33.1	26.3	22.4
	NPC	1.2	1.3	1.2	1.4	1.5	1.3	1.1
United States	PSE estimates	38.33	31.26	20.42	52.28	40.62	27.97	30.17
	PSE	24.1	16.7	10.1	23.3	15.3	7.8	7.1
	NPC	1.2	1.1	1.1	1.2	1.1	1.0	1.0
Brazil	PSE estimates	…	…	8.35	2.7	5.15	7.2	9.0
	PSE	…	…	–14.8	5.7	6.7	4.5	4.6
	NPC	…	…	0.9	1.0	1.0	1.0	1.0
China	PSE estimates	…	…	12.24	6.06	31.21	122.1	16.56
	PSE	…	…	5.5	2.3	7.4	15.3	16.8
	NPC	…	…	1.1	1.0	1.0	1.1	1.2
Indonesia	PSE estimates	…	…	2.11	1.65	1.4	2.37	2.8
	PSE	…	…	6.0	6.9	3.7	21.0	20.9
	NPC	…	…	1.1	1.1	1.0	1.3	1.3
Russian Federation	PSE estimates	…	…	5.62	0.26	6.36	15.97	13.25
	PSE	…	…	14.2	1.1	14.5	21.5	13.5
	NPC	…	…	0.9	1.0	1.1	1.2	1.1
South Africa	PSE estimates (US$ millions)	…	…	1430.8	415.7	753.3	314.6	637.0
	PSE	…	…	14.9	5.8	6.2	1.7	3.2
	NPC	…	…	1.2	1.1	1.0	1.0	1.0

Source: Compiled from OECD-Stat.

Notes
PSE = Producer Support Estimates; NPC = Nominal Protection Coefficient.

Table 2.13 Domestic support reduction commitments in aggregate measure of support (AMS) in selected countries, 1996 to 2010

Country	*Aggregate measure of support (AMS)*					*Allocation of subsidies across boxes*				
	Base year (1986–1988)	*Commitment in 2000*	*Year*	*Actual AMS reduction*	*Unused Ceiling*	*Year*	*Amber box*	*Blue box*	*Green box*	*Total domestic support*
USA (US$ in billions)	23.87	19.1	1995	6.2	12.9	1995	6.2	7	46.0	60.7
			2000	16.8	2.3	2000	16.8	0	50.1	74.2
			2005	12.9	6.2	2005	12.9	0	71.2	90.1
			2010	15.0	4.1	2009	4.3	0	103.2	114.8
EU (Euro in billions)	76.50	61.20	1995	64.4	–3.2	1995	64.4	26.9	24.2	116.6
			2000	38.9	22.3	2000	38.9	19.8	19.5	78.7
			2005	28.4	32.8	2005	28.4	13.5	40.5	83.2
			2009	11.8	49.4	2009	11.8	5.3	62.8	81.0
Japan (Yen in billions)	4966.0	3973.0	1995	3,329.7	643.3	1995	3,329.7	0	2,818.1	6,521.2
			2000	708.5	3,264.5	2000	708.5	92.7	2,595.3	3,428.2
			2005	593.3	3,379.7	2005	593.3	65.3	1,916.3	2,616.2
			2009	564.8	3,408.2	2009	564.8	21.8	1,848.4	2,608.1
China (US$ in billions)	–	–	–	–	–	1995	11.6	0	22.3	33.8
						2000	11.2	0	25.1	36.3
						2001	8.2	0	29.3	38.4
All other countries (US$ in billions)	–	–	–	–	–	1995	12.1	1.2	27.9	42.8
						2000	8.2	0.08	15.8	28.1
						2003	5.1	0.009	13.5	21.9

Sources: Author's compilation. Data for the EU, the US and Japan taken from Poczta-Wajda (2013), and data for China taken from USDA Economic Research Service.

Note
All other countries refer to the countries that had notified the WTO of their AMS by 2007.

bring down Amber box support to $19.1 billion (25 percent below the base year level) but actually brought it down to $16.8 billion by 2000, about 30 percent below the base year level. The EU committed itself to bring down its Amber box supports to €61.2 billion (25 percent below the base year level of support), but actually brought it down to €38.9 billion by 2000, about 50 percent below the base year level. Similarly, Japan committed itself to bring down its Amber box supports to ¥3973 billion by 2000, but brought it down to ¥708.5 billion, cutting it to almost one-fifth.

Interestingly, such spectacular reductions actually may have been achieved without any real cuts in domestic supports in any of these countries. Japan, for example, met its WTO commitments without actually cutting the subsidy level at all. As Table 2.13 indicates, both Amber box and Green box supports have declined in Japan over the years in nominal terms. While Amber box supports declined from ¥3329.7 billion in 1995 to ¥564.8 billion in 2009, the Green box supports declined from ¥2818 billion to ¥1848 billion, and overall agricultural support declined by more than half—from ¥6521 billion to ¥2608 billion—during the same period. But as the world market price declined in terms of yen, Japan was actually able to raise the real value of domestic supports to its mid-1980s level and still fulfill its obligations under the WTO Agreement (Poczta-Wajda, 2013).[31]

In the US and the EU—the largest providers of agricultural supports in the world—the decline in Amber box supports was actually accompanied by a simultaneously applied significant increase in Green box supports. As Table 2.13 suggests, Amber box supports in the US declined to $4.3 billion in 2009 from $16.8 billion in 2000, when Green box supports more than doubled, increasing to $103.2 billion from $50.1 billion. In the EU, Amber box supports fell to €11.8 billion in 2009 from €64.4 billion in 1995, while Green box supports increased to €62.8 billion from €24.2billion. Such a strong correlation between dwindling Amber box supports and increasing Green box supports in the post-1995 period suggests that the largest agricultural subsidy providers in the world may be craftily restructuring agricultural support packages so that they could presumably continue to maintain considerable domestic supports even after the expiry of WTO deadlines.

After all, Annex 2 of the URAA—which defines Green box supports—grants broad latitude to WTO members to designate a wide range of supports in this category, including general government services in the areas of research, infrastructure, disease control, environmental protection, food safety, food subsidy for the poor, regional development programs, as well as direct income support for producers. The only caveat is that such supports must be decoupled from current production and prices.[32]

Box 2.1 Agricultural support reforms in the United States

The evolution of agricultural support programs in the US may be traced to the Agricultural Adjustment Act (AAA) of 1933, an omnibus farm relief legislation, which sought to restore agricultural prosperity by curtailing farm production, reducing export surpluses, and raising prices during the Great Depression. The Act allowed the Roosevelt Administration to subsidize seven major crops—corn, wheat, cotton, rice, peanuts, tobacco, and milk—and to buy excess grain from farmers to sell later on if bad weather or other circumstances negatively affected output. In 1936, the US Supreme Court, however, declared the AAA unconstitutional on the grounds that the federal government lacked the authority to help farmers, which belonged to state jurisdiction. In 1938, Congress, however, passed a new bill—the Agricultural Adjustment Act of 1938—with a built-in requirement to update it every five years. The new Act, in line with the 1933 Act, encouraged agricultural conservation, governmental control in balancing agricultural prices, and established food reserves for periods of shortages. The structure of agricultural price supports laid down by the Roosevelt Administration remained virtually intact up until the mid-1980s.

A major restructuring of the US agricultural programs came with the Federal Agriculture Improvement and Reform (FAIR) Act of 1996 during the Clinton Administration. This law sought to instill a market mechanism in agriculture by introducing direct payments to farmers instead of purchasing extra grain. It removed the link between income support payments and farm prices, and authorized what is called Production-Flexibility Contract Payments which provided participating producers with fixed government payments independent of current farm prices and production. The FAIR Act also allowed participating farmers to plant 100 percent of their total contract acreage to any crop, with some limitations on fruit and vegetables. The Act eliminated an acreage reduction program, but continued nonrecourse loans (with marketing loan repayment provisions) in a modified form. While price support for milk was slated for phasing out in four years, dairy processors were allowed to obtain recourse loans on dairy products. Trade and food aid programs were reoriented toward market mechanisms, with an increased emphasis on high-value and value-added products. Programs initiated by the FAIR Act, however, led to a huge increase in farm subsidies—as direct payments supported struggling farmers, regardless of crop output.

The next major initiative came with the Farm Security and Rural Investment Act of 2002 during the George W. Bush Administration, which continued many of the provisions of the FAIR Act, but altered the farm payment program and dramatically increased agricultural subsidies. The Act introduced a Counter-Cyclical Payments (CCPs) program, expanded conservation land retirement programs and emphasized on-farm environmental practices, relaxed rules to make more borrowers eligible for federal farm credit assistance, added various commodities to those requiring country-of-origin labeling, and, above all, significantly increased agricultural subsidies, especially targeting the production of grain, oilseed, and upland cotton.

Another phase of major agricultural reforms was also introduced during the Bush Administration under the Food, Conservation and Energy Act of 2008. The Act created a new Average Crop Revenue Election (ACRE) program under which producers were permitted to participate in a state-based revenue guarantee on acres planted. The Act also strengthened the Milk Income Loss Contract (MILC) program by increasing price support to famers and established a new Disaster Assistance

Program to complement the existing crop insurance program by providing additional assistance to farmers on the basis of loss of crop revenue due to disasters such as floods or drought. The law also eliminated the so-called three-entity rule, which enabled farmers to receive twice the enacted payment limit, and tightened the adjusted gross income (AGI) eligibility test by capping non-farm income to receive farm program benefits of up to $500,000, which was prompted by uneven distribution of subsidy resulting from the 2002 Act. In 2007, for example, 10 percent of farmers received over 75 percent of federal subsidy dollars.

The Obama Administration introduced the Agriculture Reform, Food and Jobs Act, 2014, which eliminated scores of existing programs, including the Direct Payments program, the CCPs program, the ACRE program, the Supplemental Revenue Assistance Payments (SURE) program, the Dairy Product Price Support Program (DPPSP), and the MILC program. The Act raised the adjusted gross income cap for farmers to $750,000 for receiving agricultural supports and introduced several new programs, including the Agricultural Risk Coverage (ARC) program, which allows farmers to choose between coverage at the individual farm level or at the county level; the Adverse Market Payments (AMP) program, which provides payments to farmers only when prices drop below a reference price; and the Marketing Loan program, which provides upland cotton farmers with operating capital to bring them into compliance with WTO requirements.

The 2014 Farm Act also brought dairy under two new programs—the Dairy Production Market Protection Program (DPMPP), which protects producer margins equal to the difference between the all-milk price and a national feed cost, and the Dairy Market Stabilization Program (DMSP), which promotes growth while encouraging producers who participate in the program. The law also expanded crop insurance coverage for underserved crops and regions, including fruit and vegetable producers, created a stand-alone revenue protection coverage program for cotton growers, and a separate peanut revenue insurance program with an effective price for peanut growers.

The 2014 Farm Act has also significantly expanded credits and other benefits to boost US agricultural exports. Under the law, the Export Credit Guarantee program provides export credit guarantees to help ensure the availability of credit to finance exports to countries where financing may not be available; the Market Access program provides matching funds to promote US agricultural products in overseas markets; the Foreign Market Development program provides matching funds to nonprofit commodity or trade associations to aid in the long-term expansion of export markets; the Emerging Markets and Facility Guarantee Loan Program provides funding for technical assistance to promote exports to emerging markets and supports loan guarantees to establish or improve agriculture-related facilities in emerging markets; the Technical Assistance for Specialty Crops program provides financial assistance to producers and exporters of specialty crops in addressing barriers to trade for their products in overseas markets; and the Global Crop Diversity Trust provides for the storage and maintenance of seed from food crops from all over the world in a facility in the Arctic Circle in northern Norway.

As the discussion above indicates, agricultural supports and subsidies have been granted in numerous ways and forms to US farmers since 1933, and such supports have been revised and revisited every five years as a matter of law.*

Note

* For more details see official websites of the US Department of Agriculture, the Congressional Budget Office, and the Agricultural Committees of US Congress.

The tools employed for such restructuring and reorganization—in other words, reshuffling support policy measures among boxes—however, show divergent patterns. During the implementation period (1995–2000), the US met the Amber box reduction commitments by including its supports for national food aid programs and by replacing direct payments to producers with the Production Flexibility Contract (PPC) introduced under the Federal Agriculture Improvement and Reform (FAIR) Act, 1996 (see Box 2.1). Sumner (2006) showed that the AMS notifications of the US for the years 2000 to 2006 to the WTO—ranging between a low of $7.0 billion in 2004 to a high of $16.1 billion in 2000 and well below the $19.1 billion cap—would change the scenario completely if the PFC and countercyclical payments (created by the Farm Security and Rural Investment Act, 2002) were considered as Amber box payments. With these programs included, the total AMS of the US would be $29.1 billion in 2000, $25.3 billion in 2001, and $26.3 billion in 2006—far exceeding the $19.1 billion limit.[33] It is also remarkable that total domestic supports to agriculture in the US almost doubled during the 1995 to 2009 period (Table 2.13).

The EU, on the other hand, met the URAA obligations during the implementation period (1995–2000) by excluding direct payments under production-limiting programs (the Blue box) from its reduction commitments. This resulted in total AMS reduction in 2000 to 2001 to 18 percent of the value of its agricultural production, but with the addition of the Blue box payments (product-specific supports), the total AMS would be 27 percent (Hoda and Gulati 2007, 136). To meet its reduction commitments, the EU moved its compensatory payments for cereal producers, the beef and suckling cow premiums, which were part of AMS calculations during the UR negotiations, into to the Blue box, which allowed the EU to meet its Amber box reduction commitments during the implementation period without much effort (Poczta-Wajda, 2013). In subsequent years, the EU moved most of its supports to the Green box by introducing what is called the Single Payment Scheme (SPS), which decoupled direct payments by emphasizing so-called Greening programs. During the 2000 to 2009 period, however, total supports to agriculture in the EU declined considerably, compared with the 1995 level (see Table 2.13). As Box 2.2 explains, in recent years, the EU has further tightened its subsidy-driven agricultural programs, and has even frozen governmental outlays to agriculture for the 2014 to 2020 period to the 2013 level.[34]

Box 2.2 Agricultural support reforms in the European Union

The European Union's major agricultural reforms date back to the establishment of the Common Agricultural Policy (CAP) in 1962 following the Treaty of Rome signed in 1957. Under the CAP program, the EU provided massive price supports to major temperate-zone agricultural products, including cereals, dairy products, beef, pork, sugar, and certain fruits and vegetables. On top of guaranteeing prices above the international prices on all such products, the program also guaranteed minimum price for several other products such as durum wheat, olive oil, tobacco, oilseed, and sheep under deficiency payments schemes. Such price supports and deficiency payments were also supplemented by a plethora of other administrative and governmental measures such as aid to production in the area cultivated, access to inputs at lower costs, compensatory allowance for produce left in stock at the end of the marketing year, aid for private storage, payment to industries for the use of domestic products, a premium per head of sheep, and supplemented price support. Absolutely no limit was set on government expenditures and other measures of domestic supports.

Moreover, agricultural imports at prices lower than domestic prices were shut off by border measures. For cereals, where the threshold prices provided the minimum import prices, a variable levy was determined every day on the basis of the difference between the threshold price and the lowest recorded world price. For certain fruits and vegetables, the reference price was the system applied—which resulted in a de facto minimum wholesale price below which imported products were not allowed to be sold. The EU also made preferential quota arrangements for temperate-zone agricultural products—such as bovine animals, live cane or beet sugar, sheep and goat meat, butter, cheese, manioc, fresh bananas—with several of its trade partners. Market access was also restricted by a separate variable levy on processed products and specific tariffs.

By the 1970s through the 1980s, such measures led to massive increases in agricultural outputs, productivity, and technological advancement in the EU, and by the late 1980s the EU actually ran surpluses in many agricultural products. The phenomenal success of the CAP program, however, came at a huge cost: more and more marginal and environmentally sensitive lands were brought under production, solitary emphasis on production-tied compensation resulted in rewarding professional farmers and penalizing family farmers, and to top it all, the costs to the Exchequer mounted significantly.

It was in 1988 that some serious attempts were made, for the first time to curb domestic support to agriculture in the EU. Any onward increase in farm support was capped at 74 percent of the EU's GDP growth, and at the same time automatic stabilizers were introduced to limit support for each product to a maximum guaranteed quantity (MGM). In case any agricultural production exceeded the MGM for a product, it was made subject to automatic cuts in price supports the following year. The reforms, however, failed to bring any far-reaching change.

In 1992 the MacSharry Reforms were introduced, named after the European Commissioner for Agriculture Ray MacSharry, which actually sought to break away from the highly subsidized regime by injecting pro-market principles. To switch from product support (through prices) to producer support (through income support), the MacSharry reforms sought to cut price supports by as much as 29 percent for cereals, 9 percent for butter, 7.5 percent for dairy products, and 15 percent for beef. Direct payments were introduced in order to compensate for the decrease of the price support. To qualify for compensatory payments farmers were required to leave 15 percent of their land fallow, but areas left fallow were entitled to the same compensation as the areas under cultivation. The reforms also provided incentives to farmers for optimizing profits by looking beyond mere output, by developing and conserving rural areas.[a]

The next major phase of reforms in EU agriculture came with the so-called Agenda 2000, which sought to develop a more modern and sustainable agricultural sector through greater market orientation and competition. The reforms, among other things, envisaged: (1) a substantial cut in the target prices of agricultural products in order to make them more competitive on internal and external markets; (2) full compensation for drops in farmers' income without linking it to the quantities produced; and (3) recourse to measures that limited the use of the means of production, such as set-aside of arable land, withdrawal of part of the land for major crops, and limits on livestock numbers per hectare of fodder area. The reforms also sought to conserve the environment and landscape by encouraging early retirement of certain categories of farmers with the transfer of their land to other uses, and to facilitate the use of farmland for other purposes, such as afforestation or leisure.

The reforms envisaged by the Agenda 2000 represented a move in the CAP program from market price supports toward measures allowed under the exempt categories of the Blue box and Green box of the Uruguay Round Agreement in Agriculture (URAA). Implemented during the 2000 to 2006 period, it deepened the McSharry reforms of 1992 by cutting institutional prices further and increasing compensatory payments. Under this program, grain support was reduced by 15 percent, support to beef was reduced by 20 percent, and direct payment to certain other products also came down significantly. In 2003, the EU adopted the decoupled single farm payment program, replacing direct payments offered for arable crops (such as cereals, oilseed, and protein crops), and for beef and sheep premiums as well as dairy products. The next major CAP reform came in 2004, when tobacco, olive oil, and cotton were also brought under the decoupled single farm payment program. Sugar, another highly subsidized product, was also brought under the reforms in 2006, following challenges by Australia, Brazil, and the US in the WTO.

Finally, the latest round of agricultural reforms envisaged by the EU is outlined by the CAP Reform 2014 to 2020 initiative, which seeks to strengthen links between the two pillars of CAP. The first pillar of CAP supports farmers' incomes provided in the form of direct payments and market measures, and is entirely financed from the EU Agricultural Guarantee Fund. The second pillar is the support provided for the development of rural areas, which is co-financed by member states and the European Agricultural Fund for Rural Development. The new round of reforms seeks to link the two pillars under a more holistic and integrated approach.

The latest reform package emphasizes a new architecture of better targeted and more equitable direct payments, an enhanced safety net, and strengthened policies for rural development. It seeks to provide more equitable distribution of direct payments by progressively reducing the differences in the average level of direct payments received by farmers across the EU. The reforms also envisage what is called the 'greening' payment, which guarantees 30 percent of direct income support for farmers if they observe farming practices that are beneficial to the environment and the climate. Most importantly, the reform seeks to freeze the EU budgetary outlays for both pillars at the level of 2013. As a result, in real terms CAP funding is now slated to decrease in the future compared to the current period. The new CAP thus seeks to promote a competitive agricultural sector capable of competing in world markets without excessive subsidies, preserving natural resources, and adopting environmentally safe production methods.[b]

Notes

a For more details see http://ec.europa.eu/agriculture/cap-history/1992-reform/index_en.htm.

b For more details see http://ec.europa.eu/agriculture/policy-perspectives/policy-briefs/05_en.pdf.

As Table 2.13 shows, while the Amber box supports in China declined from \$11.5 billion in 1999 to \$9.1 billion in 2001, the Green box supports increased from \$22.3 billion to \$29.3 billion during the same period, when overall agricultural support increased from \$33.8 billion to \$38.4 billion. Yet the level of government subsidies in Chinese agriculture, which is one of the largest producers of major agricultural products in the world, is demonstratively far lower than the supports provided in the US, the EU, or Japan. Overall, AMS calculations reported to the WTO by all other countries by 2007 indicate that both Amber and the Green box supports declined by more than half during the 1995 to 2003 period—while Amber box supports declined from \$12.1 billion to \$5.1 billion, Green box supports fell from \$27.9 billion to \$13.5 billion, and total support declined from \$42.8 billion to \$21.9 billion during the same period.[35]

As the discussion above indicates, like tariffs, there are waters in the AMS calculations as well, which allow major agricultural subsidy providers to switch supports to different boxes in order to satisfy WTO obligations without actually reducing supports. Moreover, the AMS calculation method lends itself to questionable measurements. The calculation involves two components, namely product-specific support and non-product-specific support, and the reduction commitment applies to the total AMS—the sum of both components. This means that a country can reduce its total support while increasing its support to selected or sensitive sectors. Moreover, the price support for the AMS is calculated on the basis of the difference between a fixed world price and a domestic administered price. As the reference external price is fixed, calculation of the AMS may not correspond to the real AMS, and as a result may not measure real support. The exchange rate may also be problematic for the AMS calculation, as administrative prices are expressed in national currency, but the reference price has to be converted into domestic currency at the fixed exchange rate. In addition, a country's AMS reduction obligations may increase when it raises administered prices in response to high inflation rates. Finally, the selection of 1986 to 1988 as the benchmark period for AMS has also eroded the effectiveness of the AMS calculation. World market prices were at one of their lowest levels in the base year, which resulted in very high domestic supports (as the difference between the world prices and domestic prices were exceptionally high), which, in turn, made it easier for many developed countries to meet their AMS reduction commitments without much effort (Poczta-Wajda, 2013).[36]

Commodity subsidies

Historically, commodity subsidies have played crucial roles in agricultural production in many developed countries. Sumner (2006) showed that in the US the per acre average cost of production was above per acre market revenue for almost all major crops, including corn, wheat, rice, cotton, and soybeans, signifying that average American farmers would lose money every year if no government subsidies were available to cover their losses. The EU also massively subsidized agriculture for several decades, which eventually paved the way for the region to emerge as one of the largest agricultural producers and exporters in the world by the early 1980s. Since mid-1995, however, all developed countries, including the US and the EU, have been obligated to undertake necessary measures to reduce such supports in order to comply with URAA requirements.

As Table 2.14 indicates, over the years producer support has indeed declined quite significantly in both powerhouses of subsidized agriculture—the US and the EU—although the decline has not been so robust for the OECD countries taken as a whole. For the US, producer supports, measured in producer support estimates (PSE), fell from $36.4 billion in 1986 to 1988 (base year) to $29.9 billion in 2010 to 2012, while during the same period such supports for the EU fell from $88 billion to $79.1 billion. For the OECD as a whole, however, producer support showed a rise from $239.1 billion in 1986 to 1988 to $252.5 billion in 2010 to 2012. Many of these supports/subsidies were allocated to individual commodities under what is known as the Single Commodity Transfer (SCT). As Table 2.14 shows, for the whole OECD, SCT, as a percentage of producer support estimates (PSE), fell from 88 percent in the base year to 75 percent in 1995 to 1997, and then to 52 percent in 2010 to 2012. During the same period, the share of SCT in producer support in the US also fell from 71 percent to 33 percent—slashed by more than half. The EU-27, however, slashed commodity supports (SCT) by more than 75 percent—from 93 percent to 21 percent during the same period.

Crop-specific supports

Crop-specific government subsidies also demonstrate a similar pattern. For wheat, producer SCT, as a percentage of PSE, fell from 43.2 percent in the base year to 3.6 percent in 2010 to 2012 in the OECD countries, while it dropped from 46 percent to 6 percent in the US, and from 49 percent to under 1 percent in the EU (see Figures 2.8, 2.9, and 2.10). For corn/maize, the SCT for the whole OECD dropped from 36.2 percent in the base year to 3.1 percent in the 2010 to 2012 period, reflecting a similar drop in the US and the EU as well. Although the decline in SCT for rice was trivial for the OECD as a whole (dropping from 79.8 percent in the base year to 62 percent in 2010 to 2012), it was quite significant in both the US and the EU. In the US, the SCT for rice fell to 2 percent in 2010 to 2012 from 50 percent in the base year, and in the EU the decline was to from 59 percent to 11 percent during the same period. For sugar, the SCT in OECD countries dropped from 50.8 percent in the base year to 13.6 percent in 2010 to 2012. During the same period the SCT for sugar dropped from 56 percent to 28 percent in the US, and from 59 percent to 2 percent in the EU. For milk, the percentage of SCT in the OECD dropped from 50.3 percent in the base year to 10.1 percent in 2010 to 2012. During the same period, the drop was 35 percent to 5 percent in the US and 70 percent to 2 percent in the EU.

Evidently, in aggregate, single commodity transfers have come down significantly in OECD countries for most of the major agricultural commodities since the mid-1990s, coinciding with the integration of agriculture into the strengthened

Table 2.14 Single commodity transfers in OECD countries, 1986 to 2012 (% of total producer support)

	OECD			*USA*			*EU27*		
	1986–1988	*1995–1997*	*2010–2012*	*1986–1988*	*1995–1997*	*2010–2012*	*1986–1988*	*1995–1997*	*2010–2012*
PSE (US$)	239.5	253.9	252.5	36.4	26.6	29.9	88.0	93.8	79.1
SCT (in %)	88	75	52	71	51	33	93	70	21
Single commodity transfers (in %)									
Wheat	43.2 (1.7)	8.8 (1.1)	3.6 (1.0)	46 (1.3)	5 (1.0)	6 (1.0)	49 (2.1	11 (1.0)	0 (0.9)
Maize	36.2 (1.3)	7.4 (1.0)	3.1 (1.0)	35 (1.1)	0 (1.0)	3 (1.0)	51 (2.2)	35 (1.3)	0 (0.8)
Barley	52.3 (2.2)	12.7 (1.1)	4.3 (1.0)	41 (1.8)	2 (1.0)	4 (1.0)	58 (2.6)	13 (1.2)	0 (1.0)
Oats	31.7 (1.5)	17.4 (1.2)	2.3 (1.0)	–	–	–	33 (1.6)	25 (1.3)	0 (0.9)
Sorghum	31.0 (1.2)	2.2 (1.0)	6.9 (1.0)	36 (1.2)	2 (1.0)	7 (1.0)	–	–	–
Rice	79.8 (4.9)	75.4 (4.2)	62.0 (2.4)	50 (1.5)	8 (1.0)	2 (1.0)	59 (2.5)	33 (1.5)	11 (0.8)
Rapeseed	47.5 (1.9)	1.2 (1.0)	1.0 (1.0)	–	–	–	58 (2.4)	0 (1.0)	0 (1.0)
Sunflower	47.3 (1.9)	4.5 (1.0)	4.7 (1.0)	–	–	–	56 (2.3)	0 (1.0)	0 (1.0)
Soybean	8.7 (1.1)	(2.0) (1.0)	4.8 (1.0)	2 (1.0)	0 (1.0)	3 (1.0)	61 (2.6)	0 (1.0)	0 (1.0)
Sugar	50.8 (2.3)	41.2 (1.8)	13.6 (1.1)	56 (2.3)	37 (1.6)	28 (1.4)	59 (22.2)	50 (15.7)	2 (5.2)
Milk	59.3 (2.8)	44.7 (1.8)	10.1 (1.1)	35 (1.6)	35 (1.6)	5 (1.0)	70 (4.6)	50 (2.1)	2 (1.0)
Beef and Veal	27.9 (1.4)	25.0 (1.3)	11.0 (1.1)	1 (1.0)	0 (1.0)	0 (1.0)	51 2.1	48 (1.7)	17 (1.1)
Sheep meat	51.7 (1.8)	39.8 (1.4)	8.3 (1.1)	1 (1.0)	1 (1.0)	9 (1.1)	69 (2.7)	56 (1.7)	14 (1.1)
Wool	2.9 (1.0)	3.7 (1.0)	0.9 (1.0)	48 (1.0)	13 (1.0)	6 (1.1)	–	–	–
Pig meat	9.0 (1.2)	9.8 (1.1)	9.2 (1.1)	–1 (1.0)	0 (1.0)	0 (1.0)	–1 (1.1)	5 (1.1)	1 (1.0)
Poultry	13.3 (1.3)	13.7 (1.2)	10.4 (1.1)	9 (1.1)	0 (1.0)	0 (1.0)	13 (1.5)	31 (1.5)	25 (1.3)
Eggs	21.4 (1.3)	12.3 (1.2)	5.5 (1.1)	4 (1.1)	3 (1.0)	0 (1.0)	33 (1.6)	9 (1.1)	1 (1.0)

Source: Author's compilation from OECD statistical database.

Notes
PSE = Producer support estimates. SCT (in %) refers to the share of producer SCT in PSE. PSE of EU are in EU currencies. Numbers in parentheses reflect nominal protection coefficient (NPC).

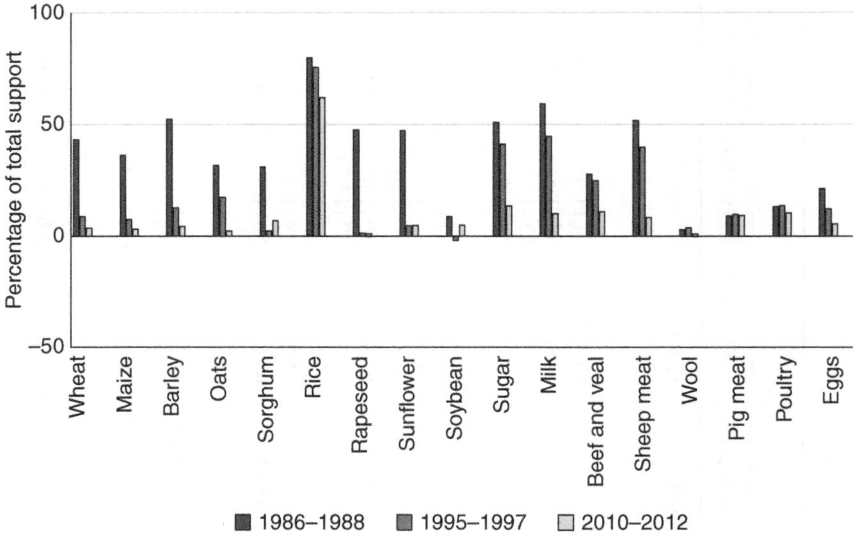

Figure 2.8 Single commodity transfers in OECD, 1986 to 2012 (in % of total support).

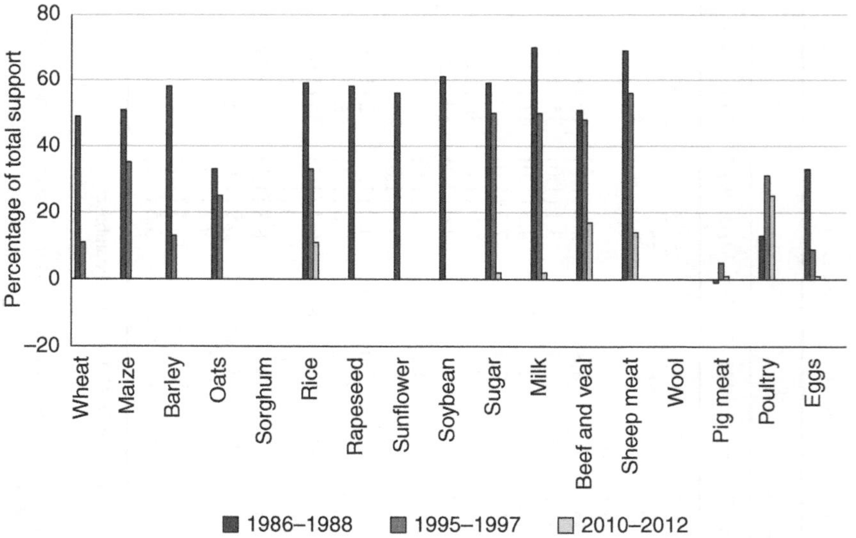

Figure 2.9 Single commodity transfers in the European Union, 1986 to 2012 (in % of total support).

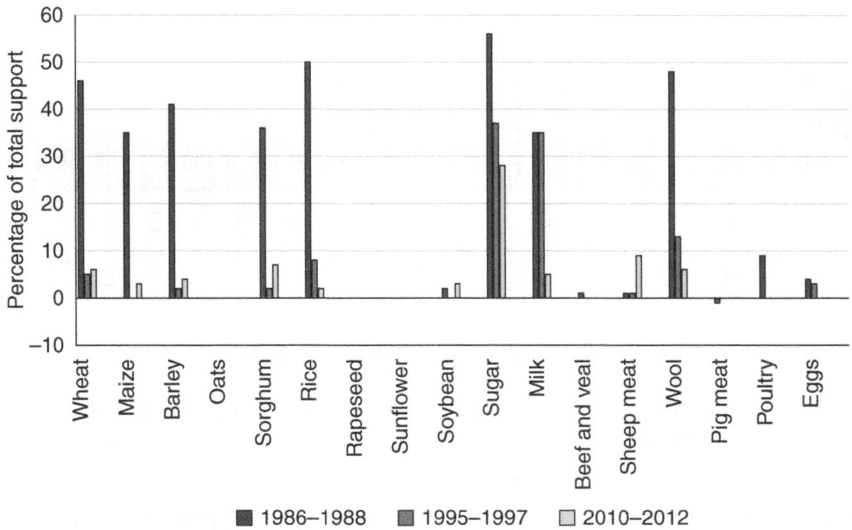

Figure 2.10 Single commodity transfers in the United States, 1986 to 2012 (in % of total support).

GATT discipline. The decline in SCT has obviously been more significant in the EU than in the US, but the EU had a very high base year support to begin with. The decline in government supports for corn and wheat in the EU and the US is also quite remarkable from the standpoint that these are also the world's largest producers of these commodities. Greater liberalization in such staple agricultural commodities should come as a very significant development for the liberalization of agriculture around the world. At the same time it is also notable that in both the EU and the US, the percentage of SCT still remains very high for rice and sugar, and in the OECD countries overall, SCT still remains at significant levels for many agricultural commodities, including milk, beef and veal, sheep meat, pig meat, sugar, rice, poultry, and sorghum.

Nominal protection coefficient of crops

Another way to determine the scale of government supports to specific crops may be measured by the nominal protection coefficient (NPC) of specific crops. The NPC—the ratio of farm price to border reference price—helps in measuring the gap between domestic prices and world prices that results from government supports to crop production. If government supports are contingent on the price gap, then the supports will be higher when international prices are higher compared with domestic prices. An NPC greater than 1 for a crop signifies that the domestic price is higher than the price on the international market, and domestic producers have been receiving support incentives to produce the crop. For example, an NPC

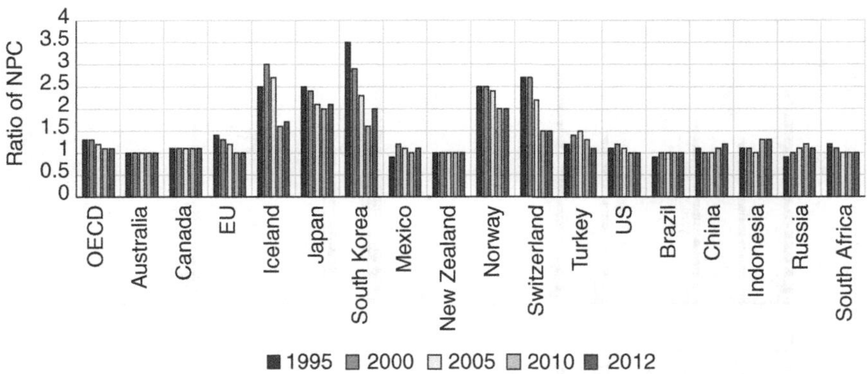

Figure 2.11 Nominal protection coefficient of producer support in agriculture in selected OECD and non-OECD countries, 1995 to 2012.

of 1.10 suggests that farmers received prices that were 10 percent above international market levels. Similarly, an NPC of 2.0 indicates that farmers received prices that were 100 percent above international market levels (OECD, 2014).

The numbers given in parentheses in Table 2.14 show producer NPC of agricultural commodities in the OECD countries, including those of the US and the EU. In the base year all major crops in OECD countries had NPC greater than 1—signifying that all of these commodities received government subsidies. Some of these commodities, such as wheat, rice, rapeseed, sunflower, milk, and sugar, had NPC 2 or greater—which means that farmers received prices that were double or more than double the international price. By 2010 to 2012, however, NPCs for all these crops had come down dramatically—only rice had an NPC of 2.4; all the other crops came down to 1.0 or 1.1 (see Figure 2.12).

In the US, all commodities listed in Figure 2.12 had NPCs of more than 1 in the base year, but the highest NPC was on sugar (2.3), followed by barley (1.8), milk (1.6), and rice (1.5). By 2010 to 2012, NPCs of most of the commodities had been brought down to 1.0, but sugar still had the highest NPC (1.4). In the EU, all commodities had NPCs greater than 1 in the base year—the highest was on sugar (a staggering 22.2), followed by milk (4.6), sheep meat (2.7), barley and soybean (each 2.6), and rapeseed (2.4). By 2010 to 2012, NPCs for the EU came down dramatically—except for sugar, which still had NPC of 5.2. While NPCs for all other products came down to 1.0 or under, beef, veal, and poultry had NPCs of 1.1, reflecting a gap of about 10 percent between domestic and border prices in these commodities (see Figures 2.13 and 2.14).

Thus, by 2010 to 2012, the protection afforded to agricultural commodities changed drastically in OECD countries, including the US and the EU. The NPCs for almost all commodities came down to 1, and only a handful of commodities still had NPCs greater than 1, which included rice, sugar, milk, beef and veal, sheep meat, pig meat, poultry, and eggs. Such an impressive scenario of decline

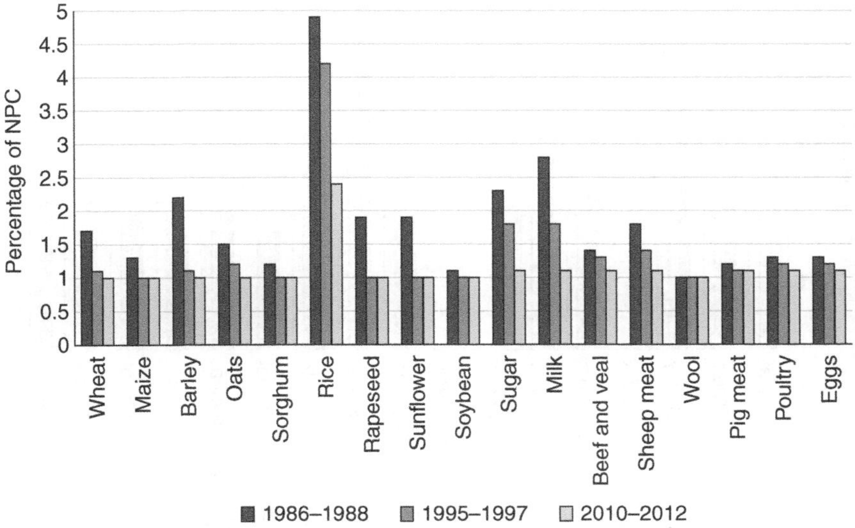

Figure 2.12 Nominal protection coefficient of single commodities in selected OECD countries, 1986 to 2012.

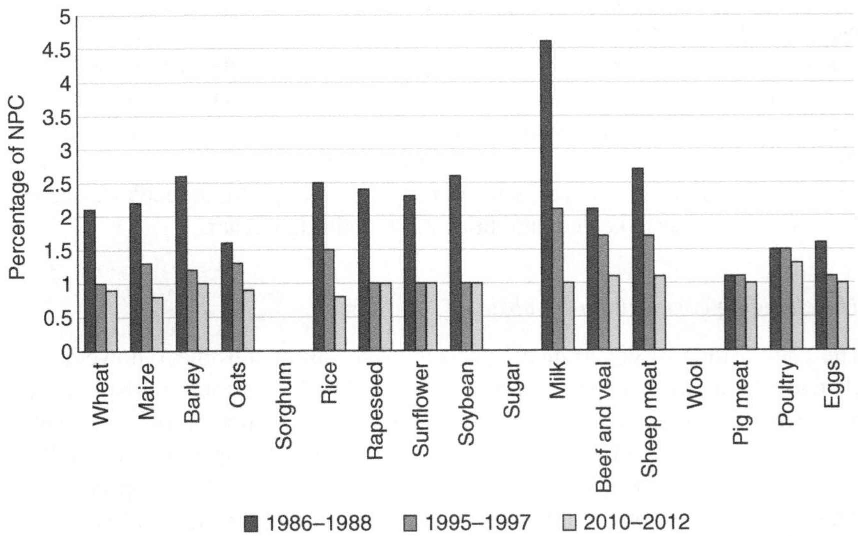

Figure 2.13 NPC of single commodities in the European Union, 1986 to 2012.

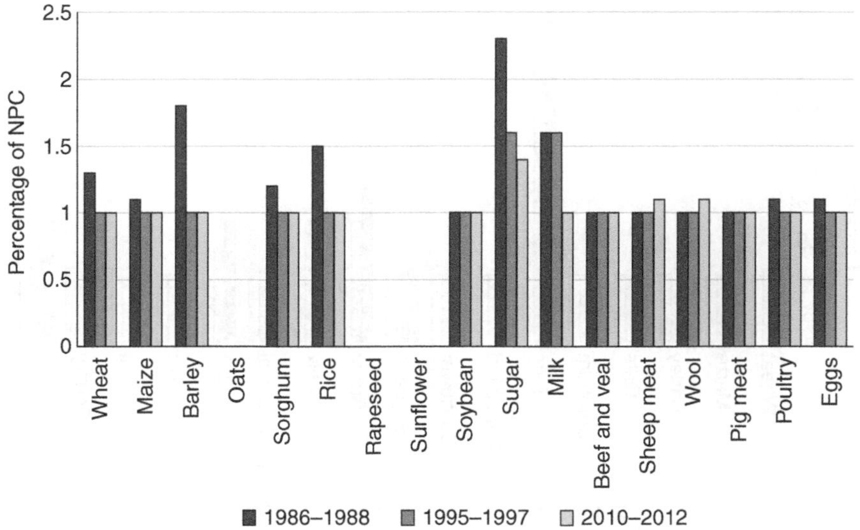

Figure 2.14 NPC of single commodities in the United States, 1986 to 2012.

in commodity subsidies in terms of both SCT and NPC, however, should be taken with a grain of salt. Much of these achievements may have been achieved by clever shuffling of the support packages. For example, between 1995 and 2012, the US government provided $292.5 billion in agricultural subsidies, of which the largest amount went to commodity supports ($177.6 billion), followed by crop insurance ($53.6 billion), conservation ($38.9 billion), and disaster ($22.5 billion) (Environmental Working Group, 2015). This means that government supports to single commodities may have declined, but overall support to agriculture had not. Moreover, supports to key commodities still remain significant.

The changing composition of subsidies

The composition of government supports (agricultural subsidies), however, has changed dramatically over recent years. As Table 2.15 indicates, in the US about a quarter of total subsidies went to conservation programs, 58 percent went to commodity-specific subsidies, and about 11 percent to crop insurance in 1995. In 2012, on the other hand, 47 percent of the subsidies went to crop insurance, while the share of commodity subsidies declined to 36 percent and that of conservation subsidies dropped to 12.4 percent. Obviously, crop insurance has become the more preferred vehicle for subsidy transfers in recent years than direct payments or commodity supports. Farmers are, however, receiving the subsidies in one form or another.

Second, governmental subsidies may not be actually declining when it comes to major agricultural products. For example, under the Direct Payment program,

Table 2.15 Allocation of agricultural subsidies in the United States, 1995 to 2012 (in US$ billions, unless otherwise indicated)

Year	*Total farm subsidies*	*Conservation subsidies*	*Disaster subsidies*	*Crop insurance subsidies*	*Commodity subsidies*
1995	8.13	1.91 (23.5)	0.66 (8.1)	0.89 (10.9)	4.68 (57.6)
2000	24.74	1.73 (7.0)	1.43 (5.8)	1.34 (5.4)	20.22 (81.7)
2005	24.31	2.96 (12.2)	3.07 (12.6)	2.34 (9.6)	16.25 (66.8)
2010	15.36	1.92 (12.5)	1.21 (7.9)	7.46 (48.8)	5.03 (32.7)
2012	14.87	1.84 (12.4)	0.79 (5.3)	6.95 (46.7)	5.32 (35.8)

Source: Author's compilation from USDA Economic Research Service (ERS).

Note
Parentheses show percentage of total.

which was mandated by the Firm Act of 2002, subsidy payments to major agricultural crops totaled $49.72 billion during 2002 to 2012 (about $5 billion on average each year), of which $12.93 billion (26 percent) went to corn—the largest recipient of commodity subsidy in the US, followed by $6.97 billion to wheat (14 percent), $4.13 billion to soybean (8.3 percent), $3.82 billion to Upland cotton (7.7 percent) and $2.63 billion to rice (5.3 percent) (see Figures 2.15 and 2.16).[37]

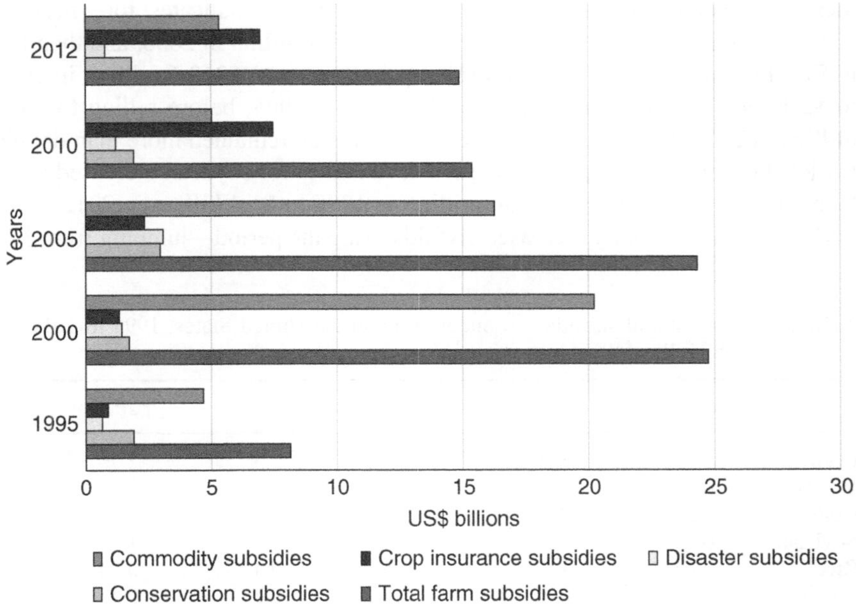

Figure 2.15 Allocation of agricultural subsidies in the United States, 1995 to 2012 (US$ billions).

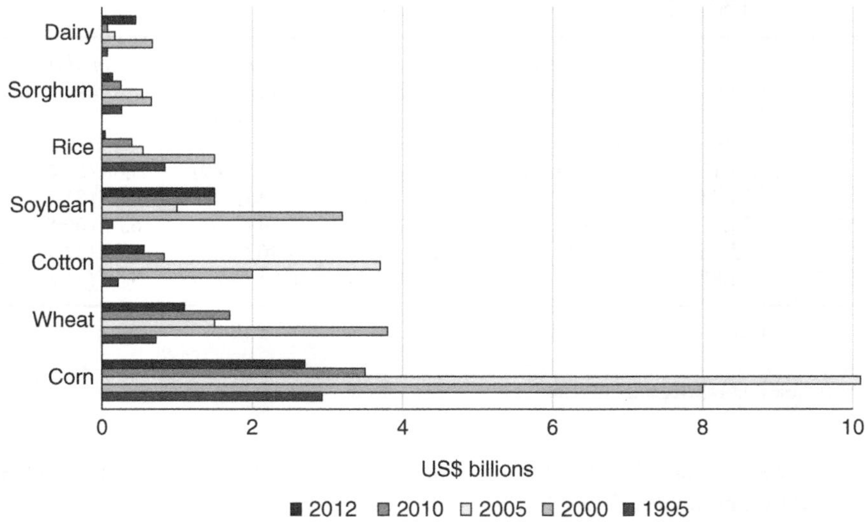

Figure 2.16 Subsidies to major agricultural products in the United States, 1995 to 2012 (in US$ billions).

Third, while subsidies for corn declined slightly—from $2.9 billion in 1995 to $2.7 billion in 2012—subsidies for wheat, cotton, soybean, and dairy increased significantly during this period. As Table 2.16 indicates, for wheat the support increased from $721 million in 1995 to 3.8 billion in 2000, and then fell to $1.1 billion in 2012. The cotton subsidy jumped from $212.6 million in 1995 to $2 billion in 2000, and then to $3.7 billion in 2005, before falling to $560 million in 2012. Even so, in 2012 the cotton subsidy remained more than double the level of 1995. During the same period, subsidies for soybean increased more than tenfold—jumping from $136 million in 1995 to $1.4 billion in 2012. Similarly, subsidies for dairy increased sixfold during the period—jumping from $73

Table 2.16 Agricultural subsidies to major crops in the United States, 1995 to 2012 (in US$ billions)

	1995	*2000*	*2005*	*2010*	*2012*
Corn	2.93	8.0	10.1	3.5	2.7
Wheat	0.72	3.8	1.5	1.7	1.1
Cotton	0.21	2.0	3.7	0.83	0.56
Soybean	0.14	3.2	1.0	1.5	1.5
Rice	0.84	1.5	0.55	0.4	0.04
Sorghum	0.26	0.66	0.54	0.25	0.14
Dairy	0.07	0.67	0.17	0.07	0.45

Source: Author's compilation from USDA Economic Research Service (ERS).

million in 1995 to $447 million in 2012. According to Sumner (2006), the ratio of subsidy to the value of production for corn was 14.7 percent in 2004, 28.8 percent in 2005, and 44.6 percent in 2006. For wheat, the ratios were 21.8 percent in 2004, 27.4 percent in 2005, and 50.9 percent in 2006. For cotton, the ratios were 27.7 percent in 2004, 80.3 percent in 2005, and 65.2 percent in 2006.

As the Upland cotton dispute with Brazil demonstrated in 2004 and the ongoing dispute of the cotton-exporting African countries (so-called Cotton-4) in the WTO platforms indicate, the magnitude of subsidies in the US may still not be in full compliance with the WTO rules. Moreover, the WTO Agreement on Subsidies and Countervailing Measures (SCM), which applies to all trade sectors, defines some subsidies, which are not specifically prohibited, as actionable subsidies when they adversely affect the interests of other WTO members. Such adverse effects may include injury to a domestic industry, nullification or impairment of benefits under WTO agreements, and serious prejudice to the interests of another WTO member. The fact that price-contingent subsidies in the US for corn, wheat, cotton, and rice are still sizable relative to the total value of production, such subsidies may well be deemed as trade-distorting subsidies which less developed countries and other major exporters of agricultural products may see as actionable subsidies under WTO rules (Sumner, 2006).

Reduction of export subsidies

Numerous studies have shown over the decades that export subsidies lower world prices and distort trade flows; since exports depend neither upon the prices of the exporter nor upon the prices of competitors in the international markets, it depends rather upon the exporting country's internal decision of how much quantity to remove from the domestic market.[38] In order to reduce export subsidies and to establish a level playing field, the URAA capped export subsidies and subjected them to annual reduction commitments. Developed countries were granted a six-year transition period so that by 2000 their subsidized exports had reached expenditure and quantity levels of 36 per cent and 21 per cent, respectively, below those of the base period (1986–1988). Developing countries were granted a 10-year transition period to reduce the volume of subsidized exports by 14 percent and the expenditure on subsidies by 24 percent. The LDCs were exempted from such reduction commitments (see Table 2.1).

The URAA covered a wide range of subsidies, such as payments in kind, subsidized stock exports, producer-financed export subsidies, export marketing, cost subsidies, export-specific transportation subsidies, and subsidies on goods incorporated into exports. The agreement also banned any new export subsidies, and required that the allowed subsidies be implemented in a way that did not undermine the cuts in export subsidies. The agreement allowed subsidized exports only by WTO members who submitted subsidy reduction commitments, and allowed them to subsidize only the products on which they had commitments to reduce the subsidies.[39] By the same token, WTO members without any reduction commitments were not allowed to subsidize agricultural exports at all (WTO, 2002).

As it turned out, only 25 WTO members submitted their exports reduction commitments, and most of the commitments were geared toward livestock and dairy products—not many commitments were made in respect of major crops or grain exports. As Table 2.17 indicates, most of the commitments came from the EU, which accounted for 90 percent of all OECD export subsidies notified to the WTO. Switzerland came second with 5.3 percent of the total notifications of export subsidy reduction commitments, followed by the US and Norway, each accounting for 1.4 percent of total commitments (FAO, 2004).

At the time of the signing of the URAA, the US and the EU—the two largest agricultural exporters in the world—were also the two largest providers of export subsidies. During the period 1995 to 2001, subsidized exports as a proportion of total exports in the EU were 43 percent for corn, 74 percent for skimmed milk powder, 66 percent for cheese, 54 percent for rice, 65 percent for sugar, and 100 percent for butter (Jank and Jales, 2004). In the US also, subsidies reduced the cost of production to farmers by an average of 51 to 58 percent for wheat, 67 percent for corn, and 77 percent for rice (Watkins, 2003). Such subsidized exports distorted global trade in many agricultural commodities including dairy, sugar, cotton, rice, peanuts, wheat, and processed goods, depressing global prices, impeding price transmission from the world market to the domestic markets, and badly affecting developing countries and the LDCs in terms of lost income and welfare.

Table 2.17 Export subsidy reduction commitments by WTO members, 2002

Australia (5)—milk products, fats, non-fat solids	Hungary (16)—wheat, coarse grains, cheese, slaughter pigs, pork, broiler chicken	Poland (17)
Brazil (16)	Iceland (2)—sheep meat, bovine meat, butter, and cheese	Romania (13)
Bulgaria (44)	Indonesia (1)	Slovak Rep (17)
Canada (11)—butter, skim milk powder (SMP), and cheese	Israel (6)	S Africa (62)
Colombia (18)	Mexico (5)	Switzerland-Liechtenstein (5) —dairy and cattle
Cyprus (9)	New Zealand (1)	Turkey (44)—poultry meat and cream
Czech Rep (16)—dairy, butter, cheese	Norway (11)—butter and cheese	United States (13)—butter, skim milk powder (SMP), cheese, poultry
EU (20)—wheat, coarse grains, rice, butter, skim milk powder (SMP), cheese, whole milk powder (WMP), beef, pig meat, and poultry	Panama (1)	Uruguay (3)
		Venezuela (72)

Source: Author's compilation from WTO (2002).

Note

The numbers of products involved for each country are given in brackets. For some countries major commodities are also shown.

Benefits of the elimination of export subsidies on some of the commodities like sugar, cotton, rice, and peanuts were estimated in billions of dollars. The liberalization of sugar, for example, was expected to result in $4.7 billion annual gains in global welfare. Similarly, the removal of protection on cotton was expected to raise the cotton price by 13 percent annually over a 10-year period, increasing global trade by 6 percent, a drop in US exports by 6.7 percent and the EU's exports by 70.5 percent, while increasing the share of exports from Africa by 13 percent and from Uzbekistan by 6 percent. Similarly, the removal of protection to rice was expected to benefit rice-growing countries like Cambodia, China, and Vietnam, and the removal of export subsidies and price supports for peanuts was expected to help countries like Gambia, Malawi, Nigeria, Senegal, South Africa, and Sudan to regain their global share in the market (World Bank, 2003, 125–129).

The implementation of export subsidy reduction commitments by the WTO members, however, showed better than expected results. Many WTO members eliminated or suspended subsidies for some or even all commodity exports exceeding the URAA requirements. As a result, the use of export subsidies dropped significantly—from $7.3 billion in 1995 to under $3.5 billion in 2002—declining by more than 50 percent in six years. As Table 2.18 shows, the EU—the largest user of export subsidies in 1995—had cut its export subsidies by 50 percent by 2002. Switzerland and Norway—two of the countries that were well known for high export subsidies—also brought down their export subsidies to 70 percent and 62 percent of their respective levels of 1995. Canada eliminated all its subsidies on grain in 1995, and Australia replaced its dairy export subsidies with rebates of a new production levy and then replaced that levy in 2000 (Josling, 2004, 30). Historically, the US did not use export subsidies so extensively, but rather provided export credits more extensively.[40] In 2002, however, the US export subsidies increased by 23 percent compared with the level of 1995. The actual amount of subsidies, however, remained very small—only $31.5 million.

Commodity-wise reductions in export subsidies, however, indicate that otherwise impressive results were accomplished without axing subsidies on many sensitive products. As Table 2.19 shows, milk products, beef, sugar, coarse grain, wheat, and poultry were among the top recipients of export subsidies in 1995. In 2002, export subsidies were cut by 13 percent for wheat, 40 percent for sugar, 30 percent for milk products, 53 percent for rice, 57 percent for coarse grain, 46 percent for poultry, and 35 percent for processed agricultural products. As these figures suggest, although the goals of export subsidy reduction as stipulated by the URAA were largely accomplished or even exceeded, still, export subsidies for many key agricultural products, such as wheat, sugar, milk products, rice, coarse grain, and processed agricultural products, still remain substantial.[41]

Despite export subsidies still remaining substantial for major agricultural products, about 50 percent reduction in such supports during the 1995 to 2002 period should be viewed as a great achievement of the URAA. Some of the

Table 2.18 Pattern of total export subsidies in selected countries, 1995 to 2002 (US$ millions)

Country	*1995*	*1996*	*1997*	*1998*	*1999*	*2000*	*2001*	*2002*	*% change between 1995–2002*
European Union	6,495.9	7,071.2	4,856.7	5,989.0	5,853.7	2,516.6	2,297.1	3,269.5	50.3
United States	25.6	121.5	112.2	146.7	80.2	15.3	54.6	31.5	123
Switzerland	454.6	392.1	294.5	292.8	268.9	187.7	138.4	137.1	30.2
Norway	83.9	77.9	99.9	76.9	126.2	44.0	32.0	NA	38.2
Rest of world	263.7	225.0	200.4	175.7	190.5	160.9	55.0	108.8	41.6
Total	7,323.6	7,887.6	5,563.6	6,681.0	6,519.5	2,924.5	2,577.1	3,547.0	48.4

Source: USDA Economic Research Service (ERS) calculations attributed to the World Trade Organization.

Table 2.19 Total export subsidies to selected commodities, 1995 to 2002 (US$ millions)

Commodities	*1995*	*1996*	*1997*	*1998*	*1999*	*2000*	*2001*	*2002*	*% change between 1995–2002*
Wheat	169.6	403.4	197.9	563.0	531.1	98.6	7.5	147.8	87.1
Coarse grain	421.6	494.4	306.2	864.7	774.9	186.5	102.0	180.4	42.8
Rice	55.3	97.7	36.3	28.7	27.5	29.4	26.9	26.0	47.0
Oilseed	83.3	50.5	10.3	2.9	1.1	3.0	0.9	0.0	0.0
Fibers	0.4	0.0	0.0	0.0	0.0	0.0	0.9	0.0	0.0
Fruits and vegetables	170.3	162.4	103.3	96.5	81.0	65.0	39.5	36.5	21.4
Sugar	512.9	692.7	900.3	913.5	510.6	363.7	442.0	306.1	59.7
Milk products	2,546.3	2,695.3	1,938.7	1,992.9	2,255.4	1,103.2	1,016.6	1,790.4	70.3
Wine	81.1	86.8	47.2	35.5	27.4	21.6	20.3	20.0	24.7
Beef	2,010.1	1,947.1	952.2	735.9	789.0	356.2	348.1	310.1	15.4
Pork	135.5	94.4	95.4	403.7	290.7	45.2	20.6	16.6	12.2
Poultry	189.2	107.1	108.1	129.7	102.6	71.5	62.9	102.2	54.0
Other meats	11.9	11.3	6.7	2.2	25.3	3.8	0.5	0.1	0.0
Livestock	26.6	14.7	1.0	1.4	2.9	4.6	5.4	4.0	15.0
Tobacco	25.8	5.9	1.0	1.5	1.7	5.8	2.6	0.0	0.0
Processed products	779.4	839.4	709.5	742.5	841.0	448.9	429.4	506.5	65.0
Other agricultural products	104.3	184.5	149.5	166.5	257.2	117.3	51.6	100.5	96.3
Total	7,323.6	7,887.6	5,563.6	6,681.0	6,519.5	2,924.5	2,577.7	3,547.0	48.43

Source: USDA Economic Research Service (ERS) calculations attributed to WTO database.

factors that contributed to such a large decrease in the use of subsidies in such a short time include: (1) export subsidies in the world, especially in the EU, reached their peak during the base period 1986 to 1990. Such a high starting base made it easier for the EU to make reduction commitments as required by the URAA; (2) in the mid-1990s, the world experienced a commodity boom, which resulted in lesser use of subsidies; (3) the reduction in intervention prices in developed countries narrowed the price gap between the world and internal markets, which brought down the rate of direct export subsidies; and finally (4) direct payments introduced around this time under the production-limiting programs enabled exporters to reduce their prices in order to compete with efficient suppliers.[42]

Consequences of the URAA implementation

After about two decades of reforms and liberalization under the strengthened GATT rules, although significant tariff and non-tariff barriers still exist and domestic supports and export subsidies continue to undermine a level playing field across countries, presumably an argument can be made that international trade in agriculture is now more liberalized than ever before. A significant transformation has taken place in global production, consumption, and trade in agriculture since the sector was brought under the URAA in 1994. Available data suggest that global agricultural production has increased considerably, both in terms of overall agricultural goods as well as processed agricultural products. Although the EU and the US still remain dominant in both exports and imports in agriculture, the share of developing countries appears to be on the rise, and a remarkable shift seems to be taking place among leading exporters and importers in the world for agricultural products and food supplies. More importantly, as a result of trade liberalization and agricultural intensification and higher productivity, more food is being produced now than is needed to feed the entire world population and such a feat has been accomplished at prices that are lower than ever (Hazel and Wood, 2008).[43]

Global production of major agricultural commodities

Available data show that global production of major agricultural crops, such as wheat, maize/corn, rice/paddy, sugar cane, and soybeans, has increased significantly since the URAA came into effect. Although how much of this increase may be attributed to the liberalization of agriculture is not yet clear, it appears that during the 1995 to 2012 period, global maize/corn production increased from 517.3 mmt to 872.8 mmt—by almost 70 percent. During the same period, the production of maize/corm increased by 46 percent and 20 percent in the US and the EU, respectively. What is remarkable is that most of the growth in corn/maize production came from the developing part of the world. As Table 2.20 indicates, net food importing developing countries increased their maize/corn production by 120 percent during this period, while low-income food-deficit

Table 2.20 Global agricultural production in selected commodities, 1995 to 2012 (in million metric tons)

Commodities	*1990*	*1995*	*2000*	*2005*	*2010*	*2012*	*% change between 1995–2012*
Sugar cane (world total)	1,053.0	1,172.3	1,256.4	1,316.3	1,700.6	1,842.2	57
European Union	144.1	139.0	137.9	136.8	105.1	115.5	–8.5
United States	25.5	27.9	36.1	26.6	24.8	29.2	4.6
Net food-importing developing countries	206.4	173.4	187.5	173.7	180.7	198.3	14.3
Low-income food-deficit countries	336.3	392.0	416.4	376.8	430.8	510.6	30.2
Least developed countries (LDCs)	30.1	32.5	37.6	–	–	–	–
Rice, paddy (world total)	515.9	544.7	596.9	632.2	702.0	738.2	35.5
European Union	–	–	–	–	–	–	–
United States	7.1	7.9	8.6	10.1	11.0	9.0	13.9
Net food-importing developing countries	68.8	76.8	97.6	113.5	136.8	138.8	80.7
Low-income food-deficit countries	218.7	231.8	262.9	286.7	326.4	349.6	50.8
Least developed countries (LDCs)	55.0	59.6	77.0	90.5	114.5	112.5	88.7
Maize/corn (world total)	483.4	517.3	592.5	713.7	851.3	872.8	68.7
European Union	37.0	49.8	53.1	65.4	59.2	59.3	19.7
United States	201.5	187.9	251.8	282.2	316.2	274	45.8
Net food-importing developing countries	26.4	28.2	33.4	41.7	56.8	62.1	120
Low-income food-deficit countries	55.4	56.6	63.1	76.9	107.6	117.2	106.7
Least developed countries (LDCs)	14.0	15.2	17.9	22.6	36.2	39.3	158.5
Wheat (world total)	592.3	542.7	585.7	626.7	649.3	671.5	23.7
European Union	116.8	120.0	133.4	136.8	137.6	136.1	3.8
United States	74.3	59.4	60.6	57.2	60.0	61.7	13.4
Net food-importing developing countries	29.4	82.8	36.8	45.0	48.5	51.5	–27.5
Low-income food-deficit countries	61.7	–	95.3	97.3	111.4	127.7	33.9
Least developed countries (LDCs)	–		–	–	–	12.7	–
Soybeans (world total)	108.4	126.9	161.3	214.6	265.0	241.1	91
European Union	–	–	–	–	–	–	–
United States	52.4	59.2	75.0	83.5	90.6	82.0	56.4
Net food-importing developing countries	–	–	–	–	–	–	–
Low-income food-deficit countries	–	–	–	–	–	–	–

Source: Author's compilation from FAOSTAT.

countries and the LDCs increased their outputs by 107 percent and 158 percent, respectively. Similarly, global wheat production also increased significantly during the same period—from 542.7 mmt in 1995 to 671.5 mmt in 2012—by 23.7 percent. The increase had been 3.8 percent and 13.4 percent for the EU and the US, respectively, but 34 percent for low-income food-deficit countries, indicating much higher growth in less developed countries than in developed countries.

Global rice/paddy production has also increased from 544.7 mmt to 738.2 mmt during the period 1995 to 2012—by more than 35 percent. Almost all of the growth came from the developing countries—when net food importing developing countries increased their production by 81 percent, the low-income food-deficit countries increased their production by 51 percent, and the LDCs increased their shares by 89 percent. Despite massive subsidies, rice/paddy production in the US registered only 14 percent growth compared with more than 35 percent global growth rate during the same period. Global sugar cane production increased from 1,172.3 mmt to 1,842.2 mmt—by 57 percent—during the 1995 to 2012 period, when output increased by only 8.5 percent and 4.6 percent, respectively, in the EU and the US. Again most of the growth came from the developing part of the world—net food importing developing countries increased their output by 14 percent, while the low-income developing countries increased their output by 30 percent.

As the discussion above indicates, developed countries have been experiencing much slower growth in major agricultural commodities (in wheat, corn/maize, rice, and sugar), compared with the developing part of the world, especially coinciding with the implementation of the URAA obligations. Whether such a slower growth in the production of major agricultural commodities in developed countries, especially in the US and the EU, compared with the developing parts of the world, has been the result of dwindling subsidies to these crops in developed countries deserves the attention of future researchers.

Historical patterns of global production, consumption, and trade

Historical patterns in global production, consumption, and trade of major agricultural commodities in the context of the pre-URAA and the post-URAA periods are explained below on the basis of a major OECD study conducted by Pete Liapis (2012), who found a relatively smooth upward trend in the production and consumption of selected agricultural products during the 1970 to 2010 period, despite many shocks stemming from severe weather, recessions, financial crisis, volatile exchange rates, and so on. The study shows that on average the production and consumption of selected commodities grew at approximately equal rates, and decade-on-decade variations were very small. On average, annual rates of growth for the production and consumption for wheat were 1.8 percent and 1.9 percent, respectively; for maize, 2.6 percent and 2.6 percent, respectively; and for soybean oil, 5.1 percent and 5 percent, respectively. On the other hand, average annual rates of growth for production and consumption were the same for rice and sugar (2.1 percent each), Soybean (4.7 percent), whole milk powder (3.1 percent), beef (1.4 percent), and butter (1.1 percent). The study found that during the 1995 to 2010 period, for all products other than maize/corn and butter, production grew at a slower pace relative to the entire period (1970–2010), but so did consumption.

According to the study, such a relatively smooth progression at the global level was possible as local production or consumption shortfalls were adequately compensated for by surpluses in other regions, while world production and consumption experienced considerable variability. The study also found that production variability was higher for products not directly depending on climatic conditions, and smaller for products subject to the vagaries of weather. As Table 2.21 indicates, during the study period, the average variability for maize/corn was the highest (7.28 and 5.02 for production and consumption, respectively), followed by soybean (10.11 and 8.30 for production and consumption, respectively), while beef and butter had the lowest volatility. For all major commodities, production volatility was at its highest in the 1970s, then it gradually stabilized in the 2000s, and the variability in world consumption was lower than the variability in production throughout the study period. The study attributes such a remarkable decline in the volatility in global consumption and production of major agricultural commodities in the 2000s to the implementation of the URAA.

The study also found that international trade has expanded substantially since the mid-1990s, reflecting increased globalization, the integration of new participants in world markets, and the reform of agricultural markets as a result of the URAA. Despite such remarkable progress, international trade in agriculture still remained thin—the ratio of exports to global production was very small, since most of the agricultural goods were consumed domestically and only a small fraction were traded internationally. International trade in all agricultural products is, however, not so thin. For example, during the 1995 to 2010 period, while only 6.6 percent of global rice production was exported, the share was 18.7 percent for wheat, 31.5 percent for sugar, 30.3 percent for soybeans, 27.0 percent for soybean oil, and 43.1 percent for whole milk powder. As Table 2.21 indicates, while rice had the lowest share of production exported, the share was the highest for whole milk powder, but exports as a share of production for most of the commodities had increased or remained fairly stable throughout the 1970 to 2010 period.

The study also found that agricultural commodities with a relatively small share of production traded, such as rice and maize, had a relatively large number of countries in the self-sufficient category, while products with a relatively large share of production traded, such as wheat, soybeans, and milk powder, had a relatively large number of countries that consistently depended upon imports to satisfy domestic consumption. The study pointed out that market shares of individual exporters had declined over the decades as international markets became more competitive than before. The Herfindahl Index of agricultural products—which measures exporting countries' market share in global markets—shows

Table 2.21 Average variability in production, consumption, and export shares of major agricultural products, 1970 to 2010

Goods	*1970–2010*	*1970–1994*	*1995–2010*	*Goods*	*1970–2010*	*1970–1994*	*1995–2010*
Wheat				Sugar			
Production	5.19	5.71	4.37	Production	4.84	4.7	4.29
Consumption	3.48	4.42	2.03	Consumption	3.83	5.07	3.1
Exports as share of production (mean, %)	18.9	19.1	18.7	Exports as share of production (mean, %)	30.0	29.1	31.5
Herfindahl Index for Exports	0.11 (2000s)	0.22 (1980s)	0.17 (1990s)	Herfindahl Index for Exports	0.09 (2000s)	0.17 (1980s)	0.12 (1990s)
Soybeans				Beef			
Production	10.11	10.97	8.77	Production	3.12	3.72	2.19
Consumption	8.3	9.01	7.2	Consumption	3.15	3.61	2.44
Exports as share of production (mean, %)	29.7	29.3	30.3	Exports as share of production (mean, %)	11.2	10.9	11.8
Herfindahl Index for Exports	0.34 (2000s)	0.64 (1980s)	0.47 (1990s)	Herfindahl Index for Exports	0.08 (2000s)	0.08 (1980s)	0.09 (1990s)
Whole milk powder				Butter			
Production	6.63	7.91	5.04	Production	6.06	4.12	9.09
Consumption	6.45	7.37	5.76	Consumption	6.15	4.22	9.16
Exports as share of production (mean, %)	39.0	34.9	43.1	Exports as share of production (mean, %)	17.5	20.3	13.1
Herfindahl Index for Exports	0.09 (2000s)	0.13 (1980s)	0.1 (1990s)	Herfindahl Index for Exports	0.09 (2000s)	0.13 (1980s)	0.10 (2000s)

Rice				Soybean oil			
Production	3.93	4.42	3.16	Production	9.26	10.06	8.0
Consumption	3.42	4.18	2.24	Consumption	8.64	9.05	7.99
Exports as share of production (mean, %)	5.0	4.0	6.6	Exports as share of production (mean, %)	23.8	21.8	27.0
Herfindahl Index for Exports	0.14 (2000s)	0.18 (1980s)	0.14 (1990s)	Herfindahl Index for Exports	0.21 (2000s)	0.16 (1980s)	0.16 (1990s)
Maize/corn							
Production	7.28	8.14	5.95				
Consumption	5.02	5.32	4.54				
Exports as share of production (mean, %)	13.4	14.3	11.9				
Herfindahl Index for Exports	0.28 (2000s)	0.45 (1980s)	0.38 (1990s)				

Source: Author's compilation from Liapis (2012).

Notes

Production and consumption numbers are average percentages. Numbers in parentheses refer to the decades to which the Herfindahl Index of Exports refers. The Herfindahl Index for Meat refers to meat of bovine animals, fresh, chilled, or frozen; for Milk refers to milk and cream—in solid form and blocks; and for Sugar refers to refined sugar and other refined sugar products.

that the soybean market remained the most concentrated (the Herfindahl Index being 0.47) while the beef market was the least concentrated (the Herfindahl Index being 0.09) during the 1995 to 2010 period. During the same period, the Herfindahl Index fell for most of the agricultural commodities compared with the 1970 to 1994 period, indicating the evolution of a more competitive international market coinciding with the liberalization of agricultural trade since the emergence of the WTO.

Shifts in global trade

Agricultural exports

Although the Herfindahl Index shows less concentration in exports, nominal export values indicate that the share of the top 15 agricultural exporters in the world increased from 66 percent in 1995 to more than 80 percent in 2010 (Table 2.22). The EU, which emerged as the largest agricultural exporter in the world by the late 1980s, due largely to massive domestic supports and export subsidies, remained so throughout the period of 1995 to 2010. In both 1995 and 2000, the combined share of exports of leading members of the EU in global agricultural exports hovered at around 40 percent, but in 2005 the EU's share in global exports increased to 43 percent. In 2010, however, the EU's share fall to 39 percent, which probably reflects the consequences of shedding domestic supports and export subsidies mandated by the URAA.

The US remained the second largest agricultural exporter throughout this period, but its share also declined from 12.7 percent in 2000 to 10.5 percent in 2010. Canada, which eliminated all agricultural subsidies in the late 1990s, succeeded in increasing its share in global agricultural exports to 6.2 percent in 2000 from 3.2 percent in 1995, but its share fell to 3.8 percent in 2010. It is also remarkable that the Triad—comprising the advanced industrialized countries, namely the US, the EU, and Canada—together controlled more than half of the total agricultural exports of the top 15 exporters throughout the period of 1995 to 2010. The Triad's share was 54 percent in 1995, 51 percent in 2000, 56 percent in 2005, and 53 percent in 2010 in the total share of top 15 agricultural exporters, when global exports surged from $361 billion to $1.4 trillion (see Figure 2.17).

Among the developing countries, Brazil succeeded in almost doubling its share in global agricultural exports during the 1995 to 2010 period—its share jumped from 2.8 percent in 1995 to 5 percent in 2010. China's share in global agricultural exports also increased during the period—from 2.8 percent in 1995 to 3.8 percent in 2010. India, on the other hand, had 1.5 percent share in world agricultural exports in 1995, which fell to 1.2 percent in 2005. The country failed to occupy a spot among the top 15 agricultural exporters in 2000 and 2010. Indonesia and Malaysia, two other developing countries, occupied spots in the top 15 agricultural exporters for the first time in 2005. Both countries increased their shares in global agricultural exports between 2005 and 2010—Indonesia

Table 2.22 Top 15 exporters of agricultural products in the world, 1995 to 2000 (in US$ billions)

Rank	*1995*			*2000*			*2005*			*2010*		
	Country	*Value*	*Share (%)*	*Country*	*Value*	*Share (%)*	*Country*	*Value*	*Share (%)*	*Country*	*Value*	*Share (%)*
1	United States	42.2	11.7	United States	70.9	12.7	EU (25)	369.7	43.4	EU (27)	532	39.1
2	Netherlands	33.8	9.3	France	36.5	6.5	United States	82.7	9.7	United States	143	10.5
3	France	30.3	8.4	Canada	34.8	6.2	Canada	41.2	4.8	Brazil	69	5.0
4	Germany	21.2	5.8	Netherlands	34.1	6.1	Brazil	35.0	4.1	Canada	52	3.8
5	Canada	11.7	3.2	Germany	27.8	5.0	China	28.7	3.4	China	52	3.8
6	Spain	11.5	3.2	Belgium	19.9	3.6	Australia	21.2	2.5	Indonesia	36	2.6
7	Belgium	11.5	3.2	Spain	16.9	3.0	Argentina	19.2	2.3	Thailand	35	2.6
8	Italy	11.2	3.1	United Kingdom	16.7	3.0	Thailand	17.8	2.1	Argentina	35	2.5
9	Denmark	10.9	3.0	China	16.4	2.9	Russian Federation[a]	14.9	1.7	Malaysia	29	2.1
10	United Kingdom	10.9	3.0	Australia	16.4	2.9	Indonesia	14.3	1.7	Australia	27	2.0
11	Thailand	10.7	3.0	Italy	16.1	2.9	Malaysia	13.4	1.6	India	23	1.7
12	China	10.0	2.8	Brazil	15.5	2.8	New Zealand	13.0	1.5	Russian Federation	21	1.5
13	Brazil	10.0	2.8	Thailand	13.3	2.4	Mexico	12.7	1.5	New Zealand	20	1.4
14	Argentina	7.2	2.0	Argentina (1999)	12.0	2.2	India[a]	10.1	1.2	Mexico	19	1.4
15	India	5.4	1.5	Denmark	10.9	2.0	Chile	10.1	1.2	Chile	15	1.1
	Top 15 total	238.5	66.0	Top 15 total	358.0	64.2	Top 15 total	704.1	82.6	Top 15 total	1,107.0	81.3
	World Total	361.4	100		557.6	100		852.4	100		1,361.6	100

Source: Author's compilation from UNCTAD website and WTO database.

Note

a Includes WTO Secretariat estimates.

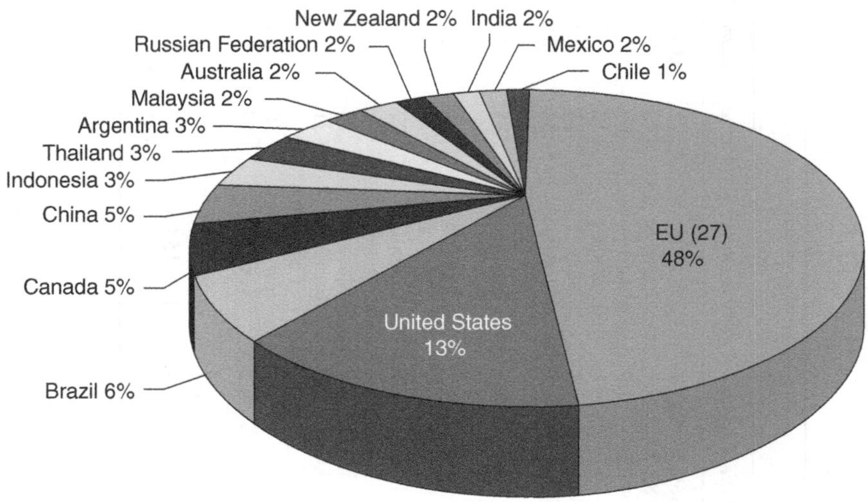

Figure 2.17 Top 15 agricultural exporters in the world, 2010 (share in %).

increased its share from 1.7 percent to 2.6 percent, and Malaysia from 1.6 percent to 2.1 percent. Thailand succeeded in maintaining a spot among the top 15 agricultural exporters in the world throughout the period of 1995 to 2010, but its share fell from 3.0 percent in 1995 to 2.6 percent in 2010.

Agricultural imports

When it comes to global agricultural imports, the EU maintained its dominant position throughout the 1995 to 2010 period, while the US and Japan swapped the distant second and third positions. As Table 2.23 indicates, during the 1995 to 2010 period, the share of the top 15 importers ranged between 65 percent and 81 percent in global agricultural imports. The EU's share in global agricultural imports hovered at around 30 percent in 1995 and 2000, but increased to 44 percent in 2005, and then fell to 39 percent in 2010. In 1995, Japan was the second largest importer of agricultural products in the world with a 12 percent share in the global market, but its share gradually declined to 10 percent in 2000, 7 percent in 2005, and 5 percent in 2010. The US had an 8 percent share in global agricultural imports in 1995, which increased to 11 percent in 2000, but declined to 10.6 percent in 2005, and to 8.2 percent in 2010. Canada maintained its share in global agricultural imports at around 2 percent throughout the period.

Among the developing countries, the Russian Federation had a 3 percent share in 1995, which came down to 2.6 percent in 2010. China, on the other hand, increased its share in global agricultural imports from 1.6 percent in 1995 to 3.2 percent in 2000, 5.0 percent in 2005, and then to 7.6 percent in 2010. Just as with exports, in imports of agricultural products also the Quad countries dominated the

Table 2.23 Top 15 agricultural importers in the world, 1995 to 2010 (US$ billions)

Rank	*1995*			*2000*			*2005*			*2010*		
	Country	*Value*	*Share (%)*	*Country*	*Value*	*Share (%)*	*Country*	*Value*	*Share (%)*	*Country*	*Value*	*Share (%)*
1	Japan	45.9	12.1	United States	66.7	11.0	European Union (25)	398.88	44.0	European Union (27)	557	39.1
2	Germany	38.1	10.0	Japan	62.2	10.3	United States	95.80	10.6	United States	116	8.2
3	United States	29.4	7.7	Germany	41.5	6.9	Japan	65.95	7.3	China	108	7.6
4	France	24.6	6.5	United Kingdom	32.5	5.4	China	45.19	5.0	Japan	77	5.4
5	United Kingdom	21.0	5.5	France	30.4	5.0	Canada[b]	21.46	2.4	Russian Federation[a]	37	2.6
6	Netherlands	19.5	5.1	Italy	29.4	4.9	Russian Federation[a]	19.29	2.1	Canada[a]	32	2.2
7	Italy	19.2	5.0	Netherlands	20.9	3.5	South Korea	16.77	1.8	South Korea	27	1.9
8	Spain	11.7	3.1	China	19.5	3.2	Mexico[b]	16.45	1.8	Mexico[a]	24	1.7
9	Russian Federation	11.3	3.0	Belgium	18.5	3.1	Hong Kong, China	11.09	–	Hong Kong, China	21	–
10	Belgium	9.3	2.5	Spain	17.0	2.8	Taipei, Chinese	9.48	1.0	India	17	1.2
11	Canada	8.2	2.2	Canada[b]	15.3	2.5	Saudi Arabia[a]	9.07	1.0	Malaysia	16	1.1
12	Hong Kong	7.5	2.0	South Korea	13.0	2.1	Switzerland	8.25	0.9	Indonesia	16	1.1
13	China	6.1	1.6	Hong Kong, China	11.7	–	India[a]	7.67	0.8	Saudi Arabia	13	0.9
14	South Korea	5.9	1.6	Mexico[b]	11.1	1.8	Malaysia	7.24	0.8	Taipei, Chinese	13	0.9
15	Saudi Arabia	4.0	1.1	Russian Federation[b]	9.9	1.6	United Arab Emirates[a,c]	7.24	0.8	Turkey	13	0.9
	Top 15 total	261.7	69	Top 15 total	394.32	65.2	Top 15 total	736.04	81.2	Top 15 total	1,080	75.7
	World total	379.27	100		604.8	100		906.4	100		1,426.7	100

Source: Author's compilation from UNCTAD website and WTO database.

Notes

a Includes WTO Secretariat's estimates.

b Imports are valued at f.o.b.

c 2004 instead of 2005.

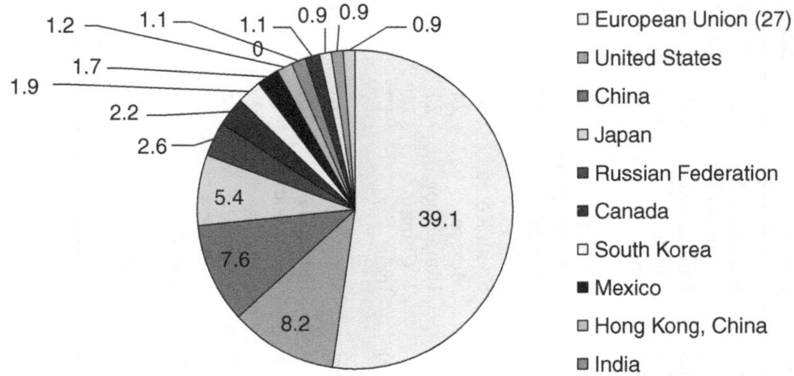

Figure 2.18 Top 10 agricultural importers in the world, 2010 (share in %).

market—their shares were 60 percent in 1995, 55 percent in 2000, 64 percent in 2005, and 55 percent in 2010—when global agricultural imports surged from $379 billion to $1.43 trillion (see Figure 2.18).

Global food trade

When it comes to food exports, the EU dominates the world, but its share in global food exports slipped from 44 percent in 2000 to 40 percent in 2010. As Table 2.24 indicates, the position of the US has also steadily declined from 17.6 percent in 1980 to 13.6 percent in 1990, to 12.6 percent in 2000, and 10 percent in 2010. Canada also experienced similar decline—from 3.5 percent in 1980 and 1990, its share slipped to 3 percent in 2010. Australia's food exports also declined from 3.3 percent in 1980 to 2.5 percent in 1990, and to 2 percent in 2010. During the same period, the share of developing countries increased significantly in world food exports. Brazil increased its share from 4.2 percent in 1980 to 5.4 percent in 2010. China's share increased almost threefold—from 1.4 percent in 1980 to 4 percent in 2010. Indonesia's share also increased threefold—from 0.7 percent in 1980 to 2.3 percent in 2010. Malaysia and Thailand almost doubled their shares between 1980 and 2010. Indian and Mexican shares in food exports also increased during the same period.

In global food imports also the EU dominates the world market—it had a commanding share of 43 percent in 2000 and 40 percent in 2010. The US had been in distant second position with a share of 8.9 percent in 1990, which increased to 11.1 percent in 2000, and then fell to 8.2 percent in 2010. Japan was the third largest food importer—its share, however, fell from 10.1 percent in 1990 to 5.4 percent in 2010. Canada's food imports increased during the period—from 1.8 percent in 1980 to 2.6 percent in 2000, then fell to 2.4 percent in 2010. Among the developing countries, China's food imports

Table 2.24 Leading food exporters and importers in the world, 1980 to 2010 (in US$ billions)

Exporters	*Value*	*Share (%) in world exports*				*Importers*	*Value*	*Share (%) in world imports*			
	2010	*1980*	*1990*	*2000*	*2010*		*2010*	*1980*	*1990*	*2000*	*2010*
European Union (27)	450	–	–	43.9	40.2	European Union (27)	469	–	–	43.4	39.7
Extra-EU (27) exports	105	–	–	10.7	9.4	Extra-EU (27) imports	124	–	–	12.4	10.5
United States	112	17.6	13.4	12.6	10.0	United States	97	8.8	8.9	11.1	8.2
Brazil	61	4.2	2.8	3.0	5.4	Japan	64	7.2	10.1	10.5	5.4
China	44	1.4	2.5	3.1	3.9	China	60	1.4	1.4	2.0	5.0
Canada	37	3.5	3.5	4.1	3.3	Russian Federation[a]	34	–	–	1.8	2.9
Argentina	34	2.3	2.2	2.7	3.0	Canada[a]	28	1.8	2.1	2.6	2.4
Indonesia	26	0.7	0.9	1.3	2.3	Mexico[a]	20	1.4	1.3	1.8	1.7
Thailand	25	1.3	2.1	2.3	2.2	Korea, Republic of	19	0.9	1.2	1.7	1.6
Malaysia	24	0.9	1.1	1.3	2.1	Hong Kong, China	12	1.0	1.2	1.3	1.1
Australia	22	3.3	2.5	2.9	2.0	Malaysia	13	0.5	0.6	0.8	1.1
India	18	1.1	0.9	1.3	1.6	Saudi Arabia[b]	12	1.8	1.0	1.2	1.1
Mexico	18	0.9	1.0	1.9	1.6	India	12	0.5	0.2	0.5	1.0
New Zealand	16	1.1	1.4	1.3	1.5	Indonesia	11	0.6	0.3	0.7	1.0
Turkey	12	0.7	0.9	0.8	1.1	United Arab Emirates	11	0.4	0.5	0.8	1.0
Russian Federation	12	–	–	0.9	1.0	Switzerland	10	1.2	1.3	1.0	0.9
Above 15	910	–	–	83.3	81.4	Above 15	873	–	–	81.2	74.0

Source: Author's compilation from WTO statistical database.

Notes
a Imports are valued f.o.b.
b Includes WTO Secretariat estimates.

jumped to 5 percent in 2010, from 1.8 percent in 1980. Similarly, imports of Mexico, Korea, Malaysia, India, and the United Arab Emirates also increased during this period.

Trade in processed agricultural products

In processed agricultural products—those that undergo some transformation prior to their final use—such as chocolates, steaks, or wines—advanced industrialized countries dominate the global market. During the 1995 to 2008 period, exports of processed products more than doubled—increasing from $211 billion to almost half a trillion, when the exports from high-income countries increased from $169 billion to $363 billion. In both the 1995 to 1997 and 2006 to 2008 periods, developed countries had over 70 percent share in global exports of processed agricultural products (Table 2.25) when the EU controlled about 60 percent of global exports, while the US had 10 percent and 7 percent shares,

Table 2.25 Top exporters and importers of procwessed agricultural products, 1995 to 2008

Top Exporters					
Exporters	*1995–1997 (US$ billions)*	*Share (%)*	*Country*	*2006–2008 (US$ millions)*	*Share (%)*
EU-15	125.7	58.1	EU-27	257.2	58.6
United States	22.1	10.2	United States	31.6	7.2
China	5.7	2.7	Brazil	19.3	4.4
Australia	5.5	2.5	China	13.6	3.1
Canada	5.1	2.3	Canada	12.3	2.8
Brazil	4.8	2.2	Australia	12.1	2.8
New Zealand	4.7	2.2	New Zealand	11.2	2.5
Argentina	2.7	1.3			
Thailand	2.6	1.2			
Share in world total		83	Share in world total		81
Top importers					
EU-15	101.8	47.0	EU-27	229.7	48.8
Japan	19.1	8.0	United States	41.4	8.1
United States	15.6	7.2	Japan	23.2	4.9
Russia	9.6	4.4	Russia	17.6	5.8
Hong Kong, China	5.5	2.6	Canada	12.9	2.7
Canada	4.4	2.0	Mexico	8.2	1.7
Singapore	2.9	1.3	Hong Kong, SAR	6.7	1.4
South Korea	2.7	1.3	Switzerland	6.5	1.4
Brazil	2.7	1.2	South Korea	5.6	1.2
Switzerland	2.7	1.2			
Share in world total		77	Share in world total		73

Source: Author's compilation from Liapis (2011).

respectively. Some developing countries–such as China, Brazil, and Thailand—made the list of top exporters of processed agricultural products during 1995 to 1997, with their share in global market ranging between 1.2 percent and 2.7 percent. In 2006 to 2008, however, Brazil and China had significantly expanded their shares in global exports of processed agricultural products—Brazil doubled its share to 4.4 percent, while China increased its share to 3.1 percent from 2.7 percent in 1995 to 1997.

Evidently, developing countries' exports of processed agricultural products have been growing much faster than those of developed countries. During the 1995 to 2008 period, the annual growth rate of exports of agricultural products in developed countries was 5.9 percent compared with 10.9 percent in the upper-middle-income countries, and 10.5 percent in the low-income countries.[44] It appears that with the implementation of the URAA, some developing economies like Brazil, China, Indonesia, and South Africa are becoming increasingly competitive in processed agricultural products. Although low-income developing countries account for a small share of trade in processed products, their share also appears to have risen in recent years (Liapis, 2011).

In respect of imports of processed agricultural products, while developed countries accounted for more than 60 percent share in the global market, the shares of middle- and low-income developing countries more than doubled during 1995 to 2008. The shares of the Russian Federation, Hong Kong-China, Singapore, and Brazil increased during the 2006 to 2008 period, compared with the 1995 to 1997 period (Table 2.25). The share of leading importers in global imports, however, fell from 77 percent in 1995 to 1997 to 73 percent in 2006 to 2008. The rising share of imports by developing countries may reflect high-income growth in some developing countries in the early 2000s, but imports from war-torn Afghanistan and Iraq also increased at the same time, which may be attributed to Western military deployment in these countries during this period.

Post-URAA issues and WTO negotiations

Although agriculture contributes only about 3 percent to the world GDP, this sector remains important for global poverty reduction and economic development through various transmission mechanisms.[45] Approximately one-third of the world's population still obtain their livelihoods from agriculture and for up to 70 percent of the world's poor who live in rural areas, agriculture is still the main source of income and employment (World Bank, 2014). For scores of developing countries and LDCs, agriculture is still the largest source of their national gross domestic products (GDPs). In 2010 to 2012, agriculture accounted for 27 percent of the GDPs of low-income developing countries, with 71 percent of the national GDP in Liberia, 57 percent in Guinea-Bissau and Sierra Leon, 52 percent in the Democratic Republic of Congo, 49 percent in Ethiopia, 39 percent in Liberia, and 35 percent in Burkina Faso. Similarly, in many developing countries and LDCs, agriculture is still the largest employer, In 2010 to 2012, agriculture's share in employment was 62 percent in Bhutan, 53.3 percent in Cameron,

48.9 percent in Liberia, 47.2 percent in India, 44.5 percent in Ghana, and 41.5 percent in Albania.[46] The developing countries and LDCs thus have a huge stake in the liberalization of agriculture under the WTO.

But the agricultural sector, in which developing countries have so much at stake, remains much less liberalized than manufacturing. As noted above, the sector was brought under the rule-based global trading system only in the mid-1990s under the URAA, while liberalization of the manufacturing sector, in which developed countries have exports interests, began in earnest immediately after World War II—precisely with the establishment of GATT in 1947. In the absence of any international discipline, both developed and developing countries erected rather elaborate infrastructures and mechanisms to protect their domestic agricultures. They, however, took contrasting routes. As explained above, while developed countries protected their agriculture and farmers through massive doses of domestic supports, export subsidies, export credits, and so on, most of the developing countries, especially up until the 1980s, taxed their agriculture by depressing their farmers' incentives through counterproductive trade and exchange rate policies.

Protectionist measures adopted by developed countries included: (1) market price supports—which covered the difference between domestic and international prices caused by border barriers such as tariffs and quantitative restrictions—accounted for about 70 percent of total protection in OECD countries; (2) direct supports—product-specific domestic producer or consumer subsidies—played a limited role as they came from state exchequers; and (3) general support to agricultural research, marketing, and infrastructure (Legg, 2003; OECD, 2005). As noted above, such support structures evolved into elephantine proportions over the course of several decades and reached their peak in the late 1980s.

In the mid-1990s, under the URAA, WTO members agreed to reduce agricultural support and protection by establishing disciplines and rules on market access, export subsidies, and trade-distorting domestic supports. Thus, much of the trade-distorting price supports, subsidies, and tariff and non-tariff barriers, which underpinned developed countries' agricultural production and trade for many decades, came under strengthened GATT discipline. With full implementation of the URAA, as discussions above suggest, much of those support structures have now been dismantled. However, the agricultural sector still remains far from full-scale liberalization, as many distortions with far-reaching economic implications continue to plague international trade in the sector.

Domestic support still remains substantial

First, the agricultural support level in developed countries still remains very high. In 2011, for example, on average, 19 percent of farmers' incomes in the OECD countries still came from governmental supports. Understandably, such supports varied from country to country—New Zealand had the lowest level of support, at just 1 percent of farm income, followed by Australia (3 percent), Chile (4 percent), the US (9 percent), Mexico (12 percent), Israel (13 percent),

Canada (16 percent), Iceland (47 percent), South Korea (50 percent), Japan (51 percent), Switzerland (56 percent), and Norway (60 percent) (OECD, 2013). In 2011, the total support to agriculture in OECD countries stood at $252 billion, a historic low, but it was more than 30 percent of combined GDPs of all LDCs in the world in 2013.[47]

Worse still, about half of the agricultural supports of the OECD countries in 2011 represented supports which distorted production and trade (OECD, 2013), and much of the supports were geared to selected agricultural products, such as dairy, sugar, rice, and cotton. In the US, for example, about 50 percent of total producer revenue for milk, sugar, and rice was attributable to farm programs (OECD, 2002), and such supports were about 35 percent for cotton producers (Sumner, 2006) and about 25 percent for maize/corn and oilseed (Hertel *et al.*, 2007).

The fact that overall support to agriculture and farming activities still remains substantial in developed countries, especially in the EU and the US, does indicate that they succeeded in fulfilling their Amber box reduction commitments without significantly reducing actual supports. Critics argue that the EU capped its AMS reduction commitments at 18 percent of the value of its agricultural production by excluding direct payments under production-limiting programs, and with the addition of such Blue box payments the EU's total AMS would be about 27 percent (Hoda and Gulati, 2007, 136). Similarly, Sumner (2006) argued that although the AMS notifications of the US for the years 2000 to 2006 remained well below the $19.1 billion cap, with the addition of the Production Flexibility Contract (PFC) and Countercyclical Payments in the Amber box, the total AMS of the US was $29.1 billion in 2000, $25.3 billion in 2001, and $26.3 billion in 2006.[48]

The underlying reason for the continuation of such a scale of agricultural support, even after full implementation of the URAA, may lie with the built-in loopholes of the URAA itself. First, the prescribed method of AMS calculation left scope for manipulation. The URAA allowed WTO members to reduce overall AMS, and thus a country could presumably reduce its overall AMS while increasing support to some selected sectors or products. That developed countries significantly reduced their domestic supports, by meeting or even exceeding their URAA obligations, while still retaining substantial supports to some selected products, does indicate that such a strategy may have been utilized. Moreover, the price support for the AMS is calculated on the basis of the difference between a fixed world price and a domestic administered price, without requiring any adjustment to inflation or exchange rate fluctuations. As a result, AMS calculations in respect of some developed countries failed to capture the actual AMS (Poczta-Wajda, 2013). In addition, the base year for AMS calculation was 1986 to 1988, when world prices were very low, which resulted in very high domestic support. As reduction commitments were based on such a high base, even the significant reduction of support did not result in significant actual reduction.

Second, considerable ambiguities in respect of essential characteristics of the Green box, Amber box, and Blue box measures continue to provide opportunities to willing WTO members to cleverly reshuffle their agricultural supports between the boxes, which may be aimed at disguising the actual magnitude of such supports, but they do frustrate the very objective of establishing a level playing field for all WTO members. Many such supports may be theoretically 'minimally trade-distorting,' but their actual impact on production and trade may be significant for many WTO members (OECD, 2000) and they may well be deemed 'actionable subsidies' under the WTO Agreement on Subsidies and Countervailing Measures (SCM). Under SCM, subsidies in any trade, including the agricultural sector, may be deemed "actionable subsidies' when such subsidies may cause 'adverse effects' to the interests of other WTO members, cause injury to a domestic industry, or lead to nullification or impairment of benefits under WTO agreements." The fact that price-contingent subsidies for many agricultural commodities, including major staples like corn, wheat, and rice, are still sizable relative to the total value of production in many developed counties, may well be considered as trade-distorting subsidies which less developed countries and other major exporters of agricultural products may view as actionable subsidies (Sumner, 2006).

As the recent Upland Cotton Case, filed by Brazil with the WTO Dispute Settlement Body, revealed, attributing supports to various boxes may even lead to far-reaching controversies.[49] The cotton subsidy issue is incredibly important, as the magnitude of supports afforded to this commodity by some countries, especially by the US, has been critically affecting the welfare of some of the world's poorest countries. Between 20 to 50 percent of the export earnings of the 'Cotton-4' of Sub-Saharan Africa—Benin, Burkina Faso, Chad, and Mali—come from cotton exports, but they have to compete with the highly subsidized cotton exports of the US. As Table 2.26 shows, in 2005 US cotton subsidies rose to $3.7 billion from only $211 million in 1995. Even in 2010, the US cotton subsidy stood at $828 million. In fact, cotton subsidies in the US jumped from a low of about 23 percent of the value of production in 2004, to about 80 percent in 2005, and remained at 65 percent of the value of production in 2006 (Sumner, 2006). Anderson and Valanzuela (2006) found that with the full removal of the subsidy in cotton, net gainers would be developing countries, as their output and exports would increase, and Sub-Saharan African countries would be able to increase cotton exports by $1.9 billion. In addition, the benefits would come from increased output and exports, not from increased prices.

Any future negotiations on domestic support reduction should thus focus on closing up such built-in loopholes of the URAA—by making domestic support reductions both product and non-product specific; targeting selected commodities in which domestic subsidies tend to be highly concentrated; carefully selecting a more meaningful base period; making AMS calculations adjustable to inflation and exchange rates; refining the definitions and essential characteristics of agricultural policies attributable to various support boxes; clearly delineating 'actionable subsidies' in agriculture, and emphasizing a level playing field for products like cotton in which poor developing countries have greater stakes.

Market access still remains restrained

Second, both tariff and non-tariff protections continue to hinder the liberalization of agricultural trade more significantly than other sectors of international trade. Although the URAA's goals of agricultural tariff reduction have been achieved, 'waters in the tariffs' still remain significant. High bound tariffs—the so-called dirty tariffication—still allow WTO members to facilitate or impede market access in response to domestic and international market conditions. On top of that, there are numerous examples of tariff peaks, tariff quotas, and tariff escalations in agriculture, which powerfully impede trade liberalization. As discussed above, the highest frequencies of high applied tariffs, tariff peaks, and tariff escalations may be found in major agricultural products, such as meat, sugar, milk, butter, cheese, cereals, tobacco, cotton, sugar, fruit, coffee, and cocoa. Many of these products are of great export interest to developing countries and LDCs.

Among various measures of tariff protections in agriculture, arguably tariff peaks and tariff escalations stand out as more formidable barriers to market access than others. Apparently, tariff peaks are utilized to protect 'sensitive products' from international competition, but this label of 'sensitivity' is left to arbitrary determination by individual WTO members. As a result, extremely high tariff peaks are applied to goods as diverse as Christmas trees to cereals or vegetables. Moreover, although the overwhelming majority of tariff peaks are in the range of 12 to 30 percent around the world, about 20 percent of tariff peaks in the US, 25 percent in the EU, 30 percent in Japan, and about 15 percent in Canada exceed 30 percent.

Tariff escalations also pose serious problems, especially for developing countries. With tariff escalations, tariff protection increases as a product undergoes additional processing, and thus the effective rate of protection squarely depends on tariff escalations. As explained above, compared with developed countries, tariff escalation rates are very high in low-income developing countries. Thus, developing countries face high barriers to exports in agricultural processed products because of their heavy dependence on imported intermediate goods from developed countries.

Market access for developing countries has also been impeded by the changing nature of the international food production and distribution system. As discussed above, only a small fraction of most of the agricultural commodities enter the international market, and in most of the major agricultural products only a handful of countries are exporters, and among them only a few are dominant. That makes the global agricultural commodity market oligopolistic in nature. Moreover, only a small proportion of global food production is traded internationally, and some food products do not have global markets at all. Global agricultural trade is further compounded by the dominance of a few transnational corporations—almost 85 to 90 percent of agricultural trade is controlled by a few transnational businesses, such as Cargill, Continental, Louis Dreyfus, Andre, and Bunge. These companies also substantially control the marketing of agricultural inputs—such as fuel, fertilizer, seeds, pesticides, and irrigation equipment. By controlling the trade of both agricultural inputs and outputs, as well as banking, processing, and shipping operations, these transnational corporations powerfully distort agricultural trade around the world, while their operations and influence remain outside the purview of the WTO (Cheng, 2007).

Any future WTO negotiations in agricultural market access should thus vigorously address a whole range of issues that currently impede market access for developing countries—including the issues of dirty tariffication, tariff peaks, tariff escalations, market concentration of food and agricultural commodity, as well as the WTO's possible oversight on oligarchic businesses in agricultural inputs and output across the world.

Imperatives for the further liberalization of agriculture

Arguably, the further liberalization of agriculture is more important than the liberalization of any other sector in the contemporary world economy. As the discussion above suggests, greater liberalization of agriculture is crucial not only for establishing a level playing field or efficient allocation of scarce agricultural resources, but also for poverty reduction and economic development in less developed countries. The URAA has recently brought this sector under the rules and disciplines of a strengthened GATT—but it has not liberalized it as yet. The WTO Agreement rather left most of the reforms necessary for the actual liberalization of the sector for future negotiations. As the discussion above indicates, the sector still remains sheltered within strong protectionist walls—a plethora of domestic supports, export subsidies, and tariff and non-tariff barriers still plague trade in this sector. The attendant cost of prolonged and widespread protections in agricultural trade, in terms of lost income and welfare to developing countries as well as to the world economy, is considered to be staggering. It is such an abysmal situation which has led some leading scholars to surmise that under the current agricultural trade regimes the wealthiest of rich country farmers predominantly gain from agricultural protection while farm households in poor countries pay the price (Anderson and Valanzuela, 2006). The implementation of the URAA thus far has undoubtedly led to some tangible progress in reducing domestic supports and tariff barriers, but as explained below, the further liberalization of agricultural trade beyond the URAA promises far greater benefits to the world economy.

Double swords of tariff and subsidy removal

Available studies, however, suggest that the removal of agricultural supports or tariffs may not be equally beneficial for all developing countries. Reduction in domestic supports in developed countries is likely to result in an increase in the world prices of agricultural commodities, which may actually harm some developing countries if they are net importers of products that developed countries subsidize and export. On the other hand, reduction in tariffs in developed countries is

Table 2.26 Estimates of welfare effects of agricultural trade liberalization (change in real income, in US$ billions)

Liberalizing region	*Benefiting regions*		
	High-income countries	*Developing countries*	*World*
High-income countries			
Anderson *et al.* (2005)	109.0	26.0	135
Hertel and Keeney (2006)	36.9	10.8	47.7
Tokarick (2005)	91.7	8.0	99.7
Developing countries			
Anderson *et al.* (2005)	19.0	28.0	47.0
Hertel and Keeney (2006)	4.8	3.3	8.1
Tokarick (2005)	2.8	21.4	24.2
Total			
Anderson *et al.* (2005)	128.0	54.0	182.0
Hertel and Keeney (2006)	41.6	14.1	55.7
Tokarick (2005)	97.8	30.4	128.2

Effects of tariff and subsidy removal on developing countries

Liberalization by high-income countries	*Impacts of real income of developing countries*
Tariff removal	
Hertel and Keeney (2006)	11.9
Tokarick (2005)	12.5
Removal of all subsidies	
Hertel and Keeney (2006)	–1.2
Tokarick (2005)	–4.5
Removal of export subsidies only	
Hertel and Keeney (2006)	–1.5

Source: Author's compilation from Tokarick (2008).

Notes

Estimates of Anderson *et al.* (2005), relative to base year 2015; Hertel and Keeney (2006), relative to base year 2001; and Tokarick (2005), relative to base year 1997.

likely to be beneficial for developing countries, as they will have greater access to developed country markets. Table 2.26 summarizes the findings of several economic models which sought to capture the costs and benefits of developing countries from the further liberalization of agriculture. According to Anderson *et al.* (2005), the removal of all agricultural trade barriers (both tariff and subsidies) by both developed and developing countries would yield a gain of $182 billion in real income for the world, while Hertel and Keeney (2006) and Tokarick (2005) projected the benefits more modestly, at $56 billion and $128 billion, respectively.[50]

Interestingly, all these models project developed countries as the largest beneficiaries of further agricultural trade liberalization: $128 billion out of total gains of $182 billion in Andersen, $42 billion out of total gains of $56 billion in Hertel and Keeney, and $98 billion out of total gains of $128 billion in Tokarick. Shockingly, disaggregated into individual developed countries, the largest beneficiaries of agricultural trade liberalization are projected to the most distorted economies—the EU, the US, Japan, and South Korea (Tokarick, 2008, 208). Developing countries as a whole are expected to gain only $54 billion (30 percent) in Anderson, $14 billion (25 percent) in Hertel and Keeney, and $30 billion (24 percent) in Tokarick. According to Hertel and Keeney (2006), trade liberalization by developed countries, without any reform by developing countries, is likely to raise real income for developing countries by $10.8 billion, while tariff elimination is likely to raise real income by $11.9 billion, and the removal of subsidies is likely to reduce real income by $1.2 billion. Tokarick (2005) projected the net gain for developing countries at $8 billion—a balance of the gain of $12.5 billion from tariff elimination and the loss of $4.5 billion from subsidy removal.

In aggregate, however, across all of these models, the impact of agricultural trade liberalization is likely to be positive for developing countries as a group, but the gains would hinge on the liberalization of their own economies. According to Hertel and Keeney (2006), developing countries would gain $10.8 billion from liberalization in high-income countries and $3.3 billion from their own liberalization, while Andersen *et al.* (2005) showed a $26 billion gain from liberalization by developed countries and $28 billion from their own liberalization. Tokarick (2005) showed the gain of developing countries at $8 billion from the liberalization of developed countries, but an overwhelming $21.4 billion from the liberalization of their own economies. In a related study, Anderson *et al.* (2006a, 190) found that the liberalization of agriculture would cause farm output and farm employment to rise in developing countries, from which the poorest people, namely farmers and unskilled laborers in developing countries, would gain the most.

Economic research thus points to further liberalization of agriculture—on both fronts—in respect of domestic supports as well as tariff protections. As greater potential benefits of liberalization will accrue to those developing countries that liberalize their own trade policies while pushing for the further liberalization of agriculture in future WTO negotiations, developing countries, even LDCs, should not seek exemption from their liberalization obligations; neither should they seek longer periods for transition. Past experiences do suggest that delayed reforms not only delay benefits; they also result in prolonging the costs for a longer period. Developing countries have already paid heavy prices in the past for pursuing counterproductive strategies.

In the 1950s and the 1960s, many developing countries were swayed by the so-called Two-Sector Model of Arthur Lewis (1955), which stipulated that economic development was a process of relocating factors of production from an agricultural sector characterized by low productivity and traditional technology to a modern industrial/manufacturing sector with higher productivity. Lewis' theory and its policy implications, however, now stand debunked, as governmental intervention to pursue industrialization by explicitly or implicitly taxing agriculture has largely been discredited (Anderson and Valenzuela, 2008; Kirkpatrick and Barrientos, 2004).

More recent economic theories, in contrast, argue that economic development results rather from rising incomes and a lower incidence of poverty among those who depend on agriculture for a living—a declining share for agriculture in national employment and GDP is an inevitable consequence, not a cause, of economic progress.[51] Economic researches now also show that as incomes grow, consumers increase their consumption of manufactured goods and services faster than their consumption of food, and higher income elasticities of demand for non-agricultural goods and services, in turn, propel growth in manufacturing and service sectors (Cervantes-Godoy and Dewbre, 2010), and through such transmission mechanisms, agriculture stimulates and sustains economic transition toward manufacturing and service-oriented economies (DFID, 2014).

Conclusions

Bringing the agricultural sector into the strengthened GATT discipline has been one of the hallmark achievements of the Uruguay Round. Prior to that, in the absence of international rules and disciplines, also because of the sensitive character of agriculture and food, many countries—developed as well as developing—raised protectionist walls of their own to shelter agricultural trade from international competition. Up until the 1980s, while developed countries provided massive doses of domestic supports to their farmers, developing countries did the opposite—they taxed their farmers. The URAA succeeded in bringing this sector under the GATT disciplines in the mid-1990s. The agreement, however, just opened the door for the sector's liberalization, and many of the reforms necessary for the actual liberalization of this important sector of trade to many developing countries have been left to future negotiations.

There is, however, no denying that considerable progress has been made with the full implementation of the URAA since 1995. Non-tariff barriers (NTBs) have been transformed into tariffication and all agricultural tariffs are now bound tariffs. Outrageous levels of domestic supports in the developed countries have been brought down to an average of 20 percent of farmers' income, many of the trade-distorting subsidies have been sidelined, and overall transparency in governmental support measures has been strengthened. Developing countries' position in the WTO is now more organized and pronounced than ever before. International trade in agriculture has expanded substantially since the mid-1990s, reflecting increased globalization, the greater integration of new participants in world markets, and the deepening of reforms in agricultural markets as a result of the URAA. The reforms have also led to considerable shifts in global agricultural trade—the shares of developing countries in global production and exports of agricultural goods, including processed products, are on the rise.

The agricultural sector, however, still remains far away from full-scale liberalization—much of the sector is still sheltered by protectionist measures, such as producer supports, export subsidies, commodity supports, high bound tariffs, tariff peaks, TRQs, tariff escalations, and so on. Even applied MFN tariffs in agriculture are still three times higher compared with those in the manufacturing sector. Considerable ambiguities still remain in respect of essential characteristics of the Green box, Amber box, and Blue box measures. The fact that domestic supports to agriculture in the powerhouses of agriculture—the EU and the US—are still very high and around 20 percent of farmers' income indicates that their compliance with WTO commitments may have been compromised by a clever reshuffling of support measures. The cost of the prevalence of such widespread protections in agricultural trade, in terms of lost income and welfare to developing countries as well as to the world economy, can hardly be overemphasized.

Projected welfare benefits of the further liberalization of agriculture for the world economy are believed to be the largest among all sectors of international trade. This is so because this sector still remains less liberalized than other international trade sectors. Developing countries are expected to benefit from further tariff reforms, as these will enhance their market access to developed country markets. With the removal of subsidies in developed countries, however, terms of trade for developing countries may worsen, as prices of currently subsidized exports would rise. In balance, however, the expected benefits would far outweigh the costs of developing countries from further liberalization of agricultural trade, especially when viewed more comprehensively—encompassing the issues of the employment of unskilled labor, poverty alleviation, farmers' income, and an increased share of global exports.

Developing countries thus have a great stake in the further liberalization of the agricultural sector. Any future WTO negotiations on domestic support reduction should focus on closing the built-in loopholes of the URAA—by making domestic support reductions both product and non-product specific, targeting commodities in which domestic subsidies tend to be highly concentrated in developed countries, adopting more effective base periods, making the AMS calculations adjustable to inflation and exchange rates, further clarifying essential characteristics of agricultural policies attributable to various support boxes, and more clearly delineating 'actionable subsidies' in agriculture. Developing countries should also focus on reforming their own economies—as reaping greater benefits from a liberalized agriculture would squarely hinge on the extent to which they liberalize their own economies.

Notes

1 Literature on agricultural trade protections and distortions has been voluminous. Some of the important studies, especially in the context of the pre-WTO period, include Anderson and Hayami (1986); Tyers and Anderson (1986); FAO (1998); Tangermann *et al.* (1994); Krueger *et al.* (1988); Schiff and Valdes (1992), and Chenery and Srinivasan (1989).

2 See GATT (1947, Article VI, Article XI.2a, Article XI.2.c, Article XVI.3, and the Addendum to Article XVI). The GATT agreement defined agricultural products as 'primary commodities,' 'foodstuffs,' and 'agricultural and fisheries products,' and so

on, to imply farm products in their natural form, or which had undergone some processing required for marketing.

3 While world grain imports increased at an annual rate of 6 percent during the 1960s through the 1970s, in the 1980s world grain imports stagnated and agricultural market prices fell due to slower growth of import demands in developing countries (Tangermann *et al.*, 1994).

4 In the 1980s, the EU accounted for 24 percent of world imports of food grain and 11 percent of world exports, while the US had a 22 percent share in global exports in food grain. About 60 percent of all trade disputes submitted to the GATT for settlement between 1980 and 1990 were concerned with agriculture, and most of those were filed by the US and the EU. For more details see Tangermann *et al.* (1994).

5 The Cairns Group at that time consisted of 14 traditional agricultural exporters from both developed and developing countries, namely Argentina, Australia, Brazil, Canada, Chile, Columbia, Fiji, Hungary, Indonesia, Malaysia, New Zealand, the Philippines, Thailand, and Uruguay.

6 The WTO asked the member countries, apart from the LDCs, to submit the Schedules by April 1994, prior to signing the UR Agreements. The LDCs were given up until April 1995 to comply with the same requirement.

7 Article 5 of the URAA, however, allowed WTO members to raise tariffs above the level stipulated in their respective Country Schedules under particular circumstances. In addition, Annex 5 of the URAA permits WTO members to retain NTBs for certain sensitive products. The URAA, however, prohibited the following NTBs: quantitative import restrictions, variable import levies, minimum import prices, discretionary import licensing, non-tariff measures maintained through state trading enterprises, voluntary export restraints, and similar border measures other than ordinary customs duties.

8 This minimum level was to be raised to 5 percent by the year 2000 in the case of developed countries and by 2004 in the case of developing countries. The market access provisions, however, did not apply if the commodity in question was a traditional staple of a developing country.

9 The agreement also protects preferential tariff rates for the developing country exporters as specified under bilateral trade agreements.

10 TRQs were, however, applicable mainly to the developed countries, as few developing countries were engaged in such tariff practices.

11 See also Martin and Winters (1996); Harrison *et al.* (1995); FAO (1998); Dowlah (2003).

12 Literature in this area is simply voluminous, and at the same time quite divergent in findings and interpretations. Some of the useful studies include Hertel *et al.* (2007); Jansen *et al.* (2002); Diaz-Bonilla and Robinson (2001); Liapis (2012); OECD (2000, 2010a, 2010b, 2012); Tokarick (2008); World Bank (2008).

13 For more details, see Anderson and Tyers (1995); Valdes and Zietz (1995); World Bank (2003, 103–139).

14 According to the website of the Cairns group, the group now represents a coalition of 19 agricultural exporting countries which account for over 25 percent of the world's agricultural exports. The new members are: Bolivia, Costa Rica, Fiji, Hungary, Pakistan, Peru, Paraguay, and South Africa. See www.cairnsgroup.org/Pages/Introduction.aspx. On the other hand, the G20—a coalition of developing countries—established in 2003 accounts for 60 percent of the world's population, 70 percent of its farmers, and 26 percent of the world's agricultural exports. Currently, 24 WTO members belong to the G20: Argentina, Bolivia, Brazil, Chile, China, Cuba, Ecuador, Egypt, Guatemala, India, Indonesia, Mexico, Nigeria, Pakistan, Paraguay, Peru, the Philippines, South Africa, Tanzania, Thailand, Uruguay, Venezuela, the Bolivarian Republic, and Zimbabwe. See www.wto.org/english/tratop_e/dda_e/negotiating_groups_e.htm.

15 Multinational organizations like the United Nations, the World Bank, and the International Monetary Fund (IMF) each classify countries on the basis of their own criteria, and thus no uniform taxonomy for classification of countries exists today. In this study, however, countries are classified in line with the World Bank taxonomy. Developing countries, in this study, include the countries that the World Bank categorizes as middle-income and low-income developing countries. Examples of middle-income developing countries would be Brazil, India, China and Korea, Hungary, Malaysia, and the Philippines, while examples of lower income developing countries would be Bangladesh, Guatemala, and Indonesia. For details on the taxonomy of the classification of countries, see Chapter 1 (this volume), and Nielson (2011).

16 Tariff peaks are defined in many different ways. The OECD website defines it as tariffs above 20 percent of its *ad valorem* equivalent. See www.stats.oecd.org/glossary/index.htm. The US defines domestic tariff peaks as those exceeding the overall average applied rate, and international tariff peaks as those exceeding 15 percent. See WTO (2012).

17 The URAA tariffication process called for setting the tariffs at a 'low or minimal' rate, without specifying any numerical rule for 'low or minimal.' As most countries set the tariffication at a very high rate, it would seem to contradict the spirit of the agreement (Gibson *et al.*, 2001, 16).

18 See WTO (2008, Attachment A).

19 In 2012, 5 percent of all tariff lines in the US had international tariff peaks (tariffs exceeding 15 percent), and 6.7 percent of all tariff lines had domestic tariff peaks (exceeding three times the overall average applied tariff rates). The percentages were 5.6 percent and 6.6 percent for domestic and international tariff peaks respectively in 2002, and 6.9 percent and 5.2 percent respectively in 2007. See WTO (2012).

20 Earlier, Gibson *et al.* (2001, 12–14) found that 18 of the 46 commodity aggregates they studied—including tobacco, dairy, meat, sugar, sweeteners, vegetables, cereals, and breeding animals—had above the global average agricultural tariff rate of 62 percent. The study also found several commodity groups with the lowest tariffs, such as coffee, fiber, several fruit categories, spices, and live horticulture.

21 For more details see Table 3.9 in Aksoy (2005, 49).

22 In 2002, for example, tariffs on final fruit products and cocoa in the US were 136 percent and 186 percent respectively, while the respective rates were 98 percent and 63 percent in the EU (Aksoy, 2005, 49).

23 Moreover, most of the agricultural commodity chains, particularly those of high-value crops and processed products, are being increasingly dominated all over the world by a few giant multinational corporations. As the incentives and ability of these global oligopolies grow stronger to maintain tariff escalations, the developing countries and consumers in developed countries pay the eventual price for such tariff escalations (Cheng, 2007).

24 The TSE is calculated by adding the Producer Support Estimates (PSE), the taxpayer cost of consumption subsidies and the provision of general services, and subtracting import tariff receipts.

25 The actual amount of TSE increases during this period were as follows: from $111.55 billion to $118.33 billion in the EU; from $60.18 billion to $135.49 billion in the US; from $7.52 billion to $10.30 billion in Canada; and from $58.24 billion to $63.64 billion in Japan.

26 In 2012, the share came down further to 18.6 percent.

27 These countries had a very small percentage of producer support in 2005 as well—3.6 percent in Australia, 5.0 percent in Chile, and 1.3 percent in New Zealand.

28 Iceland has cut down from 70 percent in 2005 to 47 percent in 2012—by one-third—but about half of farm income in the country continues to come from the state exchequers.

29 Producers' support also appears to be falling in India, another major non-OECD agricultural producer. In a study of four major developing countries—India, China, Malaysia, and Vietnam—Orden *et al.* (2007) found that India's support to agriculture has been counter-cyclical to world prices. Agricultural support increased when world prices were low, and decreased when world prices were high. In aggregate, taking into account both price support and budgetary costs, the study found a trend that showed dis-protection toward protection over the period of 1985 to 2002. India's producer support estimates are not included in Table 2.12 because of conceptual and measurement issues involved in such calculations by different sources.

30 The URAA also separates domestic subsidies from export subsidies. The agreement allows export subsidies, but only for products for which members made a commitment to phase out these subsidies and when exports above that commitment level are made without using subsidies. More details on export subsidies are given below.

31 Poczta-Wajda (2013) also maintains that the Japanese example showed that the AMS measurement, as prescribed by the WTO, could be misleading in measuring domestic support. See also Baskar and Beghin (2009) and Goodwin and Mishra (2006).

32 For greater details on coupling and decoupling practices of agricultural supports in both developed and developing countries, see Bhaskar and Beghin (2009); Jank and Jales (2004); Moise *et al.* (2013).

33 For more details see Tables 1 and 2, and Figures 1 and 2 in Sumner (2006). Such discrepancies came to light following Brazil's complaint to the WTO's dispute settlement panel, which in 2004 ruled that US subsidy programs for Upland cotton violated its WTO obligations, and in 2005 the WTO's Appellate Body upheld the panel's finding. Sumner shows that the problem of US non-compliance with WTO obligations is not confined to cotton only, and many US subsidies on numerous other commodities besides cotton may be trade distorting and vulnerable to the WTO challenge as well.

34 For more details on agricultural supports reduction in the EU and the US, especially in respect of their AMS reduction commitments, see chs 5 and 6 in Hoda and Gulati (2007).

35 In 2004, the AMS ceilings of some other countries stood as follows: Australia: A$912.1 billion; Brazil: US$3.5 million; Canada: C$344 million; Iceland: ISK12.8 billion; Israel: US$568 million; South Korea: 1490 billion Won; Mexico: Mex$2.5 billion; New Zealand: $NZ288 million; Norway: NOK2.0 billion; and Venezuela: US$1.1 billion. For further details see Economic Research Service (ERS), USDA: www.ers.usda.gov/db/wto.

36 For conceptual and methodological problems, especially in respect of calculations of the AMS in the context of developing countries, see Orden *et al.* (2007); Bhaskar and Beghin (2009); Moise *et al.* (2013).

37 For more details see Farm Subsidy Database of Environmental Working Group, www.farm.ewg.org.

38 Some of the prominent studies include Anderson and Valenzuela (2007); Anderson *et al.* (2006a); Hertel *et al.* (2007).

39 Josling (2004, 68), however, found an exception to this rule. As it turned out, following Hungary's claim that it had erroneously overlooked some export subsidies it had actually allowed in the base period, the WTO granted it a waiver to exceed its commitment for an interim period.

40 According to OECD (2000) estimates, historically, three countries' export subsidy elements of export credit operations were higher than their direct export subsidy expenditures—the US, Canada, and Australia. More details on export credits are given below.

41 The WTO (2002) suggests that the reduction of export subsidy was relatively greater in volume limits as opposed to value limits, and in OECD countries as a whole, the volume limits were exceeded almost twice as often as the value limits.

42 For more details on the export subsidy reductions in both the US and EU, see Hoda and Gulati (2007, 146–151, 172–175). The authors maintain that the reported decline in the use of direct export subsidies in the EU was 'largely an illusion' as the rate of subsidization in the EU depended on the difference between internal and international prices (per unit subsidy/world f.o.b. prices). The declining trend in subsidies for cereals and beef was the result of a reduction in intervention prices, and for products for which intervention prices had not come down appreciably, such as rice, sugar, butter, and pig meat, the magnitude of per unit export subsidy remained very high in the EU. See also Josling (2004, 2007).

43 Hazel and Wood (2008, 501) maintain that the complete dismantling of governmental supports in OECD countries might lead to about 10 to 15 percent increase in agricultural prices. The World Development Report of the World Bank (2008) also cautioned that higher import prices would have potentially disastrous consequences for poor consumers and for farmers in countries with a net deficit in food production. See also Brooks *et al.* (2008).

44 For more details, see Table 1 in Liapis (2011, 17).

45 A study by DFID (2004), which looked into four decades of development experience around the world, showed that agriculture contributed to poverty reduction and economic development through four transmission mechanisms: (1) the direct impact of improved agricultural performance on rural incomes; (2) the impact of cheaper food for both urban and rural poor; (3) agriculture's contribution to growth and the generation of economic opportunity in the non-farm sector; and (4) agriculture's fundamental role in stimulating and sustaining economic transition, as countries shift away from being primarily agricultural toward a broader base of manufacturing and services.

46 Based on Tables 3.2 and 4.2 of the World Bank (2014).

47 Harcourt (2004) puts it more bluntly: "You could fly all the cows in France around the world, business class, for the same cost of the European Union's agricultural subsidies."

48 Moreover, the US also reduced its support for the Amber box by moving food aid to the Green box, although historically food aid served as a safety valve for surpluses rather than being a humanitarian response to the problem of hunger in poor countries. On top of that, the EU continues to use export subsidies, and the US continues to use export credits—elimination of which could provide the greatest benefits to global and developing country welfare (Anderson *et al.*, 2008).

49 In September 2004, the WTO dispute settlement panel ruled that US subsidy programs for Upland cotton violated URAA obligations and recommended that the US change its policies to bring them into conformity with WTO rules. In March 2005, the WTO's Appellate Body upheld the panel's finding and Brazil, the complaining party in the dispute, demanded $1 billion in trade retaliation unless the US fully implemented the Appellate Body's recommendations. In 2006, the WTO's Dispute Settlement Board (DSB) agreed to Brazil's request to examine whether the US had brought cotton subsidy measures into compliance with its recommendations. The DSB panel, however, found that the US had failed to do so. The US appealed, and the WTO Appellate Body upheld the decision in 2008. See WT/DS267/AB/RW (adopted on June 20, 2008).

50 The differences in their estimates may be attributed to different databases, benchmark years, and other assumptions of these models. Andersen and colleagues (2005), for example, used a dynamic model of the world economy classified into 27 regions and 25 sectors, of which 13 were agricultural sectors. On the other hand, both Hertel and Keeney (2006) and Tokarick (2005) used general equilibrium models (GTAP models), but different versions. All these studies had different benchmark years.

51 For more details see Byerlee and Sadoulet (2009); Timmer (1989); Cervantes and Brooks (2009).

References

Abbott, P. and Morse, B. (2000). Tariff rate quota implementation and administration by developing countries. *Agricultural and Resource Economics Review*, 29(1), 115–124.

Aksoy, A. (2005). Global agricultural trade policies. In M. Aksoy and J. Beghin (eds), *Global Agricultural Trade and Developing Countries* (pp. 37–53). Washington, DC: World Bank.

Anderson, E. and Tyres, R. (1995). How developing countries would gain from agricultural trade liberalization in the Uruguay Round. In I. Goldin and O. Knudsen (eds), *Agricultural Trade Liberalization: Implications for developing countries*. Paris: OECD and World Bank.

Anderson, K. (2002). *Agricultural trade liberalization: Implications for Indian Ocean Rim countries*. Adelaide: Center for International Economic Studies.

Anderson, K. (2004). Agriculture, trade reform and poverty reduction: Implications for Sub-Saharan Africa. Policy Issues in International Trade and Commodities Study Series No. 22. New York and Geneva: UNCTAD.

Anderson, K. and Hayami, Y. (1986). *The Political Economy of Agricultural Protection: East Asia in international perspective.* Sydney: Allen & Unwin.

Anderson, K. and Nelgen, S. (2010). Trade barrier volatility and domestic price stabilization: Evidence from agriculture. World Bank Policy Research Working Paper No. 5511. World Bank.

Anderson, K. and Valenzuela, E. (2006). The World Trade Organization's cotton initiative: A tale of two issues. World Bank Research Working Paper No. 3918. World Bank.

Anderson, K. and Valenzuela, E. (2007). Do global trade distortions still harm developing country farmers? *Review of World Economics*, 143(1), 108–139.

Anderson, K., Cockburn, J., and Martin, W. (eds). (2008). *Agricultural Price Distortions, Inequality and Poverty.* Washington, DC: World Bank.

Anderson, K., Ingco, E, and Ingco, M. (1999). Integrating agriculture into the WTO: The next phase. Paper presented to the WTO/World Bank Conference on Developing Countries' Countries in a Millennium Round. WTO Secretariat, Geneva, 20–21 September. Available online at: www.iatp.org/files/Integrating_Agriculture_into_the_WTO_The_Next_.htm.

Anderson, K., Martin, W., and Mensburgghe, D. (2005). Market and welfare implications of Doha reform scenarios. In K. Anderson and A. Winters (eds), *Agricultural Trade Reform and the Doha Development Agenda* (pp. 333–400). Washington, DC: World Bank.

Anderson, K., Martin, W., and Mensburgghe, D. (2006a). Distortions to world trade: Impacts on agricultural markets and farm incomes. *Review of Agricultural Economics*, 28(2), 168–194.

Anderson, K., Martin, W., and Valenzuela, E. (2006b). The relative importance of global agricultural subsidies and market access. *World Trade Review*, 5(3), 357–376.

Antimiani, A., Conforti, P., and Salvatici, L. (2008). Measuring restrictiveness of bilateral trade policies: A comparison between developed and developing countries. *Review of World Economics*, 144(2), 207–224.

Bacchetta, M. and Bora, B. (2001). *Post-Uruguay Round Market Access Barriers for Industrial Products, Policy Issues in International Trade Commodities.* Study Series No. 12. Geneva: UNCTAD.

Baffes, J. (2005). Cotton market setting, trade policies, and issues. In M. Aksoy and J. Beghin (eds), *Global Agricultural Trade and Developing Countries* (ch. 14). Washington, DC: World Bank.

Balassa, B. & Associates. (1971). *The Structure of Protection in Developing Countries*. Baltimore, MD: Johns Hopkins University Press.

Bhaskar, A. and Beghin, J. (2009). How coupled are decoupled farm payments? A review of evidence. *Journal of Agricultural and Resource Economics*, 34(1), 130–153.

Blarel, B., Pursell, B., and Valdes, A. (eds). (1999). *Implications of the Uruguay Round Agreement for South Asia: The case of agriculture*. New Delhi: World Bank.

Brooks, J., Dyer, G., and Taylor, E. (2008). Modelling agricultural trade and policy impacts in less developed countries. *OECD Food, Agriculture and Fisheries Working Papers*, No. 11. OECD Publishing.

Byerlee, D. and Sadoulet, E. (2009). Agriculture for development: Toward a new paradigm. *Annual Review of Resource Economics*, 1(1), 15–31.

Cervantes-Godoy, D. and Brooks, J. (2009). Smallholder adjustment in middle-income countries: Issues and policy responses. *OECD Food, Agriculture and Fisheries Working Papers*, No. 12. Paris: OECD.

Cervantes-Godoy, D. and Dewbre, J. (2010). Economic importance of agriculture for poverty reduction. *OECD Food, Agriculture and Fisheries Working Papers*, No. 23. Paris: OECD.

Chenery, H. and Srinivasan T. (eds). (1989). *Handbook of Development Economics*. Amsterdam: North Holland.

Cheng, F. (2007). Tariff escalation in world agricultural trade. In P. Pinstrup-Andersen and F. Cheng (eds), *Food Policy for Developing Countries: Case studies*. Case Study No. 10–11. Available at: http://cip.cornell.edu/dns.gfs/1200428210.

Cross, K. (2009). United States: Subsidies on upland cotton, recourse to Article 21.5 of the DSU by Brazil. *American Journal of International Law*, 103(1), 110–116.

DFID. (2014). *Agriculture, Growth and Poverty Reduction*. London: UK Department of International Development.

Diaz-Bonilla. E. and Robinson, S. (2001). WTO, agriculture, and developing countries. Available online at: http://ifpri.org/sites/default/files/publications/tmdp8.pdf.

Dowlah, C. (2003). Agriculture and the new trade agenda in the WTO negotiations: Economic analysis of interests and options for Bangladesh. In M. Ingco (ed.), *Direction in Development: Agriculture, trade, and the WTO in South Asia* (pp. 38–95). Washington, DC: World Bank.

Dowlah, C. (2004). *Backwaters of Global Prosperity: How globalization and the GATT/WTO trade regimes marginalize the world's poorest nations*. New York: Praeger.

Environmental Working Group. (2015). Available online at: http://farm.ewg.org/region.php?fips=00000 (last accessed May 8, 2015).

European Commission. (2013). Overview of CAP Reform 2014–2020. Agricultural Policy Perspectives Brief. Available online at: http://ec.europa.eu/agriculture/policy-perspectives/policy-briefs/index en.htm.

FAO (Food and Agricultural Organization). (1998). *Impact of the Uruguay Round on Agriculture*. Rome: FAO.

FAO (Food and Agricultural Organization). (2004). Export competition: Selected issues and the empirical evidence. *FAO Trade Policy Technical Notes* No. 4. Rome: FAO.

FAO (Food and Agricultural Organization). (2010). Price volatility in agricultural markets: Evidence, impact on food security and policy responses. *Economic and Social Perspectives*, Policy Brief No. 12 (December). Rome: FAO.

Gibson, P., Wainio, J., Whitley, D., and Bohman, M. (2001). *Profiles of Tariffs in Global Agricultural Markets*. Agricultural Economic Report No. 796. USDA Economic Research Service. Washington, DC: US Department of Agriculture.

GHI (Global Harvest Initiative). (2010). *2010 GAP Report: Measuring global agricultural productivity*. Available online at: www.globalharvestinitiative.org/index.php/gap-report-gap-index/2010-gap-report/.

Goodison, P. (2007).What is the future of EU–Africa agricultural trade after CAP reform? *Review of African Political Economy*, 34 (112), 279–295.

Goodwin, B. and Mishra, K. (2006). Are 'decoupled' farm programs payments really decoupled? An empirical evaluation. *American Journal of Agricultural Economics*, 88(1), 73–89.

Harcourt, T. (2004). Milking the (trade) round for all its worth. Available online at: www.austrade.gov.au/Milking-the-trade-round-for-all-its-worth/default.aspx.

Harrison, G., Rutherford, T., and Tarr, D. (1995). Quantifying the outcome of the Uruguay Round. In W. Martin and A. Winters (eds), *The Uruguay Round and the Developing Countries*. Washington, DC: World Bank.

Hazel, P. and Wood, S. (2008). Drivers of change in agriculture. *Philosophical Transactions: Biological Sciences*, 363(1491), 495–515.

Hertel, T. and Keeney, R. (2006). What is at stake? The relative importance of import barriers, export subsidies, and domestic support. In K. Anderson and W. Martin (eds), *Agricultural Trade Reforms and the Doha Development Agenda* (pp 37–62). Washington, DC: World Bank.

Hertel, T. and Winters, A. (2006). *Putting Development Back into the Doha Agenda: Poverty impacts of a WTO Agreement*. New York: Palgrave Macmillan.

Hertel, T., Keeney, R., Ivanic, M., and Winters, A. (2007). Distributional effects of WTO agricultural reforms in rich and poor countries. *Economic Policy*, 22(50), 289–337.

Hoda, A. and Gulati, A. (2007). *WTO Negotiations on Agriculture and Developing Countries*. Baltimore, MD: Johns Hopkins University Press.

Hoekman, B., Ng, F., and Olarreaga, M. (2004). Agricultural tariffs versus subsidies: What's more important for developing countries? *World Bank Economic Review*, 18(4), 175–204.

ICTSD. (2009).Capping usually high tariffs: The Doha Round and 'tariff peaks.' ICTSD Information Note No. 9 (November). Geneva: International Center for Trade and Sustainable Development.

Ingco, M. and John, N. (2004). *Agriculture and the WTO: Creating a trading system for development*. Washington, DC: World Bank.

Jank, M. and Jales, M. (2004). On products, box and blame-shifting: Negotiating frameworks for agriculture in the WTO Round. Paper presented at the Second IDB-CEPII Conference on Economic Implications of the Doha Development Agenda for Latin America and the Caribbean. Sao Paulo, Brazil, May 14. Available online at: www.pecc.org/resources/120-on-product-box-and-blame-shifting-negotiating-frameworks-for-agriculture-in-the-wto-doha-round?path=doc_view.

Jansen, T., Robinson, S., and Tarp, F. (2002). General equilibrium measures of agricultural policy bias in fifteen developing countries. TMD Discussion Paper No. 105. Washington, DC: International Food Policy Research Institute.

Johnson, D. (1991). *World Agriculture in Disarray* (2nd edn). London: Macmillan.

Josling, T. (2004). An overview of the WTO agricultural negotiations. In J. Nash and A. McCalla (eds), *Handbook on Agricultural Negotiations* (pp. 21–73). Washington, DC: World Bank.

Josling, T. (2007).The impact of the WTO and bilateral trade agreements on U.S. farm policy. In B. Gardner and D. Sumner (eds), *Agricultural Policy for the 2007 Farm Bill and Beyond* (pp. 87–93). Washington, DC: American Enterprise Institute.

Kirkpatrick, C. and Barrientos, A. (2004). The Lewis Model after 50 years. *Manchester School*, 72(6), 679–690.

Krueger, A., Schiff, M., and Valdes, A. (1988). Agricultural incentives in developing countries: Measuring the effects of sectoral and economy-wide policies. *World Bank Economic Review*, 2(3), 255–272.

Legg, W. (2003). Agricultural support indicators, measurement, meaning and use. OECD World Forum on Key Indicators. Palermo: OECD Publishing.

Lewis, A. (1955). *The Theory of Economic Growth*. Homewood, IL: R.D. Irwin.

Liapis, P. (2011). Changing patterns of trade in processed agricultural products. *OECD Food, Agriculture, and Fisheries Papers*, No. 47. Paris: OECD Publishing.

Liapis, P. (2012). Structural change in commodity markets: Have agricultural markets become thinner? *OECD Food, Agriculture and Fisheries Working Papers*, No. 54. Paris: OECD Publishing.

Lindert, P. (1991). Historical patterns of agricultural policy. In P. Trimmer (ed.), *Agriculture and the State* (pp. 29–83). Ithaca, NY: Cornell University Press.

Martin, W. and Winters, A. (1996). *The Uruguay Round and Developing Countries*. Cambridge: Cambridge University Press.

Martin, W. and Anderson, K. (2006). The Doha agenda negotiations on agriculture: What could they deliver? *American Journal of Agricultural Economics*, 88(5), 1211–1218.

Mathews, A. (2001). The position of the developing countries in the WTO negotiations on agricultural trade liberalization. Trinity Economic Paper series, Paper No. 01/01. Trinity College.

Moise, E., Delpeuch, C., Sorescu, S., Bottini, N., and Fock, A. (2013). Estimating the constraints to agricultural trade of developing countries. *OECD Trade Policy Papers*, No. 142. Paris: OECD Publishing.

Nielsen, L. (2011). Classifications of countries based on their level of development: How it is done and how it could be done. IMF Working Paper WP/11/31. Washington, DC: IMF.

OECD (Organization of Economic Cooperation and Development). (2000). *Agricultural Policies in Emerging and Transition Economies 2000*. COM/AGRA/APM/TD/WP(2000)43/Final. Paris: OECD.

OECD (Organization of Economic Cooperation and Development). (2001). *The Uruguay Round Agreement on Agriculture: An evaluation of its implementation in OECD Countries*. Paris: OECD Publishing.

OECD (Organization of Economic Cooperation and Development). (2005). *Agricultural Policies in OECD Countries: Monitoring and evaluation*. Paris: OECD Publishing.

OECD (Organization of Economic Cooperation and Development). (2006). *A Forward-looking Analysis of Export Subsidies in Agriculture*. Paris: OECD Publishing. Available online at: www.oecd.org/trade/agricultural-trade/1911050.pdf.

OECD (Organization of Economic Cooperation and Development). (2007). *Agricultural Policies in OECD Countries: Monitoring and evaluation*. Paris: OECD Publishing. Available online at: www.oecd.org/agriculture/policies.

OECD (Organization of Economic Cooperation and Development). (2009). *Agricultural Policies in OECD Countries: Monitoring and evaluation*. Paris: OECD Publishing.

OECD (Organization of Economic Cooperation and Development). (2010a). *Comparative Advantage and Export Specialization Mobility in OECD and Selected Emerging Market Economies*. TAD/TC/WP(2006)16 (June).

OECD (Organization of Economic Cooperation and Development). (2010b). *OECD's Producer Support Estimate and Related Indicators of Agricultural Support: Concepts, calculations, interpretation and use*. Paris: OECD Publishing.

OECD (Organization of Economic Cooperation and Development). (2012). *Agricultural Policies for Poverty Reduction*. Paris: OECD Publishing.

OECD (Organization of Economic Cooperation and Development). (2013). *Agriculture and Food: Key Tables from OECD*. Paris: OECD Publishing. Available online at: http://dx.doi.otg/10.1787/pse-table-2012-1-en.

OECD (Organization of Economic Cooperation and Development). (2014). *Agricultural Policy Monitoring 2013*. Paris: OECD Publishing.

Orden, D., Cheng, F., Nguyen, H., Grote, U., Thomas, M., Mullen, K., and Sun, D. (2007). *Agricultural Producer Support Estimates for Developing Countries: Measurement issues and evidence from India, Indonesia, and Vietnam*. IFPRI Research Report No. 152. Washington, DC: International Food Policy Research Institute.

Poczta-Wajda, A. (2013). Measuring domestic agricultural support in developed countries in the light of the WTO negotiations. *Village and Agriculture*, 1(158), 44–58. Available online at: www.ceeol.com.

Samuel, L. and Yeats, A. (2007). Empirical evidence concerning the magnitude and effects of developing country tariff escalation. *Developing Economies*, 25(2), 99–123.

Schiff, M. and Valdes, A. (1992). *The Plunging of Agriculture in Developing Countries*. Washington, DC: World Bank.

Sumner, D. (2006). Reducing cotton subsidies: The DDA cotton initiative. In K. Anderson and W. Martin (eds), *Agricultural Trade Reform and the Doha Development Agenda* (pp. 29–93). Washington, DC: World Bank.

Tangermann, S. and Josling, T. (1994). Pre-accession agricultural policies for central Europe and the European Union. Brussels: Directorate General of Trade, European Commission.

Timmer, C. (1989). The agricultural transformation. In H. Chenery and T. Srinivasan (eds), *Handbook of Development Economics* (ch. 8). Amsterdam: North Holland.

Tokarick, S. (2005). Who bears the cost of agricultural support policies in OECD countries? *World Economy*, 28(4), 573–593.

Tokarick, S. (2008). Dispelling some misconceptions about agricultural trade liberalization. *The Journal of Economic Perspectives*, 22(1), 199–216.

Tyers, R. and Anderson, K. (1986). *Distortions in World Food Markets: A quantitative assessment*. Background paper for *World Bank Development Report* (January). Washington, DC: World Bank.

Tyers, R. and Anderson, K. (1992). *Disarray in World Food Markets: A quantitative assessment*. Cambridge and New York: Cambridge University Press.

USDA (United States Department of Agriculture). (2004). WTO: URAA export subsidies and domestic support in the EU. Economic Research Service, United States Department of Agriculture. Available online at: www.ers.usda.gov/db/wto.

Valdes, A. and McCalla, A. (1996). The Uruguay Round and agricultural policies in developing countries and economies of transition. *Food Policy*, 21(4/5), 419–431.

Valdes, A. and Zietz, J. (1995). Distortions in world food markets in the wake of GATT: Evidence and policy implications. *World Development*, 23(6), 913–926.

Watkins, K. (2003). Northern Agricultural Policies and World Poverty: Will the Doha Development Round Make a Difference? Oxfam paper presented at the Annual World Bank Conference on Development Economics. Paris, May 15–16. Available online at: http://documents.worldbank.org/curated/en/2003/05/3262739/northern-agricultural-policies-world-poverty-doha-development-round-make-difference.

Woodward, A. (2007). The impact of U.S. subsidies on West African cotton production. In P. Pinstrup-Andersen and F. Cheng (eds), *Food Policy for Developing Countries: Case studies*. Case Study No. 10–5. Available online at: http://cip.cornell.edu/dns.gfs/1200428204.

World Bank. (1996). *Trade Policy Reform for Improving Incentive Regime*. Washington, DC: World Bank.

World Bank. (2003). *Global Economic Prospects: Realizing the development promise of the Doha Agenda*. Washington, DC: World Bank.

World Bank. (2008). *World Development Report: Agriculture for development*. Washington, DC: World Bank.

World Bank. (2014). *World Development Indicators. Agriculture and rural development*. Available online at: http://data.worldbank.org/topic/agriculture-and-rural-development.

WTO (World Trade Organization). (1995). *The Results of the Uruguay Round of Multilateral Trade Negotiations: The legal text*. Geneva: WTO.

WTO (World Trade Organization). (2000). Tariff and other quotas. G/AG/NG/S/7 (May 23). Geneva: WTO.

WTO (World Trade Organization). (2002). Secretariat background paper. Export subsidies. TN/AG/S/8. Geneva: WTO. Available online at: www.wto.org/english/tratop_e/agric_e/negs_bkgrnd08_export_e.htm.

WTO (World Trade Organization). (2008). Revised draft modalities for agriculture sensitive products: Designation. TN/AG/W/5 (December 6). Geneva: WTO.

WTO (World Trade Organization). (2008–2014). *World Tariff Profiles* (various issues). Geneva: WTO.

WTO (World Trade Organization). (2012). Trade Policy Review—Report by the Secretariat. WT/TPR/S/275. WTO Trade Policy Review Body, No. 12–6166. Geneva: WTO.

WTO (World Trade Organization). (2014). Communication from the United States to the WTO Committee on Agriculture, No. 14–3252, G/AG/W132 (June 4). Geneva: WTO.

3 Liberalization of the textiles and clothing sector

Introduction

In the eighteenth through the twentieth centuries, the textiles and clothing (T&C) sector had been at the forefront of the industrialization of the Western world, especially in the United States, the United Kingdom, and Germany. In the twentieth century, especially since World War II, this sector paved the way for industrialization and economic growth for scores of post-colonial countries. In the 1950s and early 1960s, the sector played a crucial role in the industrial transformation of Japan; in the early 1970s, it played a similar role in the industrialization and export-led economic growth of the East Asian Tigers—Hong Kong-SAR, Taiwan, Singapore, and South Korea; in the 1980s, the sector made inroads into mainland China and several Southeast Asian countries; and in the 1990s, the sector moved to South Asia, Central America and the Caribbean, Mexico, the Mediterranean, as well as Sub-Saharan African countries (Dickerson, 1991).

The transformative power of clothing, a rudimentary manufacturing activity, is thus fascinating. It requires simple technology, low start-up and fixed costs, relatively less challenging entrepreneurial skills, and low-skilled labor (Nordas, 2004; Jones, 2001), but quickly turns into a powerful harbinger of industrialization through its multidimensional backward and forward linkages. As the industry grows, it creates backward linkages with more capital and scale-intensive textile sector, and forward linkages with global value chains through sophisticated production and marketing networks (Gereffi and Memedovic, 2003).

It is thus not surprising that by the 2000s, less developed countries emerged as the dominant producer and exporter of T&C products worldwide, triumphantly demonstrating their inherent and evolving competitive advantage in this highly labor-intensive manufacturing sector. The day of eventual triumph of less developed countries in the T&C sector, however, arrived several decades late, arguably because of the prolonged and protracted protection of this sector in the developed countries. In fact, this sector came under the same overriding rules and conditions similar to all other internationally traded manufacturing products only recently: in 2009, to be precise. If history is any guide, advanced industrialized countries, otherwise committed to freer global trade regimes, restrained trade in this sector by adopting numerous protectionist measures, such as quantitative restrictions, quotas, tariffs, licenses, and so on, for at least four decades.

Presumably, advanced industrialized countries found the advantageous position of less developed countries in this manufacturing sector hugely incompatible with their domestic political and economic interests. Worse still, while both tariff and non-tariff barriers to many manufacturing products, especially in which developed countries enjoyed comparative advantage, fell sharply under successive rounds of GATT negotiations,[1] the T&C sector faced movement in the opposite direction ((Dowlah, 2004, 51–76). Eventually, the Uruguay Round Agreement on Textiles and Clothing (ATC) brought this sector into the strengthened GATT discipline in 1994, providing a 10-year transition period for eliminating all protectionist measures by 2005.

The following section presents a brief background of the international trade regimes that proliferated in the T&C sector during the GATT period. The third section explains the major features of the ATC and the challenges the agreement confronted during its implementation phases. The post-ATC transformation of global T&C trade is explained the fourth section in order to assess the consequences of full liberalization of this sector. The fifth section examines post-ATC issues and WTO negotiations in this sector with a special emphasis on the economic interests and options for developing and least developed countries. The final and fifth section concludes the chapter.

T&C trade regimes under the GATT

The original GATT envisaged three fundamental principles to promote rule-based multilateral trade: reciprocity, most-favored nation (MFN), and national treatment. The principle of reciprocity implies that negotiations among GATT contracting parties are undertaken voluntarily and on a reciprocal basis—a contracting party with export interests offers concessions to penetrate another contracting party's import market. Once a contracting party offers to lower its tariff to increase the market access to another contracting party, the principle of non-discrimination called MFN kicks in—the same lower tariff and terms of market access must be granted to all other GATT contracting parties. The principle of national treatment is also rooted in non-discrimination—once a foreign-produced good enters an import market, it has to be treated just like a nationally produced good. A GATT contracting party is required to treat foreign firms operating within its borders in the same way as it treats its own firms.[2]

The framers of the GATT, however, preferred not to subject the T&C sector to such magnificent principles of international trade—they rather decided to leave the sector out of the jurisdiction of GATT altogether by designating it as a 'special case.'[3] Apparently, the farmers argued that the principle of reciprocity, which required trade concession by a country when it received a similar concession from another country, was intended for manufactures only. As most of the newly independent developing countries at that time were principally primary good producers, they would be incapable of making such concessions.

But the underlying motivation for designating the T&C sector as a 'special case' lay precisely in the implications of 'low-cost' imports from less developed countries for employment and economic growth in the developed countries (Dickerson, 1991, 303). The MFN principle of GATT also did not bode well for many industrialized countries in respect of the T&C sector—often they chose not to comply with this principle, considering injurious effects of T&C imports on their domestic industries or other economic and political interests.[4] As a result, highly discriminatory and restrictive trade regimes proliferated in the T&C sector throughout the GATT period, seriously impeding industrialization and economic growth in many less developed countries.

Short-Term Arrangement (STA)

Before it was absorbed by the WTO in 1994, the GATT had eight rounds of negotiations,[5] but the T&C sector was brought up for serious discussion for the first time in the Dillion Round (1960–1961). Named after Douglas Dillion, then under-secretary of state of the United States, the Round was attended by 26 GATT contracting parties, and succeeded in cutting 44,000 tariffs covering $4.9 billion of trade. When it came to the T&C sector, the Dillion Round, however, agreed to what came to be known as the Short-Term Arrangement Regarding International Trade in Cotton Textiles (STA).

The STA, among other things, provided for: (1) a significant increase in access to T&C markets that were restricted at the time; (2) an orderly access to T&C markets that were relatively open; and (3) certain measures of restraints on T&C products on the part of exporting countries, such as voluntary export restraints (VERs), to avoid market disruptions in developed countries. The STA, which came into force on October 1, 1961, thus allowed T&C importing developed countries to negotiate quantitative restraints (QRS) as well as other import restrictions on 'low-cost' T&C imports from less developed countries on a selective basis to avoid possible 'market disruptions.'

Ironically, the STA came as a serious assault on the multilateral trade regime under the GATT in general and for trade in T&C products in particular. By sanctioning quantitative restrictions, the participating contracting parties threw away one of the most basic principles of the GATT—negotiation on prices, not on quantities. Second, by imposing quantitative restrictions on T&C trade on the basis of unilateral agreements, the STA violated another GATT principle—the principle of MFN—which stipulates that trade measures taken by GATT contracting parties must not discriminate between supplying countries.[6] Moreover, developed countries began to impose quantitative restrictions during a period when scores of developing countries—such as India, Japan, Hong Kong-SAR, Korea, Pakistan, Portugal, Spain, Taiwan, and the United Arab Emirates—began to demonstrate a competitive advantage in the manufacturing and export of T&C products.[7]

Long-Term Arrangement (LTA)

A year later, in 1962, the STA was renegotiated to pave the way for what is known as the Long-Term Arrangement Regarding International Trade in Cotton Textiles (LTA), which was designed as a more comprehensive framework for regulating T&C trade bilaterally on an item-by-item basis. The agreement, initially signed for a five-year period, was extended twice—in 1967 and 1970—each time for three further years. In general, the LTA was applicable to cotton textiles—defined as textiles containing cotton over 50 percent of the fiber content—but some countries, especially the US, followed what is called the 'chief value method,' under which the value of the textile product in question had to contain more than 50 percent of cotton only.

Originally, the LTA was signed by 19 contracting parties of the GATT, but the number had swelled to 82 by 1973. The LTA retained the restrictive nature of the STA by allowing importing countries, in case they faced real or perceived threats of market disruption, to renegotiate bilateral agreements with exporting countries and to impose unilateral restraints in case no agreements could be reached. The agreement, however, barred importing countries from lowering quotas from the amount of actual imports during the previous period, and provided for 5 percent annual increase in quotas. This provision benefited many developing country exporters, while adversely affecting more efficient ones by limiting their growth potentials.

Multi-Fiber Arrangements (MFAs)

In the late 1960s, textiles trading arrangements confronted new challenges as several T&C exporting countries began to use synthetic fibers, especially polyester and acrylic, and other innovations in knitting technology. At the same time, some newly industrializing developing countries, facing export restrictions on cotton textile products, began to shift their exports to hitherto uncontrolled fiber product areas. By 1973, such developments led the GATT contracting parties to frame a broader agreement called the Multi-Fiber Arrangement Regarding International Trade in Textiles (MFA). The agreement incorporated products made of manufactured fibers as well as wool[8] and determined export quota restraints (QRS) on the basis of weight, or by the number of items on the basis of product description. Originally signed by 50 contracting parties of the GATT, the agreement came into force in January 1974, initially for a four-year period.

Apparently, the MFA envisaged expansion as well as progressive liberalization of T&C trade while ensuring orderly and equitable trade in the sector so that market disruptive effects could be avoided in both importing and exporting countries. To further economic and social development of developing countries by substantially increasing their export earnings from this sector, the agreement also granted them certain flexibilities to adjust to changing market conditions, export demands, and their own capabilities. Moreover, the agreement mandated that when a restraint was renewed, the new quota could not be lower than the previous level, and in the case of continuing quotas the annual growth rate could not be less than 6 percent. The agreement also allowed T&C exporting countries to use carry-over (utilizing the previous year's unutilized quotas) and carry-forward (utilizing part of the following year's quota in the current year) in combination for up to 10 percent of the original quotas.

The MFA also provided some safeguards for avoiding disruptive effects on individual markets and individual lines of production, and imposed stricter rules for determining market disruption. In cases of actual market disruptions, importing countries were allowed to impose import restrictions unilaterally if a mutually agreed resolution could not be made, but in situations of real risk of market disruptions only bilateral restraint agreements were allowed. Neither the LTA nor the MFA, however, specifically defined what constituted market disruptions.[9] Finally, the MFA provided for a multilateral surveillance institution, called the Textiles Surveillance Body (TSB), for monitoring compliance of all parties to the agreements. A GATT Textiles Committee was also established as the final arbiter, as a court of appeal for the disputes that could not be resolved at the TSB level.

Adverse effects of the MFA regimes

The MFA was extended five times before its eventual and final expiration in 1994 when the GATT itself was replaced by the WTO.[10] The MFA turned out to be one of the most discriminatory trade regimes in the entire history of multilateral trade. During the period of the first two extensions, quota restraints were intensified, country and product coverage enlarged, and importing countries often adopted additional restrictive measures.[11] By the mid-1980s, more than 70 percent of T&C products imported to developed country markets were subject to non-tariff barriers (NTBs), both within and outside the MFA (UNCTAD, 1986).[12] In the late 1960s, with mounting pressures from developing country exporters under the auspices of the UNCTAD, the MFA-III (1982–1986) replaced the so-called 'reasonable departures' clause with a less restrictive 'anti-surge' provision, granting special restraints in the event of 'sharp and substantial increases' in imports of sensitive products with previously underutilized quotas only. At the same time, the claims by developed countries of so-called 'market disruptions' were tightened further by requiring them to show proof of a decline in the growth of their per capita consumption.[13]

The last two MFA extensions—the MFA-V (1991–1993) and the MFA-V1 (1993–1994)—coincided with the Uruguay Round negotiations (1986–1994) when T&C trade came under more intense scrutiny. At that time, about 60 percent of global T&C trade was subject to some type of restraint. The Uruguay Round replaced the MFA altogether with the Agreement on Textiles and Clothing (ATC) with effect from January 1, 1995. In December 1994, on the last day of the MFA regime, the MFA-VI had 44 signatories with 102 bilateral restraint agreements, of which 32 belonged to the US, 25 to Canada, 15 to the EU, 17 to Norway, seven to Finland, and six to Australia (GATT, 1994, 16).

During the period of MFA regimes less developed countries' exports of T&C products to developed countries increased significantly. Several studies, however, suggest that the exports as well as the earnings of developing countries could increase many times in the absence of such regimes. Kirmani and colleagues (1984), for example, showed that in the absence of the MFA regimes developing countries' annual exports to major OECD countries could increase by 82 percent for textiles and 93 percent for clothing. In a more conservative estimate, Yang (1993) showed that developing countries' exports could increase by 26 percent for clothing and 10 percent for textiles in the absence of MFA restraints. Similarly, a United Nations study (UNCTAD, 1996) suggested that the complete liberalization of T&C could increase developing countries' exports of clothing by 135 percent and of textiles by 78 percent. A USITC (1989) study suggested that the value of exports of constrained supplies to the US market could rise by 20.5 percent for textiles and 36.5 for clothing, or an average of 35 percent in both product groups in the absence of any MFA restraints.

The MFA regimes have also been criticized for generating rent transfers from importing to exporting countries through export quotas. For example, USITC (1989) estimated the quota premium on clothing products at 16.8 percent, and Trela and Whalley (1990) estimated quota premiums of between 78 and 300 percent. Earlier, Hamilton (1988) showed that import tariff equivalents of voluntary export restraints (VERs) on clothing from Hong Kong-SAR in the EC countries over the period 1980 to 1984 were about 14 percent, while they were about 28 percent for the US. The MFA regimes have also been criticized for sheltering inefficient producers in developing countries by guaranteeing them a share of exports which they could lose under a more competitive trade regime. Moreover, the MFA regimes required exporting countries to administer their own licensing system which stippled domestic competition, as many developing countries protected existing firms against efficient or new ones.

MFA quota hopping and Sub-Saharan African countries

The MFA restraints also resulted in what is known as 'quota hopping'—a search for countries with unused quotas or no quota restrictions by T&C investors from countries with full quota utilization. Under the MFA regimes developed countries granted quota-restricted access to their markets to many developing countries; while some of them fully used their quotas, some did not or could not. That, in turn, opened up a window of opportunity for T&C producers from countries with full utilization of quotas to look for countries with unused or less than fully used quotas in order to take advantage of unused quotas of foreign countries.

Such motivation, also buoyed up by the availability of lower wage labor, propelled clothing investors of Hong Kong-SAR to move to Macau in the mid-1970s, and then to Sri Lanka and Indonesia in the late 1970s. In the 1980s, Chinese and Korean companies invested in countries like Bangladesh and Vietnam in order to take advantage of unused quotas (Dowlah, 1999). Similarly, in the 1990s, the search for countries with underused or unused quotas or unrestricted quotas led many T&C investors from China, Hong Kong-SAR, Korea, and Taiwan to spread their business operations in Latin America and the Caribbean, and Sub-Saharan Africa (SSA). With the liberalization of T&C trade in the early 2000s, many of these companies pulled out their business operations from foreign countries, which, as discussed below, led to disastrous consequences, especially in some SSA countries.

MFA regimes contradicted fundamental GATT principles

The MFA regimes, as explained above, tipped the non-discrimination principles of GATT upside down by permitting countries to regulate T&C trade through bilateral agreements. The MFA regimes also violated GATT principles by allowing quota restrictions, and imposing quota restrictions on T&C exports from developing countries, while not doing so in respect of imports from developed countries. Many other provisions of the MFA regimes, such as market disruption, non-compensation for imposing import restrictions, and so on, contradicted the fundamental GATT principles and contributed to institutionalized derogation. Moreover, the MFA was originally envisaged as a temporary arrangement to provide 'breathing space' to the developed world to adjust to increased competition from developing countries, but gradually it took on a permanent shape, jeopardizing rule-based trade in the T&C sector.

MFA regimes brought mixed benefits for developed countries

In the end, many developed countries indeed reaped mixed benefits from the restrictive MFA regimes—instead of protecting domestic jobs, many of them ended up protecting machines. As labor-saving measures, such as automation and computerization, proliferated in T&C production, job creation shifted to developing countries. Between 1995 and 1998, the share of the Americas in the total world employment in clothing fell from 17.6 percent to 11.4 percent, while that of Europe dropped from 31.3 percent to 21.3 percent; at the same time Asia's share rose substantially, from 45 percent to 62 percent. In fact, job losses in textiles, clothing, and footwear began much earlier—during the 1980 to 1993 period—when job losses in these areas were 61.7 percent in Finland, 65.4 percent in Sweden, 51 percent in Poland, and 45.5 percent in France, while job gains surged to 344.6 percent in Mauritius, 177.4 percent in Indonesia, 166.5 percent in Morocco, 160.8 percent in Jordan, and 101.7 percent in Jamaica (ILO, 2000; Dowlah, 2004, 84–86).

The MFA regimes also cost developed country consumers dearly. According to Hufbauer and Elliott (1994, 11–13), the annual cost to American consumers for import protection in T&C was $4.3 billion. The Economic Report of the US President (1988) put the cost of protection of T&C between $200 and $400 per year per household. An OECD (1985) study found that the burden of protection of T&C fell largely on the lower income households, as clothing accounts for a large share of their consumption expenditure.

Francois and colleagues (2000) found that in 1997 the average cost of protection in T&C products was ECU270 for a family of four, which was approximately similar to the cost in the US.

Integration of the T&C sector into the GATT

As the discussion above suggests, by the early 1980s, adverse effects of keeping T&C outside the GATT discipline—that is, continuing bilaterally negotiated quota regimes under the umbrella of successive MFA regimes—began to unravel. As a response, the GATT Ministerial Conference of 1982 established a Working Party on Textiles and Clothing (WPTC) to consider three broad options for liberalization of the sector: (1) full application of the GATT provisions with a movement toward liberalization; (2) full application of GATT provisions combined with liberalization of trade measures irrespective of their GATT conformity; and (3) liberalization under existing frameworks (GATT, 1985).

With the WPTC failing to make any progress, the next GATT Ministerial Conference, held in Punta del Este in 1986, approved a special mandate to formulate modalities that would permit the integration of the T&C trade into 'strengthened GATT rules and disciplines.' In 1987, a Negotiating Group on Textiles and Clothing (NGTC) was established to examine the techniques and modalities for such integration. The NGTC, however, failed to complete its work before the next WTO Ministerial Conference held in Montreal in 1988, largely because the developed countries sought to renew the MFA regime beyond 1991, while the developing countries demanded a clear timetable for phasing out MFA restrictions and full integration of the sector into the GATT discipline.

In 1989, the Trade Negotiation Committee (TNC), however, agreed on modalities for phasing out the MFA and other GATT-inconsistent restrictions in the sector. Negotiations were still very intense, as the developing countries demanded: (1) immediate integration of certain products like children's clothing, products of vegetable fibers and silk blends, hand-woven fabrics and products made thereof, and the immediate removal of restrictions on small suppliers and least developed countries (LDCs); (2) a programmed elimination of restrictions on the basis of the stages of processing—the restrictions on tops and yarns to be removed initially, followed by those on fabrics, and then on made-up articles and, in the final stage, restrictions on clothing to be eliminated; and (3) an accelerated expansion of the quotas while they awaited phasing-out. The developed countries, on the other hand, sought to dismantle the restrictions gradually during an agreed-upon transition period. In December 1991, the so-called 'Dunkel Draft,' named after the then GATT Director General Arthur Dunkel, provided a compromise formula, paving the way for the liberalization of this sector under the Uruguay Round agreements.

Major features of the Agreement on Textiles and Clothing (ATC)

Eventually, the Marrakesh Ministerial Conference, held in April 1994 at the successful conclusion of the Uruguay Round, succeeded in bringing the T&C sector into the jurisdiction of the strengthened GATT discipline. The Uruguay Round Agreement on Textiles and Clothing (ATC) called for the progressive phasing out of all MFA restrictions and other discriminatory measures within a period of 10 years, so that at the end of the transitional period, January 1, 2005, the era of discriminatory and bilateral quota measures could be eliminated completely, and the T&C sector in its entirety would be brought under the strengthened GATT rules and discipline. Under what is known as the 'single undertaking approach,' the ATC was made mandatory to all signatories to the WTO Agreement. The ATC also outlined a product coverage encompassing yarns, fabrics, made-up textile products and clothing, provided for a special safeguard mechanism to domestic producers during the transition period, and established a Textiles Monitoring Body (TMB) to supervise the implementation of the agreement. Major features of the ATC are as follows.

Product coverage

The ATC covered all products which were subject to the MFA or the MFA-type quotas in at least one importing country, and listed the products in the Annex to

Table 3.1 Quota phase-out mechanisms of the WTO Agreement in Textiles and Clothing (ATC)

Stages	*Deadline*	*Integration share of clothing and textiles trade*[a] *(base: 1990 import volume)*	*Increase in size of quota for clothing and textile trade still subject to quotas base: previously agreed growth rates*
Stage I	January 1, 1995	16% (total 16%)	16% higher than initial rate (example: from 3% to 3.48%)
Stage II	January 1, 1998	17% (total 33%)	(25%) (example: from 3.48% to 4.35%)
Stage III	January 1, 2002	18% (total 55%)	(27%) (example: from 4.35% to 5.52%)
Stage IV (end of transition)	January 1, 2005	45% (total 100%)	(100%) full integration

Source: Author's compilation from the WTO website.

Note

a Importing countries are free to choose the products that they integrate at each stage, as long as products are included from the four groupings: tops and yarn, fabrics, made-up textile products, and clothing.

the ATC. It brought all MFA restrictions maintained by the GATT contracting parties under its jurisdiction, and required all WTO members to provide the TMB—a quasi-judicial standing body of the WTO responsible for implementation of the agreement—with the following information: (1) justifications for the existing restrictions; (2) actions taken by members under the provisions of the transitional safeguard mechanism; and (3) products already integrated into GATT-1994 in accordance with the integration scheme under transitional safeguard mechanisms. The agreement, however, granted special treatment to three categories of WTO members: (1) small suppliers and new entrants in the T&C sector; (2) those who had not accepted the MFA Protocols since 1986; and (3) the cotton-producing exporting countries.

Phases of integration

The ATC provided a 10-year transition period for full integration of the T&C products into the GATT discipline, and ruled out any possibility of extension. The agreement provided a list of products to be integrated in four stages and each stage's integration was based on a percentage of the total volume of imports in 1990 (see Table 3.1). The phases and integration ratios were organized as follows: Stage I—on the date of entry into force of the WTO Agreement (that is, by January 1, 1995), members were required to integrate into the GATT-1994 products which accounted for no less than 16 percent of their total volume of 1990 imports of the products in the Annex, in terms of HS lines or categories; Stage II—on the first day of the thirty-seventh month (that is, by January 1, 1998), members were required to integrate products which accounted for no less than a further 17 percent of the total volume of their 1990 imports of the products in the Annex; Stage III—on the first day of the eighty-fifth month (that is, by January 1, 2002), members were required to integrate products which accounted for no less than a further 18 percent of the total volume of their 1990 imports of the products in the Annex; and Stage IV—on the last day of the 10-year transition period (that is, by January 1, 2005), the entire textile and clothing sector had to be integrated into the strengthened GATT discipline, with the remaining 49 percent of the total volume of 1990 imports integrated, and thus all restrictions removed at the end.

The integration ratios were, however, neither the maximum limits nor mandatory—members were free to integrate their imports into the strengthened GATT discipline to the extent they wished, provided that they met the requirement of integrating the minimum percentages needed. The agreement also provided that all GATT-inconsistent, non-MFA restrictions be brought into conformity with strengthened GATT discipline by December 31, 1995, or be phased out progressively according to a program not exceeding the 10-year transition period.[14]

Transitional safeguards

The ATC called upon all WTO members to: (1) improve access to markets for T&C products through tariff reductions and bindings, reduction or elimination of non-tariff barriers, and facilitation of customs, administrative, and licensing formalities; (2) ensure fair and equitable trading conditions and policies in such areas as dumping and anti-dumping, subsidies and countervailing measures, and protection of intellectual property rights; and (3) avoid discrimination against imports when taking measures for general trade policy reasons. At the same time, the agreement also provided that tariff concessions on T&C products could be withdrawn on items of specific interest to a given country, or quota growth rate increases could be denied to countries that violated market access commitments. Moreover, it allowed selective safeguard actions during the transition period to protect domestic markets against damaging surges in imports.[15]

Implementation phase of the ATC

The ATC, coming as a milestone in the history of global trade in the T&C sector, accomplished several far-reaching goals. First of all, it succeeded in integrating the T&C sector into the mainstream, rule-based global trading system of GATT. Such integration brought an end to the discriminatory and restrictive MFA trade regimes, which severely penalized exports and economic growth in developing countries for several decades. More specifically, the ATC eliminated many of the harsh MFA provisions, including: (1) 'exceptional circumstances,' which enabled developed countries to escape from major market obligations; (2) 'minimum viable production,' through which small importing countries could evade obligations and transfer the burden of import adjustment from dominant to less significant suppliers; and (3) 'mutually acceptable terms,' which served as a vehicle for importing countries to deviate from obligations in negotiating bilateral agreements with developing countries; and, of course, (4) so-called 'market disruption,' which was never defined in operational terms.

The ATC, however, did not bring an immediate end to quota restrictions. At the time of the signing of the ATC, developed countries maintained bilateral quantitative restrictions on imports with more than 70 developing countries. For example, the US and the EU maintained such restrictions with 41 countries and 13 countries respectively, while Canada and Norway maintained such restrictions with 43 countries and 20 countries, respectively (WTO, 1995). Although per annum growth rates of quotas for the majority of the restricted products ranged between 6 to 7 percent, for many Asian clothing and textiles producers, such as China, Hong Kong-SAR, Taiwan, and South Korea, the US quota growth rates ranged between 0.5 and 3 percent, and the number of products restricted by quotas was much higher than other countries. For example, in 1994, while Costa Rica faced quotas on exports of five product categories, China faced such quotas for approximately 110 product categories (Kowalski and Molnar, 2009, 17). As the ATC provided for a 10-year transition period, the MFA regime remained effective until the final day of full integration of the sector.

Second, by allowing developed countries to select import-restrained products for integration into the GATT discipline in different phases while leaving as much as 49 percent of the products for integration on the final day of the transition period, the ATC enabled T&C importing countries to avoid the liberalization of sensitive products in early stages. Moreover, different MFA quotas had different restrictiveness and the commitments of WTO members were fixed in terms of volume, not in terms of value. The implementation records of the ATC indicate that import-restraining countries took full advantage of such flexibilities by back-loading liberalization. In the early stages, the liberalization of T&C products covered mostly Section XI of the HS Code, products such as soft luggage, umbrellas, seat belts, and so on, which are not even strictly T&C products. On the other hand, most sensitive products, for which growth rates are lowest and quota levels consistently filled, were left out for integration at the final stage. For example, the values of the US and the EU quota-restricted clothing products integrated into the ATC were 6.6 percent and 8.7 percent, respectively in the first phase of integration, while the values were 89 percent and 70 percent, respectively in the final stage of integration (Knappe, 2003; Kowalski and Molnar, 2009).[16]

Post-ATC transformation of global T&C trade

Although December 31, 2004 was the scheduled day of elimination of the quota-ridden international trade regimes in the T&C sector, the final day of elimination was delayed by four more years, to 2009. Evidently the delay was prompted by more than 20 percent rise in Chinese T&C exports in 2005, in the immediate aftermath of elimination of the final phase of the MFA restrictions.[17] Although China had a similar growth rate even the year before, in 2005 it became a matter of great concern as Chinese exports of the newly integrated products increased by about 90 percent to the EU and almost 200 percent to the US (ILO, 2005). Such a development prompted several countries—the US, the EU, Argentina, Brazil, Columbia, South Africa, and Turkey—to impose temporary safeguard measures on Chinese exports to which China voluntarily complied.[18] As the safeguard measures came to an end in December 2008, global trade in T&C products finally and eventually graduated into a fully quota- and license-free regime—subject to the same rules and conditions of international trade as other industrial products—beginning in January 2009 (Gereffi and Frederick, 2010).

As expected, the eventual abolition of quotas and other restrictions has unleashed massive adjustments in global T&C production and trade. The liberalization, however, did not result in sweeping or unwieldy consequences, as many doomsayers had predicted. Some studies, for example, predicted that in the post-ATC world, the T&C markets would be swamped by Chinese exports with severe adverse effects on other developing country exporters,[19] but most of these predictions proved to be mere exaggerations. As mentioned above, in 2005 Chinese exports did surge, but the surge was a rather one-off incident—it leveled off in subsequent years (Kowalski and Molnar, 2009). Moreover, about 20 percent annual growth in Chinese T&C exports did not signify any significant departure from the country's routine export performance in recent years—the country's T&C exports jumped from $62 billion in 1990 to $1.2 billion in 2007, averaging at 20 percent growth per annum during the 17-year period (Iacovone *et al.*, 2009).

Similarly, dire consequences predicted for clothing-exporting countries which thrived under the quota-based system proved to be gross exaggerations. Oxfam (2004), for example, predicted that in the quota-free post-ATC world, Bangladesh would lose at least one million jobs, and Sri Lanka would lose half of all its factories—neither of which materialized. Such predictions, however, came true for some other countries. With Chinese exports of clothing soaring by 22 percent in 2005 and 32 percent in 2006, Sub-Saharan African (SSA) exports to the EU and the US fell by 7 percent in 2004, and by 17 percent in 2005 (Keane and Velde, 2008, 32–33). Similarly, an 11.1 percent drop in clothing exports of Hong Kong-SAR and a 2.9 percent drop in Mexico's exports, and similar declines in US clothing exports may be attributed to the surge in Chinese supplies (Martin, 2007).

It is, however, clear that the expiration of quota regimes in T&C products immediately resulted in a huge gain for the less developed countries and similar losses for the developed and semi-developed countries, including the US, the original EU members, the Asian Tigers, and some Middle Eastern and Eastern European countries. Besides, as explained below, the expiry of quotas also resulted in a significant fall in T&C prices, a considerable rise in the global market share of developing countries vis-à-vis developed countries, and remarkable shifts in global production, technology, trade flows, and employment in T&C products.

Shifts in global T&C trade

Trends of global T&C trade

Both clothing and textiles experienced phenomenal growth during the 1985 to 1990 period, when their annual growth rates averaged at 15 percent and 18 percent, respectively (see Table 3.2). Subsequently, however, the growth rates cooled off. During 1990 to 1995, average growth rates in both clothing and textiles were slashed by almost half—down to 8 percent. During 1995 to 2000, coinciding with the period when the T&C sector underwent transition for integration into the GATT discipline, the growth rates fell even further—textiles registered no growth at all, while clothing grew by only 5 percent annually. During 2000 to 2005, however, both textiles and clothing exports bounced back, registering annual growth rates of 5 and 7 percent, respectively. Then, during 2005 to 2010, in the first five years of the post-ATC period, growth slowed down slightly—textiles grew by 4 percent annually, while clothing grew by 5 percent (see Figure 3.1). A comparison of overall growth rates of T&C products between pre-1995 and post-1995 periods shows that on average textiles grew by 8 percent annually during 1980 to 1995, but the growth rate halved during the 1995 to 2013 period. Clothing exports also declined during the post-GATT period, but only by 1 percent.

But trade in the T&C sector eventually became free like any other manufacturing sector since 2009—has it made any difference in growth rates of the

Table 3.2 Growth rates of world exports in manufactures, textiles, and clothing, 1995 to 2013 (US$ billions)

	Annual percentage changes										
	1980–1985	*1985–1990*	*1990–1995*	*1980–1995*	*1995–2000*	*2000–2005*	*1995–2005*	*2005–2010*	*2011–2013*	*2005–2013*	*1995–2013*
Manufactures	2	15	9	8.7	5	9	7	6	6	6	6.4
Textiles	–1	15	8	7.3	0	5	2.5	4	7	5	4
Clothing	4	18	8	10	5	7	6	5	9	6.5	7

Source: Author's calculation from WTO statistics database and *International Trade Statistics.*

Figure 3.1 Annual growth rates of manufactures, textiles and clothing, 1995 to 2013.

sector since then? It appears that in 2010 and 2011, in the first two years after the sector became truly liberalized, both textiles and clothing registered remarkable growth rates. Textiles grew annually by 19 percent and 17 percent, while clothing grew by 12 percent and 18 percent, respectively, in 2010 and 2011. In 2012, however, growth plummeted for both products—while textiles registered negative growth, clothing managed to grow by just 1 percent. In 2013, growth picked up again, but it was less robust than in 2010 and 2011. Overall, during the 2011 to 2013 period, textiles grew by 7 percent annually while clothing grew by 9 percent, which was very close to the growth scenario of the sector during the 1980 to 1995 period.

T&C's share in manufacturing trade

During the period 1995 to 2013, global T&C exports increased from $311 billion to $766 billion, by almost 2.5 times (see Table 3.3). In 1995, in the first year when the phasing out of the MFA restrictions began, the T&C sector had 5.7 percent share in global merchandise exports, which fell to 5.5 percent in 2000, then to 4.7 percent in 2005 and to 4.5 percent in 2010 and 2013 (see Figure 3.2). Overall, the shares of T&C exports in global merchandise trade showed a declining trend throughout the 1995 to 2013 period, when global textiles exports doubled, increasing from $152 billion to $306 billion, and global clothing exports almost tripled, increasing to $460 billion from $158 billion (Table 3.2).

This declining trend in the share of T&C (in nominal value terms) in the global merchandise trade in the post-1995 period brings to the surface at least

Table 3.3 World exports in merchandise, manufactures, textiles, and clothing, 1995 to 2013 (US$ billions)

	1995	*2000*	*2005*	*2010*	*2013*
Merchandise	5,168	6,457	10,508	15,300	16,850
Manufactures	3,719	4,691	7,312	9,962	11,848
	(72.0)	(72.6)	(69.6)	(65.1)	(70.3)
Textiles	152.3	154.8	203	251	306
	(2.9)	(2.4)	(2.0)	(1.9)	(1.8)
Clothing	158.3	197.8	276	351	460
	(3.1)	(3.1)	(2.7)	(2.6)	(2.7)
T&C exports combined	310.6	352.6	479	602	766
	(5.7)	(5.5)	(4.7)	(4.5)	(4.5)

Source: Author's calculation from WTO statistics database and *International Trade Statistics.*

Note
Numbers in parentheses reflect shares in world merchandise exports.

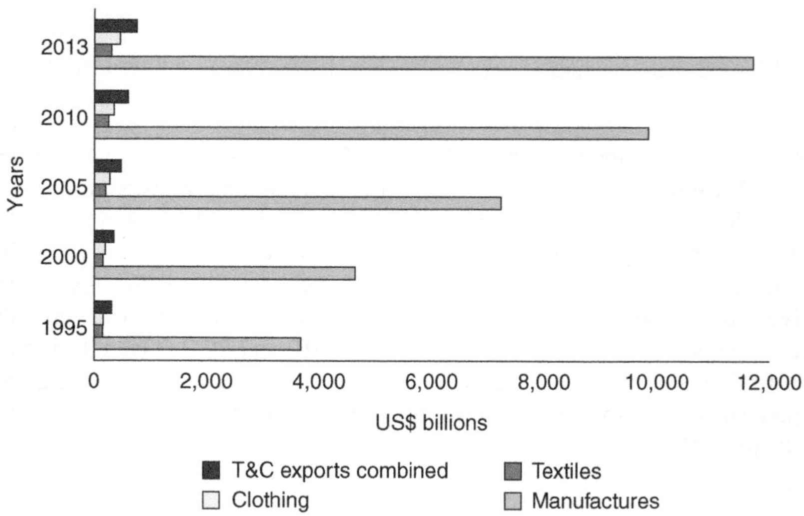

Figure 3.2 World exports of manufactures, textiles and clothing, 1995 to 2013 (in US$ billions).

two major developments. First, due to increased competition among major suppliers, export prices of T&C products must have fallen dramatically in the post-ATC period. In 2005, for example, China's exports volume soared by 150 percent, but its export prices plunged by 10 percent—due mainly to a 40 percent drop in the prices of previously constrained goods. The same year, Pakistan's T&C export of previously constrained goods grew by over 100 percent, but export prices dropped by 18 percent. In respect to India, Bangladesh, and the Philippines, quantities of previously constrained goods increased by around 50 percent, but export prices fell by about 9 percent (Harrigan and Barrows, 2009; Hayashi, 2007).[20]

Second, the share of T&C in global merchandise trade has been falling, also due to the fact that the share of textiles in the T&C trade has been declining consistently over the years. In the 1960s through the 1980s, textiles was the dominant component of T&C trade, representing between 80 and 85 percent of world trade in the sector, but since the mid-1990s the share of clothing exceeded that of textiles in the T&C trade consistently. As Table 3.3 shows, textiles' share in global merchandise trade fell from 2.9 percent in 1995 to 2.4 percent in 2000, then to 2.0 percent in 2005, and to 1.8 percent in 2013. Throughout this period, the share of clothing had been consistently around 3 percent, indicating that a fall in textiles trade may be responsible for the shrinking size of T&C in global merchandise exports since 1995.

It is also notable that the declining share of T&C in global merchandise trade as well as falling profit margins in the sector have been accompanied by a slower growth rate of this sector compared with other manufacturers. In 2011, for example, the share of dominant manufacturing sectors in the world were as follows: food and beverages (11.6 percent), chemicals and chemical products (11.2 percent), machinery and equipment (8.9 percent), and basic metals (8.6 percent). In 2013, the share of dominant manufacturing sectors were as follows: chemicals (10.9 percent), followed by office and telecom equipment (9.6 percent), and automotive products (7.4 percent). Obviously, the T&C's share was very small compared with other sectors. In addition, fast-growing manufacturing sectors in the world during 2007 to 2011 were as follows: radio, television, and communications; office, accounting, and computing machinery; electrical machinery and apparatus; and other transport equipment. Obviously, the T&C sector did not feature as one of the fast-growing manufacturing activities (UNIDO, 2013, 26–27; WTO, 2014).

Changing shares of leading T&C exporters

There have been some sea changes in the shares of major textile exporters in the world during the period 1980 through 2013. As Table 3.4 shows, during this period China's share increased almost eightfold—from 4.6 percent to 34.8 percent in world exports. During the same period India also increased its share in textiles exports by about two and a half times—from 2.4 percent to 6.2 percent of global share. The other major textiles exporters whose share increased during the period include Turkey, Pakistan, Vietnam, Thailand, Indonesia, and the United Arab Emirates. On the other hand, shares in global textiles exports decreased for major industrialized countries. While the share of the US declined from 6.8 percent in 1980 to 4.6 percent in 2013, that of Japan declined by more than 75 percent, from 9.3 percent to 2.2 percent during the same period. The share of the EU also declined by almost 40 percent, from 36.7 percent in 2000 to 23.6 percent in 2013 (see Figure 3.3).

During the 1995 to 2013 period, a latecomer in the business, Vietnam, with less than 2 percent share in global market, recorded a very impressive average

Table 3.4 Changing shares of leading textiles exporters in the world, 1980 to 2013 (in US$ billions, and percentages)

	Value	*Share in world exports*				*Annual percentage change*			
	2013	*1980*	*1990*	*2000*	*2013*	*2005–2013*	*2011*	*2012*	*2013*
China[a]	107	4.6	6.9	10.4	34.8	13	23	1	12
European Union (28)	72	–	–	36.7	23.6	0	13	–10	3
Extra-EU (28) exports	23	–	–	9.9	7.5	2	15	–6	3
India	19	2.4	2.1	3.6	6.2	11	20	0	24
United States	14	6.8	4.8	7.1	4.6	1	14	–3	3
Turkey	12	0.6	1.4	2.4	4.0	7	20	3	10
Korea, Republic of	12	4.0	5.8	8.2	3.9	2	13	–3	1
Hong Kong, China	11	–	–	–	–	–3	0	–7	2
Domestic exports[b]	0	1.7	2.1	0.8	0.1	–15	–19	–8	–11
Re-exports[d]	10	–	–	–	–	–3	0	–6	0
Chinese Taipei	10	3.2	5.9	7.7	3.3	1	13	–7	0
Pakistan	9	1.6	2.6	2.9	3.1	4	16	–4	7
Japan	7	9.3	5.6	4.5	2.2	0	13	–3	–12
Vietnam[b]	5	–	–	0.2	1.6	27	23	3	23
Indonesia	5	0.1	1.2	2.3	1.5	4	16	–5	2
Thailand	4	0.6	0.9	1.3	1.3	4	8	–14	10
United Arab Emirates[b,c]	3	0.1	0.0	0.8	0.9	9	6	16	23
Mexico[a]	2	0.2	0.7	1.7	0.8	2	11	5	9
Above 15	281	–	–	90.5	91.8	–	–	–	–

Source: Author's calculation from WTO statistics database and *International Trade Statistics*.

Notes
a Includes significant shipments through processing zones.
b Includes Secretariat estimates.
c Mainly re-exports.
d In 2013, China reported imports of textiles from China amounting to $3.2 billion.

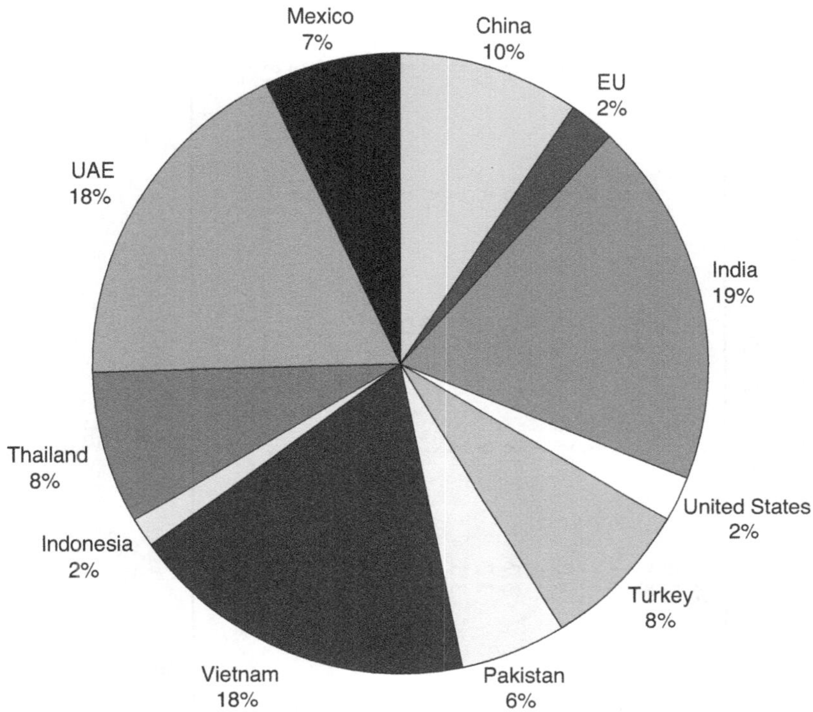

Figure 3.3 Shares of leading textile exporters in the world, 2013.

growth rate of 27 percent per annum. China, the largest textiles exporter in the world, also registered an impressive double-digit annual growth rate of 13 percent per annum. During the same period, India's growth rate averaged at 11 percent, and that of the United Arab Emirates averaged at 9 percent. In 2013, about 92 percent of textiles exports in the world were controlled by the top 15 exporters, out of which only one-third—30 percent—was controlled by the industrialized Triad countries—the US, the EU, and Japan. In 2000, the Triad had a share of more than 48 percent in the 91 percent exports controlled by the top 15 exporters.

The changes in the share of leading clothing exporters during the 1980 to 2013 period are no less fascinating. As Table 3.5 indicates, in 1980, China had only 4 percent share in global clothing exports, which increased almost tenfold by 2013, when its share jumped to 37 percent. Malaysia, Pakistan, and Sri Lanka managed to increase their shares in global clothing exports 2.5 times between 1980 and 2013. India also more than doubled its share in global clothing exports during the same period. Bangladesh made its debut in global clothing markets with less than 1 percent share in 1990, but managed to increase its share more than eightfold by 2013. Similarly, Vietnam, which joined the global clothing

Table 3.5 Changing shares of leading clothing exporters in the world, 1986 to 2013 (US$ billions, and percentages)

	Share in world exports					*Annual percentage change*			
	2013	*1980*	*1990*	*2000*	*2013*	*2005–2013*	*2011*	*2012*	*2013*
China[a]	177	4.0	8.9	18.3	38.6	12	18	4	11
European Union (28)	118	–	–	28.7	25.6	4	17	–6	7
Extra-EU (28) exports	31	–	–	6.5	6.7	6	26	3	8
Bangladesh	24	0.0	0.6	2.6	5.1	17	29	3	19
Hong Kong, China	22	–	–	–	–	–3	2	–8	–3
Domestic exports[b]	0	11.5	8.6	5.0	0.0	–35	–14	–29	–11
Re-exports[d]	21	–	–	–	–	1	2	–8	–5
Vietnam[b]	17	–	–	0.9	3.7	18	27	10	19
India	17	1.7	2.3	3.0	3.7	9	31	–6	22
Turkey	15	0	3	3.3	3.3	3	9	2	8
Indonesia	8	0.2	1.5	2.4	1.7	6	18	–6	2
United States	6	3.1	2.4	4.4	1.3	2	12	7	4
Cambodia[b]	5	–	–	0.5	1.1	11	31	8	19
Malaysia[a]	5	0.4	1.2	1.1	1.0	8	18	0	1
Pakistan	5	0.3	0.9	1.1	1.0	3	16	–7	8
Mexico[a]	5	0.0	0.5	4.4	1.0	–6	6	–4	2
Sri Lanka[b]	5	0.3	0.6	1.4	1.0	6	21	–5	13
Thailand	4	0.7	2.6	1.9	0.9	0	6	–6	–4
Above 15	410	–	–	79.0	89.0	–	–	–	–

Source: Author's calculation from WTO statistics database and *International Trade Statistics*.

Notes

a Includes significant shipments through processing zones.
b Includes WTO Secretariat estimates.
c Imports are valued f.o.b.
d Excludes retained imports of Hong Kong, China.

market with less than 1 percent share in 2000, had increased its share fourfold by 2013. Cambodia also had only 0.5 percent share in world clothing exports in 2000, but more than doubled it by 2013. At the same time, the shares of the US, the EU, Hong Kong-SAR, and Mexico declined during the same period. The share of the EU fell from 28.7 percent in 2000 to 25.6 percent in 2013, while that of the US declined from 3.1 percent in 2000 to 1.3 percent in 2013 (see Figure 3.4).

What is still more fascinating is that many of the top developing country clothing exporters registered double-digit annual growth rates during the 2005 to 2013 period, which reflected the post-MFA period. For example, annual growth rates of clothing exports averaged at 18 percent in Vietnam, 17 percent in Bangladesh, 12 percent in China, and 11 percent in Cambodia during the same period. India, Malaysia, and Sri Lanka, however, recorded more modest growth rates, which averaged at 9 percent, 8 percent, and 6 percent, respectively during the 2005 to 2013 period (see Table 3.5).

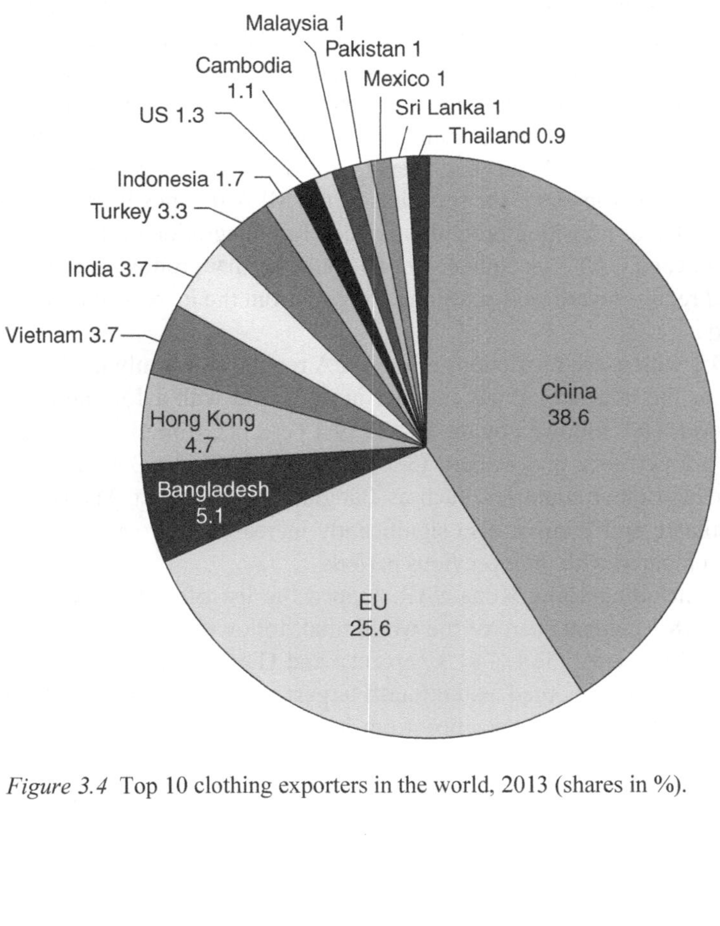

Figure 3.4 Top 10 clothing exporters in the world, 2013 (shares in %).

Shifts in global clothing trade

Clothing exports

In 1980, Hong Kong-SAR was the largest clothing exporter in the world, accounting for 11.5 percent of the world total, followed by Italy (11.3 percent), the Republic of Korea (7.3 percent), Germany (7.1 percent), and China (4.8 percent), but taken together the developed countries remained the largest clothing exporters in the world. In 1990, the EU-25 was the largest exporter of clothing in the world with a commanding share of 36.9 percent, followed by Hong Kong-SAR (14.2 percent), China (8.9 percent), and South Korea (7.4 percent), but Asian countries taken together emerged as the largest clothing exporters. In 1990, the share of Asian countries in global clothing exports increased to 44 percent of the world total, compared with 42 percent of Western Europe (ILO, 2000, 7–11; Keane and Velde, 2008, 47).

In the mid-1990s, the integration of the clothing sector into the WTO added fresh impetus to the evolving trade patterns. It is around this time that the share of clothing began to exceed that of textiles in the T&C trade. This came as a significant development, as clothing, which is relatively more labor intensive than textiles, emerged as a key export-generating manufacturing activity for many low-income and middle-income countries in Asia, Africa and Central America and the Caribbean, including Bangladesh, Cambodia, Guatemala, Lesotho, Madagascar, Mauritius, Nepal, Pakistan, Sri Lanka, and Vietnam. Second, beginning in 1995, the restraints of the MFA regimes began to crumble under the 10-year transition program aimed at full integration of this trade under the strengthened GATT discipline. Not all countries that profited from the MFA-restrained regimes were well positioned to gain from the increasingly liberalized T&C trade.

In 1995, with quota restrictions of the MFA regime still firmly in place, China emerged as the largest clothing exporter in the world with a 15.2 percent share of the world total, followed by the EU-25 (9.4 percent), Hong Kong (6 percent), the US (4.2 percent), and Turkey (3.9 percent) (see Figure 3.4). By the mid-1990s, several other countries, such as Bangladesh, Indonesia, Malaysia, Pakistan, Thailand, and Tunisia, also significantly increased their shares in clothing exports, compared with their previous periods.

China, including Hong Kong-SAR, topped the list of clothing exporters in 2000 with 18.1 percent share of the world total, followed by Italy (6.6 percent), Mexico (4.4 percent), the US (4.3 percent), and Germany (3.4 percent). In the same year, Mexico emerged as the fourth largest clothing exporter in the world, pushing the US to the fifth position from its fourth position in 1995. Mexico's rise to the top five clothing exporters in the world in 2000 clearly reflected regional trade effects of the North American Free Trade Agreement (NAFTA), which came into force in January 1994.

In 2005, in the last year of the transition period when almost all quantitative restrictions on clothing trade came to an end, albeit with the exception of

Table 3.6 Shifts in top 15 clothing exporters in the world, 1995 to 2012 (value in US$ billions, shares—percentages of total exports)

Rank	1995			2000			2005			2010			2013		
	Country	*Value*	*Share*	*Country*	*Value*	*Share*	*Country*	*Value*	*Share*	*Country*	*Value*	*Share*	*Country*	*Value*	*Share*
1	China[a]	24.0	15.2	China[a]	36.07	18.1	EU (25)	80.35	29.2	China[a]	130	36.9	China[a]	177	38.6
2	EU (27)	14.9	9.4	Hong Kong[a,b]	24.22	–	China[a]	74.16	26.9	EU (27)	99	28.1	EU (27)	118	25.6
3	Hong Kong[a,b]	9.5	6.0	Italy	13.22	6.6	Hong Kong[a,b]	72.29		Hong Kong[a,b]	24	–	Bangladesh[b]	24	5.1
4	US	6.7	4.2	Mexico[a]	8.70	4.4	Turkey	11.82	4.3	Bangladesh[b]	16	4.5	Hong Kong[a,b]	22	4.7
5	Turkey	6.1	3.9	US	8.65	4.3	India[b]	8.29	3.0	Turkey	13	3.6	Vietnam	17	3.7
6	South Korea.	5.0	3.1	Germany	6.84	3.4	Mexico[b]	7.27	2.6	India[b]	11	3.2	India[b]	17	3.7
7	Thailand	5.0	3.1	Turkey	6.53	3.3	Bangladesh	6.42	2.3	Vietnam[b]	11	3.1	Turkey	15	3.3
8	Indonesia	3.4	2.1	France	5.43	2.7	Indonesia	5.11	1.9	Indonesia	7	1.9	Indonesia	8	1.7
9	Taiwan	3.2	2.0	India[b]	5.15	2.8	US	5.00	1.8	US	5	1.3	US	6	1.3
10	Mexico[a]	2.7	1.7	South Korea	5.03	2.5	Vietnam[b]	4.81	1.7	Mexico[a]	4	1.2	Cambodia[b]	5	1.1
11	Philippines	2.4	1.5	Indonesia	4.73	2.4	Romania	4.63	1.7	Thailand	4	1.2	Malaysia[b]	5	1.0
12	Malaysia	2.3	1.4	UK	4.11	2.1	Thailand	4.09	1.5	Pakistan	4	1.1	Pakistan	5	1.0
13	Tunisia	2.3	1.4	Thailand	3.95	2.0	Pakistan	3.60	1.3	Malaysia[a]	4	1.1	Mexico[a]	5	1.0
14	Poland	2.3	1.4	Belgium	3.94	2.0	Tunisia	3.33	1.2	Sri Lanka[b]	3	1.0	Sri Lanka[b]	5	1.0
15	Bangladesh[b]	2.0	1.3	Taiwan	2.97	1.5	Sri Lanka	2.88	1.0	Tunisia[b]	3	0.9	Thailand	4	0.9
	Total 15	**127.5**	**80.5**	**Total 15**	**125.24**	**63.1**	**Total 15**	**228.98**	**83.1**	**Total 15**	**314**	**89.4**	**Total 15**	**410**	**89.0**
Share of developing countries in top 15			**43**			**37**			**47.7**			**57.7**			**60.4**

Source: Author's calculation from WTO statistics database and *International Trade Statistics*.

Notes
a Includes significant shipments through processing zones.
b Includes Secretariat estimates.

Chinese exports, the EU-25 emerged as the top clothing exporter in the world. China, being still subject to QRS, especially in the EU and the US as a condition for entry into the WTO, was relegated to the second rank. China, however, could still be considered as the number one exporter of clothing in 2005, if Hong Kong-SAR's share is included in the Chinese exports. Taken together, China and Hong Kong-SAR's exports in 2005 totaled $146.45 billion, compared with $80.35 billion of the EU (see Figure 3.5).

Turkey and India occupied the fourth and fifth slots among the top 15 exporters in 2005,[21] while Mexico, which ranked fourth in 2000, ended up as the sixth, and the US, which had the fifth slot in 2000, was relegated to the ninth position. Another remarkable feature of clothing exports in 2005 was the emergence of Bangladesh—an LDC—as the seventh largest clothing exporter in the world with a 2.3 percent share in exports. Between 1990 and 2005, the country's clothing exports increased tenfold—from $643 million to $6.4 billion.[22]

In 2010, the change in global clothing exports was still more dramatic. With the ability to export clothing without any quantitative restrictions to the world's largest markets—the EU and the US—it was easy for China to reoccupy the first rank among the world's top clothing exporters by relegating the EU-27 to the second position.[23] This was a good year for Bangladesh, which moved through the ladder further to emerge as the fourth largest clothing exporter in the world, graduating from the fifteenth place in 1995. Much of this, however, may be attributed to duty-free and quota-free access to the EU market under its 'Everything but Arms' initiative. Another developing country, Vietnam, which secured tenth place in 2005, emerged as the seventh largest clothing exporter in the world in 2010.

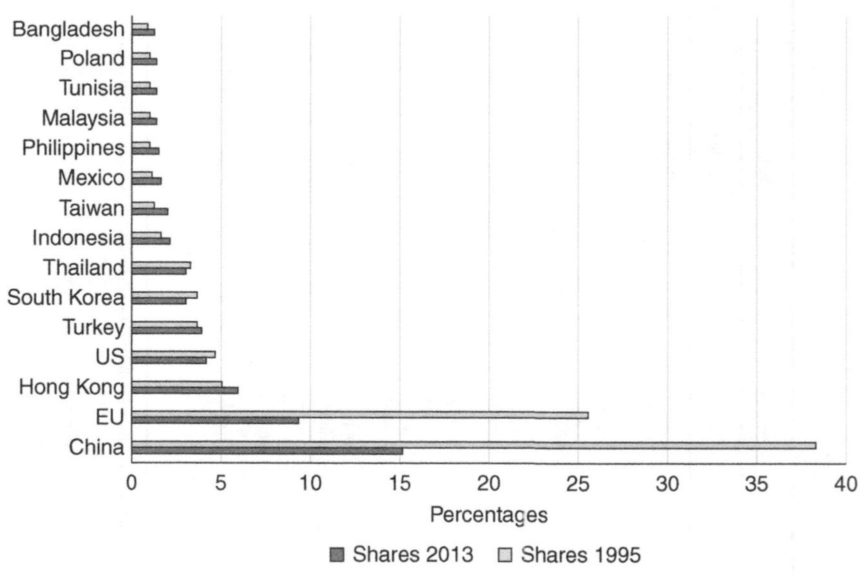

Figure 3.5 Shift in shares of top clothing exporters in the world, 1995 and 2013 (in %).

It is also remarkable that Mexico, which ranked fourth among the top 15 clothing exporters in the world in 2000, was relegated to the tenth position in 2010. As mentioned above, Mexico's emergence as one of the topmost clothing exporters in the late 1990s may be attributed to the NAFTA which enabled the country to gain major access to the US clothing market. In the 2000s, however, the situation changed dramatically—with a significant cost advantage over Mexico, many developing countries, such as China, Bangladesh, India, Indonesia, and Vietnam, could easily displace Mexico's dominance in the US clothing imports in an increasingly quota-free world. As a result, between 2000 and 2009, China's share in the US's clothing imports almost tripled in a matter of nine years—increasing from 13.3 percent to a staggering 39.1 percent. The share of Bangladesh in the US's clothing imports also increased from 3.4 percent to 5 percent during the same period, despite, and unlike in the EU, the country receiving no preferential treatment in garments exports to the US. During the same period, India's share also increased from 3.2 percent to 4.3 percent, and Indonesia's share increased from 3.5 percent to 5.8 percent, and of course, during the same period, Mexico's share in the US's clothing imports dipped to 5 percent from 13.1 percent.[24]

In 2013, China maintained its topmost position among global clothing exports when its share increased to 38.6 percent, compared with 36.9 percent in 2010. This represented a small change in terms of percentage, but not in terms of exports revenue, as in 2013 just 1 percent share in global clothing exports signified $4.6 billion. During the same year, although the EU maintained its second position in global clothing exports, its share fell by more than 2 percent compared with that of 2010. The year 2013 also brought two remarkable changes: Bangladesh, an LDC, emerged as the third largest clothing exporter in the world, overtaking Hong Kong-SAR, and Cambodia, another LDC, joined the top 15 clothing exporters' club for the first time with 1.1 percent share in global exports. The year also saw Vietnam as the fifth largest exporter of clothing in the world—it was the sixth largest in 2010.

Gainers and losers

As the discussion above indicates, striking changes have taken place in the global clothing exports market since the beginning of the phasing out of the MFA restrictions in 1995. Among the developing countries, China emerged as the clear winner, both in terms of market share and the nominal value of clothing exports during the period. The country's share in global clothing exports increased from 26.2 percent in 2005 to 38.6 percent in 2013, when the nominal value of its exports more than doubled—increasing from $74.6 billion to $177 billion.[25]

Among the low-income developing countries, Bangladesh, Cambodia, and Vietnam were clearly among the greatest beneficiaries of the transition in the post-ATC period. Bangladesh had a 2.3 percent share in global clothing exports in 1995, which increased to 5.1 percent in 2013, when the nominal value of its exports increased almost fourfold—from $6.4 billion to $24 billion. In addition, during the 1995 to 2013 period, the country's clothing exports increased 12 times—jumping from $2 billion to $24 billion. Vietnam made the top 15 club of clothing exporters for the first time in 2005 with a share of 1.7 percent, which more than doubled by 2013, when the nominal value of its clothing exports almost quadrupled—increasing from $4.8 billion to $17 billion. Another clear beneficiary in the post-ATC period is Cambodia—from a virtually non-existent base in the 1990s, the country emerged as one of the top 15 clothing exporters in the world in the 2010s.

Among the mid-income developing countries, Indian exports surged in the post-ATC period. In 1995, India did not make the list of the top 15 clothing exporters, but it emerged as the fifth largest clothing exporter in 2005. During the 2005 to 2013 period, India's share in global clothing exports increased from 3 percent to 3.7 percent, when the nominal values of its exports more than doubled—increasing from $8.3 billion to $17 billion. During the 2000 to 2013 period Indian clothing exports increased more than sixfold—from $2.8 billion to $17 billion.

When it comes to the losers of liberalized trade in clothing, Mexico perhaps tops the list among the developing countries. In 2000, when MFA restrictions were still firmly in place, Mexico's share in global clothing exports was 4.4 percent, but in 2005 its share fell to 2.6 percent, and then plummeted to just 1 percent in 2013—reflecting about 80 percent decline in its share over a period of 13 years. Much of Mexico's rise and fall as a leading clothing exporter, as mentioned above, had to do with US imports. In the early 1990s, Mexico emerged as the fourth largest clothing supplier to the US, but following the NAFTA's coming into force in 1994, the country emerged as the second largest exporter to the US clothing market in 1996, and in 1999 it emerged as the largest clothing exporter to the US with a share of 14.8 percent. The country maintained that position up until 2001, but in 2002 its fortunes reversed, as China re-emerged as the largest clothing exporter to the US. Mexico, thus, lost out in the global clothing exports market way before the complete phasing out of the MFA restrictions (Martin, 2007, 15; Iacovone *et al.*, 2009; Gereffi and Memedovic, 2003, 10).

Several East Asian Tigers also lost out in the post-ATC period. For example, South Korea had a share of 3.1 percent in global clothing exports in 1995, which fell to 2.5 percent in 2000, and the country has not occupied a spot among the top 15 list since. Similarly, Taiwan had 2 percent share in global clothing in 1995, which fell to 1.5 percent in 2000, and has failed to make the top 15 list since. Thailand had a 3.1 percent share in global clothing exports in 1995, which dropped to 1.5 percent in 2005. The country failed to make the top 15 list in 2010, but came to occupy the lowest slot in the top 15 list in 2013 with less than a 1 percent share. Hong Kong-SAR had a 6 percent share in global clothing exports in 1995, but its share fell to 4.7 percent in 2013 (see Figure 3.5).

Some of the traditional clothing exporters, such as Turkey, Indonesia, and Tunisia, however, have been experiencing transitional pressures of the liberalization of the clothing trade mainly because of cost advantages of low-income developing countries. In the post-ATC period (2005–2013), Turkey's share in global clothing exports fell from 4.3 percent to 3.3 percent, Indonesia's share fell from 1.9 percent to 1.7 percent, and Tunisia's share fell from 1.2 percent to less than 1 percent.

Among advanced industrialized countries, in the post-ATC period (2005–2013), the EU's share in global clothing exports slipped from 29.2 percent to 25.6 percent, and the share of the US slipped from 1.8 percent to 1.3 percent. In fact, the US has been one of the major losers in the liberalization of the clothing market—it had a 4.2 percent share in global clothing exports in 1995, but shredded that share by 70 percent by 2013.

Much of these shifts in clothing production and exports clearly demonstrate a movement along the path envisaged by neoclassical economics—in a freer market, specialization gravitates in favor of low-cost producers. At the same time, it should also be noted that the East Asian Tigers, especially South Korea, Taiwan, and Hong Kong-SAR, began to lose their shares in global clothing exports beginning in the 1980s, and much of the losses could be attributed to technological advancement and diversification into higher value-added products (ILO, 2000, 10). Similarly, many of the high- and medium-income developing countries, such as Malaysia, Indonesia, India, Brazil, and Mexico, have been diversifying into medium and high-tech manufacturing activities, such as radio, television and communications, office products, transport equipment, and accounting, computing and electrical machinery and apparatus (UNIDO, 2013, 27).

Shifts in clothing imports

In the global clothing imports market, the EU and the US maintained topmost positions throughout the period 1995 to 2013, although their shares in the market had shrunk considerably (see Table 3.7). The number of member countries of the EU nearly doubled during the same period—increasing from 15 to 28—but its share in global clothing exports fell from 44.5 percent in 1995 to 37.9 percent in 2013. A declining trend in its share, however, was pronounced more recently. Even in 2010, the EU had a commanding share of 44.7 percent in global clothing imports. In terms of nominal values, the EU's clothing imports, however, more than doubled during the same period—increasing from $74 billion in 1995 to $182 billion in 2013. The US remained the second largest clothing importer in the world throughout the period, but its share in global clothing imports fell from 25.4 percent in 1995 to 19.7 percent in 2013, when nominal values of its imports more than doubled—increasing from $41.8 billion to $91 billion. Japan had an 11.5 percent share in global clothing imports in 1995, which fell to 7.0 percent in 2013 (see Figure 3.6).

Overall, the Triad—the EU, the US, and Japan—remained the largest destination of global clothing exports, but its combined share in global imports of clothing declined from 80.2 percent in 1995 to 74.3 percent in 2010, and then to 64.6 percent in 2013. Throughout the 1995 to 2013 period, the shares of the US and

Table 3.7 Shifts in top 15 clothing importers in the world, 1995 to 2012 (values in US$ billions, shares—percentages of total imports)

Rank	*1995*			*2000*			*2005*			*2010*			*2013*		
	Country	*Value*	*Share*	*Country*	*Value*	*Share*	*Country*	*Value*	*Share*	*Country*	*Value*	*Share*	*Country*	*Value*	*Share*
1	EU (15)	74.2	45.5	US	66.39	31.6	EU (25)	128.70	44.8	EU (27)	164	44.7	EU (28)	182	37.9
2	US	41.8	25.4	Japan	19.71	9.4	US	80.07	27.9	US	82	22.3	US	91	19.7
3	Japan	18.8	11.5	Germany	19.31	9.2	Japan	22.54	7.8	Japan	27	7.3	Japan	34	7.0
4	Hong Kong[a,b]	12.7	–	Hong Kong[a,b]	16.01	–	Hong Kong[a,b]	18.44	–	Hong Kong[a,b]	17	–	Hong Kong[a,b]	16	–
5	Switzerland	3.8	2.3	UK	12.99	6.2	Russia[b]	7.84	2.7	Canada[c]	8	2.3	Canada	10	2.1
6	Canada	2.7	1.7	France	11.48	5.5	Canada[c]	5.98	2.1	Russia[c]	7	2.0	Russia	9	1.9
7	Mexico	1.9	1.2	Italy	6.07	2.9	Switzerland	4.72	1.6	Switzerland	5	1.4	South Korea	8	1.6
8	Singapore	1.6	1.0	Netherlands	4.83	2.3	Australia[c]	3.12	1.1	Australia[c]	5	1.3	Australia	6	1.3
9	Norway	1.4	0.9	Belgium	4.81	2.3	South Korea	2.91	1.0	South Korea	4	1.2	Switzerland	6	1.2
10	Australia	1.3	0.8	Spain	3.77	1.8	Mexico[a,c]	2.52	0.9	Turkey	3	0.8	China[a,b]	5	1.1
11	UAE[b,c]	1.3	0.8	Canada	3.69	1.8	Singapore	2.13	0.7	UAE	3	0.7	UAE[b,c]	4	0.8
12	South Korea	1.1	0.7	Mexico[a]	3.41	1.6	Norway	1.86	0.6	China[a]	3	0.7	Saudi Arabia	3	0.7
13	China[a]	1.0	0.6	Switzerland	3.22	1.5	UAE[b,d]	1.67	0.6	Norway	3	0.7	Mexico[a]	3	0.7
14	Taiwan	0.9	0.5	Russia	2.96	1.4	China[a]	1.63	0.6	Mexico[a,c]	2	0.6	Turkey	3	0.7
15	Russia	–	–	Austria	2.47	1.2	Saudi Arabia[b]	1.57	0.5	Singapore	2	0.5	Singapore	3	0.6
	Total 15	**151.3**	**92.9**	**Total 15**	**166.83**	**79.4**	**Total 15**	**267.26**	**93.1**	**Total 15**	**318**	**86.5**	**Total 15**	**368**	**76.4**

Source: Author's calculation from WTO Statistics database and *International Trade Statistics*.

Notes

a Includes significant shipments through processing zones.

b Includes Secretariat estimates.

c Imports are valued f.o.b.

d 2004 instead of 2005.

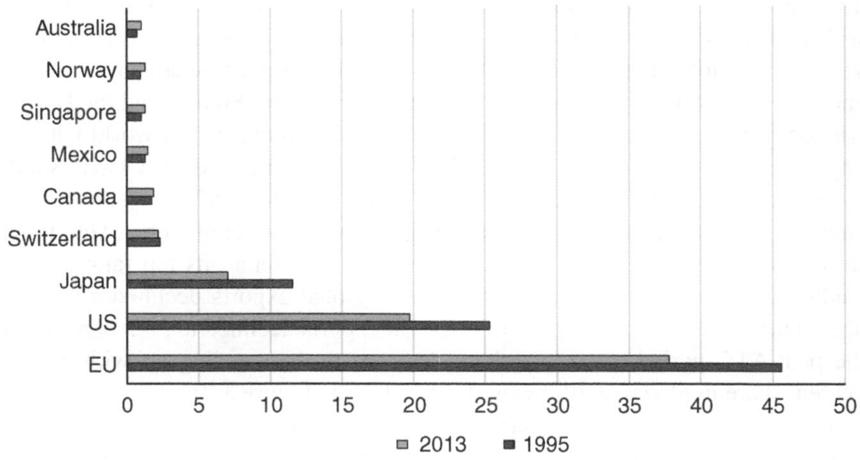

Figure 3.6 Shift in top clothing importers in the world, 1995 and 2013.

Japan in global clothing imports declined consistently, while the share of the EU demonstrated some ups and downs. Clothing import penetration—the value of imports divided by the value of apparel consumption—however, remained deep in all of these regions. In 2008, the ratio was 94 percent in the US, 93 percent in Japan, 95 percent in the United Kingdom and Germany, 85 percent in France, and 65 percent in Italy (Gereffi and Frederick, 2010).

Shifts in global textiles trade

Textiles exports

Textiles is a more capital-intensive manufacturing activity than clothing, and it requires more skilled labor as well. It is thus easier for low-income developing countries to excel in clothing than in textiles. Until the mid-1990s, Western European countries were the largest exporters of textiles—in 1980 they accounted for more than 50 percent of world textiles exports (including intra-trade), while Asia had a share of about 25 percent. In the early 1990s, while Western Europe's share in textiles exports remained about the same, Asia's share rose to 35 percent. In 1997, Asia emerged as the leading region of textile exports with a 44 percent share in world trade, when Western Europe's share declined to about 40 percent. During the 1980 to 1997 period, textiles exports from Asia increased four and a half times, while Western European exports more than doubled (ILO, 2000, 7–8). In the mid-1990s, another significant development took place. As mentioned above, textiles' share in global T&C trade began to fall as competition in textiles exports became fiercer with the phasing out of the MFA restrictions.

In 1980, the largest textile exporter in the world was Germany, which accounted for 11.4 percent of world global exports. Japan was the second largest with a share of 9.3 percent, and Italy was the third largest with a 7.6 percent share in the global market (ILO, 2000, 8–9). With dominant shares of Germany and Italy, also with considerably large shares of Belgium, France, and the United Kingdom, in 1995 the EU was the largest textiles exporter in the world with an approximately 40 percent share in the global total, followed by China, South Korea, Taiwan, the US, and Japan (see Table 3.8). In 1997, however, China emerged as the largest exporter of textiles, followed by South Korea, Germany, Italy, and Taiwan. In 2000, the EU was still able to retain its top rank among leading exporters of textiles, but its share in global exports declined considerably. Then, in 2005, the EU's share in global exports declined to 33.5 percent. In the post-ATC period, the EU's share declined further, ending up with a 23.6 percent share in global textiles exports in 2013 (see Figure 3.7).

During the 1995 to 2013 period, Japan also saw a dramatic decline in its shares in global textiles exports. The country had a share of 4.7 percent in textiles trade in 1995, which has consistently fallen ever since, ending up with less than half—just a 2.2 percent share—in 2013. The US, however, avoided such a dramatic drop in its textiles exports. It had about a 5 percent share in global textiles exports in 1995, which actually increased to 7 percent in 2000, but then gradually fell, and ended up with 4.6 percent in 2013. China, on the other hand, tripled its share in global textiles trade between 1995 and 2013. It doubled its share between 2000 and 2005, and by 2010, by tripling its exports, China overtook the EU as the largest textiles exporter in the global market. In 2013, China controlled more than one-third of global textiles exports. In nominal terms, the

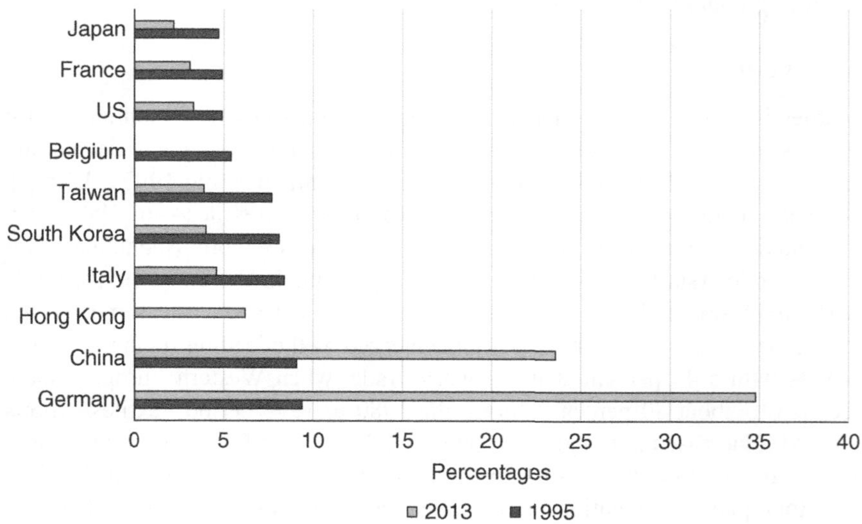

Figure 3.7 Shifts in shares of top textiles exporters in the world, 1995 and 2013.

Table 3.8 Shifts in top 15 textiles exporters in the world, 1995 to 2012 (value in US$ billions, shares in percentages of total)

Rank	*1995*			*2000*			*2005*			*2010*			*2013*		
	Country	*Value*	*Share*	*Country*	*Value*	*Share*	*Country*	*Value*	*Share*	*Country*	*Value*	*Share*	*Country*	*Value*	*Share*
1	Germany	14.3	9.4	China[a]	16.14	10.2	EU-25	67.98	33.5	China	77	30.7	China[a]	107	34.8
2	China[a]	13.9	9.1	Hong Kong[a,b]	13.44	–	China[a]	41.05	20.2	EU (27)	67	26.8	EU (28)	72	23.6
3	Hong Kong[a,b]	13.8	–	South Korea	12.78	8.1	Hong Kong[a,b]	13.83	–	India[b]	13	5.1	India[b]	19	6.2
4	Italy	12.8	8.4	Italy	11.96	7.6	US	12.38	6.1	US	12	4.9	US	14	4.6
5	South Korea	12.3	8.1	Taiwan	11.69	7.4	South Korea	10.39	5.1	Hong Kong[a,b]	11	–	Turkey	12	4.0
6	Taiwan	11.8	7.7	Germany	11.02	7.0	Taiwan	9.71	4.8	South Korea	11	4.4	South Korea	12	3.9
7	Belgium	8.2	5.4	US	10.96	7.0	India[b]	7.85	3.9	Taiwan	10	3.9	Hong Kong[a,b]	11	–
8	US	7.4	4.9	Japan	7.02	4.5	Pakistan	7.09	3.5	Turkey	9	3.6	Taiwan	10	3.3
9	France	7.4	4.9	France	6.76	4.3	Turkey	7.07	3.5	Pakistan	8	3.1	Pakistan	9	3.1
10	Japan	7.2	4.7	Belgium	6.40	4.1	Japan	6.91	3.4	Japan	7	2.8	Japan	7	2.2
11	UK	5.0	3.3	India[b]	5.09	3.4	Indonesia	3.45	1.7	Indonesia	4	1.7	Vietnam[b]	5	1.6
12	India[b]	4.3	2.8	Pakistan	4.53	2.9	Thailand	2.76	1.4	Thailand	4	1.5	Indonesia	5	1.5
13	Pakistan	4.2	2.7	UK	4.21	2.7	Canada	2.46	1.2	Vietnam[b]	3	1.1	Thailand	4	1.3
14	Indonesia	2.7	1.8	Turkey	3.67	2.3	Mexico[a]	2.13	1.1	Mexico[a]	2	0.8	UAE[b,c]	3	0.9
15	Switzerland	2.3	1.5	Indonesia	3.51	2.2	UAE[b,c]	1.70	0.9	Canada	2	0.8	Mexico[a]	2	0.8
Total 15		**109.6**	**71.9**		**116.90**	**74.5**		**183.52**	**90.5**		**228**	**91.1**		**281**	**91.8**
Share of developing countries in top 15			**29.4**			**36.5**			**46.1**			**55.9**			**61.9**

Source: Author's calculation from WTO Statistics database and *International Trade Statistics*.

Notes

a Includes significant shipments through processing zones.

b Includes Secretariat estimates.

c Imports are valued f.o.b.

value of Chinese exports rose by 12 times in 18 years—increasing from $9.1 billion in 1995 to $107 billion in 2013.

Another remarkable beneficiary of the liberalization of textiles trade has been India. In 1995, it was the twelfth largest textiles exporter in the world with a share of 2.8 percent in global trade; in 2013 it emerged as the third largest textiles exporter with a share of 6.2 percent in global trade. During the same period, the nominal value of India's textiles exports rose by more fourfold—increasing from $4.3 billion in 1995 to $19 billion in 2013. During the same period, Pakistan's share in global textiles exports also increased, although not so sharply. Its share increased from 2.7 percent in 1995 to 3.1 percent in 2013. More remarkable progress was made by Turkey—its share in global textiles exports increased from 2.3 percent in 2000 to 4.0 percent in 2013, when the nominal value of its textiles exports increased more than threefold.

Besides advanced industrialized countries like the EU and Japan, and to some extent the US, top losers of the liberalization of the textiles trade also included the newly industrialized economies of South Korea and Taiwan. South Korea had an 8.1 percent share in global textiles in 1995, which fell to 3.9 percent in 2013, when Taiwan's share dropped from 7.7 percent to 3.3 percent. Like Japan, South Korea and Taiwan also lost more than half of their textiles exports during the 1995 to 2013 period. Despite huge losses, the Triad—the US, the EU, and Japan—still control over 30 percent of the capital-intensive textiles export market in the world. At the same time, it also appears that competitions from relatively well-off developing countries like China, India, Turkey, Pakistan, Indonesia, Thailand, Tunisia, Philippines, and Mexico are being intensified. For example, Indonesia remained one of the top 15 textiles exporters throughout the 1995 to 2013 period with a share of around 1.7 percent; Turkey increased its share from 3.7 percent in 2000 to 4 percent in 2013; and Pakistan remained competitive throughout the period by maintaining about a 3 percent share in global textile exports.

Textiles imports

With the shares of all its constituent members taken together, the EU remained among the top textiles importers in the world throughout the 1995 to 2013 period (see Table 3.9). In 1995, the US was the fourth largest textiles importer in the world, when the second and third slots went to Hong Kong-SAR and mainland China. In 2000, however, the US emerged as the second largest textiles importer with a 9.4 percent share in the global total, followed by China (7.7 percent), Mexico (3.6 percent), and Japan (2.9 percent). During the 2005 to 2013 period, the combined share of the EU and the US—the two largest textiles importers in the world—declined from 41.3 percent to 32.6 percent. Similarly, the share of Canada also declined during the same period—from 2.0 percent in 2005 to 1.4 percent in 2013. Japan, however, maintained a 2.7 percent share uniformly throughout the period—the country, however, had a larger share in textiles imports during the transition period of the MFA regime. Overall, during the

Table 3.9 Shifts in top 15 textiles importers in the world, 1995 to 2010 (values in US$ billions, shares in percentages of total)

Rank	*1995*			*2000*			*2005*			*2010*			*2013*		
	Country	*Value*	*Share*	*Country*	*Value*	*Share*	*Country*	*Value*	*Share*	*Country*	*Value*	*Share*	*Country*	*Value*	*Share*
1	Germany	12.5	8.0	US	15.71	9.4	EU (25)	65.83	30.8	EU (27)	73	27.5	EU (28)	78	24.2
2	Hong Kong[a,b]	16.8	–	Hong Kong[a,b]	13.72	–	US	22.54	10.5	US	23	8.8	US	27	8.4
3	China[a,d]	10.9	7.0	China[a,d]	12.83	7.7	China[a,d]	15.50	7.2	China[a,d]	18	6.7	China[a,d]	22	6.7
4	US	10.4	6.6	Germany	9.32	5.6	Hong Kong[a,b]	13.79	–	Hong Kong[a,b]	11	–	Vietnam[b]	11	3.3
5	France	7.5	4.8	UK	6.91	4.1	Mexico[a,c]	6.02	2.8	Japan	7	2.7	Hong Kong[a,b]	10	–
6	UK	7.2	4.6	France	6.75	4.0	Japan	5.81	2.7	Turkey	7	2.5	Japan	9	2.7
7	Italy	6.5	4.1	Italy	6.12	3.7	Turkey	4.43	2.1	Vietnam[b]	6	2.3	Turkey	7	2.1
8	Japan	5.9	3.8	Mexico	6.10	3.6	Canada[c]	4.32	2.0	Mexico[a,c]	5	1.9	Bangladesh[b]	6	1.9
9	Belgium	4.5	2.9	Japan	4.94	2.9	South Korea	3.54	1.7	Bangladesh[b]	5	1.9	Mexico[a,b]	6	1.9
10	South Korea	3.9	2.5	Canada	4.13	2.5	Vietnam[b]	3.33	1.6	South Korea	5	1.8	Indonesia	6	1.8
11	Netherlands	3.5	2.2	Belgium	3.63	2.2	Romania	3.31	1.5	Indonesia	4	1.6	South Korea	5	1.6
12	Canada	3.2	2.0	Spain	3.32	2.0	UAE[b,c]	3.22	1.6	Canada[c]	4	1.6	Canada	5	1.4
13	Spain	2.6	1.7	South Korea	3.00	1.9	Russia[c]	2.68	1.3	Russia[b]	4	1.4	Russia[c]	4	1.3
14	Poland	2.2	1.4	Netherlands	2.64	1.6	India[b]	2.10	1.0	Brazil[c]	4	1.4	Brazil	4	1.3
15	Singapore	2.1	1.3	Poland	2.43	1.5	Thailand	1.99	0.9	India	3	1.0	India	4	1.1
Top 15 total		**82.9**	**52.9**		**89.27**	**53.4**		**145.19**	**67.9**		**168**	**63.2**		**184**	**59.8**

Source: Author's calculation from WTO statistics database and *International Trade Statistics*.

Notes

a Includes significant shipments through processing zones.

b Includes Secretariat estimates.

c Imports are valued f.o.b.

d Excludes retained imports of Hong Kong, China.

post-MFA period (2005–2013), the combined share of the Quad countries—the EU, the USA, Canada, and Japan—in global textiles imports declined from 46 percent to 36.7 percent.

Among the developing countries, mainland China's share in global textiles imports remained more or less steady at around 7 percent throughout the 1995 to 2013 period, and India's share also remained steady at 1 percent of global textiles imports during the post-MFA period. What is remarkable, however, is that the share in global textiles imports rose sharply for several low-income developing country clothing exporters. Vietnam, for example, came to occupy the tenth slot in 2005 with a 1.6 percent share in global textile imports, but its share doubled by 2013, when it emerged as the fourth largest textiles importer in the world. The same year, Bangladesh, another low-income developing country clothing exporter, came to occupy the eighth slot among the top textile importers in the world with 1.9 percent share. Such a high level of imports of textiles of Vietnam and Bangladesh indicates the heavy dependence of these countries on imported textiles for their export-oriented clothing industries.

Changing patterns of production, trade, and investment

Developments since the beginning of the phasing out of the restrictive MFA regimes, as explained above, indicate that over the years the global market for T&C has deepened and widened significantly, and the share of the less developed countries in the global T&C market has been on the rise, while that of the developed countries has been declining. The tide seems to have turned—the less developed countries now account for more than half of the world's textile exports and almost three-quarters of the world's clothing exports. The accompanying transformations in global production and employment structures, technological infusion and investment flows, and trade patterns under a freer trade regime in the T&C sector since 1995 have also been phenomenal.

As mentioned above, the T&C had been the harbinger of industrialization in the Western world in the eighteenth through nineteenth centuries, and it has been at the forefront of the industrialization of almost all countries ever since. But industrial transformation for most of the developing countries began in the aftermath of World War II, when newly independent primarily agricultural nations stepped into the rudimentary stage of manufacturing T&C products. Since then, the world of T&C has undergone several production migrations: (1) first migration: from North America and Western Europe to Japan in the 1950s and early 1960s; (2) second migration: from Japan to the East Asian Tigers—Hong Kong-SAR, Taiwan, Singapore, and South Korea—in the early 1970s; and (3) third migration: from the East Asian Tigers to other developing economies—to mainland China and several Southeast Asian countries in the 1980s, and to South Asia, Central American and Caribbean, Mediterranean, as well as Sub-Saharan African countries in the 1990s.[26]

Traditionally, industrialized countries have dominated global T&C exports, but the Asian developing countries, especially the Asian Tigers, emerged as top

T&C exporters in the world by the mid-1990s. Although the dominance of developed countries, such as the US and the EU, still continues in the more capital-intensive textile sector, the Asian Tigers are no longer at the forefront of T&C exports. In 2005 alone, in the last year when MFA restrictions were originally scheduled to be phased out, clothing exports of Hong Kong-SAR, South Korea, and Taiwan slipped by 11 percent, 24 percent, and 20 percent, respectively (Harrigan and Barrows, 2009; Martin, 2007). At the same time, coinciding with the phasing out of the MFA restrictions, mainland China emerged as the most dominant T&C exporter in the world. In 1995, China had only a 15 percent share in global clothing exports, which doubled by 2005. By 2013, the country increased its share in global clothing exports to 39 percent. Similarly, the country had only a 9 percent share in global textiles exports in 1995, which more than doubled by 2005. By 2013, China had a 35 percent share in global textiles exports. China is now the number one single country exporter of both textiles and clothing in the world, commanding more than one-third of global trade in both sectors.

Much of the phenomenal success of China may well be attributed to the abundance of low-cost labor, which afforded the country a natural comparative advantage in the labor-intensive clothing sector, and the country is well positioned to expand its clothing exports further in the post-MFA trading system under the WTO as long as it is able to benefit from low wages. But there are several other developing countries who also enjoy such a natural advantage. Some of them—Bangladesh, Cambodia, India, Pakistan, and Vietnam—have already made remarkable inroads into global T&C trade, where the sector has emerged as a major source of exports, foreign exchange, and employment (Keane and Velde, 2008). One reason why the second migration T&C exporters sought expansion into the third migration countries was that wages were rising in their domestic markets. That was the time when Hong Kong-SAR, for example, expanded to mainland China, taking advantage of the opening up of the Chinese economy. Now, with the Chinese cost of labor increasing, scores of African countries, especially those in Sub-Saharan Africa, which also enjoy a natural comparative advantage in low-cost labor, are being gradually integrated into global T&C trade (Kaplinsky *et al.*, 2007).

There can be no dispute that many of the less developed countries have an inherent advantage in the expansion of the clothing sector, as it requires relatively little capital, relatively low entrepreneurial skills, and unskilled labor. In addition, there is no dearth of evidence that this sector allows the less developed countries to import more advanced technologies financed through the revenues gained from clothing exports, and thus use the sector as a stepping stone for economic development (Brenton and Hoppe, 2006). But the extent to which a developing country can use its clothing sector as a stepping stone for development largely depends on what type of production system is being used for its clothing exports.

Gereffi and Memedovic (2003), for example, identify three types of T&C production systems around the world. First, what they call an assembly-type production system refers to industrial subcontracting, as may be seen in the Export Processing Zones (EPZs), under which foreign investors supply domestic firms with sewing machines with imported inputs for assembly. Domestic value addition would be very small under this system. Second, what they call original equipment manufacturing (OEM) is a form of commercial subcontracting under which the supplying firm makes a product according to a design specified by the buyer and the product is sold under the buyer's brand name. Third, what they call original brand-name manufacturing (OBM) refers to the upgrading of the production expertise domestic manufacturers from OEM to design and sell their own brand products.

The authors maintain that the key to East Asia's success was the move from mere assembly-type production to a more domestically integrated and higher value-added form of exporting under an OEM-type production system also known as full-package supply. Such successes were underpinned by these manufacturers' ability to establish links with a wide range of lead firms which served as the primary source of material inputs, technology transfer, and knowledge in buyer-driven value chains. Value addition is larger under the full-package supply, as retailers and marketers in the developed countries tend to rely on full-package sourcing networks. The OEM model also allows a greater degree of local learning about the upstream and downstream segments of the apparel chain. Then, much of the success of Japanese companies and certain firms in the East Asian Tigers stemmed from their ability to move on from OEM exports to OBM, by supplementing their production expertise with the design and then the sale of their own branded merchandise at home and abroad. Obviously, the highest value addition comes from the OBM system of production.

The case of China

Mainland China, a country with more than one billion people, for example, began its journey in the T&C sector in the early 1980s with a Special Economic Zone (SEZ) in Shenzhen, across the border of Hong Kong-SAR. Gradually such economic zones, which provided an assembly-type production system, spread throughout the east coast, in Guangdong, Zhejiang, and Jiangsu provinces. Chinese T&C flourished under private ownership dominated by foreign direct investments, most of which came from Hong Kong-SAR and Taiwan-based companies (Ngai, 2005). Over the years, the Chinese T&C sector has achieved phenomenal success—topping the list of global clothing and textiles exporters numerous times (see Table 3.6 and Table 3.8). According to the *Chinese Statistical Yearbook* of 2006, the country's T&C sector employed 8.2 million workers in 1995, but due to major downsizing during the 1996 to 2001 period when the country attempted to make the domestic industries more competitive after its accession to the WTO, employment in the sector fell to 4.2 million in 2001, rising to 4.4 million by 2005.[27]

Aside from the abundance of cheap labor, the Chinese T&C sector has also benefited through its lower dependence on imported intermediate inputs. Chinese dependence on imported raw materials for its T&C products has been one of the lowest in the world—in 2001, only 6 percent of is clothing and 8 percent of its textiles inputs were procured from outside (see Table 3.10 and Figure 3.8). This means that China enjoys the advantage of procuring most of its clothing and textile inputs directly from domestic sources which, in turn, helps the country to meet shorter turnaround delivery requirements (Audet, 2004, 12). Many developing country competitors of China, such as Bangladesh, Cambodia, and Vietnam, on the other hand, depend heavily on imported inputs. Moreover, as

Table 3.10 Imported value addition in clothing manufacturing in selected countries, 2001

Country	*Imported value addition in clothing (in %)*	*Import value addition in textiles (in %)*
Canada	19.8	24.2
United States	13.8	9.7
France	24.3	22.0
Italy	13.3	35.0
Japan	7.8	11.8
Hong Kong-SAR	13.0	5.8
South Korea	15.9	20.0
Taiwan	10.9	10.2
China	5.7	8.1
India	1.8	4.0
Vietnam	28.9	34.3
Czech Republic	28.9	35.1
Morocco	37.9	44.3

Source: Author's compilation from Nordas (2004).

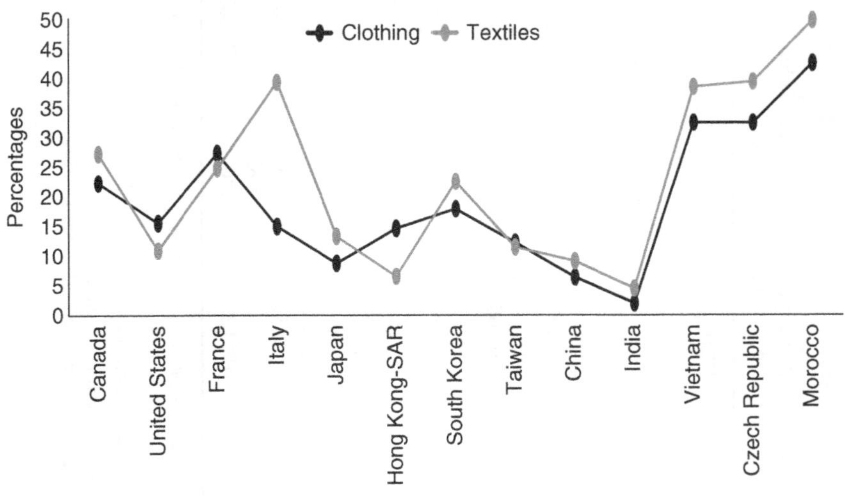

Figure 3.8 Imported value addition in textiles and clothing, 2001.

Table 3.11 Clothing exports and the shares of clothing exports in the merchandise trade in selected developing countries, 1990 to 2013 (in US$ millions, and shares in percentages)

Country	*1990*	*2000*	*2005*	*2010*	*2013*	*Share in 2005 (in economy's total merchandise exports)*	*Share in 2010 (in economy's total merchandise exports)*	*Share in 2013 (in economy's total merchandise exports)*
Bangladesh[a]	643	5,067	6,418	15,660	23,501	74.1	81.6	80.7
Cambodia[b]	45 (1998)	970	2,199	3,041	5,095	71.5	60.5	54.8
China[c]	9,669	36,071	74,163	129,838	177,435	9.7	8.2	8.0
India	2,530	5,965	8,290	11,246	168,43	8.8	5.2	5.4
Indonesia	1,646	4,734	5,106	6,820	7,692	5.7	4.3	4.2
Malaysia[c]	1,315	2,257	2,479	3,880	4,586	1.8	2.0	2.0
Mexico[c]	587	8,631	7,271	4,363	4,530	3.4	1.5	1.2
Pakistan	1,014	2,144	3,604	3,930	4,549	22.5	18.4	18.1
Sri Lanka[b]	638	2,812	2,877	3,491	4,511	45.3	41.1	45.3
Thailand	2,817	3,759	4,085	4,300	4,100	3.7	2.2	1.8
Turkey	3,331	6,533	11,818	12,760	15,408	16.1	11.2	10.2
Vietnam[b,c]	–	1,821	4,805	10,839	17,230	14.4	15.0	13.0
World	108,129	19,7635	275,639	315,464	460,268	2.7	2.4	2.5

Source: Author's calculation from WTO statistics database and *International Trade Statistics*.

Notes

a Figures refer to fiscal year.

b Includes secretariat estimates.

c Includes significant exports from processing zones.

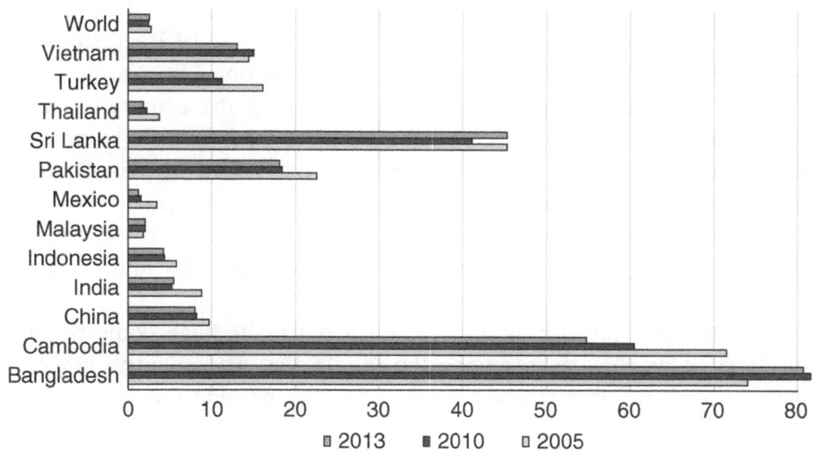

Figure 3.9 Shares of clothing exports of selected countries in world merchandise trade, 2005 to 2013.

explained below, the modernization of the Chinese T&C sector has also enabled it to successfully venture into vertical integration, especially in one of the fastest growing segments of textiles known as technical textiles.

The share of T&C trade in the overall share of merchandise exports of China, however, appears to be declining. As Table 3.11 indicates, in 2005, T&C exports had a 9.7 percent share in Chinese merchandise exports, which fell to 8 percent in 2013 (also see Figure 3.9). During the same period, the share of Chinese textiles exports in its merchandise exports also fell—from 5.4 percent to 4.8 percent (see Table 3.12). But China still remains the largest employer in T&C products in the world—in 2010, China employed 11.2 million workers in its T&C sector—6.7 million in textiles and 4.5 million in clothing—and over 80 percent of the workers were females (see Table 3.13).[28]

The case of India

India, another country with more than one billion people and thus an abundance of cheap labor, on the other hand, had a dominant textile industry for a long time. Like China, India's T&C sector also has very minimal dependence on imported intermediate inputs, and is largely shaped by the state. The liberalization of Indian textiles and the apparel industry, and thus integration with global markets, began in the 1980s, but it was ushered in by domestic policies, not driven by foreign investment or preferential market access (Tewari, 2006). In addition, India's T&C sector was largely self-dependent. In 2001, for example, the country's clothing sector's dependence on foreign inputs was less than 2 percent when the textiles sector's dependence was 4 percent (see Table 3.10).

Historically, T&C products played a significant role in India's exports basket. Between 1985 and 1990, the country's apparel exports increased from $914 million to $2.5 billion—an annual compound growth rate of 19.3 percent, when textiles exports increased from $1.0 billion to $2.2 billion (Tewari, 2006). In 2003, India's T&C sector accounted for 23 percent of the country's exports basket, employed 35 million workers (10 percent of the country's workforce), and accounted for 14 percent of the country's value added in manufacturing (Ananthakrisnan and Jain-Chandra, 2005). Much of the employment, however, was in informal sectors. According to the ILO (2013), in 2009, formal employment in the Indian T&C sector totaled 2.2 million workers—1.4 million in textiles and 863,000 in clothing (see Table 3.13).[29]

Traditionally, the Indian clothing sector catered to its huge domestic market—in 1995, it was not even among the top 15 list. The country, however, joined the global export markets robustly after the phasing out of the MFA restrictions began in 1995. By 2000, it emerged as one of the topmost exporters of clothing in the world with a global share of 2.8 percent, which increased to 3.7 percent in 2013. India, however, was one of the top 15 textiles exporters in 1995 with a share of 2.8 percent, which more than doubled by 2013, increasing to 6.2 percent. In 2013, India's T&C exports reached a total of $36 billion ($19 billion in textiles and $17 billion in clothing)—making it the sixth largest in the clothing trade and the third largest in textiles trade in the world (see Tables 3.6 and 3.8). In addition, available research suggests that India has some valuable assets to succeed in the liberalized T&C trade, such as the availability of several natural fibers domestically, clusters of expertise in man-made fibers, low manufacturing wages, an increasingly affluent and skilled middle class, a large domestic market, and an ability to manufacture a wide range of products (Audet, 2004; USITC, 2004).

Based on such assessments, many analysts predicted that with the phasing out of the MFA restrictions, both China and India would emerge as dominate figures of world trade in the T&C sector (Nordas, 2004, 34). The prediction, however, has not come true for India. Between 2005 and 2013, the share of Indian clothing exports, in its overall merchandise exports, fell from 8.8 percent to 5.4 percent (see Table 3.11), and, during the same period, its share of textiles exports in its merchandise trade fell from 8.4 percent to 6 percent (see Table 3.12 and Figure 3.10). India's failure to widen its share in quota- and restriction-free T&C trade has, however, been attributed to its domestic policy constraints and business environment, such as lack of labor market flexibility, obstacles to achieving economies of scale, a long turnaround time for delivery, high transaction costs, and poor infrastructures (Abras, 2012).

The case of Bangladesh

Bangladesh, one of the least developed and populous countries in the world, is now second only to China in single country global clothing exports. The country stepped into export-oriented clothing production in the late 1970s and early

Table 3.12 Values of selected textiles exporters in the world trade and the share of textiles in merchandise trade, 1990 to 2013 (in US$ millions, and percentages)

Country	*1990*	*2000*	*2010*	*2013*	*Share in economy's total merchandise exports (2005)*	*Share in economy's total merchandise exports (2010)*	*Share in economy's total merchandise exports (2013)*
Canada	687	2,204	1,907	1,906	0.7	0.5	0.4
China[a]	7,219	16,135	76,900	106,578	5.4	4.9	4.8
EU (27)	–	56,737	67,108	72,150	1.7	1.3	1.2
India[b]	2,180	5,593	12,872	18,907	8.4	6.0	6.0
Hong Kong[a,b]	8,213	13,441	11,307	10,718	4.7	2.8	2.0
Indonesia	1,241	3,505	4,150	4,632	3.9	2.6	2.5
Japan	5,871	7,023	7,086	6,841	1.2	0.9	1.0
Mexico[a]	713	2,571	1,928	2,446	1.0	0.6	0.6
Pakistan	2,663	4,532	7,848	9,341	44.2	36.7	37.1
South Korea	6,076	12,710	10,968	12,043	3.7	2.4	2.2
Taiwan	6,128	11,891	9,753	10,246	4.9	3.6	3.4
Thailand	928	1,958	3,761	3,874	2.5	1.9	1.7
Turkey	1,440	3,672	8,964	12,157	9.6	7.9	8.0
UAE[b,c]	6	1,289	1,812	2,736	1.4	1.0	0.7
United States	5,039	10,952	12,168	13,924	1.4	1.0	0.9
Vietnam[b]	–	299	2,660	4,786	2.2	3.7	3.6
World	104,354	154,860	250,652	305,898	2.0	1.7	1.7

Source: Author's calculation from WTO statistics database and *International Trade Statistics.*

Notes

a Includes significant shipments through processing zones.

b Includes Secretariat estimates.

c Imports are valued f.o.b.

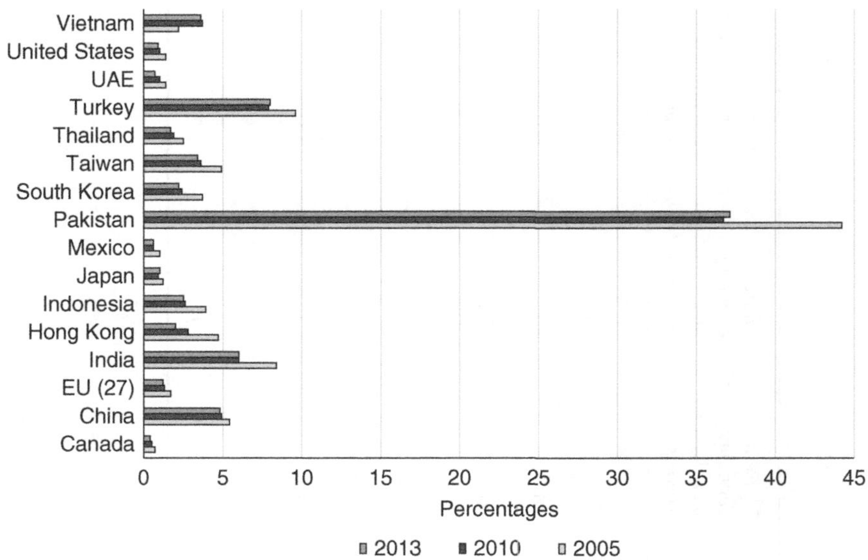

Figure 3.10 Shares of textiles exports in merchandise trade in selected countries, 2005 and 2013.

1980s largely as a part of the third migration of clothing manufacturing when some East Asian countries began investing in the country in search of quota hopping and low-cost labor. Over the course of the past three decades, foreign investment, the MFA quota system, preferential access to the EU, supportive governmental policies, and the emergence of a vibrant local entrepreneurial class played a central role in transforming the country into a successful competitor in the global clothing sector (Staritz, 2011; Dowlah, 1998).

Bangladeshi factories follow what is called a full-package model—industrial subcontractors supply products according to designs specified by buyers and the products are sold under the buyers' brand name, which allows greater domestic value addition than assembly-type production, but less than an OBM-type production system. The sector is, however, owned overwhelmingly by the domestic private sector. During 1983 and 2006, aggregate FDI in the T&C sector (directed primarily to backward linkages) was only about $500 million, and, out of more than 4,000 T&C firms in the country, only 83 were wholly or partially owned foreign firms, and all were located in the EPZs (Dunn, 2008).

Between 1995 and 2013, the country's clothing exports expanded 12 times—increasing from $2 billion to $24 billion (see Table 3.6). In 2005, clothing exports accounted for 74 percent of the country's merchandise trade, but the share exceeded 80 percent by 2010 (see Table 3.11 and Figure 3.10). In 2011, the T&C sector received another shot in the arm with graduation to GSP+ status in the EU market, which relaxed the rules-of-origin requirement to single

Table 3.13 Formal employment in textiles and clothing industries in selected countries, 2006 to 2010

Country	*Employment in textiles industry (thousands)*	*Employment in clothing industry (thousands)*	*Total employment in T&C (thousands)*	*Country*	*Employment in textiles industry (thousands)*	*Employment in clothing industry (thousands)*	*Total employment in T&C (thousands)*
China (2010)	6,700	4,501	11,201	Taiwan (2006)	114	87	201
India (2009)	1,379	863	2,242	Romania (2010)	28	155	183
Vietnam (2010)	196	844	1,040	South Korea (2008)	88	77	165
Brazil (2010)	308	671	980	Morocco (2010)	35	130	165
Indonesia (2009)	498	465	963	Poland (2009)	50	109	159
Thailand (2006)	312	346	658	Portugal (2009)	48	98	144
Turkey (2009)	266	330	596	Philippines (2008)	17	106	123
Pakistan (2006)	439	62	501	Germany (2009)	77	44	121
United States (2008)	291	130	421	Bulgaria (2010)	12	100	112
Italy (2008–2009)	183	199	382	Spain (2009)	44	62	106
Sri Lanka (2010)	35	260	295	France (2009)	49	49	98
Japan (2010)	138	138	276	Malaysia (2010)	30	55	85
Mexico (2010)	84	163	247	United Kingdom (2009)	55	28	83
Egypt (2010)	131	103	234	Jordan (2010)	38	34	37

Source: Author's compilation from ILO (2013).

Note
Year in parentheses refers to the year of data.

transformation (Abras, 2012, 97). In 2013, the country's T&C sector employed about four million mostly female workers, and accounted for 45 percent of the country's industrial workforce. The industry's contribution to GDP, however, is very small, only about 5 percent, due to the fact that the industry is heavily dependent on imported raw materials and inputs. The dependence on imported inputs has, however, declined slightly over the years. In 1991, for example, the country's import value of textiles was about 60 percent of its export value of clothing, but this figure declined to about 40 percent in 2001, indicating the development of backward linkages in the country (Nordas, 2004, 6).

But the progress in backward linkages has not been robust; about 75 percent of fabrics used in woven textiles are still imported. Progress in backward linkages is hindered by the fact that investment in textiles is more capital intensive than in clothing. In addition, some regional countries such as India, China, and Pakistan are highly competitive in fabrics production with regard to price, quality, lead times, and availability, casting doubts about the cost-effectiveness of producing yarns and woven fabrics locally (Staritz, 2011, 146; Abras, 2012). Moreover, the country's clothing exports are still highly concentrated in a few products, and clothing exports are also concentrated in a few destinations, such as the US, the EU, and Japan. The industry also lacks diversification into higher value-added products. Moreover, the country's labor costs may be lower, but its labor productivity is among the lowest as well (World Bank, 2005).

The case of Cambodia

Cambodia, another LDC, stepped into the clothing exports business in the 1990s. Like Bangladesh, the clothing sector in Cambodia also resulted from the search for MFA quota hopping, low-cost labor, and preferential market access by East Asian investors. But, unlike Bangladesh, most of the garments units of Cambodia, almost 95 percent, are owned by foreign investors mainly from Taiwan, Hong Kong-SAR, and mainland China. Most of its garments factories are also located in EPZs in the coastal region of Silhanoukville and the Mekong corridor, providing links to southern China and the newly industrialized economies of East Asia.

Although a latecomer, the country made spectacular progress by emerging as the twelfth largest clothing exporter in the world by 2012. In 2013, it moved further up the ladder, occupying the tenth slot among the top 15 clothing exporters in the world with over $5 billion in export revenues (see Table 3.6). In 1995, the country's clothing exports fetched less than $50 million. Thus, Cambodia's clothing exports grew 100 times in less than 18 years. In 2008, the country's booming garment industry accounted for more than 80 percent of its manufacturing exports, while providing about 65 percent of formal employment, and contributing to 10 to 12 percent of its GDP (Keane and Velde, 2008, 36–37).

Several factors contributed to such an exceptional feat. First of all, when the clothing sector started, Cambodia faced no quota restrictions to the EU and the US, as it was not part of the MFA regime. Then, in 1996, the country was granted MFN status by the WTO. In 1999, the country received quota-free and duty-free access to the EU, which continued under the Everything-But-Arms initiative beyond 2001. In 1989, the country's exports received another major shot in the arm under the United States–Cambodia Bilateral Textiles Agreement, which granted a very generous fixed quota for the 12 largest categories of clothing exports from Cambodia to the US market (Staritz, 2011, 105). As most of its exports were directed to the US and the EU—the world's largest markets where it enjoyed almost totally quota-free and duty-free access—the country's clothing exports grew in leaps and bounds.

Everything about Cambodia's clothing industry is not, however, so glossy. Aside from almost complete foreign ownership of its factories, the country follows an assembly-type production system, which leaves little for domestic value addition. Moreover, Cambodia's clothing production is overwhelmingly—over 70 percent—concentrated in what is called cut-make-trim (CMT), a downstream segment of the clothing value chain, which barely contributes to generate domestic value additions, skills development, productivity gains, or technological advancement. Thus, the country's clothing industry is almost entirely—over 90 percent—dependent on imported yarn, fabrics, and accessories (see Figure 3.9). The country is a net importer of textiles—there is almost no backward linkage in the country. In addition, the country lacks diversification in terms of export products and destinations—outputs are concentrated in only a few clothing lines, and the exports market is overwhelmingly concentrated on the EU and the US only.[30]

The case of Sub-Saharan Africa

Among the developing country losers of the MFA phase-out are many Sub-Saharan African (SSA) countries, such as Kenya, Lesotho, Madagascar, Swaziland, and Mauritius. Many of these countries developed an export-oriented clothing sector in the 1970s through the 1990s with heavy investments from East Asian investors who sought to take advantage of cheap labor, unused quotas under the MFA regimes, and preferential access of these countries to Western markets. Most of the clothing exporting firms in the SSA countries are, however, foreign owned, and nearly all FDI to these countries' clothing sector came from greater China—mainland China, Hong Kong-SAR, and Taiwan (Fontaine, 2008; Morris, 2006).

Among the SSA countries, Mauritius emerged as a successful T&C exporter in the 1980s, and was also able to move into increasing value-added clothing activities, benefiting especially from preferential access to the European markets (Gereffi, 2002). In the 1990s, the lower end T&C productions of Mauritius relocated to neighboring Madagascar, and soon other SSA countries, such as Kenya, Swaziland, and Lesotho, also established EPZs to attract FDI in the sector. A further impetus to clothing industries of the SSA countries came from the African Growth and Opportunity Act (AGOA) of the US during 2000/2001.

Clothing exports of the SSA countries grew exceptionally, even up until the fag-end of the MFA regime. Between the 1995 and 2004 period, clothing exports of SSA countries more than doubled—jumping from $1.6 billion to $3.2 billion. But with the phasing out of the MFA regime by 2004, SSA exports began to fall gradually—in 2008, earnings fell to $2.7 billion.[31] Several studies suggest that with the phasing out of the MFA quota restrictions, many of the East Asian investors moved their businesses back to their home countries, and increased competition from the MFA phase-out not only reduced orders but also decreased prices for SSA exports, resulting in a precipitous decline in production, exports, and employment in these countries (Fontaine, 2007; Morris, 2006; Kaplinsky *et al.*, 2007).

Like Bangladesh and Cambodia, lack of diversification in exports products and destinations is a serious problem for SSA countries as well. In 2008, for example, more than 96 percent of exports from Lesotho, Swaziland, and Kenya were destined for the US market, and Madagascar and Mauritius had over 96 percent of their exports directed to the US and the EU. At the same time, their exports are concentrated in a few product lines. The clothing sector of SSA countries depends almost entirely on imported yarn, fabrics, and accessories, which makes it harder for these countries to meet rules-of-origin requirements of preference-granting countries. Moreover, labor may be cheap, but they are less productive (Staritz, 2011, 66–83; Brenton and Hoppe, 2006).

Other countries which also persistently lost out on clothing exports due to the phasing out of the MFA regimes include Canada, and some South American countries, such as Guatemala and the Dominican Republic, and Mexico. In the textiles sector, some traditional textile exporting nations, such as Belgium, France, Germany, Japan, Taiwan, Turkey, Mexico, and Canada, saw significant declines in their exports values since 1995, and especially since 2005.

Nexus between the low cost of labor and low productivity

Understandably, lower wages has been one of the main driving forces for migration of T&C manufacturing toward low-income developing countries for many decades. As Table 3.14 indicates, per-hour labor cost in many developing countries is still only a tiny fraction of the wage in advanced countries. In fact, it is still less than a dollar in scores of low-income and middle-income developing countries, such as Bangladesh, Cambodia, Vietnam, Indonesia, Sri Lanka, India, Pakistan, Vietnam, Madagascar, Swaziland, Kenya, and Lesotho (see Figure 3.11). Low-income developing countries and LDCs thus still provide greater cost advantages in T&C production, especially in the labor-intensive clothing sector. At the same time, however, it is equally important to note that value added per worker in T&C production is the lowest in the LDCs ($536.4), followed by low-income developing countries ($1,749), lower middle-income developing countries ($2,791.1) and upper middle-income developing countries ($1,846.7) (Keane and Velde, 2008, 9).

Table 3.14 Average clothing manufacturing wages per hour in selected countries

Country	*Rate per hour (US$)*[a]	*Country*	*Rate per hour (US$)*[a]	*Country*	*Rate per hour (US$)*[b]
Bangladesh	0.31	Kenya[c]	0.56	Germany	25.80
Cambodia	0.33	Swaziland[c]	0.86	Canada	24.23
Madagascar[c]	0.33	Mauritius[c]	1.25	France	21.06
Vietnam	0.38	South Africa[c]	1.38	Japan	18.32
Indonesia	0.44	China	1.44	United Kingdom	21.16
Sri Lanka	0.46	Mexico	2.17	United States	23.32
Lesotho[c]	0.5	Turkey	2.44	Australia	28.55
India	0.51			Switzerland	34.29
Pakistan	0.56			Denmark	34.78

Source: Author's compilation from Fontaine (2008); ILO (2013).

Notes

a Hourly wages for garment workers in developing countries in 2007.

b Hourly direct pay for manufacturing in 2010 in industrialized countries taken from ILO (2013).

c Taken from Fontaine (2008).

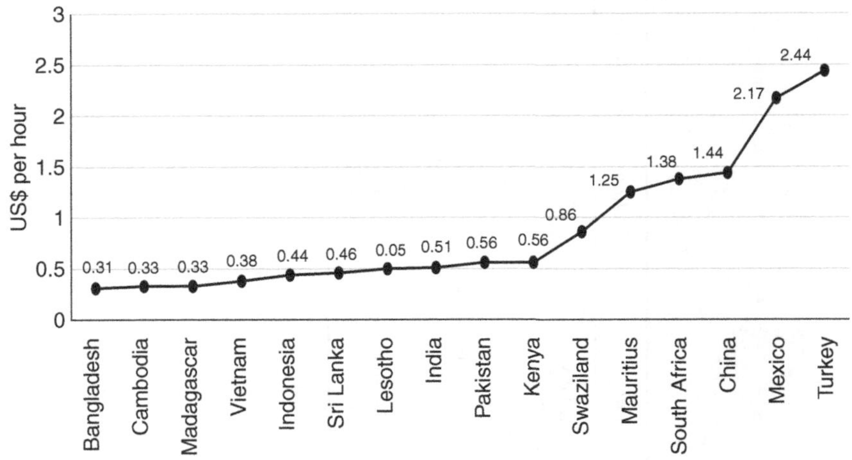

Figure 3.11 Average hourly wages of clothing workers in selected countries.

Erosion of preferences

Second, the phenomenal success of many developing countries in T&C exports also hinges on preferential market access granted by the US and the EU—the largest destination of T&C exports in the world. Both the US and the EU offer non-reciprocal concessions to developing countries under the Generalized System of Preferences (GSP) schemes granted under the Special and Differential Treatment (SDT) provisions of the GATT. The GSP schemes of both the US and the EU—which grant tariff preference to imports from developing countries on a non-reciprocal basis—have undergone many extensions and modifications since their introduction in the early 1970s (Dowlah, 2008; UNCTAD, 2003, 8–41).

Since 2001, however, the EU has provided something called 'Everything but Arms' (EBA), which grants duty-free and quota-free access to all products from all LDCs, with the exception, of course, of arms and ammunition, and some 'sensitive' agricultural products. The US also provides non-reciprocal concessions under a similar program called the African Growth and Opportunity Act (AGOA). Passed in 2000 and extended up until 2015, this law provides expanded GSP benefits to 37 of the 48 countries of Sub-Saharan Africa (SSA), including limited duty and quota-free access to the US market for textiles fabricated with the US and third country yarn and fabrics.[32] In 2003 Canada granted duty-free and quota-free entry to all textiles and clothing imports originating from the LDCs that met the 25 percent content requirement originating from any LDCs, GSP beneficiaries, or Canada. Similarly, Japan, the third largest clothing importer in the world, also grants duty-free access to clothing from LDCs, but subject to rules-of-origin requirements.

Consolidations and differentiations

Another consequence of the post-ATC wave of trade/consolidation has been that production plants both from low-cost, low-productivity, and high-cost countries have been relocating to the most productive and relatively low-cost countries (Kowalski and Molnar, 2009). Under the quota-driven system of the MFA, FDI outfows in T&C were directed to countries with lower productivity but under-used quotas, or to countries not subject to quotas, which resulted in dispersed and inefficient production of T&C around the globe. The removal of the quota system has facilitated efficiency-enhancing consolidation in the sector as declining trade and investment barriers, along with decreasing transportation and communication costs, led to further slicing of the value-added chain (Jones and Kierzkowski, 1990).

The liberalization of trade restrictions in the T&C has also resulted in both vertical and horizontal strategic adjustments in T&C value chains in the advanced countries. According to the OECD (2009), productivity increases in developed countries were accompanied by significant reductions in numbers of T&C firms, numbers of workers per firm, and to some extent revenue per firm, suggesting vertical differentiation, a move toward smaller scale and higher quality production. For example, nearly 80 percent of other competitors' products in the US markets are less than a quarter of the Italian unit price in a limited number of product categories in which Italy specializes strategically.

Technical textiles

One of the offshoots of such vertical integration involves a new direction of non-clothing applications of textiles, called technical textiles. Such textiles are differentiated by their technical and performance properties rather than by their aesthetic or decorative characteristics, and they are used for diverse purposes in furniture, automotive, health and hygiene, transportation, construction, environment, and so on. As the process involves complex technical textiles machinery as well as physical human capital, technical textiles are mostly concentrated in developed countries (OECD, 2004). However, it appears that some developing countries, especially China, Turkey, India, and Pakistan, have been acquiring advanced textiles technologies for moving into such vertical differentiation (Kowalski and Molnar, 2009). According to Hayashi (2007, 8), almost 60 percent of technical textile production has already shifted to the developing countries. As Table 3.15 shows, global exports of technical textiles increased from $70 billion in 2000 to $92 billion in 2007: more than 30 percent in three years. What is still more remarkable is that while China has succeeded in increasing its share in global technical textiles exports three times between 2000 and 2007, the shares of Taiwan, South Korea, the US, Japan, and France have declined. While Italy retained its share at 6 percent in both years, Germany succeeded in increasing its share slightly, from 8 percent in 2000 to 9 percent in 2007 (see Figure 3.12).

Table 3.15 Top 10 exporters of technical textiles products in the world, 2000 and 2007

Country	*Values (in billion US$)*		*Share in all countries' exports (%)*	
	2000	*2007*	*2000*	*2007*
All countries	69.9	91.9	100	100
China	4.4	17	6	18
Germany	5.4	8.0	8	9
Taiwan	7.6	6.6	11	7
South Korea	8.0	5.6	12	6
United States	5.3	5.3	8	6
Italy	4.2	5.2	6	6
Japan	4.7	4.6	7	5
Hong Kong, China	4.1	3.0	6	3
Indonesia	2.4	3.0	3	3
France	2.7	2.7	4	3

Source: Kowalski and Molnar (2009).

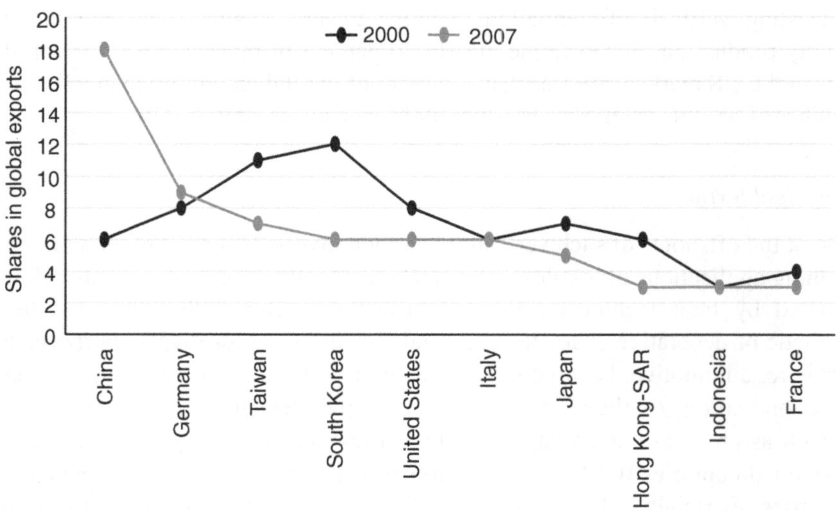

Figure 3.12 Top technical textiles exporters in the world, 2000 and 2007.

It also appears that as a result of enhanced competition in major markets, many producers are now concentrating on horizontal differentiation—producing fewer product categories in order to increase their shares in major markets. Besides the efficiency gains, such a strategy also allows for better exploitation of economies of scale, thereby benefiting both importers and producers. Producers from two countries with very similar structures of export commodities, for instance, can differentiate their products by quality or, if the quality of their products is also similar, they can enter into price competition in global markets.[33]

They can also geographically slice markets. For example, in the trading of clothing products (HS Chapters 60–63), Bangladesh has reduced its overlap with other countries except Italy and Turkey between 1990 and 2007. China, on the contrary, exports increasingly similar products to the EU countries. India has reduced its overlap with China over the past 15 years and increased it with Italy and the Netherlands. Thus, lower cost producers try to avoid competition with each other and, when they can, move into product categories supplied by higher cost exporters.

Changing patterns of employment

As the discussion above suggests, production and trade structures of the T&C sector have undergone radical changes since the transition of the MFA phase-out began in 1995. A plethora of factors, such as the phasing out of quotas, cost-competitiveness, preferential market access, upgrading of production along the global value chains, vertical and horizontal differentiations, and diversifications of products and exports markets shaped such a massive transformation. The resultant transformation in respect of employment in the T&C sector has been quite sweeping as well. Broadly, employment soared in many developing countries, while it fell dramatically in many developed and semi-developed countries.

During the initial onslaught of the MFA phase-out between 1995 and 1998, the share of the Americas in the total world employment in clothing fell from 17.6 percent to 11.4 percent, while that of Europe declined from 31.3 percent to 21.3 percent, when Asia's share in employment increased from 45 percent to 62 percent (ILO, 2000). Between 1995 and 2000, overall employment in the T&C sector declined from 1.5 million to 1.1 million in the US (37 percent), from 361,000 to 258,000 in the UK (40 percent), from 271,000 to 214,000 in France (27 percent), from 383,000 to 339,000 in Germany (13 percent), from 596,000 to 558,000 in Italy (6 percent), and from 146,000 to 139,000 in Canada (5 percent) (ILO, 2005; Nordas, 2004, 10).

In the next phase of the MFA phase-out, during the 2000 to 2006 period, T&C sector job losses in the OECD countries ranged between 12 percent and 49 percent—50 percent in Ireland, 44 percent in the US, 41 percent in Hungary, 37 percent in France, 36 percent in South Korea, 35 percent in Austria, 34 percent in the Czech Republic, and around 30 percent in the Netherlands, Norway, Germany, and Australia (see Table 3.16).

Between 1995 and 2009, the T&C sector's employment in Germany fell from 383,000 to 121,000, by about 70 percent; in Italy from 596,000 to 382,000, by about 46 percent; in Spain from 225,000 to 106,000, by more than 50 percent; in France, from 27,000 to 98,000, by more than 65 percent; in the UK from 361,000 to 83,000, by about 80 percent; in Portugal from 242,000 to 146,000, by about 40 percent.[34]

The loss of T&C sector jobs has been spectacular in the US as well. From 1.6 million in 1995, employment in the US T&C sector fell to 1.3 million in 2005—about 300,000 jobs lost, coinciding with the phasing out of the MFA restrictions.

Table 3.16 Employment in textiles and clothing industries in selected OECD countries, 2000 to 2006

Country	*2000*	*2001*	*2002*	*2003*	*2004*	*2005*	*2006*	*% of total manufacturing employment in 2006*[a]	*% reduction 2000–2006*[a]	*% reduction in total manufacturing, 2000–2006*
Australia	77,761	69,902	68,998	62,138	55,315	54,957	–	–	–29.33	–4.48
Austria	35,634	33,718	31,392	28,839	25,824	24,142	23,335	3.70	–34.51	–4.56
Belgium	54,233	52,388	48,896	45,963	43,269	40,692	38,635	6.49	–28.76	–9.33
Canada	142,681	145,982	139,490	125,089	117,107	111,364	105,326	5.00	–26.18	–4.21
Czech Republic	130,063	124,744	118,743	107,485	102,829	93,957	85,994	6.19	–33.88	1.65
Denmark	13,199	12,485	11,459	10,594	9,607	8,912	–	2.32	–32.48	–13.37
Finland	16,800	16,500	16,000	14,700	13,500	12,900	12,300	2.81	–26.79	–4.98
France	216,162	205,123	190,180	173,480	153,432	137,314	–	4.07	–36.48	–8.58
Germany	247,000	238,000	217,000	197,000	187,000	175,000	–	2.33	–29.15	–8.29
Hungary	130,342	125,232	117,873	111,343	98,673	83,914	77,217	8.96	–40.76	–7.95
Ireland	12,683	11,889	10,807	9,333	7,890	7,202	6,422	2.38	–49.37	–9.82
Italy	661,000	662,200	663,000	660,200	637,900	600,800	582,100	11.64	–11.94	–0.06
Korea	622,623	580,181	547,176	489,916	440,899	397,283	–	9.38	–36.19	–2.93
Luxembourg	700,800	1,200	1,200	1,200	1,300	1,400	–	4.15	100.00	1.81
Netherlands	28,756	28,030	26,035	24,120	21,640	20,430	19,963	2.18	–30.58	–11.76
Norway	7,500	6,600	6,000	7,005	3,005	2,005	200	1.95	–30.67	–10.74
Portugal	275,128	268,564	261,828	247,837	239,198	225,171	–	24.02	–18.16	–10.41
Spain	275,900	272,000	255,700	245, 00	229,200	226,300	205,400	6.61	–25.55	4.65
Sweden	12,923	12,554	12,277	11,446	10,636	9,900	–	1.38	–23.39	–9.45
United States	1,151,957	1,015,488	907,617	812,706	743,471	689,605	646,624	4.16	–43.87	–17.79

Source: Kowalski and Molnar (2009, 49).

Note

a For countries for which 2006 data were not available the figures refer to 2005.

But job losses in the sector have accelerated further since 2005. In 2006, the T&C sector's employment in the US fell to 646,000, which declined further to 373,000 in 2012. Thus, between 1995 and 2012, the T&C sector in the US shredded about 1.3 million jobs. The US Bureau of Labor Statistics projects that the country's apparel manufacturing industry will shred another 85,800 jobs (or 50 percent of all jobs in the industry) by 2022 when it will employ only 62,300 people.[35]

Several studies, however, suggest that this trend of job losses in developed countries cannot be directly attributed to the phasing out of the MFA restrictions in T&C trade. According to these studies: (1) the trend of job losses in the T&C sector in developed countries has been fully in place since the early 1990s, even before the MFA phasing out of quota restrictions began; (2) although job losses had been much deeper in the T&C sector, most of the developed countries also experienced significant job losses in the manufacturing sector as a whole; and (3) some of the job losses may be attributed to the efforts of many low-cost OECD producers to boost productivity, reduce firm sizes, and focus on higher value and niche products (see Table 3.16; Kowalski and Molnar, 2009; Martin, 2007). According to Murray (1995), during the period 1973 to 1995, the US T&C sector lost 30 percent of their combined workforce due mainly to gains in productivity and increased competition from abroad.

The T&C sector employment, on the other hand, surged in less developed countries since the phasing out of the MFA regime began. In China, for example, employment in the Chinese T&C sector increased from 14.7 million to 19 million during the 1995 to 2004 period (ILO, 2005; UNCTAD, 2013). Between 2001 and 2009, employment in the T&C sector surged from 1.6 million to 3.1 million in Bangladesh, almost double; from 1.3 million to 2.5 million in Pakistan, again almost double; from 34 million to 35 million in India, from 355,000 to 937,000 in Vietnam, an increase of 2.6 times; and from 187,000 to 325,000 in Cambodia, an increase of more than 70 percent (Savchenko and Lopez-Acevedo, 2012, 206). In 2010, formal employment in the T&C sector was 11.2 million in China, 2.2 million in India, 1.1 million in Vietnam, and 501,000 in Pakistan (see Table 3.13).

While the phasing out of the MFA restrictions in general resulted in significant growth of production and employment in T&C in many developing countries, some of these countries were also adversely affected. For example, foreign investors in ready-made garments factories in Fiji, the Maldives, Mongolia, and Nepal shifted their production elsewhere following the expiry of the quota system, resulting in huge job losses in the sector (Adhikari and Yamamato, 2007, 189). Similarly, many Sub-Saharan countries like Swaziland, Lesotho, and Madagascar lost production, exports, and employment when East Asian investors moved back to their home countries following the expiry of the MFA regime (Kaplinsky *et al.*, 2007). Similarly, Mexico and some Latin American and Caribbean countries, such as Guatemala and the Dominican Republic, experienced significant declines in their production and employment in the T&C sector due to huge losses in exports to the US. At the same time, several East Asian

Tigers—especially Hong Kong-SAR, South Korea, and Taiwan—lost huge production and employment in T&C due mainly to the upgrading of their T&C production.

Changing dynamics of global supply and demand

As the discussion above suggests, the transformation in global T&C trade, production, and employment has been quite dramatic in the post-ATC world. Liberated from the world of quota restrictions, global buyers can now source their T&C products from any country in the world at any amount. At the same time, developing country T&C producers are confronting more intensified competition and price pressures from their peers now than ever before to capture global markets and upgrade their products through global value chains. In the context of the MFA phase-out, the evolving global T&C value chain thus faces two underlying structural changes: (1) asymmetric market and power relations within global clothing value chains; and (2) changing global supply and demand structures (Staritz, 2011, 26–40).

First, evolving asymmetric market and power relations. The clothing value chain is considered to be a classic example of a buyer-driven value chain because of its globally dispersed production networks, which are coordinated by lead firms who control design, marketing, and branding at the retail end, but generally do not get involved in production (Gereffi and Memedovic, 2003). Sourcing strategies and practices of the global buyers, often dubbed as sourcing geography, thus profoundly affect global clothing value chains in terms of market share and upgrading possibilities of globally dispersed T&C producers (Bair and Gereffi, 2003). In the post-MFA world, however, the sourcing strategies and practices, often described as 'supply chain rationalization,' appear to be playing more critical roles as global buyers have increasingly been consolidating supply chains of their products in order to reduce costs and lead times, and ensure greater control over product quality and labor and environmental compliance. Such strategies, in turn, have been resulting in greater consolidation of supply base and sourcing countries, with increasing concentration on core suppliers with large scales and production capacities (Palpacuer *et al.*, cited in Staritz, 2011, 38).

Second, there have been significant structural changes in the pattern of global demand and supply of the clothing sector since 2000. In the 1970s through the 1990s, the global clothing sector was characterized by the replacement of production in the developed countries, which propelled the production and exports of the developing countries. In the 2000s, however, demand for clothing began to stagnate in developed countries as import penetration levels in the world's largest clothing markets—the US, the EU, and Japan—reached between 80 and 100 percent. In addition, the future growth of clothing demand is likely to be slower in major developed country markets compared with fast-growing emerging economies, such as China, Eastern Europe, the Russian Federation, India, Turkey, and Brazil (Staritz, 2011, 38–40). At the same time, unlike in the past, in the post-MFA world, clothing supply has been concentrated in a few developing countries with large scale and production capacities, and overcapacity in high-income developing countries like China and India, which has been constraining market potentials for other less developed countries (Morris, 2006; Kaplnisky and Messner, 2008).

Trade patterns since 1995 also demonstrate a declining trend in T&C imports by leading importers. In 1995, for example, the share of top 15 clothing importers in the world was 93 percent of the global total, which declined to 79.4 percent in 2000. In 2005, however, the share returned to 93 percent, but then declined to 86.5 percent in 2010, and then fell to 76.4 percent in 2013 (see Table 3.17). At the same time, the shares of the largest clothing importers in the world—the US, the EU, and Japan—appear to be declining as well. As Table 3.17 indicates, the share of the EU in global clothing imports declined from 41.1 percent in 2000 to 37.9 percent in 2013, when the share of the US declined from 33 percent to 19 percent, and that of Japan declined from 9.7 percent to 7 percent. In 2000, the three largest clothing importers in the world had a combined share of 83.8 percent in the global total, which decreased to 63.8 percent by 2013—a hefty 25 percent decline in a matter of little more than a decade. At the same time, the shares in the global clothing imports market appear to be rising in countries like Australia, Canada, China, the Russian Federation, Saudi Arabia, South Korea, the United Arab Emirates, and Turkey. In 2000, these countries had a combined share of 5.8 percent in global clothing imports, which increased to 10.9 percent in 2013, thereby almost doubling during the period.

The EU and the US, however, still remain the major exporters of T&C products in the world. In 2013, the EU-28 was the second largest clothing exporter with 25.6 percent share in the global market, and the second largest textiles exporter with 23.6 percent share of the world market. Similarly, although the US had a smaller share in global clothing exports—1.3 percent in 2013—it was the fourth largest textiles exporter in the world with a 4.6 percent share in the global market. As Table 3.18 and Figure 3.13 indicate, the share of the less developed countries in global textiles imports has been on the rise for several decades now. In 2000, for example, the combined share of Bangladesh, Brazil, India, Indonesia, the Russian Federation, Turkey, and Vietnam was 3.8 percent of global textiles imports, which increased more than 330 percent to 12.8 percent in 2013. During the same period, the combined share of the EU, the US, and Japan declined from 20.6 percent to 17.4 percent of global textiles imports. During 1999 to 2006, more than 80 percent of T&C machinery imported by the low-cost T&C producers—close to 50 percent of all OECD countries' T&C machinery exports—originated from the OECD countries (Kowalski and Molnar, 2009). During the 1980s through the 1990s, four leading T&C machinery exporters—Germany, Italy, Japan, and Switzerland—maintained nearly two-thirds control over the global exports of competitive textile and clothing machinery (Audet, 2004, 13).

Table 3.17 Changing shares of leading clothing importers in the world, 1980 to 2013 (in US$ billions, and percentages)

	Value	*Share in world exports/imports*				*Annual percentage changes*			
	2013	*1980*	*1990*	*2000*	*2013*	*2005–2013*	*2011*	*2012*	*2013*
European Union (28)	182	–	–	41.1	37.9	4	15	–10	6
Extra-EU (28) imports	95	–	–	19.6	19.7	5	15	–11	5
United States	91	16.4	24.0	33.0	18.9	2	8	–1	3
Japan	34	3.6	7.8	9.7	7.0	5	23	3	–1
Hong Kong, China	16	–	–	–	–	–1	4	–5	1
Retained imports	…	0.9	0.7	0.9	…	…	…	…	…
Canada[c]	10	1.7	2.1	1.8	2.1	7	15	–2	6
Russian Federation[b,c]	9	–	–	0.1	1.9	33	23	0	–2
Korea, Republic of	8	0.0	0.1	0.6	1.6	13	38	3	20
Australia[c]	6	0.8	0.6	0.9	1.3	9	21	4	3
Switzerland	6	3.4	3.1	1.6	1.2	4	16	–7	3
China[a,d]	5	0.1	0.0	0.6	1.1	16	59	13	18
United Arab Emirates[b]	4	0.6	0.5	0.4	0.8	12	21	13	10
Saudi Arabia, Kingdom of[b]	3	1.6	0.7	0.4	0.7	11	28	5	14
Mexico[a,c]	3	0.3	0.5	1.8	0.7	3	20	8	9
Turkey	3	0.0	0.0	0.1	0.7	19	15	–18	17
Singapore	3	0.3	0.8	0.9	0.6	4	19	2	22
Above 15[d]	**368**	–	–	**93.1**	**76.4**	–	–	–	–

Source: *International Trade Statistics* (WTO, 2014).

Notes

a Includes significant shipments through processing zones.

b Includes WTO Secretariat estimates.

c Imports are valued f.o.b.

d Excludes retained imports of Hong Kong.

Table 3.18 Changing shares of leading textiles importers in the world, 1980 to 2013 (in US$ billions, and percentages)

	Value	*Share in world exports/imports*				*Annual percentage change*			
	2013	*1980*	*1990*	*2000*	*2013*	*2005–2013*	*2011*	*2012*	*2013*
EU-28									
Extra-EU (28) imports	29	–	–	9.9	9.0	4	17	–14	7
United States	27	4.5	6.2	9.8	8.4	2	8	2	4
China[a,d]	22	1.9	4.9	7.8	6.7	4	7	5	9
Vietnam[b]	11	...	...	0.8	3.3	15	24	4	17
Hong Kong, China[b]	10	–	–	–	–	–3	–2	–6	1
Retained imports[b]	0	3.7	3.8	0.9	0.0	–20	...	...	...
Japan	9	3.0	3.8	3.0	2.7	5	28	–2	–3
Turkey	7	0.1	0.5	1.3	2.1	5	16	–15	5
Bangladesh[b]	6	0.2	0.4	0.8	1.9	12	48	–12	6
Mexico[a]	6	0.2	0.9	3.6	1.9	0	14	2	3
Indonesia	6	0.4	0.7	0.8	1.8	29	34	–1	4
Korea, Republic of	5	0.7	1.8	2.1	1.6	5	17	–14	7
Canada	5	2.3	2.2	2.5	1.4	1	8	2	–1
Russian Federation[b]	4	–	–	0.4	1.3	17	25	5	–6
Brazil	4	0.1	0.2	0.6	1.3	18	14	0	–2
India[b]	4	0.1	0.2	0.4	1.1	8	22	–2	8
Above 15	**193**	–	–	**70.0**	**59.8**	–	–	–	–

Source: *International Trade Statistics 2014* (WTO, 2014).

Notes

a Includes significant shipments through processing zones.

b Includes Secretariat estimates.

c Mainly re-exports.

d In 2013, China reported imports of textiles amounting to $3.2 billion.

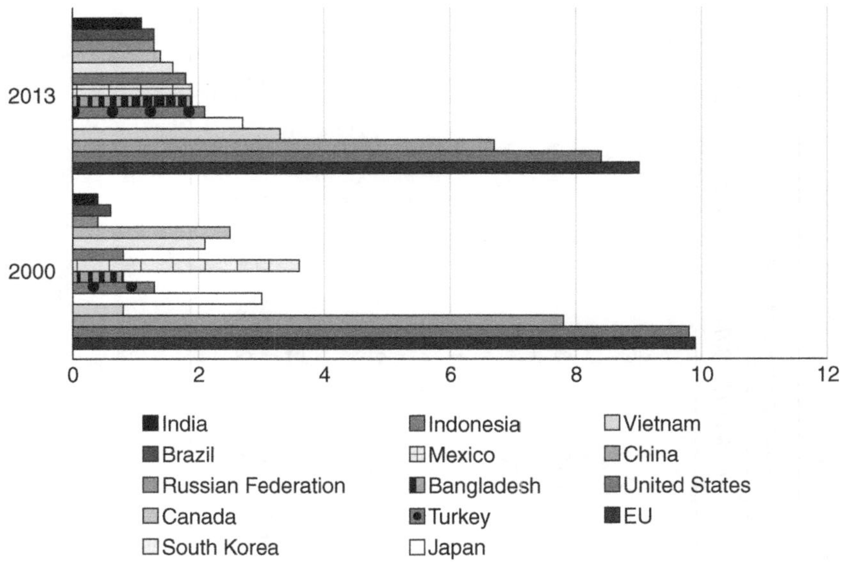

Figure 3.13 Changing shares of leading textile importers, 2000 and 2013.

Post-ATC issues and WTO negotiations

Although, with the complete phasing out of MFA restrictions by 2009, T&C trade is now as free as any other manufacturing activity in international trade under the strengthened GATT discipline, this sector continues to confront certain tariff and non-tariff barriers, which pose considerable challenges for many developing countries to tap their inherent and evolving potentials in this vital sector of their exports interests.

Tariff barriers

As discussed above, successive rounds of GATT negotiations over the decades succeeded in bringing down manufacturing tariffs in the developed countries to a historical low—the worldwide manufacturing tariff now averages at around 3 percent (Hayashi, 2007; Brenton and Hoppe, 2007). But the scenario is not the same for the recently integrated T&C sector. Compared with other manufacturing sectors, international trade in this sector, in which developing countries have major exports interests, still faces very high tariff rates, tariff peaks, and tariff escalations in developed country markets.

First of all, average MFN tariffs are still more than double in the T&C sector compared with other manufacturing sectors. While the average manufacturing MFN tariff in the OECD countries is 6.2 percent, average import tariffs on textiles and clothing are 9.4 percent and 16.1 percent, respectively (see Table 3.19

Table 3.19 Worldwide tariff averages applied to the textiles and clothing sector compared to tariff averages of the manufacturing sector

A Average import tariffs in manufactures, textiles, and clothing

Region/country	*Manufactures*	*Textiles*	*Clothing*
OECD countries	6.2	9.4	16.1
Japan	2.9	5.1	10.8
European Union	4.4	6.9	12.0
United States	4.0	7.8	12.3
Australia	5.4	9.9	23.6
Mexico	17.3	19.9	35.0
Developing countries	13.5	18.1	23.0
Hong Kong-SAR	0.0	0.0	0.0
Chile	0.0	0.0	0.0
Dominican Republic	14.6	5.7	19.9
China	9.6	20.1	23.5
Bangladesh	22.1	28.4	36.9
Morocco	28.2	35.9	49.8

B MFN tariff rates of selected clothing products in the United States (in %)

Cotton-based clothing	*MFN tariff rate*	*Synthetic-based clothing*	*MFN tariff rate*
Knitted men's shirts	19.7	Knitted women's skirts	14.9
Knitted shirts	16.5	Knitted sweaters	32.0
Woven men's trousers	10.3	Woven men's suites	27.3
Woven women's dresses	8.4	Woven women's dresses	16.0

Source: Author's compilation from European Community (2011, 39); Staritz (2011, 10).

and Figure 3.14). In the EU, MFN tariffs for manufactures average at 4.4 percent, but the averages for textiles and clothing stand at 6.9 percent and 12 percent, respectively. In Japan, manufacturing tariffs average at 2.9 percent, but average tariffs on textiles and clothing stand at 5.1 percent and 10.8 percent, respectively. In the US, average MFN tariffs on manufactures stand at 4 percent, but average tariffs in textiles and clothing are 6.9 percent and 12 percent, respectively. Table 3.19 also shows that in the US, MFN tariffs for key cotton-based clothing products range between 8.4 percent and 19.7 percent, while MFN tariffs for key synthetic-based clothing products range between 14.0 percent and 32.0 percent—much higher than overall average tariffs on textiles and clothing. Overall, around the world, average tariff rates are much higher in T&C products than in manufactures, and in labor-intensive clothing products than in capital-intensive textiles products.[36]

Second, although the average bound tariffs for apparel range between 6 percent and 12 percent in the largest T&C markets in the world—the US and the EU—there are considerable tariff peaks that can range up to 32 percent. As Table 3.20 shows, in the US, 16 to 20 percent tariffs are applied to 21 percent of

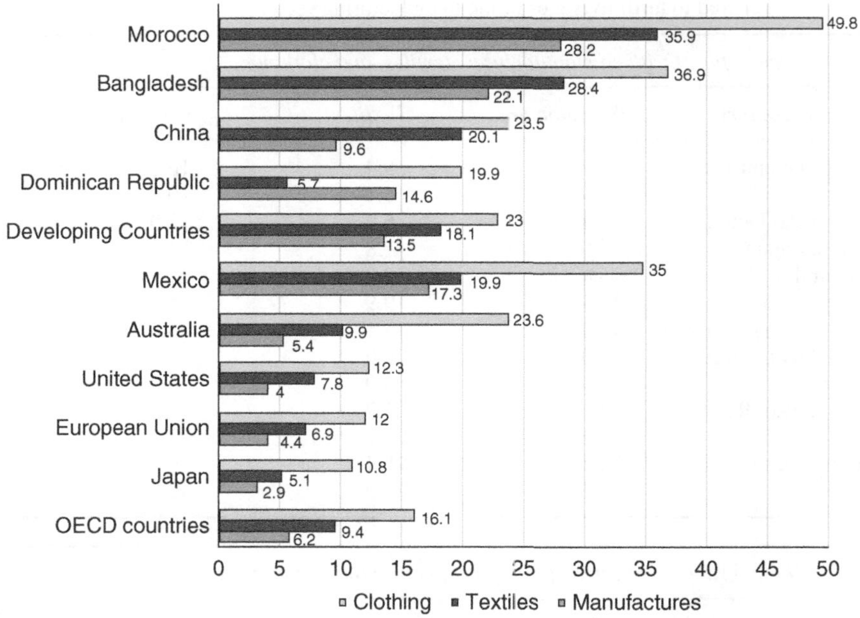

Figure 3.14 Average MFN tariffs in manufactures, textiles and clothing.

tariff lines in man-made filaments, 29 percent of tariff lines in man-made staple fibers, 20 percent of tariff lines in apparel with knitted fabrics, and 10 percent of tariff lines for apparel with non-knitted fabrics. In addition, tariff rates of 21 percent to 25 percent are applied to 4 percent of tariff lines for apparel with knitted fabrics and 3 percent of tariff lines for apparel with no-knitted fabrics. Similarly, applied tariff rates for textiles are also very high—36 percent of tariff lines have tariff rates of 10 percent to 15 percent. In the EU, the majority of the apparel and textiles tariffs are fixed at 12 percent—this is also much higher than average applied manufacturing tariffs (Hayashi, 2007, 10–11).[37]

Thus, the reduction of average and bound tariffs as well as tariff peaks for T&C products should be a prime concern for developing countries in the Doha Development Round (DDR) negotiations now underway under the banners of Non-Agricultural Market Access (NAMA) issues. But, as Hayashi (2007) points out, tariff reductions in T&C may impact the developing countries and the LDCs differently. As LDCs are exempt from the NAMA tariff reduction obligations, they do not have to reduce their tariffs, while most developing countries have to adhere to any such tariff reduction mandated by the negotiations.

Moreover, further tariff reduction will inevitably result in further erosion of preference margins for many developing countries, especially the LDCs. This is especially significant as, in recent years and decades, there has been mushrooming growth of preference programs. In the US, they are implemented either

Table 3.20 Tariff structure of the United States and the European Union for textiles and clothing (in %)

Product (HS codes)	*United States*							*European Union*					
	% over total imports of T&C	*Simple average bound rate*	*Simple average applied rate*	*Duties of 10% to 15%*	*Duties of 16% to 20%*	*Duties of 21% to 25%*	*Duties of 26% to 30%*	*% over total imports of T&C*	*Simple average bound rate*	*Simple average applied rate*	*Duties of 5% to 8%*	*Duties of 9% to 12%*	*Duties of 12%*
Cotton yarn and fabrics (52)	2	8	8	48	0	0	0	5	6	6	60	0	0
Man-made filaments (54)	2	10	10	36	21	0	0	4	6	6	55	0	0
Man-made staple fiber (55)	2	11	11	46	29	0	0	3	6	7	50	0	0
Apparel with knitted fabrics (61)	36	12	12	30	20	4	6	31	12	12	1	99	88
Apparel with non-knitted fabrics (62)	41	10	10	32	10	3	1	40	11	11	11	89	88
Other made-up textile articles (63)	9	7	7	36	0	0	0	7	10	10	16	80	61

Source: Author's compilation from Hayashi (2007).

through reciprocal arrangements, such as the NAFTA or the EU–Turkey customs union, or unilateral initiatives such as the Caribbean Basin Trade Partnership Act (CBTPA), the African Growth and Opportunity Act (AGOA), and the Andean Trade Preferences Act (ATPA). The EU also accords similar preferential programs under the Euro-Mediterranean Association Agreements, the Africa Caribbean Pacific (ACP) Trade Agreement, and the Everything-but-Arms (EBA) Initiative with the LDCs. Some of these preference programs have resulted in huge benefits for some apparel exporting developing countries and the LDCs as they could substantially increase their exports of apparel to the US and the EU, which would not have been possible if they had faced the same tariff rates as other apparel exporters. The interests of the preference receiving countries thus run counter to further tariff reductions as envisaged by the current NAMA negotiations.

The Swiss Formula

The Doha Round's tariff reduction negotiations under NAMA are being guided by something called the Swiss Formula, presented at the sixth WTO Ministerial Conference held in Hong Kong in 2006. The Formula, defined as [Final bound tariff = ([initial bound tariff] × [coefficient])/([initial bound tariff] + [coefficient])], provided separate coefficients for developed countries (15, 5, and 2), and the developing countries (40, 25, and 15) to determine the final bound rate. A higher coefficient, as envisaged for developing members, meant lower reductions in tariffs.

The latest negotiating text of the Formula brought down the coefficients to 8 for developed members and 20, 22, and 25 for developing countries, implying that while all developed countries have to apply the formula with the same coefficient, developing countries will have flexibilities to choose their coefficients. Developing countries were given three options in respect of choosing the coefficients and flexibilities: (1) a member choosing to apply the lowest coefficient of 20 would be entitled to make smaller or no cuts in 14 percent of its most sensitive industrial tariff lines, provided that these tariff lines do not exceed 16 percent of the total value of its NAMA imports; (2) a member choosing to apply a coefficient of 22 would be entitled to make smaller or no cuts in a smaller number of products—up to 10 percent of its most sensitive industrial tariff lines from the full effect of the formula—provided that these tariff lines do not exceed 10 percent of the total value of its NAMA imports; and finally (3) a member choosing to apply the highest coefficient of 25 will have to apply it to all of its products without exceptions.[38]

With the potential implementation of the Swiss Formula, as outlined above, the maximum tariff in developed countries would be below 8 percent, with average bound tariffs below 3 percent, and tariff peaks below 8 percent on their most sensitive products. For the developing countries, the majority of tariff lines would be less than 12 to 14 percent, depending on the coefficient and the flexibilities used. Average bound tariffs would be between 11 and 12 percent, and only a limited number of tariff lines would have levels above 15 percent. In the end, differences between bound rates and those actually applied would be substantially reduced.

Ultimately, however, it all depends on the success of the Doha Round itself. In addition, there has not been any meaningful progress in respect of the Swiss Formula for several years now. But in the event that the Formula is eventually adopted, it will result in a substantial reduction in the differences between bound tariffs and actual tariffs on the one hand, and in preference margins on the other. A UNCTAD/World Bank World Integrated Trade Solution (WITS) tariff simulation showed that coefficients of 5 for developed countries would result in the effective disappearance of preference margins in their entirety (Hayashi, 2007, 11). Thus, interests of preference receiving countries will be at odds with those of non-preference receiving developing countries.

Rules-of-origin controversy

Another contentious issue for the developing countries in T&C negotiations involves the Rules of Origin (ROO) for non-reciprocal preference programs. The WTO Rules of Origin Agreement provides a broad framework by requiring members to ensure that the ROOs are transparent and that they do not restrict, distort, or disrupt international trade, and that they are administered in a consistent, uniform, and reasonable manner. Preference granting countries are thus left with their own mechanisms for determining the origin of a product, and as a result there are wide variations in the way they apply the ROO—some apply the criterion of change of tariff classification, some apply the *ad valorem* percentage criterion, and some use the criterion of manufacturing stages or processing operations—there is no harmonization in the ROO.

Apparently, when it comes to T&C products, most preference granting countries use the criteria of *ad valorem* percentage or manufacturing or processing operations, which make it hard for many developing countries to use preferential market access as they lack domestic textiles capacities. The EBA scheme of the EU, for example, extends duty-free access to T&C products from LDCs, but to qualify for duty-free treatment, apparel articles must undergo a double transformation; for example, imported yarns must be transformed into fabric and apparel. Most Sub-Saharan African countries, many of whom are LDCs, lack the capacity to produce fabrics or to provide competitive fabrics that may be used as inputs to exports, and as a result fail to qualify for preferential treatment under the EBA.

Even Bangladesh, a leading LDC, which has emerged as one of the largest clothing exporters in the world, finds the EBA ROO difficult to comply with, particularly for woven fabric apparel. The country has over the years developed the domestic capacity to produce knitted and crocheted fabrics, and 80 percent of its exports of apparel articles made with these fabrics entered the EU market duty-free in 2005. However, the corresponding figure for woven fabric apparel was less than 30 percent.[39] Similarly, due to lack of domestic textile capacities, less than 50 percent of apparel articles made with knitted or crocheted fabrics (HS Chapter 61) from countries like Indonesia, the Philippines, Sri Lanka, Thailand, and Vietnam benefited from the EU GSP scheme in 2005, and the corresponding figure for non-fabric apparel articles (HS Chapter 62) was even lower: less than 30 percent. On the other hand, the US GSP schemes exclude most T&C products, and reduce average tariffs only marginally—from 7.54 percent to 7.36 percent for textiles and from 10.67 percent to 10.64 percent for clothing (Staritz, 2011, 11).

When it comes to the AGOA, the third country fabric rule provides flexibility in ROO for the AGOA beneficiary countries, and AGOA beneficiary countries also enjoy significant tariff concessions, as opposed to non-GOA developing country T&C exporters to the US, but uncertainties concerning the extension of AGOA, preference erosions, and the inability of some SSA countries to meet ROO requirements have already contributed to a significant decline in apparel exports from the AGAO countries to the US in recent years. Moreover, Brenton and Ikezuki (2005) have shown that the overall value preferences to the SSA countries under the AGOA had been very small—in 2002, such preferences amounted to 1.3 percent of the value of exports to the US, and the top five beneficiaries accounted for almost three-quarters of the value of preferences.

Complex ROO requirements are often justified on the ground that they are necessary to encourage substantial value-added activities in T&C exporting countries, so that these countries can develop integrated production structures individually or through regional cumulation, which would also maximize the impact on their employment, but such arguments have become redundant in the light of technological changes and global trade liberalization that resulted in the fragmentation of production processes and the development of global networks of sourcing (Brenton and Ozden, 2005). Many other researchers also agree that stringent ROO requirements are geared to protect the more capital-intensive textiles sector than the professed objectives of maximizing developmental impacts on the less developed countries (Bair and Gereffi, 2003; Morris, 2006). Thus, a more friendly and useful nature of ROO is required in order not to restrict, distort, or disrupt international trade, as envisaged by the WTO Rules of Origin Agreement.

Other non-tariff barriers

In addition to ROO, the developing countries and the LDCs also face other important non-tariff barriers (NTBs), such as conforming to customs and other documentation formalities, non-uniform classification practices with respect to the same products, technical barriers to trade requirements, and social condition-related requirements. Many international standards such as 'social clauses,' 'core labor standards,' 'environmental protection.' 'label requirements,' 'combatting drug regimes,' and so on, which may well be imposed with legitimate concerns, may go beyond legitimate policy objectives and end up as unnecessary barriers to trade as many developing countries and LDCs may find the implementation of such standards extremely costly (Hayashi, 2007, 19; Dowlah, 2008).

At the same time, the concentration of apparel retailing in developed countries in a few major companies, with significant control over global commodity chains and prices, has left developing country apparel exporters with little or no bargaining power—their profit margins are increasingly being squeezed, thereby limiting their capacity to modernize and provide better wages and working conditions.[40] While developed country governments and buyers have been demanding better working conditions and social and environmental protections, the global apparel retailers are making it impossible for developing country producers to adhere to such principles.

There are also concerns about domestic supports. Some countries encourage domestic production by creating obstacles to imports (such as import licensing) and incentives for domestic production (such as government procurement or trade agreements with rules of origin). Several countries (including the EU and China) extend subsidies that are applied equally to all industries, thus providing opportunities to benefit their domestic T&C sectors. These types of subsidies are allowed by the WTO and are not considered to be protectionist measures, but they may be interpreted as a WTO-prohibited subsidy.[41] There are also problems with bound tariffs. Although the WTO requires that binding tariffs are applied equally to all trading partners, some countries apply their bound tariff rates differently. There have been several such cases in the T&C sector in recent years, all of which, however, involved the developing countries. India, Brazil, Ecuador, and Egypt, for example, targeted other developing countries for such violation in textile products, such as yarn, fabric, and cotton.[42]

Conclusions

Bringing the T&C sector into the trajectory of the strengthened GATT discipline through a 10-year transition period under the Agreement on Textiles and Clothing (ATC) has been a hallmark achievement of the Uruguay Round. Similarly, bringing a determined end to the 40-year streak of the discriminatory and protectionist MFA regimes, through the full and faithful implementation of the ATC without any extension, has been a historic achievement of the WTO. International trade in the T&C sector is now as free as any other manufacturing sector under the WTO. The tides unleashed by the liberalization have been sweeping the world since the very beginning of the phasing out of the MFA regimes. Increasingly competitive dynamics of cost advantage, intensified competition, pricing pressures, buyer-driven strategic sourcing decisions, and labor and environmental concerns are reshaping the whole landscapes of T&C production and trade across the world.

The developing countries, in demonstrating their natural and evolving comparative advantage in this labor-intensive sector, had already emerged as the leading exporters of T&C products by the mid-1990s, and the trend continues. While hitherto dominant developed countries lost their shares in global exports and experienced massive unemployment, production, exports and employment soared in the developing part of the world. At the same time, the global market is more competitive than ever before, both horizontal and vertical integration have been leading to greater efficiency in the allocation of resources and concentration of production in the countries with real comparative advantage, T&C prices have been falling, and consumers are now better off across the world than ever before.

Although predictions of many doomsayers did not come true, the experience over the course of the past two decades, since the emergence of the WTO and the integration of the T&C sector into the GATT discipline, does indicate that all developing county T&C exporters did not do equally well—rising tides did not raise all boats. While some developing countries, especially in Asia, succeeded in increasing their T&C exports without preferential market access, some others with preferential access, especially in Latin America and Africa, experienced a decline in their exports.

This experience demonstrates that factors like the availability of low-cost labor, proximity to a buyers' market, dependence on assembly-type production systems, preferential rules of origin that prohibit the use of competitive inputs, and so on may not guarantee success in an environment of fiercely competitive liberalized trading in the T&C sector. Developing countries that have been doing well under the liberalized system are those which have succeeded in supplementing their low-wage labor with better backward linkages, low dependence on value additions from imports, low turn-over time, and moving into highervalue-added products through both vertical and horizontal differentiation in global value chains.

Some LDCs have done exceedingly well by using preferential or duty-free access to developed country markets. These countries, however, may face a very serious erosion of preference margins; such margins may even disappear if the Doha Round negotiations on NAMA tariff reductions materialize. Many of these countries also depend on assembly-type production systems and imported materials, which lead to smaller value addition to their GDPs. These countries need to develop backward linkages to reduce dependence on imports, and move to higher value-addition products in order to be competitive in preference-eroded or preference-free trade regimes in the future.

Although the T&C sector is now as liberalized as any other manufacturing sector, average tariffs in this sector are much higher than those in other manufacturing sectors, and the sector still faces a very significant number of high bound tariffs, tariff peaks, and tariff escalations. The sector also faces significant non-tariff barriers, such as non-harmonized rules of origin, non-universalized customs and documentation formalities, non-uniform classification practices with respect to many products, 'social clauses,' 'core labor standards,' 'environmental protection,' 'label requirements,' and so on. At the same time, a buyer-driven global market imposes significant pressures on global demand and prices for T&C products; a few lead firms have been squeezing the profits of developing country apparel exporters which often results in poorer working conditions for T&C workers. Therefore, the less developed countries will have high stakes in the WTO negotiations in the T&C sector in the future.

Notes

1 As explained in Chapter 1, the General Agreement on Tariff and Trade (GATT) was established in 1947 as an interim global trade agreement, while negotiations were being conducted to create an International Trade Organization (ITO), a third pillar of the Breton Woods economic structure along with the International Monetary Fund (IMF) and the World Bank. As the ITO could not be established due to the resistance of US Congress, the GATT continued to provide a platform for a rule-based global trade.

2 The MFN principle is outlined in Article 1 of the GATT 1947, and the National Treatment principle is outlined in Article 111. The MFN principle, however, has exceptions. For example, countries may grant lower tariffs to members of a free trade agreement for goods traded within the group, and deny similar treatment to goods from non-members. In addition, the developed countries may grant the developing countries special access to their markets for certain products, as provided under the GATT waiver called Special and Differential Treatment to developing countries. A GATT member may also raise trade barriers against products from some countries to avoid unfair trade. For more details see GATT (1972); Bagwell and Staiger (2009); Michalopoulos (1999); Whalley (1990).

3 See Articles XII and XIX of GATT: 'Restrictions to Safeguard the Balance of Payments,' and 'Emergency Action on Imports of Particular Products' (GATT, 1972).

4 Developed countries could ignore the MFN principle as GATT was basically a voluntary organization without any coercive power—it lacked authority to bar any contracting party from violating its rules on the ground of domestic concerns (Murray, 1995, 9–10). Second, the GATT Articles XII and XIX, as mentioned above, indeed authorized such exceptions in the case of 'market disruptions.' Finally, up until the launching of the Uruguay Round in 1986, the GATT was essentially a club of the developed countries, where the developing countries merely served as onlookers (Dowlah, 2004, 30–46).

5 The Rounds were: the Geneva Round (1949), the Annecy Round (1949), the Torquay Round (1951), the Geneva Round (1956), the Dillion Round (1960–1961), the Kennedy Round (1964–1967), the Tokyo Round (1973–1979), and the Uruguay Round (1986–1994). For more details see Chapter 1 (this volume), and the WTO website, The GATT Years: From Havana to Marrakesh. https://www.wto.org/english/thewto_e/whatis_e/tif_e/fact4_e.htm

6 The GATT Article XI (General Elimination of Quantitative Restrictions) explicitly prohibits quantitative restrictions (and related import and export licensing), except under a small number of exceptional circumstances (such as export restrictions to temporarily relieve domestic food shortages). Moreover, the GATT Articles I (MFN Treatment) and XIII (Non-discriminatory Administration of Quantitative Restrictions) state that any trade measures taken by countries must not discriminate between supplying countries (GATT, 1972; Naumann, 2006).

7 Apparently, the STA was strongly backed by the Kennedy Administration. During his election campaign, President Kennedy pledged to protect the domestic textile industry which felt threatened by 'low-cost' imports from developing countries. In addition, the US used the STA most extensively—cotton textile imports from scores of countries, such as Spain, Taiwan, Colombia, Israel, the United Arab Republic, Hong Kong-SAR, and Portugal were restricted. Hong Kong-SAR's initial unwillingness to voluntarily restrain exports (VERs) resulted in limiting its exports to the US by 35 percent below its previous levels. The European countries also used similar quantitative restrictions on textile imports from 'low-cost' developing country exporters (Blokker, 1989, 127).

8 The MFA, however, excluded handloom fabrics and cottage products as well as traditional ethnic handicraft products from its coverage.

9 The MFA vaguely provided a description of market disruption by linking it to the existence, or threat, of serious damage to the domestic industry, which could be assessed by sales, market share, profits, employment, and production, and so on. The agreement also linked disruption to a sharp and substantial increase in imports from a particular source, and/or at the prices lower than those prevailing in the market for similar products from domestic as well as other import sources. Interpretation of damage to the domestic industry or sharp and substantial increases, and so on was thus left to importing developed countries.

10 The MFA protocols were extended five times—each of the first four MFAs lasted four years, but MFA-V lasted three years (1991–1993) and MFA-VI lasted one year (December 1993 to December 1994). In 1993, the MFA had 44 members, when six major T&C exporters—Austria, Canada, the EEC, Finland, Norway, and the U.—maintained a total of 98 trade-restraining agreements. Two MFA members (Switzerland and Japan), however, never applied restraints. Sweden left the MFA in 1991, but after it joined the EC in 1995 it became subject to the EC's quota restrictions. China was not a member of the GATT at that time, but was a member of the MFA. For more details, see Dowlah (2004, 77–106).

11 MFA II (1977–1982), for example, permitted something called 'jointly agreed reasonable departures,' which worked against the interests of developing country exporters as importing countries could reduce quotas, deny flexibility provisions, and allow less than 6 percent growth rates in quota as envisaged by the original MFA.

12 Still, T&C lobbies in both the US and the EU considered the MFA-II restrictions not adequate to slow down the tide of cheap imports from the developing countries and indeed mounted intense pressure during the Kennedy Round (1964–1967) and the Tokyo Round (1973–1979) against the further liberalization of trade in the sector. As a result, U.S. Congress granted conditional negotiating authority to its trade delegations to the MFA-III (1982–1986) in order to forestall the further liberalization of trade in the sector (Dickerson, 1991, 314).

13 Critics, however, argue that despite the fact that the MFA III protocols granted favorable treatment to small country suppliers and new entrants, in aggregate, restraints under the regime were actually more extensive and restrictive than before.

14 Such non-MFA restrictions included the restrictions imposed by the MFA signatories to other MFA signatories, restrictions imposed by the MFA signatories against non-MFA signatories, and other restrictive measures maintained by both the MFA and non-MFA signatories. See Dowlah (2004, 77–106) for more details.

15 The ATC, however, asked the MFA signatories to use transitional safeguards as sparingly and as consistently as possible in order to facilitate the effective implementation of the integration process. The Agreement identified circumvention by trans-shipment, rerouting, false declaration concerning country of origin, and falsification of official documents as a major hindrance for integration of the sector, and required WTO members to establish the necessary legal provisions and administrative procedures to take action against such acts of circumvention.

16 The EU website (accessed October 7, 2013), however, showed that at the first stage of integration (1995–1997), the EU had 16.2 percent of its 1990 imports under the (quota-free) GATT umbrella, and in the second stage (1998–2002), it had added a further 17.1 percent. With the addition of another 18 percent, it had liberalized up to 65 percent of its restricted trade by the third stage. The remaining 35 percent was liberalized by the final day—on December 31, 2004.

17 In 2005, Chinese textile exports rose to $107.7 billion, from $88.8 billion in 2004, and its clothing exports jumped from $62 billion to $74 billion, signifying 21.3 percent growth in textiles and 19.4 percent growth in clothing exports. In addition, the share of China in global T&C exports would be much higher if those of Hong Kong-SAR and Macau Special Administrative Regions were included as Chinese exports.

18 The ATC, as explained above, allowed WTO members to adopt selective (product-specific) safeguard actions during the transition period to protect the domestic market against damaging surges in imports. The US imposed quotas on seven products in May 2005, and the EU imposed sanctions against two products (flax yarn and T-shirts) in June 2005. China, however, was not the only country whose exports surged in 2005. Evidently, exports from several other developing countries, such as India, Bangladesh, Cambodia, Egypt, Madagascar, and Vietnam, also increased significantly during the same year. In fact, India and China together captured 85 percent of the increase in clothing trade in both 2004 and 2005. Obviously, the size of Chinese 20 percent growth was much greater than other exporters, and Chinese T&C exports literally swamped the US and EU markets. See Martin (2007) and Brenton and Hoppe (2006) for more details.

19 Numerous studies painted such grave scenarios, pointing to China's huge reservoir of low-cost labor and potentially unconstrained access to the global market in the post-ATC world. See, for example, USITC (2004); Knappe (2003); Applebaum (2005); Nordas (2004).

20 In 2004/2005, the unit price of US imports of man-made fiber (MMF) apparel fell by 26 percent for imports from China, 8 percent from Pakistan, 6 percent from Bangladesh, 8 percent from Honduras, 12 percent from Mauritius, and 16 percent from South Africa. See Tables 3–5 in Hayashi (2007). Such drastic falls in import prices due to increased competition also resulted in reduced profits and the exit of many garment companies in developing countries (ILO, 2005).

21 Turkey was the fifth and seventh largest clothing exporter in 1995 and 2000, respectively, while India was the ninth largest exporter in 2000, but had no slot among the top 15 exporters in 1995.

22 Bangladesh, however, was not alone in registering such phenomenal growth in clothing exports. Between 1980 and 1997, clothing exports of Turkey increased by 51 times, China by 20 times, Indonesia by 30 times, and Malaysia by 16 times (ILO, 2000, 10).

23 This time around, mainland China came to occupy the topmost rank without including the exports of Hong Kong-SAR.

24 Based on Table 2 in Gereffi and Frederick (2010).

25 China emerged as the largest exporter of textiles in 1997, followed by South Korea, Germany, Italy, and Chinese-Taipei. In 1980, the largest textile exporter was West Germany, accounting for 11.4 percent of world exports, followed by Japan (9.3 percent) and Italy (7.6 percent) (ILO, 2000, 8–9). In 2012, however, Chinese exports dropped to $95 billion. As its share in the global market increased further in 2012 compared with 2010, this drop had to do with the slump in the global market in that year rather than Chinese exports. It is also remarkable that the Chinese export market is not concentrated in some countries or regions. China rather demonstrates an impressive pattern of export destinations. In 2007, for example, China's top clothing export markets were the EU-15 (17.4 percent), the US (16.3 percent), and Japan (14.3 percent), which together represented 48 percent of its total clothing exports. China also had considerable market share in Australia and African countries (Frederick and Gereffi, 2009a, 2009b).

26 For more details, especially of the underlying reasons for such migrations, see Gereffi and Memedovic (2003, 68–89).

27 Employment data of the Chinese T&C industry are very murky. According to the ILO, in 1995 the Chinese T&C industry employed 8.3 million workers (6.7 million in textiles and 1.7 million in clothing), and the number fell to 6.7 million in 2001 (4.7 million in textiles and 2.0 million in clothing). See Nordas (2004, 12–13); Also Ngai (2005).

28 Oxfam, however, claims that in 2007, the Chinese T&C sector employed about 15 million workers, of whom more than 80 percent were females. Available online at: www.labourbehindthelabel.org/jobs/item.

29 According to the ILO (2005), in 1995, formal employment in India's clothing sector numbered 1.8 million and in the textiles sector it was 264,000. In 2000, employment increased to 1.3 million in clothing and to 331,000 in textiles. See Table 4 in Nordas (2004, 12).

30 For more details see Staritz (2011, ch. 4).

31 See Table 3.1 in Staritz (2011, 50).

32 In 2009, U.S. Congress tabled what was called the Tariff Relief Assistance for Developing Economies Bill of 2009, which sought to grant duty-free access to imports of manufactures from certain selected LDCs, including key T&C exporters, such as Bangladesh, Cambodia, Nepal, and Sri Lanka. The Bill, however, failed to pass.

33 For example, countries like Bangladesh, India, Pakistan, Vietnam, and Indonesia have been exporting to the US and the EU similar quality products as China, but they adjust their prices to China—over half of clothing exported to these markets had a unit price very close to China's price. This strategy of 'following' Chinese prices became particularly apparent after 2005.

34 For 2009 figures, see Table 3.13.

35 Available online at: www.bls.gov/opub/mlr/2013/article/industry-employment-and-output-projections-to-2022.htm (accessed July 1, 2014).

36 In developing countries also manufacturing tariffs are much lower than tariffs in textiles and clothing. While MFN tariffs average at 13.5 percent for manufactures, the average tariff rates are 18.1 percent and 23 percent, respectively in textiles and clothing. In some developing countries, such as China, Bangladesh, and Morocco, average import tariffs on textiles and clothing are above 20 percent.

37 It is also notable that significant tariff barriers—including tariff peaks and tariff escalations—are also evident in some developing countries, such as China, India, and South Africa, which have significant T&C sectors as well as large end markets (Staritiz, 2011, 10).

38 See www.wto.org/english/tratop_e/dda_e/status_e/nama_e.htm (accessed July 11, 2014).

39 The EBA, however, grants partial regional accumulation within some regional groups such as ASEAN, the South Asian Association for Regional Cooperation (SAARC), and the Central American Common Market and the Andean Group. Under such 'regional cumulation,' a product manufactured in or with inputs from two or more countries belonging to the same group of countries is treated as if they originated in the exporting beneficiary country. See Dowlah (2008) and the EU website for greater details.

40 For details see Gereffi and Memedovic (2003).

41 In particular, the US cotton subsidy has been a highly contentious matter for many years. The issue is discussed in greater detail in Chapter 2 (this volume) in the context of agricultural trade liberalization.

42 The WTO Anti-Dumping Agreement allows members to add anti-dumping duty to an imported product in order to bring the price closer to a normal value or remove the injury to the domestic industry in the importing country. In 2008, the WTO was notified of 208 anti-dumping investigations and 139 anti-dumping measures—39 of the investigations (18.8 percent) and 10 of the anti-dumping measures (7.2 percent) were in the T&C sector, and the majority of investigations were carried out by a few developing countries—Turkey, Brazil, Argentina, India, and Pakistan. The developed countries, primarily the US and the EU, accounted for the largest number of anti-dumping duty impositions.

References

Abras, A. (2012). Success and upgrading after the end of the MFA. In G. Lopez-Acevedo and R. Robtertson (eds), *Sewing Success? Employment, wages, and poverty following the end of Multi-Fiber Arrangement* (pp. 87–125). Washington, DC: World Bank.

Adhikari, R. and Yamamoto, Y. (2007). The textile and clothing industry: Adjusting to post-quota world. In *Industrial Development for the 21st Century Series* (pp. 183–234). New York: UNDP.

Ahmed, N. (2009). Sustaining ready-made garments exports from Bangladesh. *Journal of Contemporary Asia*, 39 (4), 597–618.

Ananthakrishnan, P. and Jain-Chandra, S. (2005). The impact of India of trade liberalization in the textiles and clothing sector. IMF Working Paper WP/05/214. Washington, DC: International Monetary Fund.

Applebaum, R. (2005). TNCs and the removal of the textiles and clothing quotas. Center for Global Studies, University of Santa Barbara, Paper 3. Geneva: UNCTAD.

Audet, D. (2004). Structural adjustments in textiles and clothing in the post-ATC trading environment. OECD Trade Policy Paper No. 4, TD/TC/WP. Paris: Organization of Economic Cooperation and Development.

Bagwell, K. and Staiger, R. (2009). The WTO: Theory and practice. WTO Working Paper ERSD-2009–11, November. Geneva: World Trade Organization.

Bair, J. (2008). Surveying the post-MFA landscape: What prospects for the global south post-quota? *Competition and Change*, 12(1), 3–10.

Bair, J. and Gary, G. (2002). NAFTA and the apparel commodity chain: Corporate strategies, inter-firm networks, and industrial upgrading. In G. Gereffi, D. Spencer, and J. Bair (eds), *Free Trade and Uneven Development: The North American apparel industry after NAFTA* (pp. 23–50). Philadelphia, PA: Temple University Press.

Bair, J. and Gereffi, G. (2001). Local clusters in global chains: The causes and consequences of export dynamism in Torren's blue jeans industry. *World Development*, 29(11), 1885–1903.

Bair, J. and Gereffi, G. (2003). Upgrading, uneven development, and jobs in the North American apparel industry. *Global Networks*, (3)2, 143–169.

Blokker, N. (1989). *International Regulation of World Trade in Textiles: Lessons for practice, a contribution to theory*. The Netherlands: Martinus Nijhoff/Kulware Academic, USA.

Brenton, P. and Hoppe, M. (2006). Life after quotas? Early signs of the new era in trade of textiles and clothing. In R. Newfarmer (ed.), *Trade, Doha, and Development: A window into the issues* (pp. 151–160). Washington, DC: World Bank.

Brenton, P. and Ikezuki, T. (2005). *The Value of Trade Preferences for Africa*. Washington, DC: World Bank.

Brenton, P. and Ozden, C. (2005). Trade preferences for apparel and the role of rules of origin: The case of Africa. Trade and Development Research Group (DECRG). Washington, DC: World Bank.

Dickerson, K. (1991). *Textiles and Apparel in the International Economy*. New York: Macmillan.

Dowlah, C. (1998). *The Consequences of the GATT Uruguay Round for the Textiles and Clothing Sector in Bangladesh*. Dhaka: GTZ/DCCI Business Advisory Services.

Dowlah, C. (1999).The future of the readymade clothing industry of Bangladesh in the post-Uruguay Round World. *The World Economy*, 22(7), 933–953.

Dowlah, C. (2004). *Backwaters of Global Prosperity: How globalization and the GATT/WTO trade regimes marginalize the world's poorest nations*. New York: Praeger.

Dowlah, C. (2013).An assessment of U.S. GSP Schemes from the perspective of the Least Developed Countries. In L. YongShik, H. Gary, and C. Won-Mog (eds), *Law and Development Perspective on International Trade Law* (pp. 334–356). New York: Cambridge University Press.

Dunn, J. (2008). The ready-made garments industry in Bangladesh: An update. IMF Working Paper. Washington, DC: International Monetary Fund.

European Commission. (2011).The Textile and Clothing Sector and the EU Trade Policy. February 2011. Available online at: http://trade.ec.europa.eu/doclib/docs/2011/october/tradoc_148259.pdf.

Fontaine, T. (2007). Trade preferences—End of quotas hits African textiles. IMF Working Paper. Washington, DC: International Monetary Fund.

Fontaine, T. (2008). Responding to the challenges in the global trading regimes for Swaziland's textiles and sugar sectors. IMF Working Paper. Washington, DC: International Monetary Fund.

Francois, J., Glismann, H., and Spinanger, D. (2000). The cost of EU trade protection in textiles and clothing. March. Institute of World Economics, Kiel. Available online at: www.frihandel.nu/pdf/textilrapport.pdf.

Frederick, S. and Gereffi, G. (2009a). Protectionism in textiles and apparel. In S. Evenett, B. Hoekman, and O. Cattaneo (eds), *Effective Crisis Response and Openness: Implications for the trading system* (pp. 321–344). Washington, DC: World Bank.

Frederick, S. and Gereffi, G. (2009b). *Review and Analysis of Protectionist Actions in the Textiles and Apparel Industries*. Washington, DC: World Bank.

Frederick, S. and Staritz, C. (2012). Developments in the global apparel industry after the MFA phase-out. In G. Lopez-Acevedo and R. Robtertson (eds), *Sewing Success? Employment, wages, and poverty following the end of Multi-Fiber Arrangement* (pp. 41–86). Washington, DC: World Bank.

GATT (General Agreement on Tariff and Trade). (1972). *Basic Agreements and Selected Documents.* Eighteenth Supplement. Geneva: GATT.

GATT (General Agreement on Tariff and Trade). (1994). *Results of the Uruguay Round of Multilateral Trade Negotiations.* Geneva: GATT.

Gereffi, G. and Frederick, S. (2010). The global apparel value chain, trade and the crisis: Challenges and opportunities for developing countries. World Bank Policy Research Working Paper No. 5281. Washington, DC: World Bank.

Gereffi, G. and Memedovic, O. (2003). *The Global Apparel Value Chain: What prospects for upgrading by developing countries.* Geneva: United Nations Industrial Development Organization.

Gereffi, G., Spencer, D., and Bair, J. (2002). *Free Trade and Uneven Development: The North American apparel trade after NAFTA.* Philadelphia, PA: Temple University Press.

Hamilton, C. (1988). Restrictiveness and international transmission of new protectionism. In R. Balwin, C. Hamilton, and A. Sapir (eds), *Issues in US–EC Trade Relations*. Chicago, IL: National Bureau of Economic Research.

Harrigan, J. and Barrows, G. (2009). Testing the theory of trade policy: Evidence from the abrupt end of textile and apparel of the multi-fiber arrangement. *Review of Economics and Statistics*, 91(2), 282–294.

Hayashi, M. (2007). *Trade in Textiles and Clothing: Assuring development gains in a rapidly changing environment.* Geneva: UNCTAD.

Hufbauer, G. and Elliott, K. (1994). *Measuring the Costs of Protection in the United States*. Washington, DC: Institute for International Economics.

Iacovone, L., Rauch, F., and Winters, A. (2009). Trade as engine of creative destruction—The Mexican experience with Chinese competition. Development Research Group. Washington, DC: World Bank.

ILO (International Labor Organization). (2000). Global employment levels in textile, clothing and footwear industries holding stable as industries relocate. ILO press release, October 16. Available online at: www.ilo.org/global/about-the-ilo/media-centre/press-releases/WCMS_007911/lang–en/index.htm

ILO (International Labor Organization). (2005). Promoting fair globalization in textiles and clothing in a post-MFA environment. TMTC-PMFA/2005. Available online at: www.ilo.org/wcmsp5/groups/public/-ed._dialogue/-sector/documents/meeting-document/kd00003.pdf.

ILO (International Labor Organization). (2013). *World Wage Report 2012/13: Wages and equitable growth*. Geneva: ILO.

Jones, R. (2001). Horizontal aspects of vertical fragmentation. In L. Cheng and H. Kierzkowski (eds), *Global Production and Trade in East Asia*. Boston, MA: Kulwer Academic.

Jones, R. and Kierzkowski, H. (1990). The role of services in production and international trade: A theoretical framework. In R. Jones and A. Krueger (eds), *Political Economy of International Trade* (pp. 31–48). Oxford: Blackwell.

Kaplinsky, R. and Morris, M. (2008). Do the Asian drivers undermine export-oriented industrialization in SSA? *World Development*, 36(2), 254–273.

Kaplinsky, R. and Messner, D. (2008). Introduction: The impact of Asian drivers on the developed world. *World Development*, 36(2), 197–209.

Kaplinsky, R., McCormick, D., and Morris, M. (2007). The impact of China on Sub-Saharan Africa. Working Paper No. 291. Institute of Development Studies, University of Sussex.

Keane, J. and Velde, D. (2008). *The Role of Textile and Clothing Industries in Growth and Development Strategies. Investment and Growth Program*. London: Overseas Development Institute.

Kirmani, N., Molajani, P., and Mayer, T. (1984). Effects of increased markets access on exports of developing countries. IMF Staff Papers 31: 661–684. Washington, DC: International Monetary Fund.

Knappe, M. (2003). Textiles and clothing: What happens after 2005? Geneva: International Trade Center. Available online at: http://traadeforum.org/news/fullstory.php/aid/611/Reaching_Out_to_Garmout_Manufacturers.html.

Kowalski, P. and Molnar, M. (2009). Economic impacts of the phase-out in 2005 of quantitative restrictions under the Agreement on Textiles and Clothing. OECD Trade Policy Paper No. 90. Paris: OECD Publishing.

Ludema, R., Mayda, A., and Mishra, P. (2010). *Protection for Free? The political economy of US tariff suspensions*. Washington, DC: International Monetary Fund.

Martin, M. (2007). US clothing and textile trade with China and the world: Trends since the end of quotas. CRS Report for Congress (RL34106). Washington, DC: US Congress.

Michalopoulos, C. (1999). The role of special and differential treatment for developing countries in GATT and the World Trade Organization. Policy Research Working Paper. Washington, DC: World Bank.

Mittlelhauser, M. (1997). Employment trends in textiles and apparel, 1973–2005. *Monthly Labor Review* (August), 24–34.

Morris, M. (2006). Globalization, China, and clothing industrialization strategies in Sub-Saharan Africa. In H. Jauch and R. Traub Merz (eds), *Future of the Textiles and Clothing Industry in Sub-Saharan Africa*. Bonn: Freiderich-Ebert-Stifftung.

Murray, L. (1995). Unraveling employment trends in textiles and apparel. *Monthly Labor Review* (August), 62–72.

Naumann, E. (2006). The Multifibre Agreement—WTO Agreement on Textiles and Clothing. Tralac Working Paper No. 4/2006. Available online at: www.fibre2fashion.com/industry-article/pdffiles/the-multifibre-agreement.pdf.

Ngai, P. (2005). Global production, company codes of conduct and labor conditions in China: A case study of two factories. *The China Journal* (54), 101–113.

Nordas, H. (2004). The global textile and clothing industry post the Agreement on Textiles and Clothing. WTO Discussion Paper No. 5. Geneva: World Trade Organization.

OECD (Organization for Economic Cooperation and Development). (2004a). *A New World Map in Textiles and Clothing—Adjusting to change*. Paris: OECD.

OECD (Organization for Economic Cooperation and Development). (2004b). Structural adjustment in textiles and clothing in the post-ATC trading environment. TD/TC/WP(2004)/23/Final. Paris: OECD.

OECD (Organization for Economic Cooperation and Development). (2005). *Trade and Structural Adjustment—Embracing globalization*. Paris: OECD.

OECD (Organization for Economic Cooperation and Development). (2007). *Globalization, Jobs and Wages*. OECD Policy Brief, June. Paris: OECD.

OECD (Organization for Economic Cooperation and Development). (2010). *Seizing the Benefits of Trade for Employment and Growth*. Report prepared for submission to the G-20 meeting, Seoul (Korea), November 11–12.

Oxfam (Oxfam International). (2004).Stitched up: How rich-country protectionism in textiles and clothing trade prevents poverty alleviation. Briefing Paper No. 60, April. Oxford: Oxfam.

Savchenko, Y. and Lopez-Acevedo, G. (2012). Female wages in the apparel industry post-MFA: The cases of Cambodia and Sri Lanka. World Bank eLibrary. dx.doi.org/10.1596/1813-9450-6061.

Singh, J. (2008). Indian textile and clothing sector poised for a leap. In M. Mikic (ed.), *Unveiling Protectionism: Regional responses to remaining barriers in the textiles and clothing trade*. Bangkok: UNESCAP (United Nations).

Spinanger, D. (2001). What happens when MFN principles govern T&C trade beyond 2004 and China is a WTO member? Paper presented to the World Bank Conference on WTO Accession Policy Reform and Corporate Strategies for Globalization. Beijing, October 29 to November 1. Available online at: http://worldbank.org/INTRANET-TRADE/Resources/DeanSpinanger1.pdf.

Staritz, C. (2011). *Making the Cut: Low income countries and the global clothing value chain in a post-quota and post-crisis world*. Washington, DC: World Bank.

Tewari, M. (2006). Is price and cost-competitiveness enough for apparel firms to gain market share in the world after quotas? A review. *Global Economy Journal*, 6(4), 1–18.

Trela, I. and Whalley, J. (1990). Global effects of developed country trade restrictions on textiles and apparel. *Economic Journal*, 100(403), 1190–1205.

UNCTAD (United Nations Conference on Trade and Development). (1986). *Protectionism and Structural Adjustment*. New York: United Nations.

UNCTAD (United Nations Conference on Trade and Development). (2004). *Trade and Development Report, 2004*. New York and Geneva: United Nations Publications.

UNCTAD (United Nations Conference on Trade and Development). (2005). *Weaving a New World: Realizing development gains in a post-ATC trading system*. Geneva: United Nations.

UNCTAD (United Nations Conference on Trade and Development). (2013). *Trade and Development Report, 2004*. New York and Geneva: United Nations Publications.

UNIDO (United Nations Industrial Development Organization). (2009). The impact of world recession on the textiles and garment industries of Asia. Research and Statistics Branch Working Paper 17/2009. Vienna, Austria: UNIDO.

UNIDO (United Nations Industrial Development Organization). (2013). Industrial Development Report 2013: Sustaining employment growth. UNIDO ID/446. Vienna, Austria: UNIDO.

USAID (US Agency for International Development. (2005). *Measuring Competitiveness and Labor Productivity in Cambodia's Garment Industry*. Phnom Penh: USAID.

US Department of Labor. (2013). Industry employment and output projections to 2022. Monthly Labor Review, December. Available online at: www.bls.gov/opub/mlr/2013/article/industry-employment-and-output-projections-to-2022.htm

USITC (US International Trade Commission). (1989). *Economic Effects of Significant US Import Restraints.* Publication No. 2222, October. Washington, DC: USITC.

USITC (US International Trade Commission). (2004). Textiles and apparel: Assessment of the competitiveness of certain foreign suppliers to the US market. Publication No. 3671. Washington, DC: USITC.

Whalley, J. (1990). Non-discriminatory discrimination: Special and differential treatment under the GATT for developing countries. *Economic Journal*, 100(403), 1318–1328.

World Bank. (2004). *Trade Polices in South Asia: An overview.* Report No. 29949. Washington, DC: World Bank.

World Bank. (2005). Bangladesh growth and competitiveness. Report No. 31394-BD, South Asia Region. Washington, DC: World Bank.

World Bank. (2012). *World Development Indicators*. Washington, DC: World Bank.

WTO (World Trade Organization). (1995). *Options for Least Developed Countries to Improve their Competitiveness in the Textiles and Clothing Business.* WT/COMTD/LDC/W/37. Geneva: WTO.

WTO (World Trade Organization). (2006). *World Trade Report, 2006.* Geneva: WTO.

WTO (World Trade Organization). (2014). *World Trade Report, 2014.* Geneva: WTO.

WTO (World Trade Organization). (2001–2014). *International Trade Statistics*. Geneva: WTO.

WTO (World Trade Organization). (2001–2013). *World Trade Profiles.* Geneva: WTO.

Yang, Y. (1993). The impact of the phasing out on world clothing and textile markets. National Center for Development Studies, Australian National University, Australia.

Yang, Y. and Zhong, C. (1998). China's textile and clothing exports in a changing world economy. *The Developing Economies*, 36(1), 3–23.

4 Liberalization of cross-border labor mobility

Introduction

As discussed in previous chapters, over the course of the past few decades phenomenal progress has been made in respect of the liberalization of global merchandise trade. Available estimates suggest that over 70 percent of merchandise production is now contested internationally, and such liberalization has brought forth extraordinary gains for the global economy (WT0, 2011; Hoekman *et al.*, 2002). But the liberalization of the services trade, on the other hand, lagged far behind. Currently about 20 to 25 percent of services are traded internationally despite this sector accounting for more than 70 percent of global gross domestic products—more than double the contribution that may be attributed to the manufacturing sector (World Bank, 2009a, 2009b).[1] In 2013, global exports of services reached $4.7 trillion, representing 20 per cent of total exports of goods and services (UNCTAD, 2014, 6), but the actual share of trade in services, when considered in terms of value-added in the global value chain (GVC), may approach 45 to 50 percent of world exports (Francois and Hoekman, 2010; WTO, 2009; UNCTAD, 2013).

Available research suggests that far greater benefits would accrue to the world economy from the further liberalization of trade in services than in merchandise trade, mainly because benefits from the further liberalization of merchandise would be nominal, as the sector has already been largely liberalized (Mattoo *et al.*, 2008; Anderson and Winters, 2008). During the period of the GATT (1947–1994), both tariff and non-tariff barriers in merchandise trade fell sharply, but not much progress was made in respect of the services trade, as the sector remained largely outside the GATT discipline As a result, in the post-GATT period, international trade in services not only remains smaller in size, but also faces greater trade protections and obstacles than trade in merchandise (Moses and Latnes, 2004; WTO, 2004; Adlung and Roy, 2005; Gootiz and Mattoo, 2009).

Such challenges are still greater for what is known as the Temporary Movement of Natural Persons across borders as service suppliers, as envisaged by Mode-4 of the General Agreement on Trade in Services (GATS) of the Uruguay Round Agreement. Although the services covered by Mode-4 account for a tiny share in global trade, it remains one of the most debated and controversial issues in the services trade, mainly due to the nature of complexities involved in such trades (Kemekliene, 2007; Dowlah, 2012; Francois and Hoekman, 2010). Understandably, cross-border labor mobility—no matter whether permanent or temporary—is a highly contentious and politically charged subject, especially in the developed countries, as most of the people who seek to migrate originate from the less developed countries (Czaika and Hass, 2013; Dowlah, 2014). Currently, approximately 3.2 percent of the global population live in a country where they were not born.[2]

Available demographic projections suggest that the world population will increase to 8.1 billion by 2025, and to 9.6 billion by 2050, from the current level of 7.2 billion, and almost all of the additional people will enlarge the population of developing countries, while populations of developed countries will decline considerably (UNDESA, 2013a; UNFPA, 2014). Such a dramatic transformation in global demographics will hugely increase both demand and supply of cross-border labor mobility in the future, but no credible multilateral institution exists now to serve as a watchdog for managing the evolving challenge. Presumably, the only multilateral platform available now is the GATS Mode-4, but it can serve the purpose only partially and only for the temporary movement of labor across borders. Moreover, the effectiveness of GATS Mode-4 squarely depends on the progress to be made in multilateral negotiations under the WTO.

Based on a review of relevant theoretical and empirical literature, this chapter argues that: (1) a basic convergence of economic interests appears to be emerging between the labor-sending and -receiving countries for the liberalization of the temporary movement of natural persons across national borders as service suppliers; (2) despite growing anti-immigration sentiments in developed countries, credible progress is currently being made both bilaterally and multilaterally, especially under the auspices of some regional trading blocs, for promoting cross-border temporary labor-mobility; and (3) Mode-4 of GATS may actually emerge as a great window of opportunity for the liberalization of temporary cross-border labor mobility across the world by mitigating against controversial effects of permanent or other forms of labor migration.

This chapter is organized as follows. The second section provides a brief description of different modes of services trade as acknowledged by the GATS. The third section examines empirical trends in global labor migration and remittance flows around the world in recent decades. The fourth section reviews the existing literature on the relationship among remittance inflows, economic development, and the brain-drain from the less developed countries. The fifth section explores the rationale for temporary labor mobility across national borders from theoretical as well as empirical standpoints. The sixth section explores the potential of GATS Mode-4 as a unique platform for promoting temporary cross-border labor mobility, as opposed to permanent or other forms of migration, and the current state of the WTO negotiations for the liberalization of Mode-4 services. The seventh section examines current trends of temporary labor mobility from both bilateral and multilateral perspectives. The eighth section concludes the chapter.

The GATS and global labor mobility

As mentioned above, the GATT focused primarily on manufactures, while the agriculture and service sectors were left behind. Eventually, the Uruguay Agreement, which established the WTO in 1994 by replacing the GATT, opened the doors for the liberalization of trade in agriculture and service sectors as well. The service sector was brought under what is called the GATS, which identified the following four modes of the supply of services.

> Mode-1: cross-border supply—supply of services from the territory of one member to another member; for example, the delivery of services through technological means, such as international telephone calls.
>
> Mode-2: consumption abroad—supply of services in the territory of one member to the service consumer of another member, such as the cross-border movement of patients for healthcare, or foreign travelers involved in tourism.
>
> Mode-3: commercial presence—supply of services by a service supplier of one member in the territory of another member through commercial presence; for example, foreign direct investment, such as opening a healthcare center, or a branch of a clinic abroad, or opening a bank branch in another country.
>
> Mode-4: the temporary cross-border movement of natural persons in an individual capacity, or as part of an establishment to provide the service overseas, such as the temporary movement of healthcare professionals to deliver services across borders.

The GATS envisages the temporary nature of migration in two critical ways: the temporariness of duration and functional specificity. Paragraph 2 of the Annex on the Movement of Natural Persons Supplying Services under the GATS Agreement makes it clear that Mode-4 does not actually guarantee access to the host country's labor market; service providers are more likely to be pre-employed by the host country's industries and screened by the host country's government before they enter the host country. Next, Paragraph 1 of the Annex provides for the movement of temporary persons for specific services only, which are not interchangeable among other modes or sectors. In addition, GATS Article 1:2(d) suggests that while any service provider from a developing country may freely gain access to developed countries' service markets, the actual levels of market access via Mode-4 would depend on a national schedule of commitments of a host country.

The framework of Mode-4, however, raises several perplexing legal and economic issues for both labor-sending and -receiving countries. For example: (1) how to define temporary employment; (2) how to determine the length of stay of a temporary worker; (3) what skill levels are covered under temporary services; and finally (4) what will be the nature of contract with the temporary service supplier? The Annex on the Movement of Natural Persons Supplying Services under GATS recognizes two categories of temporary labor migration: (1) those who are affecting 'service suppliers of a member,' and (2) those who are 'employed by a service supplier of a Member, in respect of the supply of a service.' Although the framers have clearly delineated that none of the GATS modes apply to measures affecting individuals seeking access to the labor market of a member country, or to measures regarding citizenship, residence, or employment on a permanent basis, the definition of temporary employment remains highly ambiguous. Often questions are raised whether natural persons 'employed by a service supplier of a Member' include foreigners employed by a foreign firm only, or those employed by host country firms as well (Winters *et al.*, 2003).

Second, GATS Mode-4 covers only the temporary movement of natural persons, but does not define the length of employment that would be legally deemed temporary. Instead, the length of employment is left to the discretion of individual WTO members. Such ambiguities and discretions have resulted in divergent practices. Some countries, for example, grant 90-day visas for the temporary entry of ordinary service providers without renewal, while some countries allow temporary work-visa holders, especially in respect of intra-corporate transfers, to stay for up to five years. Moreover, immigration systems often do not separate migration in terms of service or non-service activities. Currently, visa categories for trade do not make a distinction whether they are truly commercial or whether they involve trade for GATS purposes.

Third, the GATS left it open to member countries to decide what skill levels to cover for temporary labor movement across borders. As a result, many developed countries are increasingly seeking only skilled foreigners, leading to something called the 'brain-drain'—a higher proportion of migration of tertiary educated people from the less developed countries, which implies a net transfer of human capital and scarce resources from low- to high-income countries (Liepziger, 2008). Fourth, the service contract becomes complex when it involves the use of more than one mode of delivery of services from the same individual or company. It is plausible that the same person may provide services as a commercial presence (Mode-3) and, at the same time, as a temporary service by a natural person (Mode-4) (Magdeleine and Maurer, 2008).

Empirical trends in global labor migration and remittance flows

Global labor mobility

Although a phenomenal increase in the mobility of goods and services across the world has been the hallmark of the contemporary phase of globalization, clearly cross-border mobility of labor has not been nearly as robust. A look at the broader global migration pattern may provide useful insights into the evolving pattern of global mobility. During 1960 to 2000, the global migration rate even failed to keep up with the growth of the world population. In 1960, the global migration rate was 3.1 percent of the world population, which fell to 2.7 percent in 2000. During the same period, the absolute number of international immigrants increased from 93 million to 167 million—by 80 percent—while the world population increased from 2.98 billion to 6.07 billion—by 104 percent (Czaika and Hass, 2013, 12–13).

Since 2000, however, the global migration rate has picked up significantly. Between 2000 and 2010, the absolute number of international migrants increased from 174.5 million to 220.7 million—an increase of 26 percent in a decade (see Table 4.1). By 2013, the number of global migrants swelled to 231.5 million. Thus, between 1960 and 2013, the number of the world's migrants tripled—increasing from 75 million to 231.5 million.[3] Falling transportation and travel costs, the globalization of information flows, improvements in education, and more openness to human mobility across borders (even in this age of terrorism), may be some of the factors behind such an uptick in global migration.

In the 1990s, global migrant stock grew on average by about two million per year, but the number more than doubled to 4.6 million annually in the 2000s. During 2010 to 2013, the migration flow slowed down slightly to 3.6 million per year, compared with the previous decade. In terms of annual percentages of growth, global migrant stocks grew by 1.2 percent in the 1990s, 2.3 percent in the 2000s, and by 1.6 percent in the 2010 to 2013 period. Overall, between 1990 and 2013, the numbers of international migration increased by 50 percent. In 2013, 3.2 percent of the global population were international migrants, the highest rate since 1960.

Concentration of migrants' origins and destinations

Although the total number of migrant stock is still relatively small, compared with about 7.2 billion inhabitants in the world today, its magnitude and relative importance in terms of movement and concentration in certain parts of the world is quite remarkable. As Figure 4.1 indicates, between 1990 and 2013, migrant stocks in developed regions increased from 82.3 million to 135.6 million—demonstrating an average annual increase of 2.1 million in the 1990s, 2.6 million in the 2000s, and 1.9 million in 2010 to 2013, with an average annual growth rate of 2.3 percent between 1990 and 2010, and a 1.5 percent growth rate during the period 2010 to 2013. During the same period, the migrant stocks of developing countries increased from 71.9 million to 95.9 million, registering an annual average growth rate of only 1.4 percent. Developing countries in fact experienced negative growth in migrant stocks in the 1990s, but the rate picked up to 2.5 percent in the 2000s, but then fell again to 1.8 percent during the 2010 to 2013 period.

Between 1990 and 2013, the number of international migrants in the North (advanced countries) increased by 53 million (by 65 percent), while the migrant

Table 4.1 International migrant stock by development level and major area, 1990 to 2013

	International migration stock (millions)				*Average annual changes in migrant stock (millions)*			*Average annual growth rate in migrant stock (%)*		
	1990	*2000*	*2010*	*2013*	*1999–2000*	*2000–2010*	*2010–2013*	*1999–2000*	*2000–2010*	*2010–2013*
World	154.2	174.5	220.7	231.5	2.0	4.6	3.6	1.2	2.3	1.6
Developed regions	82.3	103.4	129.7	135.6	2.1	2.6	1.9	2.3	2.3	1.5
Developing regions	71.9	71.1	91.0	95.9	–0.1	2.0	1.6	–0.1	2.5	1.8
Africa	15.6	15.6	17.1	18.6	0.0	0.2	0.5	0.0	0.9	2.8
Asia	49.9	50.4	67.8	70.8	0.1	1.7	1.0	0.1	3.0	1.5
Europe	49.0	56.2	69.2	72.4	0.7	1.3	1.1	1.4	2.1	1.5
Latin America and the Caribbean	7.1	6.5	8.1	8.5	–0.1	0.2	0.2	–0.9	2.2	1.8
North America	27.8	40.4	51.2	53.1	1.3	1.1	0.6	3.7	2.4	1.2
Oceania	4.7	5.4	7.3	7.9	0.1	0.2	0.2	1.5	3.1	2.6

Source: UNDESA (2013a).

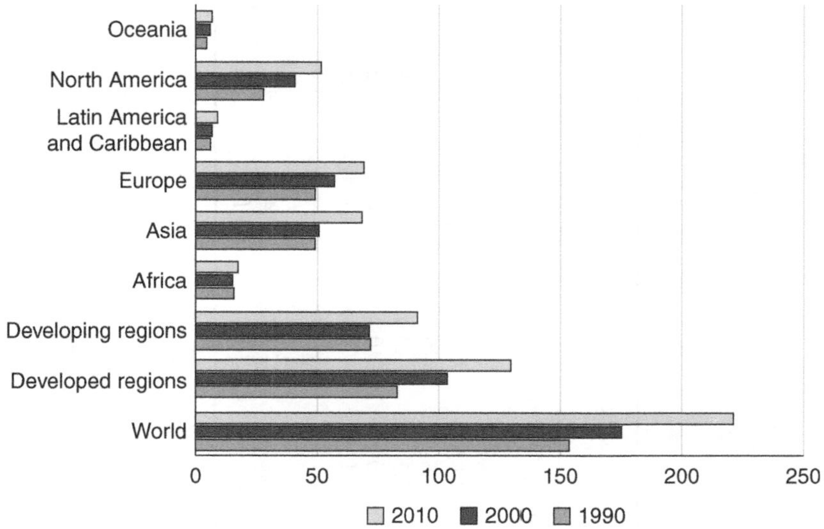

Figure 4.1 International migrant stocks by major areas, 1990 to 2010 (in millions).

population in the South (developing countries) grew by 24 milion (by 34 percent). In 2013, 60 percent of international migrants lived in the developed countries, compared with 43 percent in the 1960s. As a result, the share of international migrants in the developed country population is on the rise—in 2013, the share was nearly 11 percent, compared with less than 9 percent in 2000. Although, in the 2000s, the average annual growth rate for the migrant stock in the South was 2.5 percent per annum compared with 2.3 percent in the developed world, the proportion of international migrants to the total population in the developing countries remained under 2 percent in 2013 due to high population growth in those countries.

The US remains the prime destination of global migration throughout the 1960 to 2013 period (see Table 4.2). In 1960, the US was home to only 12 percent of all international migrants, but that share increased continuously over the years. In 2013, the US was home to 20 percent of total global migrants. There were, however, considerable shifts in the position of other migrant-receiving countries over the course of time. Germany, France, Canada, and Australia, for example, remained among the top 10 destinations of international immigrants, but their ranks shifted back and forth during the past five decades. While Argentina and Brazil were among the top 10 destinations of migrants in the 1960s, they subsequently receded to the back-burner. By the 2000s, some Middle Eastern countries like Saudi Arabia and the UAE emerged as top destinations for migration, and by the 2010s, the Russian Federation emerged as the second largest destination of international migrants, only next to the US. As Figure 4.2 indicates, in 2013, the majority of international migrants lived in

Table 4.2 Shifts in international migration stocks, 1960 to 2013 (in millions)

1960			*2000*			*2013*		
Rank	*Country*	*Net stock*	*Rank*	*Country*	*Net stock*	*Rank*	*Country*	*International migrants*
1	US	9.85	1	US	32.63	1	US	45.8
2	Argentina	2.45	2	Germany	7.53	2	Russian Federation	11.0
3	France	2.31	3	Saudi Arabia	4.91	3	Germany	9.8
4	Germany	1.66	4	France	4.51	4	Saudi Arabia	9.1
5	Canada	1.63	5	Canada	4.30	5	UAE	7.8
6	Hong Kong	1.57	6	Australia	3.56	6	United Kingdom	7.8
7	Indonesia	1.54	7	UAE	2.21	7	France	7.5
8	Australia	1.53	8	Hong Kong	1.94	8	Canada	7.3
9	Brazil	1.25	9	Côte d'Ivoire	1.67	9	Australia	6.5
10	Israel	0.97	10	Israel	1.66	10	Spain	6.5

Source: Author's compilation from Czarika and Hass (2013) and OECD-UNDESA (2013).

Note

Net stock implies balance of immigration to and emigration from a country. International migrants refer to the number of migrants moving into that county.

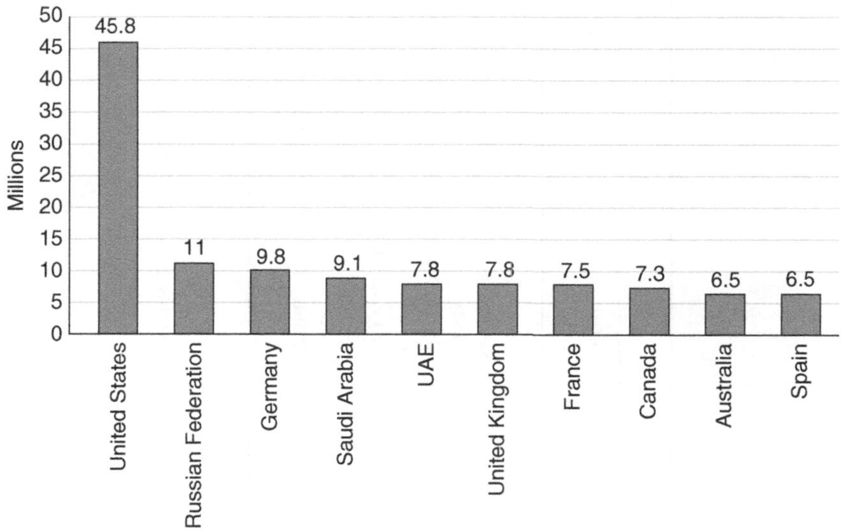

Figure 4.2 Top 10 international migrant stocks, 2013 (in millions).

developed countries. It is also remarkable that in the 2000s, about half of all international migrants resided in the top 10 countries of migration destination in the world (OECD-UNDESA, 2013).

In 2013, over 60 percent of migrants to developed regions originated from the developing countries, in which Asia's share was the largest (47.5 percent), followed by Latin America and the Caribbean (38 percent), and Africa (13.8 percent) (see Table 4.3). Among the 95.9 million migrant stock that migrated to developing regions, 82.3 million (86 percent) were from the developing countries themselves—reflecting what is called South–South migration (see Figure 4.3). Globally, 164 million—over 70 percent of global migrants—originated from the developing countries, in which Asia was the largest source (56 percent), followed by Latin America (22 percent), and Africa (19 percent). Half of the migrants to the OECD countries came from the developing countries in which Mexico topped the list with 11 million, followed by China (3.8 million), and India (3.4 million). Other developing countries with significant migration to OECD countries included the Philippines, Morocco, Vietnam, Algeria, and small island states like Tonga, Guyana, Jamaica, Albania, Barbados, Trinidad and Tobago, Belize, Fiji, El Salvador, and Malta.

Changing patterns of labor migration

In the 1960s, on the other hand, countries like the United Kingdom, Italy, Spain, Greece, China, Poland, and Russia were prime countries of emigration. In the 2000s, a host of new countries like Mexico, Bangladesh, India, the Philippines,

Table 4.3 International migrant populations by destinations and origin, 2013 (in millions)

Destination	*Origin*									
	Developed regions	*Developing regions*	*Africa*	*Asia*	*Europe*	*Latin America and the Caribbean*	*North America*	*Oceania*	*Other*	*World*
Developed regions	53.8	81.8	11.3	38.9	48.8	31.0	2.4	1.6	1.6	135.6
Developing regions	13.7	82.3	19.7	53.7	9.7	5.7	1.9	0.2	5.1	95.9
Africa	1.3	17.3	15.3	1.1	0.8	0.0	0.1	0.0	1.4	18.6
Asia	9.7	61.2	4.4	54	7.6	0.7	0.6	0.1	3.6	70.8
Europe	40.1	32.4	8.7	18.7	37.9	4.5	1.0	0.3	1.5	72.4
Latin America and the Caribbean	2.7	5.9	0.0	0.3	1.2	5.4	1.3	0.0	0.2	8.5
North America	9.6	43.5	2.0	15.7	7.9	25.9	1.2	0.3	0.0	53.1
Oceania	4.1	3.9	0.5	2.9	3.1	0.1	0.2	1.1	0.1	7.9
World	67.5	164.0	30.9	92.6	58.5	36.7	4.3	1.8	6.7	231.5

Source: UNDESA (2013a).

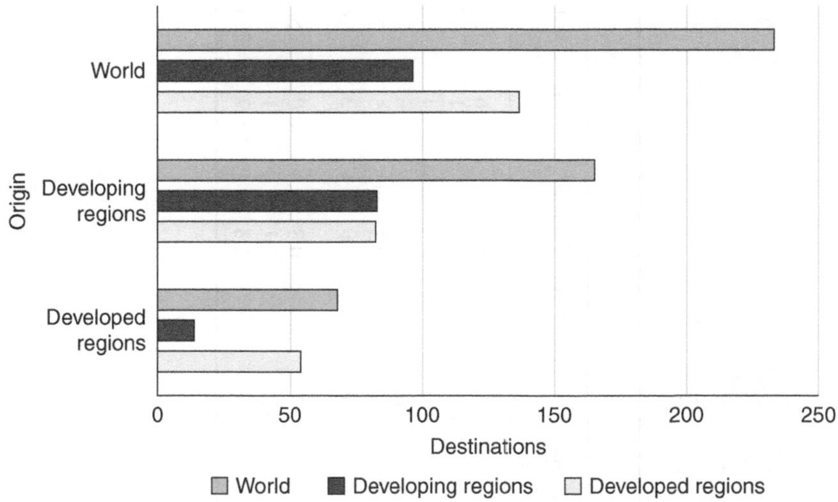

Figure 4.3 International migrant populations by destinations and origins, 2013 (in millions).

Egypt, Poland, Turkey, Vietnam, Indonesia, Morocco, and many small countries and island states of Africa, Latin America, and the Caribbean, like Jamaica, Tonga, Mauritius, Belize, and Fiji. Both Poland and China remained a prime country of origin throughout the 1960s and into the 2000s, but the Chinese figures are relatively low compared with its population (Czaika and Hass, 2013).

Unlike in the past, the recent migration pattern also demonstrates increasing shares of females and tertiary educated workers in the migrant stocks. According to UNDESA (2013b), in the first decade of this century, about 48 percent of the migrant stock were females with varying shares in different regions of the world. For example, their shares were 51.9 percent in Europe, 51.6 percent in Latin America and the Caribbean, 51.2 percent in North America, 50.2 percent in Oceania, 45.9 percent in Africa, and 41.6 percent in Asia.

Second, increasing proportions of migrants in recent years demonstrate what is called 'brain-drain' syndrome—the proportion of tertiary educated immigrants to the OECD countries increased by more than 70 percent in the 2000s. More than 20 percent of the new tertiary educated migrants came from three Asian countries—India (two million), China (1.7 million), the Philippines (1.4 million)—while 2.9 million migrated from African countries. In addition, the share of women in tertiary educated migrant stock was higher than men in the 2000s. At the same time, intra-OECD migration among tertiary educated migrants increased from Germany, the United Kingdom, Poland, France, and the US. Most of the migrants, however, originated in the developing countries (OECD-DESA, 2013b).

Third, recent migration trends also demonstrate that migration can no longer be viewed just as a South-to-North phenomenon. In 2013, out of 135.6 million migrants to developed regions in the world, 53.8 million (about 40 percent) originated in the developed regions (see Figure 4.3). Globally, out of a total of 231.5 million migrants in 2013, 67.5 million (30 percent) originated from developed regions. In fact, since 2000, emigration rates to the OECD countries have increased significantly from several non-Southern countries, such as Albania (9.1 percent), Romania (8.3 percent), the Republic of Moldova (6.3 percent), Bulgaria (4.6 percent), and Lithuania (4.5 percent).

Global remittance flows

More than 90 percent of the migrant stock in the world are considered economic migrants,[4] and thus, increased migration implies an increase in workers' remittances—the monetary transfers that migrants make to their country of origin. During 1970 to 2010, such remittance flows totaled a staggering amount at $6.21 trillion—larger than the combined GDPs of India, Italy, and the Russian Federation in 2013. Growth patterns of remittance inflows have been spectacular as well. From a scanty amount of $1.9 billion in 1970, remittance inflows increased to 35.8 billion in 1980—registering a 19-fold increase in a decade. Then, from $64.1 billion in 1990, remittance inflows increased to $452 billion in 2010—registering a sevenfold increase in two decades (see Table 4.4). The growth of remittance inflows has thus been more spectacular in recent decades. While, in the 1970s and 1980s, annual remittance inflows averaged at $12.6 billion and $43.8 billion, respectively, in the 1990s and 2000s the annual averages were $99 billion and $305 billion, respectively.

Top remittance recipient countries in the world

During 1970 to 2012, an overwhelming 64.3 percent of total remittance inflows of $5.67 trillion went to the top 20 recipient countries (see Table 4.5). The top 10 remittance recipient countries during the period were: India, China, Mexico, France, the Philippines, Germany, Egypt, Nigeria, Spain, and South Korea. During the same period, the top 20 remittance-providing countries had only a 30 percent share in global outflows of remittances. The top 10 remittance-providing countries were: the US, Saudi Arabia, the Russian Federation, Switzerland, Germany, Kuwait, Italy, Spain, France, and Luxembourg.

Understandably, most of the remittance-receiving countries were developing countries, but some developed countries were also among the top recipients. As Table 4.5 indicates, the inflows and outflows of remittances for some developed countries like Italy, Spain, South Korea, France, and Germany were about the same. For the US, the largest remittance provider in the world, however, the gap between receipts and outflows of remittances had been quite large. During the 1970 to 2013 period, the US received remittances of $94 billion, while its outflows of remittances totaled $259 billion. During the same period, remittance outflows had also been very significant for several Gulf countries, including Saudi Arabia, Kuwait, and the United Arab Emirates, as their shares in remittance inflows had been very insignificant.[5]

Table 4.4 Remittance, FDI, and ODA inflows to developing countries, 1970 to 2010 (in US$ billions)

	Years					*Average 1970–1980*	*Average 1981–1990*	*Average 1991–2000*	*Average 2001–2010*
	1970	*1980*	*1990*	*2000*	*2010*				
Global remittance inflows	1.9	35.8	64.1	130.2	452	12.6	43.8	99.3	305.4
Developing countries	1.3	25.1	44.9	91.1	325.0				
Least developed countries	0.09	1.7	3.1	6.4	25				
FDI inflows to developing countries	3.8	7.5	34.8	264.5	637	5.3	23.3	141.6	205.9
Least developed countries	0.01	0.05	0.06	4.1	18.7	–	0.05	3.0	12.1
ODA inflows to developing countries	8.3	43.1	75.0	48.0	156.2	21.5	48.9	66	98.3
Least developed countries	0.08	9.8	17.3	12.2	45.3	4.4	11.9	14.7	29.5

Source: Author's calculation based on World Bank remittance database, OECD statistics, and UNCTADSTAT.

Note

The remittance amounts of LDCs and developing countries are approximate numbers, derived on the basis of ahistorical pattern of 70 percent going to developing countries and 7 percent going to LDCs; 2010 shows actual figures of remittances.

Table 4.5 Top 20 countries of remittance inflows and outflows, 1970 to 2012 (in US$ billions)

Inflows		*Outflows*	
India	547.7	United States	258.7
China	427.0	Saudi Arabia	133.2
Mexico	321.7	Russian Federation	130.0
France	273.5	Switzerland	118.3
Philippines	251.4	Germany	77.3
Germany	189.1	Kuwait	63.5
Egypt, Arab Republic	171.5	Italy	61.3
Nigeria	163.5	Spain	60.5
Spain	155.6	France	57.2
Korea, Republic of	137.3	Luxembourg	53.9
Italy	137.2	Netherlands	52.0
Pakistan	123.7	Korea, Republic of	45.9
Portugal	121.8	Oman	31.5
Bangladesh	104.7	Canada	26.4
Morocco	100.9	Lebanon	22.3
United States	93.8	Norway	22.3
Belgium	92.9	Japan	21.4
Turkey	82.9	Qatar	21.3
Poland	82.6	Belgium	21.2
United Kingdom	67.3	Australia	20.5
Top 20 (64.3%)	3.65 trillion	Top 20 (29.3%)	1.30 trillion
Global total	5.67 trillion		4.43 trillion

Source: Author's calculation from World Bank remittance database.

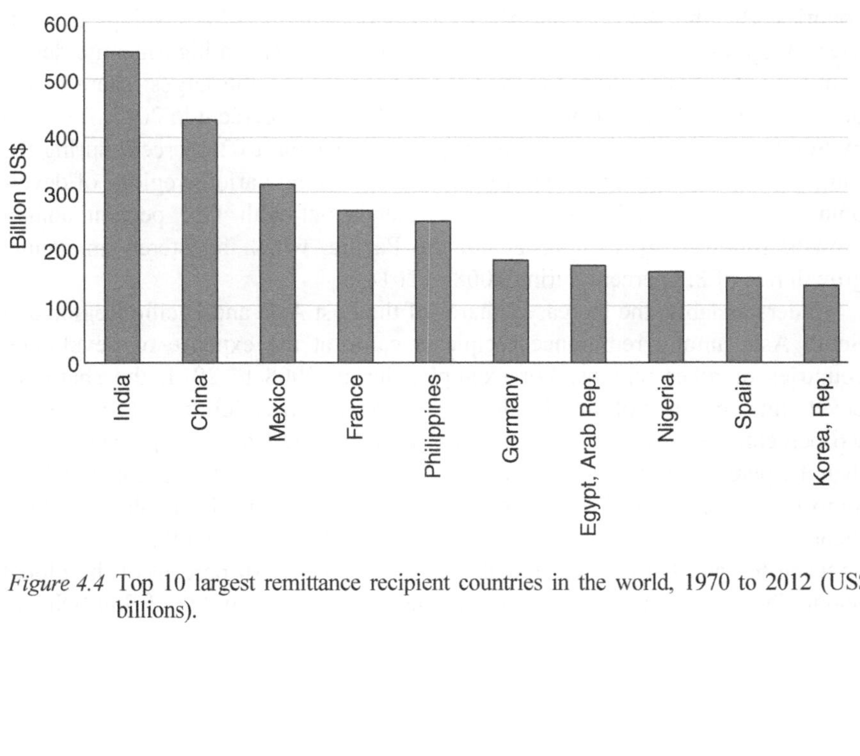

Figure 4.4 Top 10 largest remittance recipient countries in the world, 1970 to 2012 (US$ billions).

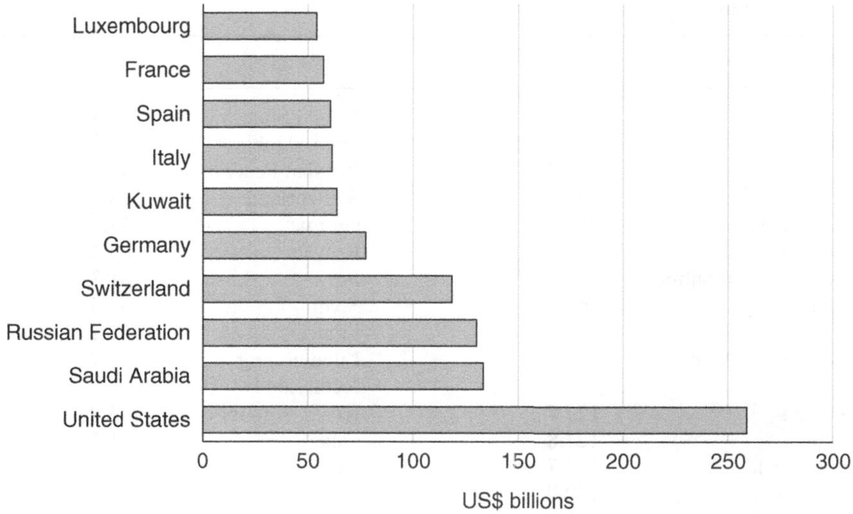

Figure 4.5 Top 10 largest remittance source countries in the world, 1970 to 2012 (US$ billions).

Changing shares of the developing countries in remittances

As the above discussion suggests, in recent years, workers' remittance has emerged as a great source of external finance for developing countries. As Table 4.6 shows, during the 2008 to 2014 period, in each of these years more than 70 percent of increasingly robust inflows of remittances accrued to the developing counties. But the share of the pie varied widely among the developing countries—the bulk of the remittances, over 92 percent, went to high-income developing countries. The East Asia and Pacific region had the largest share of the pie—its share increased from 26 percent in 2008 to 29 percent in 2013, followed by South Asia whose shares increased from 22 percent to 26 percent during the same period. In terms of growth of remittances among various regions of developing countries, South Asia, however, stands out with 11.5 percent annual growth, followed by East Asia and the Pacific, which registered an annual growth rate of 8.7 percent during 2008 to 2014.

Understandably, the increased shares of the East Asia and Pacific Region and South Asia among remittance recipients came at the expense of developing countries of other regions. For example, during 2008 to 2014, the shares of developing countries of the Middle East and North Africa fell from 11 percent to 9.6 percent, the shares of Europe and Central Asia fell from 14 percent to less than 12 percent, and the shares of Latin America and the Caribbean fell from almost 20 percent to 17.5 percent. During the same period, the share of low-income developing countries in the global inflow of remittances hovered between 6.8 and 8.4 percent. For the LDCs—home of 10 percent of the global population—the share ranged between 7 and 8 percent, and that of Sub-Saharan

Table 4.6 Remittance flows to developing countries, 2008 to 2014 (in US$ billions)

	2008	*2009*	*2010*	*2011*[a]	*2012*[b]	*2013*[b]	*2014*[b]
World	456	429	449	483	514	550	593
	(15.9)	(–5.8)	(4.6)	(7.5)	(6.4)	(7.1)	(7.7)
High-income countries	132	123	124	132	137	144	152
Percentage growth	(14.7)	(–7.1)	(1.1)	(6.3)	(4.1)	(4.9)	(5.7)
All developing countries	324	307	325	351	377	406	441
Percentage growth	(16.4)	(–5.2)	(6.0)	(8.0)	(7.3)	(7.9)	(8.4)
Share in global remittance inflows	71%	71.6%	72.4%	72.7%	73.3%	73.8%	74.4%
Low-income developing countries	22	23	25	28	30	33	37
Percentage growth	(32.8)	(3.7)	(8.9)	(12.0)	(9.4)	(10.4)	(11.5)
Share in remittance to developing countries (%)	6.8	7.5	7.7	8.0	7.9	8.1	8.4
Middle-income developing countries	302	284	301	324	347	373	404
Percentage growth	(15.4)	(–5.9)	(5.8)	(7.6)	(7.1)	(7.6)	(8.2)
Share in remittance to developing countries (%)	93.2	92.5	92.6	92.3	92.0	92.0	91.6
Least developed countries (LDCs)	23	24	25	27	29	32	35
Percentage growth	(32.5)	(2.0)	(4.9)	(8.5)	(8.5)	(9.1)	(9.6)
Share in global remittance inflows	5.0%	5.5%	5.6%	5.6%	5.6%	5.8%	5.9%
Share in remittance to developing countries	7.0%	7.8%	7.7%	7.7%	7.7%	7.9%	7.9%
East Asia and Pacific	85	85	94	101	109	117	127
Percentage growth	(18.8)	(0.4)	(10.2)	(7.6)	(7.3)	(8.0)	(8.7)
Share in remittance to developing countries (%)	26.2	27.7	28.9	28.8	28.9	28.8	28.8
Europe and Central Asia	45	36	36	40	44	48	53
Percentage growth	(16.3)	–(19.8)	(–0.1)	(11)	(8.8)	(10.1)	(11.4)
Share in remittance to developing countries (%)	13.9	11.7	11.1	11.4	11.7	11.8	12.0
Latin America and the Caribbean	64	57	57	61	66	71	77
Percentage growth	(2.2)	(–12.2)	(1.2)	(7.0)	(7.6)	(7.9)	(8.1)
Share in remittance to developing countries (%)	19.7	18.6	17.5	17.4	17.5	17.5	17.5
Middle East and North Africa	36	34	35	36	37	39	42
Percentage growth	(12.0)	(–6.7)	(3.3)	(2.6)	(5.0)	(5.3)	(5.5)
Share in remittance to developing countries (%)	11.1	11.1	10.8	10.2	9.8	9.6	9.5
South Asia	72	75	82	90	97	105	114
Percentage growth	(32.6)	(4.8)	(9.5)	(10.1)	(7.4)	(7.9)	(8.4)
Share in remittance to developing countries (%)	22.2	24.4	25.2	25.6	25.7	25.9	25.8
Sub-Saharan Africa	22	20	21	23	24	26	28
Percentage growth	(15.8)	(–7.0)	(4.5)	(7.4)	(6.3)	(6.8)	(7.3)
Share in remittance to developing countries (%)	6.8	6.5	6.4	6.5	6.4	6.4	6.3

Source: Author’s calculation on the basis of World Bank (2011b).

Notes

a Estimate.

b Forecast. Numbers in parentheses are percentages of annual growth.

Africa—the third world of the Third World—the share remained at around 6 percent throughout the period.

Importance of remittances in the GDPs of developing countries

Workers' remittances have also emerged as a dominant segment of GDPs in many developing countries. Between 1995 and 2010, the share of remittances in developing countries' GDPs almost doubled—an increase from 0.95 percent to 1.75 percent.[6] In developed countries, however, the share of remittances in GDP hovered around 0.2 and 0.3 percent during the same period. Among the developing countries, the share of remittances in GDP was 2.2 percent for low-income countries, 1.5 percent for middle-income countries, and 0.8 percent for high-income countries, indicating the relatively higher importance of remittances in the GDP of low-income developing countries (UNDP, 2011, 127–128). As Table 4.7 shows, in 2012, the top remittance recipients among the developing countries in terms of shares in their GDPs were Tajikistan, Kyrgyz, Nepal, Moldova, Samoa, Lesotho, Armenia, Haiti, Liberia, and Kosovo (see Figure 4.6).

However, most of the top remittance-receiving countries in the world are relatively well-off developing countries. In 2013, for example, the top 10 remittance recipient developing countries in the world were India, China, the Philippines, Mexico, Nigeria, Egypt, Pakistan, Bangladesh, Vietnam, and Ukraine—most of whom are high-income developing countries. The same year, $266 billion (65 percent) of the $406 billion that accrued to the developing countries went to the top 10 remittance recipient countries, of which $178 billion, more than 40 percent of total receipts of all developing countries, went to four countries: India, China, the Philippines, and Mexico (see Figure 4.7).

Table 4.7 Top 10 remittance recipients and top 10 countries with largest shares of remittances in their GDPs (in US$ billions)

Top 10 remittance recipient countries (2013)	*Remittance (US$ billions)*	*Top 10 countries with largest shares in GDPs (2012)*	*Share in GDP (%)*
India	70	Tajikistan	52
China	60	Kyrgyz Republic	31
Philippines	25	Nepal	25
Mexico	23	Moldova	25
Nigeria	21	Samoa	23
Egypt	17	Lesotho	23
Pakistan	15	Armenia	21
Bangladesh	14	Haiti	21
Vietnam	11	Liberia	20
Ukraine	10	Kosovo	17

Source: Author's calculation from World Bank remittance database.

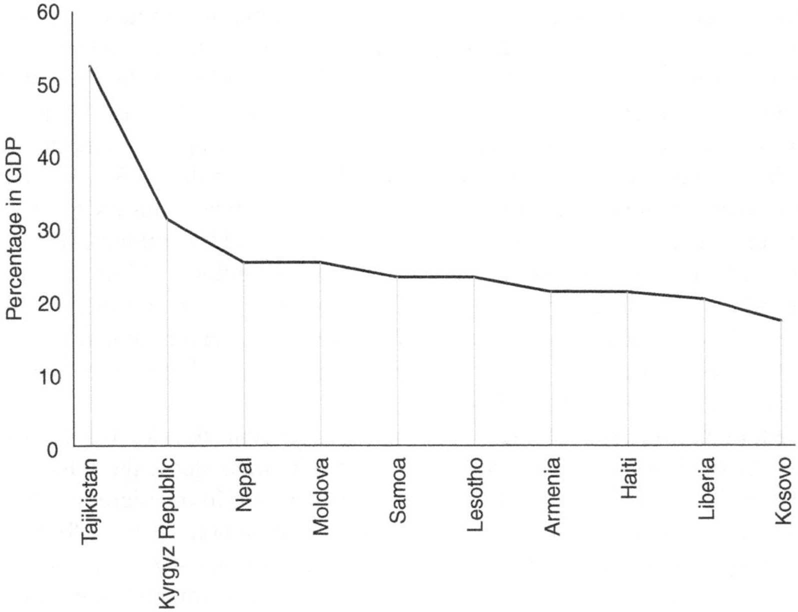

Figure 4.6 Top 10 countries with largest share of remittance in their GDPs, 2012 (%).

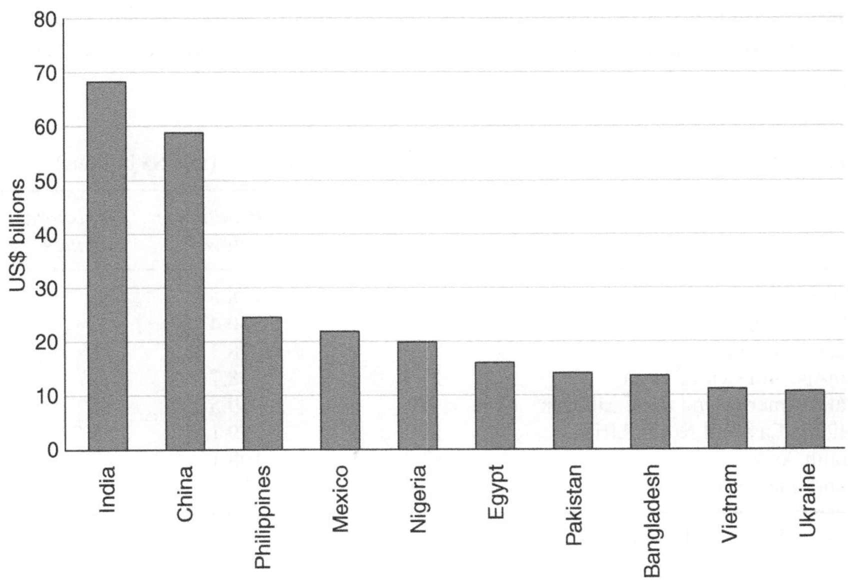

Figure 4.7 Top 10 remittance recipient countries in the world, 2013 (US$ billions).

Regional variations on remittance inflows

Regional variations in the developing countries in terms of remittance inflows and migrant stocks are quite remarkable as well. As Table 4.8 shows, Sub-Saharan Africa as a region had a remittance inflow of $26.7 billion in 2012, although it had the largest migrant stock (17.6 million), while the East Asian and Pacific region, with about one-third of migrant stock (5.4 million) had almost three times larger remittance inflows ($78.3 billion). Similarly, South Asian migrant stocks totaled 12.2 million in 2012, with remittance inflows of 108.1 billion for virtually the same number of migrant stock (11.9 million), and the Middle East and North African region had a remittance inflows of less than half ($39.1 billion). Such differences may be explained by discrepancies in the income and skills patterns of migrants, the propensity to send remittances back home, the use of official channels to transmit remittances, and other such factors (World Bank, 2011a; Chami *et al.*, 2008).

In addition, diaspora savings vary among different developing country regions. In 2012, for example, with 5.4 million migration stock, the East Asia and Pacific diaspora saved $116 billion, while with 17.6 million migration stock Sub-Saharan Africa region's diaspora saved only 37 billion (see Table 4.8). Similarly, Europe and Central Asia's 15.3 million migrant stock saved $93 billion, while Latin America and the Caribbean region's 6.1 million migrant stock saved $146 billion. In the end, the factors that affect diaspora savings include: (1) the size of diaspora stocks in different host countries; (2) average incomes of diaspora members, and (3) diaspora members' propensity to save. The World Bank (2011b) estimates that diaspora savings, as a share of GDP, may range between 2.3 percent in middle-income countries and as high as 9 percent in low-income countries, and annual total diaspora savings of all developing countries may be in the range of $400 billion, with a $34 billion share of low-income countries.

Table 4.8 Global remittance inflows and diaspora savings in 2012 (in US$ billions)

	Migration stock (in millions)	*Remittance inflows*	*Diaspora savings*
World	213.3	478.5	
Developing countries	68.7	350.4	
East Asia and Pacific	5.4	78.3	116
Europe and Central Asia	15.3	38.7	93
Latin America and the Caribbean	6.1	59.5	146
Middle East and North Africa	11.9	39.1	47
South Asia	12.2	108.1	72
Sub-Saharan Africa	17.6	26.7	37

Source: Author's calculation from World Bank remittance database.

Table 4.9 Inflows of foreign direct investment, official development assistance, and remittances, 2001 to 2011 (in US$ billions)

	Year											*Average 2001–2011*
	2001	*2002*	*2003*	*2004*	*2005*	*2006*	*2007*	*2008*	*2009*	*2010*	*2011*	
FOREIGN DIRECT INVESTMENT (FDI)												
World	836.0	626.1	601.2	734.1	989.6	1480.6	2002.7	1816.4	1216.5	1408.5	1651.5	1214.8
Developing economies	224.1	169.2	193.7	280.3	334.5	432.1	589.4	668.4	530.3	637.1	735.2	435.8
Least developed countries	7.1	6.8	10.2	8.5	7.5	11.5	15.0	18.8	17.6	18.7	21.4	13.0
Sub-Saharan Africa	15.2	11.4	14.2	12.4	20.9	16.9	29.8	38.4	36.5	29.9	42.0	24.3
OFFICIAL DEVELOPMENT ASSISTANCE (ODA)												
World	59.4	62.4	64.7	71.9	112.3	96.1	115.7	146.1	165.0	167.2	163.0	111.3
Developing economies	54.2	54.8	57.8	65.3	106.4	89.2	108.4	135.6	155.0	156.2	151.0	103.1
Least developed countries	13.6	16.8	25.2	25.0	25.7	27.7	33.3	40.8	42.0	45.3	43.0	30.8
Sub-Saharan Africa	12.2	20.2	24.2	23.7	30.6	29.6	30.1	36.5	42.5	41.6	43.2	30.4
REMITTANCE INFLOWS												
World	131.5	170.0	221.0	237.0	274.9	317.0	385.0	456.0	429.0	449.0	483.0	323.0
Developing countries	96.0	116.0	144.0	161.0	191.0	235.0	278.0	324.0	307.0	325.0	351.0	229.8
Least developed countries	6.8	8.4	9.6	10.8	11.8	14.0	17.0	23.0	24.0	25.0	27	16.1
Sub-Saharan Africa	4.7	5.0	5.9	8.0	9.3	13.0	19.0	22.0	20.0	21.0	23.0	13.7

Source: Author's calculation based on World Bank remittance database, OECD statistics and UNCTADSTAT.

Trends in external financial inflows to developing countries

Historically, inflows of Official Development Assistance (ODA) and Foreign Direct Investment (FDI)[7] had been the largest sources of external finance for most of the developing countries, but in recent years the tide appears to have turned. During the 1970 to 2010 period, inflows of remittances to developing countries increased from $1.3 billion to $325 billion, while FDI inflows to developing countries increased from $3.8 billion to $637 billion—both 168 times. During the same period, ODA inflows to developing countries increased from $8 billion in to $156 billion—less than 20 times (see Figure 4.8). More recently, during the 2001 to 2011 period, annual average remittance inflows to the developing countries totaled $229 billion, while FDI inflows averaged at $435 billion, and ODA inflows averaged at $103 billion—thus remittance inflows have surpassed ODA inflows, although FDI inflows still remain above remittance inflows (see Table 4.9).

When it comes to the LDCs and Sub-Saharan Africa, however, remittances averaged at $16 billion and $13.7 billion, respectively during the 2001 to 2011 period, when ODA averaged at $30.8 billion and 30.4 billion, respectively, and FDI averaged at $13 billion and $24 billion, respectively. This means that, in the context of the LDCs and Sub-Saharan African countries, remittance inflows are now on a par with FDI inflows, although ODA inflows still exceed remittances as a source of external finance.

Remittance and economic development

Empirical lessons

As the discussion above indicates, inflows of workers' remittances to the developing countries have been rising phenomenally in recent years and decades, and

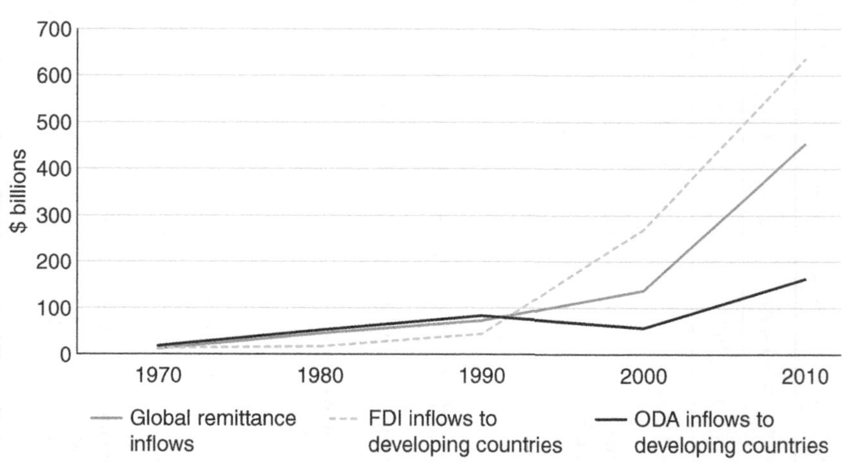

Figure 4.8 Remittance, FDI and ODA inflows to developing countries, 1970 to 2010 ($ billions).

by the early 2000s these inflows exceeded other external sources of finance, such as FDI or ODI, or the combined inflows of both, in many developing countries (Ratha and Shaw, 2007). Thus, such "golden eggs," as Haas (2005) puts it, received from "millions of powerless working class emigrants," have now emerged as a viable alternative to foreign aid, foreign loans, or foreign private investment in many developing countries. Some labor-sending countries, such as the Philippines, Bangladesh, and Nepal, have not only managed to offset large trade deficits, but also succeeded in maintaining a current account surplus in recent years due to the large inflow of remittances (World Bank, 2010a). Remittances also provide a distinct advantage over other sources of external finance—they are not subject to the whims of donor governments or private investors, or burdensome conditions of multilateral institutions. More importantly the remittances are not likely to be siphoned off by corrupt government officials (Kapur and McHale, 2003). While such extraordinary benefits associated with inflows of remittances can hardly be overemphasized, considerable debate does persist on the role of remittances in respect of domestic investment and economic growth, poverty reduction, foreign exchange, and exports, and the 'brain-drain.'

Investment and growth

Available literature suggests an evolving scenario of the relationships between remittances and domestic investment and economic growth. Several powerful studies in the early 1970s through the early 1990s embraced what is called a 'conventional approach' by stipulating that labor migration could be a "slippery slope to political instability and random social change" (Keely and Tran, 1989); that "the decline in the volumes of remittances is inevitable" (Birks and Sinclair, 1980); and that "an over-reliance on labor exporting as a strategy for economic development generally produces disappointing results" (Taylor *et al.*, 1996, 182). More recent studies, expounded since the mid-1990s coinciding with the phenomenal growth in the inflows of workers' remittances, however, reflect a 'revisionist approach,' and which tend to portray remittances rather as a sound and viable vehicle for raising the levels of national savings, reducing chronic poverty, increasing consumption, and inducing economic growth and development in remittance-receiving countries.[8]

First, let us focus on the findings of the earlier studies. During the 1960s through the 1980s, Turkey exported more than 800,000 workers to European countries, especially to Germany, under a massive state-sponsored migration policy. Several studies, however, found that not only did such a massive migration fail to contribute to substantial capital formation in Turkey, but also resulted in a significant shortage of trained manpower for domestic industrial projects. Similar studies carried out in other developing countries, such as Greece, former Yugoslavia, Spain, Portugal, Yemen, Morocco, Algeria, Lesotho, and Sudan, also found that returning migrant workers settled in urban rather than in rural areas, and spent most of their income on conspicuous consumption, housing construction, and durable goods, with little or no contribution toward domestic investment or economic growth. Although returning migrants in some Latin American and Caribbean countries appeared to have channeled some remittances into savings and investment—for example, 5.7 percent in El Salvador, 9.4 percent in Guatemala, and 8 percent in Nicaragua—most of the remittances to these countries ended up in the purchase of land, the construction of houses, and imports of consumer goods, resulting in higher inflation and lower agricultural production (Taylor *et al.*, 1996, 168–200).

Several studies on Asian economies, conducted in the late 1980s, however, found that remittances had significant positive effects on GDP, production, employment, and investment in labor-sending developing countries. Studies on Pakistan, for example, found that remittances boosted the country's economic growth by increasing domestic savings and providing scarce foreign exchange, although the economy came under inflationary pressures. Studies on India found that remittances contributed 6 percent to domestic savings and 7 percent to gross domestic capital formation in the mid-1980s. Studies on South Korea, however, found that migrant remittances played a significant role in the country's GNP growth during 1976 to 1981. Studies on Bangladesh, the Philippines, and Thailand, on the other hand, suggested that a significant share of remittances went to land, housing, education, and conspicuous consumption (Taylor *et al.*, 1996, 168–200). Overall, earlier studies, as Haas (2005) points out, were largely 'one-sided'—they focused on the interests and consequences of labor migration for receiving countries and societies, and thus undermined "the potential contribution of migration to enhancing welfare and well-being in both the sending and the receiving countries."

More recent studies, however, found far better use of workers' remittances in many remittance-receiving developing countries. Massey and Parrado (1994), for example, found that 20 percent of new business enterprises in 30 communities surveyed in Mexico could be attributed to workers' remittances. Dustmann and Kirchcamp (2002) found that about half of the returned migrant population in Turkey became active in entrepreneurship and 32 percent returning emigrants created jobs in entrepreneurial activities. McCormick and Wahba (2001) showed that overseas savings played a significant role in the development of entrepreneurship in Egypt. Adams (2005) found that remittances had a significant effect on rural asset accumulation in Pakistan. Korovilas (1998) found that the relative success of the Albanian economy in the 1990s rested largely on the inflow of remittances, and Giuliano and Ruiz-Arranz (2005) showed that remittances contributed to growth in those less developed countries with underdeveloped financial sectors by investing their savings in small businesses, real estate, or other assets.

Similarly, several studies conducted in the 2000s found a positive correlation between remittances and educational improvement (the development of human capital) in labor-sending developing countries. For example, Cox-Edwards and Ureta (2003) showed that remittances significantly reduced the probability of school drop-outs in El Salvador, and Hanson and Woodruff (2003) showed that remittance inflows improved school attendance among Mexican boys and girls.

Similarly, Mckenzie and Rapoport (2007) showed that migration reduced educational inequality, especially among girls.

Chami *et al.* (2005), on the basis of panel data from 113 countries, found that remittances "may increase investment, facilitate human capital formation, enhance total factor productivity (TFP), and may have a favorable effect on the financial system, all of which potentially contribute positively to economic growth." The authors, however, also point out that remittances may give rise to moral hazard problems leading to negative effects on the economic growth of less developed countries as remittance recipient households tend to work less, save less, restrict efforts to work, and make riskier investments. Several related studies, however, indicate that although remittance recipient families might work less, the decline in mothers' outside work due to remittance inflows lowered the incidence of infant mortality in Mexico (Duryea *et al.*, 2005), and although remittances reduced labor force participation, they contributed to increasing schooling among Pilipino children (UNDP, 2011, 129)

As the empirical evidence elaborated above indicates, the impact of remittances on economic growth remains inconclusive. Several recent studies, however, asserted stronger linkages between remittances and economic growth in labor-sending developing countries. A study of 39 developing countries covering the period 1980 to 2004, for example, found a positive impact of remittance inflows on economic growth of labor-sending countries (Pradhan *et al.*, 2008). Similarly, a study on 18 Latin American countries for the period 1980 to 2005, and another study on African economies for the period 1980 to 2004 found that remittances significantly and positively affected the economic growth of these economies (UNDP, 2011, 131–132).

Exports and foreign exchange

Theoretically, large inflows of international remittances should result in the appreciation of the real exchange rate, which, in turn, would reduce export competitiveness of the remittance-receiving country. Remittance from abroad may also affect export competitiveness of a labor-sending country due to increases in the demand for non-tradable goods, which drives labor away from the export sector. In a study on several Latin American and Caribbean countries, Amuedo-Dorantes and Pozo (2004) found that the real exchange rate appreciated by approximately 0.2 percent following an increase of 1 percent in remittance inflows. Lopez-Cordova and Olmedo (2006) showed that on average a 10 percent increase in remittance inflows (as a fraction of GDP) reduced exports between 2 to 4 percent depending on the use of the estimation strategy. While these findings raise concerns of so-called Dutch Disease—resource discoveries resulting in real exchange rate appreciation and shifting of resources from the traded to the non-traded sectors—Ratha (2007) points out that although there is no dispute that remittances may cause currency appreciation, the evidence so far suggests that there is no such 'Dutch Disease.'

Poverty reduction

Most of the available studies suggest a strong linkage between remittance inflows and poverty reduction in labor-sending countries. For example, on the basis of a study of many labor-exporting developing countries, Adams and Page (2004) concluded that a 10 percent increase in the share of remittances in a country's GDP leads to a decline in the incidence of poverty by 1.1 percent. Subsequently, Adams (2005) reported a 20 percent reduction in the severity of poverty in Guatemala due to the inflow of international remittances. Ratha (2007) showed that remittances reduced the poverty–headcount ratio significantly in low-income countries—11 percent in Uganda, 6 percent in Bangladesh, 5 percent in Ghana, and 3 to 5 percent in Nepal—and concluded that a 10 percent increase in per capita official remittances leads to 3.5 percent decline in the share of poor people.[9]

Earlier, Adelman and Taylor (1990) estimated that with every dollar brought into Mexico as remittance increased to $2.69 to $3.18, depending on which household group received these remittances. The study also found that remittances produce larger income multiplier effects when they go to rural households, whose consumption and expenditure patterns favor goods produced domestically with relatively labor-intensive production technologies and few imported inputs. Conversely, when remittances go to urban households, multiplier effect tends to fall, as more of the remittance dollar leaks out of the country in the form of import demand. Some earlier studies (e.g., Massey and Parrado, 1994) also found that the multiplier effect of remittances was much higher when remittances went to lower strata of society (Das and Serieux, 2010).

The brain-drain and development dilemma

Finally there is the age-old question of the 'brain drain'—the net transfer of human capital and scarce resources from labor-sending low-income countries to developed countries. As mentioned above, the number of tertiary educated immigrants in the OECD countries has increased by 70 percent in the past decade to 27 million in 2010/2011, and one-fifth of them originated from three Asian countries—India, China, and the Philippines. Earlier, the World Bank (2008) pointed out that over 80 percent of Indian migrants aged 25 years and over in industrialized countries had a university degree, compared to 2.5 percent of that age group back in India.

Available data of 137 countries for 2010/2011 indicate that for virtually all countries of origin the emigration rate of the highly skilled had exceeded the total emigration rate, and the migration rates of highly skilled were 20 times those of the total emigration rates for many countries, such as Burundi, Lesotho, Malawi, the Maldives, Mozambique, Namibia, Niger, Papua New Guinea, the United Republic of Tanzania, and Zambia (OCED-UNDESA, 2013). The report also points out that the brain-drain problem is particularly acute in small countries and island states of Africa, and Latin America and the Caribbean. In 2010, for example, close to 90 percent of highly skilled persons born in Guyana lived in OECD countries, and more tertiary educated persons lived outside Barbados, Haiti, and Trinidad and Tobago than in those countries. In addition, almost all physicians trained in Grenada and Dominica emigrated abroad, and some other smaller countries like St. Lucia, Cape Verde, Fiji, São Tomé and Principe, and Liberia were among the countries with the highest emigration rates of physicians.

As Table 4.10 indicates, in 2000, in as many as 20 countries at least 60 percent of their tertiary educated professionals migrated to the OECD countries, and most of these were small countries and island states of Africa, and Latin America and the Caribbean. In some of these countries and island states, such as Guyana, Jamaica, St. Vincent and the Grenadines, Grenada, Haiti, Cabo Verde, and Palau, more than 80 percent of their tertiary educated professionals migrated to the OECD countries. Compared with such small countries and island states, in countries with large populations, such as Brazil, China, India, and the Russian Federation, emigration rates of their highly skilled professionals were below 3.5 percent in 2000.[10]

The migration syndrome known as the brain-drain is thus real for all practical purposes. The question is no longer whether global labor migration entails the

Table 4.10 Top 20 countries with highest percentage of migrants with tertiary education to OECD countries

Country	*Migration stock (in thousands), 2010*	*% tertiary educated to OECD (2000)*
Guyana	12	89.2
Jamaica	30	84.7
St. Vincent and the Grenadines	9	84.6
Grenada	13	84.3
Haiti	35	83.4
Cabo Verde	12	82.4
Palau	6	80.9
Trinidad and Tobago	34	78.9
St. Kitts and Nevis	5	78.5
Seychelles	11	77.3
Tonga	1	75.6
Samoa	9	73.4
St. Lucia	10	68.6
Antigua and Barbuda	21	68.5
Gambia	290	67.8
Suriname	39	65.8
Belize	47	65.5
Tuvalu	0	64.9
Dominica	6	63.9
Fiji	19	62.8
Barbados	28	62.6

Source: Compiled from World Bank remittance database.

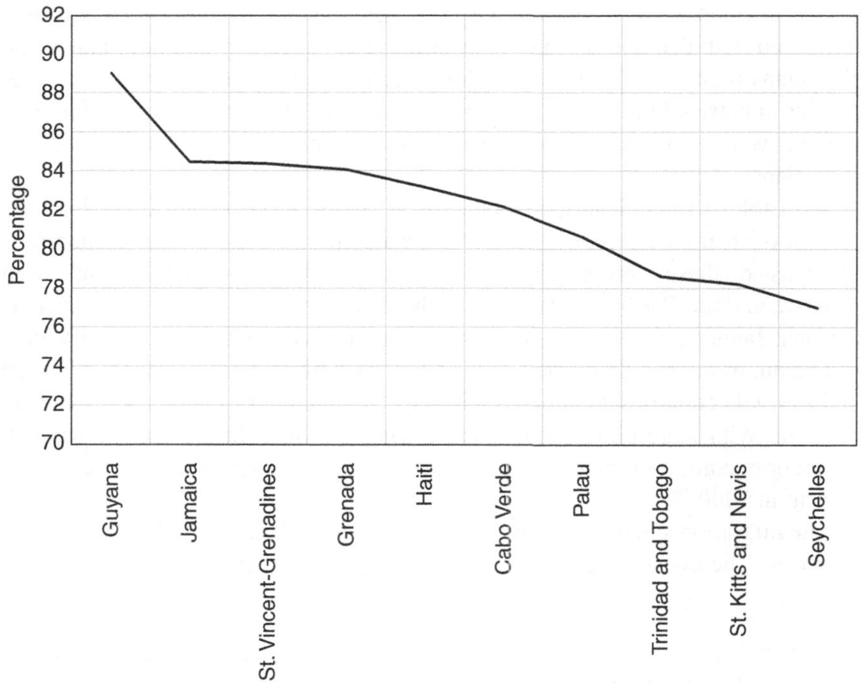

Figure 4.9 Countries with highest percentages of tertiary educated migration to OECD countries.

'brain-drain,' but how to assess and address controversial effects of the brain-drain on labor-sending low-income countries and labor-receiving developed countries. The crux of the issue lies with public investment in education—when workers migrate, precious little investment which the migrant-sending country made in the migrating individuals might be a total loss to that society, unless, of course, the losses are somehow offset by remittance inflows or some other kind of return. Thus, the brain-drain issue raises two central questions: (1) why some labor choose to migrate and why some labor-sending countries choose to export labor in the first place; and (2) if skilled labor migrates, how that helps labor-receiving countries and adversely affects labor-sending countries.

Why do workers tend to migrate?

First, let us focus on the first question: why some workers tend to migrate. Neo-classical economics, for example, provide a sound rationale for labor migration. A rational utility-maximizing individual will take advantage of differentials in wages and employment conditions between countries and immigration costs, and conceive a movement as an income-maximization decision. According to the labor migration models of Lewis (1954) and Ranis and Fei (1961), workers from low-wage countries migrate to high-wage countries, and thus drive up wages in labor-rich countries and drive down wages in capital-rich countries. Sjaastad (1962) and Todaro (1969), in their macro-analyses of labor migration, also postulated that individual rational actors decide to migrate in accordance with cost–benefit calculations with the expectation of a positive net return from such a movement.

The central tenant of neoclassical economic theories—a linear relationship between wage differentials and migration flows—however, has been challenged by many since the 1970s. The Dual Market Theory, developed by Piore (1979), for example, views international migration as a natural consequence of economic globalization and market penetration across national boundaries (Massey *et al.*, 1993, 432). According to this theory, international migration is caused by a permanent demand for immigrant labor that is inherent to the economic structure of developed nations—it is not caused by 'push factors' in sending countries (such as low wages or high unemployment); it rather results from 'pull factors' in receiving countries (a chronic and unavoidable need for workers).

Since people work not only for income, but also for the accumulation and maintenance of social status, advanced countries create demand for low-skilled jobs which domestic workers refuse to take. Stark and Bloom (1985), in their new economics of migration, showed that international migration is not solely based on the rational calculations of labor, but is rather a resource maximization decision of families or households, and labor migration does not necessarily stop when wage differentials were eliminated across national boundaries—incentives for labor migration would remain for the failure of other markets in labor-sending countries (Massey *et al.*, 1993, 439–440).

The World Systems Theory, put forward by Wallerstein (1979) and other sociological theorists, stipulated that with the pace of globalization the penetration of capitalist economic relations into peripheral, non-capitalist societies creates a mobile population that is prone to migrate abroad (Silver, 2003). This propensity of migration is intensified by structural disparities between areas with stagnant economies but high rates of fertility and areas with fast-growing economies but declining fertility (Hugo, 1998). At the same time, a rapidly aging population—lack of a working-age population—leads to a severe labor shortage in industrialized economies, especially in low-skilled jobs. Thus, due to both strong pull and push factors, demand for 3D jobs (dirty, demanding, and dangerous jobs) is on the rise in advanced countries (Massey *et al.*, 1993, 444).

There are also several other theories that deserve attention in respect of workers' willingness to migrate. First, the Network Theory explains how diaspora influences migrants' destinations, how migration patterns tend to form so-called migration regimes, and why migration continues even when wage differentials cease to exist (Dustmann and Glitz, 2005; Faist, 2000). Second, the Migration Systems Theory emphasizes the 'developmental' context of migration—how migratory movements arise in response to prior links between labor-sending and -receiving states, such as colonial ties, trade, or investment flows

(Castles and Miller, 2009; Haas, 2005). Finally, the Theory of Transnational Migration explains how migrants stay connected and participate in both the home and host country's political, economic, social, and cultural environments (Bretell and Hollifield, 2008).

As the discussion above indicates, scores of theories explain the reasons, and the pull and push factors of migration in divergent ways.[11] Obviously some are influenced by the factors highlighted by neoclassical economics—given freedom to choose, a rational labor will try to exploit wage differences by migrating from low-wage jobs in home countries to high-wage jobs in developed countries. Then, others may be more concerned with non-income factors as well, such as the accumulation and maintenance of social status, and sociological, motivational, and developmental factors as emphasized by other theories. Considerable empirical evidence, however, suggests that wage and income inequalities serve as a powerful force for migration and the propensity to emigrate increases with skills and education. For example, the rate of emigration of skilled workers is often as high as 20 times that of ordinary emigration rates (UNDESA, 2013). In addition, at least 12 percent of the doctors trained in India live in the UK, about 50 percent of graduates of South African and Pakistani medical schools emigrated to industrial countries, and Jamaica had to train five doctors and Grenada 22 to keep just one at home (Page and Plaza, 2006, 313). Such a level of migration of qualified professionals from the developing countries does suggest that wage and income inequalities serve as powerful forces for migration and that the propensity to emigrate increases with skills and education (Carrington and Detragiache, 1998; Nakosteen and Zimmer, 1980).

Why do some countries export labor?

Why do some countries choose to export labor, wherein lies the interest of labor-sending developing countries? As mentioned above, most labor-sending developing countries are overpopulated, and according to demographic projections, most of the future population growth will take place in those countries. According to United Nations (2012) projections, from 7.2 billion now, the world population is set to increase to 8.1 billion by 2025, and to 9.6 billion in 2050. Almost all of these additional people will enlarge the population of the developing countries, which is projected to rise from 5.9 billion in 2013 to 8.2 billion in 2050. Much of the overall increase between 2013 and 2050 is projected to take place in high-fertility countries, mainly in Africa, as well as in countries with large populations such as India, Indonesia, Pakistan, and the Philippines. Population growth is expected to be particularly dramatic in the LDCs, which are projected to double in size from 898 million inhabitants in 2013 to 1.8 billion in 2050 (Docquier and Rapoport, 2009).

First of all, over-population breeds poverty, unemployment, and political and economic instability—a heady cocktail of push factors for migration. Second, many developing countries have huge numbers of skilled and educated people, and may be deliberately creating such a surplus pool of tertiary educated labor for export. The importance of international migration to such labor-sending countries is obvious—individual and collective gains from the migration of such skilled labor are more likely to outweigh the costs or losses of migration. Several studies suggest that migration of highly skilled individuals may have beneficial effects in labor-sending countries in the form of counter-flows of remittances, investments, trade relations, new knowledge, innovations, attitudes, and information (Lowell and Findlay, 2002; Stark *et al.*, 1997; Haas, 2005). Even those countries that are sending labor at the lower end—unskilled labor—are benefiting from receipts of migrants' savings and remittances, which help them pay for their imports and maintain a sound balance of payments.

How does the brain-drain affect labor-sending countries?

The second question focuses on the consequences of the brain-drain for labor-sending and -receiving countries. Proponents of the 'brain-drain' theory tend to point out that the brain-drain phenomenon may have several adverse effects on the well-being of labor-sending countries, such as: (1) the labor-sending economy bears the cost of the formation of emigrants but does not receive the returns to its investment in human capital; (2) emigration may cause adverse consequences for economic development—as the most skilled workers are generally among the richest taxpayers, the sending economy loses a substantial source of income which could be taxed and redistributed (Bhagwati, 1976); and (3) as economic growth partly comes from human capital accumulation (Lucas, 1990), it may be argued that the loss in human capital induced by the emigration of relatively skilled workers reduces productivity and slows down growth in the labor-sending economy. Skilled labor's contribution to the economy is not limited to what they directly contribute; they also exert positive effects on the productivity of others—the emigration of skilled people eliminates this indirect benefit to the economy at large. In addition, skilled labor's migration may discourage foreign direct investment and transfer of technology in labor-sending countries (Reichlin and Rustichini, 1998).

The critiques of the brain-drain theory, as mentioned above, argue that the migration of highly skilled individuals may have beneficial effects for labor-sending countries in the form of counter-flows of remittances, investments, trade relations, and the flow of knowledge and technology. They also argue that historically emigration of labor provided substantially more benefits to many labor-sending countries, especially for labor-abundant countries, than costs (Stahl, 1982). Available evidence also suggests that skilled migrants improve economic welfare back in their home countries through sending a relatively larger flow of remittances. Based on cross-country regressions on the relationship between education and remitting behavior in 11 major migration destination countries, Bollard *et al.* (2011) found an overall positive effect of education on the amount remitted.[12] Earlier, Dos Santos and Postel-Vinay (2003) found that when workers freely choose their location, some natives may rationally decide to return to their home country after they have accumulated a certain amount of knowledge abroad, while some will prefer to stay permanently in the same economy (either at home or abroad), and that such two-way worker mobility can have an expansionary effect on the labor-sending economy, and that in the long run, as the sending economy develops, fewer natives are likely to emigrate and more migrants are likely to return.

Migrants may return to their home country for a variety of reasons: they may have made their initial decision to emigrate based on erroneous information and return migration may also have been planned as part of an optimal life-cycle relocation sequence (Dustmann, 1996; Borjas and Bratsberg, 1996). Several studies suggest that not only should the total proportion of migrants in the population fall as the source economy develops and catches up with the 'developed world,' but also this should occur partly through an intensification of return migration (Stark *et al.*, 1997; Djajic and Milbourne, 2002). Thus, the so-called brain-drain may actually increase the incentive to accumulate human capital in the source economy and eventually have a positive impact on growth, especially by fostering investment in human capital in the source economy (Mountford, 1997).

In addition, when skilled emigrants contribute to the growth-inducing innovation process in the receiving region, where the returns on research and development (R&D) are higher, the source economy may benefit from the stimulation of growth in the receiving economy through imitation and knowledge diffusion (Schiff, 2005).[13] Biene *et al.* (2001), for example, found that for some developing countries the stock of human capital has a positive relationship with the immigration rate, indicating what is called a 'beneficial brain-drain.' At the same time, the magnitude of benefits of labor migration to labor-sending countries would depend on their domestic economic structure and policies, and the capabilities of their financial systems in handling remittances properly (Chami *et al.*, 2008; Dowlah, 2011a).

Rationale for the liberalization of global labor mobility

With a significant increase in the growth of international migration and remittance flows in recent decades and a greater awareness of its developmental impacts, it is hardly surprising that cross-border labor migration has now emerged as the third leg of globalization—the other two being international trade and international capital flows (Caglar *et al.*, 2011). It is now increasingly being accepted that trade liberalization in either the labor-sending or -receiving country is likely to increase migration in the long run, as it reduces the costs of migration (Schiff, 1994), rather than causing a decline in labor migration as predicted by earlier theories. The Factor Price Equalization theorem of Heckscher-Ohlin, for example, implied that trade liberalization would lead to a decline in international migration by reducing international price differentials between factors. Ever-increasing flows of migration from low-cost developing countries seem to have upstaged such postulations. Even the NAFTA agreement between the US, Canada, and Mexico was sold on the premise that by creating jobs in Mexico,

NAFTA would be able to stem the tide of Mexican migration to the US—that did not materialize either.

It is becoming increasingly clear that labor migration will significantly rise in the future because of both push and full factors. While falling transport and communication costs, rising unemployment and poverty, and political instability in many developing countries, the widening income gap between the developed and developing countries, and the phenomenal increase in population in developing parts of the world will serve as powerful push factors, a dramatic demographic transition in Western countries—characterized by an aging population and dwindling population growth—will greatly propel demand for migrants in the coming decades.

As mentioned above, the world population is projected to increase from 7.2 billion now to 8.1 billion by 2025, and to 9.6 billion in 2050, and much of the increase is projected to take place in the developing part of the world, while the populations of developed countries are projected to decline (UN, 2012). The over-65 population in developed countries is projected to increase from 34.7 million (28.4 percent) in 2010 to 53.9 million (28.6 percent) in 2040, while that of ages 15 to 65 is projected to decline from 124.2 million (65.9 percent) to 107.3 million (56.9 percent) in Western Europe, and from 235.8 million (67.1 percent) to 265.6 million (61.6 percent) in the US and Canada. At the same time, the population of this age is projected to increase in Sub-Saharan countries from 470.5 million (54.5 percent) to 976.6 million (63.6 percent) (Docquier and Rapaport, 2009). Remarkably, the population of Western countries is projected to age considerably at a time when the largest cohort of young people is expected to enter the global labor market from low-income countries.[14]

Such sea changes in global migration, as well as the increasing globalization of the production of goods and services, have in recent years resulted in a greater focus on labor migration issues around the world. Although multilateral mechanisms for cross-border movement of goods, services, and capitals are in place, international migration of labor is, however, still confined mostly to bilateral agreements, albeit with the exception of some regional arrangements, as outlined below. As labor migration involves global externalities and requires the concurrent cooperation of many nations, an awareness seems to be brewing for a multilateral system of rules and principles under a new organization called the World Migration Organization (WMO) to provide architecture and governance for global migration (Page and Plaza, 2006). Until such a day arrives, labor migration will presumably be governed mostly by bilateral and regional agreements, while the only multilateral architecture available for migration governance will be the GATS Mode-4 of the WTO, which is the focus of this study.

When it comes to the GATS Mode-4, presumably the central questions will be as follows: (1) whether existing economic literature provides a strong rationale in support of the temporary movement of natural persons across borders as service providers; (2) whether political developments around the world will be conducive to promoting an agenda for the temporary movement of natural persons as service providers across borders; and (3) how effective the GATS

Mode-4 will be as a multilateral governance structure for promoting the temporary movement of natural persons across borders as service providers.

Economic rationale

As explained above, the economic basis of international trade is the principle of comparative advantage that envisages exploiting differences—the larger the differences, the larger the potential gains. Trade in merchandise demonstrates numerous such examples on a daily basis—people buy coffee from Columbia, olive oil from Italy, oil from the Middle East, cars from Japan, and so on—and the mobility of such merchandise across borders faces few or no barriers all around the world. Global trade in commercial services, such as tourism, transport, insurance, and so on has also been sharply increasing in recent decades. In 2012, for example, world merchandise exports totaled $18.3 trillion, almost tripling from $6.5 trillion in 2002. That same year, trade in commercial services totaled $4.4 trillion, more than doubling from $2.1 trillion in 2002 (WTO, 2014).

Capital is on the move as well—each year, trillions of dollars move across national borders as equities, debts as well as foreign direct investment (FDI). Such flows (FDI, equity, debt) fluctuated between 2 and 6 percent of world GDP during the period 1980 to 1995, but since then has increased to 14.8 percent of GDP, and in 2006 they totaled $7.2 trillion, more than tripling since 1995 (IMF, 2008). In 2012, the FDI inflows alone totaled $1.5 trillion (UNCTAD, 2014).

The global mobility of labor, however, still faces multifarious socio-political problems and stringent governmental restrictions in both developed and developing countries alike. In the late 1950s, Mundell (1957) showed that trade in products could be a perfect substitute for trade in capital and labor. In the early 1980s, Markusen (1983) showed how trade in factors of production could complement trade in goods and services, and how freeing up both could yield greater gains to the world economy. Hamilton and Whalley (1984) estimated that by allowing labor to move until real wages equalized worldwide, thereby eliminating all barriers to migration, world GDP could double.

More recent estimates of expected benefits of freeing mobility of labor across borders are more precise, although very diverse. For example, an OECD (2002) study predicted potentially large gains if medium and less skilled workers, who are relatively abundant in the less developed countries, and for whom the gap between home and host country wages was greatest, are allowed to move around and provide their services in the developed countries.

Winters *et al.* (2003) found that the partial liberalization of labor mobility, capped at 3 percent of the OECD's existing labor force, would result in a total gain of 0.6 percent of world income ($156 billion in 1997 prices), but it would be comparable to removing all remaining restrictions on merchandise trade. Earlier, Rodrik (2002) estimated direct income gains at $200 billion if the temporary movements of foreign skilled and unskilled workers were to be capped at the same 3 percent level of developed countries' labor force. Cline (2004, 180) estimated that moving to complete free trade in labor would increase world GDP by 0.93 percent ($228 billion at 1997 prices), of which approximately 40 percent would accrue to developing countries. Moses and Latnes (2004), however, found that the gains of freeing up labor mobility would be around 10 percent of world GDP ($3,390 billion in 1998 dollars)—even with the assumption that developing countries' workers were less productive than those in developed countries.

Walmsley *et al.* (2005) estimated that if the labor force of developed countries increased by 3 percent as a result of freeing up the movement of skilled and unskilled workers from developing countries, real incomes of permanent residents in the developed countries would increase by an average of $200 per person, while those of the developing countries would increase by $24 per person, and new skilled and unskilled migrants themselves would gain in real terms: $9,200 and $9,400 per person, respectively.

The World Bank (2006) estimated that for the same 3 percent increase in developed countries' labor force, the gain from the liberalization of trade in labor would total $356 billion. The study also found that the extra 3 percent gain in high-income countries' workforce would represent a loss of merely 0.4 percent to the developing countries' workforce, and even in the developing countries' skilled category, it would represent only 1.7 percent loss of workers. Anderson and Winters (2008) found that even if the increased migration was only 0.5 instead of 3 percent, it would generate the same proportional comparative static gain as the Doha Development Round might achieve via the liberalization of the entire merchandise trade.

Obviously, the estimated benefits of liberalization of cross-border labor mobility vary widely, largely due to differing assumptions about wage gaps of labor in source and host countries as well as in the differences of modeling frameworks used by the researchers, but in general all these studies show that estimated gains from the free movement or even the partially free movement of labor across national borders would far exceed those of completely freeing up trade in merchandise. One reason for this is that because of the 'globalization of everything but labor' over the course of the past few decades, an increase in the mobility of labor has been small compared with the greatly increased mobility of goods and capital, and economic gains from the further liberalization in goods and capital markets will be far smaller compared with potential gains from the increased mobility of labor across borders (Pritchett, 2006, 20–21).

Political dynamics

When it comes to politics and political expediencies or sensitivities, it is, however, a different ball-game altogether. Although the Chinese did not build the China Wall and the Egyptians did not build pyramids without migrant labor, labor migration has always been a highly contentious political issue around the world. In addition, it is hardly surprising that the perspectives of the developing (labor-surplus and labor-sending) countries and those of the developed (labor-scarce and labor-receiving) countries on labor migration issues differ almost diametrically around the world.

Perspectives of the developing countries

First of all, demand for labor from the developing countries will increase in the developed countries in the future. Pritchett (2006, 16–40), in his book *Let their People Come*, identifies "Five Irresistible Forces" which will propel such greater labor mobility in the near future. First, gaps in wages and income between the developed and developing countries are becoming wider than ever. In the nineteenth century, the gaps in unskilled wages ranged between 2 to 1 and 4 to 1 between immigrant-sending and -receiving countries, but such a small gap was sufficient to cause massive migration flows. Now that gap stands at 10 to 1, and the ratio of incomes between the top and the bottom countries has increased from 10 to 1 in 1870 to something like 50 today. Second, the difference in demographic futures is becoming starker—as differences create trade, dramatic differences in demographics will create ever greater pressure in developed countries to accept greater labor inflows and similar pressures in developing countries for greater outward flows of labor.

Third, because the world has thus far followed the strategy of globalization of everything but labor, potential economic gains from the increased mobility of labor will be greater than potential gains from the further liberalization of merchandise trade. Fourth, as many jobs in the developed countries for low-skill services cannot be outsourced, such as jobs for home health aides, janitors, cashiers, and fast food workers, such forces will generate a greater demand for labor mobility from the developing countries. Finally, the market forces of demand and supply will come to play a role. If labor is geographically mobile and hence labor supply is elastic, then large declines in labor demand in developing parts of the world and increased demand in the developed countries will lead to larger outward migration from the developing countries.

At the same time, the developing countries will have a strong incentive to encourage labor mobility. As explained above, they have vested interests in boosting labor exports, as migrants' savings and remittances have emerged as a formidable and risk-free source of external finance for their economies. Moreover, increasing populations, poverty, and unemployment will induce labor-surplus developing countries to push labor exports. On top of that, some of these countries face environmental and ecological disasters. The semi-arid areas of North Africa, for example, are vulnerable to the ability of agriculture to provide livelihoods, and in several parts of the developing world, large numbers of 'ecological refugees' seem inevitable as global warming may result in rising sea levels, and extreme weather events such as droughts, storms, and floods. Such natural disasters may result in the displacement of more than 50 million ecological refugees by 2020, and migration across borders may be a major adaptation strategy for such ecological refugees (IOM, 2009).

Presumably, the only major concern for developing countries lies with the so-called 'brain drain.' Although the debate on the brain-drain dates back to the 1960s, no one has yet had the last word. As elaborated above, however, the understanding of the brain-drain phenomenon has evolved over the decades—

scholars now believe that labor migration may provide substantially more benefits to labor-sending countries than costs with the appropriate supportive mix of macroeconomic policies and infrastructure, and it may even function as a dynamic force for promoting higher education, poverty reduction, economic growth, and national development (Biene *et al.*, 2001; D'Costa, 2008; Liepziger, 2008; Haas, 2005; Dowlah, 2012).

Perspectives of the developed countries

The developed countries, although net beneficiaries of tertiary migration from the developing countries, have increasingly been tightening their immigration policies in recent years and decades, especially in respect of less skilled migration. As mentioned above, between 1990 and 2013, the number of international migrants worldwide rose by 77 million (50 percent)—an average of two million per annum during 1990 to 2000 and 3.6 million per annum during 2010 to 2013—of which developed regions gained 53 million (69 percent).[15] The increasing concentration of migrants to the developed countries as well as post-September 11 concerns for terrorism have resulted in increasingly tightening borders and tougher immigration policies in the developed countries (Anderson and Winters, 2008).

Second, public opinion and governmental policies in the developed countries are increasingly concerned that some immigrants may become a welfare burden. Most of the developed countries with the largest gains in their migrant stock during the 1990 to 2013 period have witnessed a deceleration in economic growth in recent years, constraining governmental abilities to provide benefits to fresh migrant inflows (OECD-UNDESA, 2013). Third, domestic labor unions in many of the developed countries have been hardening their stance against migrants—there has been a progressive increase in political voice among those who are likely to be hurt by labor market competition from relatively lower skilled immigrants. On the other hand, those who stand to gain from immigration—mainly consumers—are too dispersed, and the migrants themselves are not part of the political process in the receiving country, at least *ex ante* (Winters and Mattoo, 2011). Fourth, many developed country governments see migration and imports as substitutes to some extent—more economic gains in relaxing imports and political gains in limiting immigration. Trade is thus seen as a national and essentially economic matter, while immigration is seen as a local and essentially social and political issue (Greenway and Nelson, 2006, 25).

Fifth, immigration is also viewed as a national security issue in many advanced countries in the post-September 11 world. People always feel very differently about different cultural heritages, ethnicity, language, historical background, and so on, but September 11 has worsened such attitudinal and sentimental issues. As Anderson and Winters (2008) point out, a major challenge to global labor mobility "is greater doubt among predominantly Christian western countries of allowing more immigrants from Moslem countries where recent global terrorism seems to have emerged." Pritchett (2006) also identifies risks of crime and terrorism—in the wake of September 11 and similar bombings in London and Madrid—as one of the "Eight Immovable Ideas" in Western minds when it comes to cross-border movements of people. Moreover, intensified state actions justified on the ground of addressing perceived global security threats in recent years have resulted in a significant extension of state power in respect of immigration control in developed countries, especially in the US and the EU (Mitsilegas, 2012).

Fifth, trade is based on comparative advantage, while migration is based largely on absolute advantage—to many developed countries immigration is more a one-way trade; developing countries have little or nothing to reciprocate. Moreover, labor migration is becoming increasingly polarized in the contemporary world—most labor-receiving countries are becoming more selective and seeking only skilled foreigners. The OECD countries have increasingly been adopting restrictive policies toward unskilled workers, as jobs at low qualification levels are expected to fall across all occupational groups. As a result, in the foreseeable future, demand for migrant labor will be geared principally to skilled workers in response to specific shortages, and migrants will be accepted as long they are seen as essential to retaining international competitiveness and increasing productivity (World Bank, 2010a).[16]

On top of all this, because of what Pritchett (2006, 63–104) calls "Eight Immoveable Ideas," ordinary people in the Western world remain firmly opposed to any increase in the levels of immigration. Pritchett's "Immovable Ideas" may be summarized as follows: (1) nationality is a morally legitimate basis for discrimination—it is morally legitimate to limit people's chances of migration on the basis of race, ethnicity, and religion; (2) proximity or physical presence in the same political jurisdiction is all that matters for moral obligations—people suffering abroad is not the concern, but if they somehow arrive in their country, the moral obligation shifts dramatically; (3) development is exclusively about nation-states, not about nationals; (4) labor movements across borders are not necessary to raise living standards—trade in goods and capital flows would be sufficient in equalizing wage/income across countries; (5) the increased migration of unskilled labor will lower wages and worsen the distribution of income in the receiving countries; (6) immigrants raise fiscal costs because they use more services than they pay in taxes; (7) allowing movement across borders creates risks of crime and terrorism; and finally (8) they are not like us—they don't share the cultural cohesion of the society they move into.

It is thus not surprising that a survey by the United Nations (2002) found that more than 75 percent of respondents in Germany and Italy, and more than 60 percent in the UK, the Netherlands, Sweden, and Norway oppose any increase in immigration. In the US, the percentage of respondents who wanted immigration to be reduced remained the same at 42 percent during the 1977 to 2002 period, although there had been temporary increases in these percentages in the early 1980s and in early 1990s. Interestingly, the survey found that only 5 percent of developing country governments thought that the level of emigration from their countries was too low, while 23 percent thought that it was too high, and only 6 percent said their policy aim was to increase emigration while 22 percent said their aim was to reduce it. Baffled by such a trend, Hatton (2007) asks, “If gains from remittances are so significant and valuable to developing countries—why would they wish to discourage emigration?”

Due to highly contentious perspectives of the developing and developed countries, labor migration remains less globalized than international markets in goods and capital. In most countries, the ratio of imports to GDP far exceeds the ratio of immigrants to total population. In fact, since the 1960s, the worldwide ratio of immigrants to population has increased only modestly, while the ratio of imports to GDP has doubled. Average tariffs in Europe and North America fell from more than 15 percent in 1950 to about 4 percent in 2000, in Asia from 30 percent in 1960 to 10 percent in 2000, while the proportion of developed country government policy aims to reduce immigration has increased from less than 20 percent in the mid-1970s to more than 40 percent in the mid-1990s. The share of the world’s population that is foreign-born increased from 2.2 percent in 1965 to about 3 percent in the 2000s, while the ratio of imports to GDP is 10 percent. In OECD countries, the average share of immigrants is about 6 percent, while their share of imports to GDP is 27.5 percent.

From economic research standpoints, however, there is little dispute that the liberalization of labor will raise economic gains and global welfare. Even Dani Rodrik, the author of *Has Globalization Gone Too Far?* (1997), in his ‘Feasible Globalizations’ (2002, 314), made the point that gains from cross-border labor mobility would be so huge that “if international policy makers [are] really interested in maximizing worldwide efficiency … they would all be busy at work liberalizing immigration restrictions.” Emphasizing urgency in the liberalization of cross-border labor mobility, Walmsley and Winters (2005) showed that restrictions on temporary labor migration were inducing costs to both developed and developing countries alike in the range of about $150 billion annually. Pritchett (2006, 108–109) asks,

> If there can be a justice-based movement for animal rights, certainly there can be a justice-based movement for labor mobility.… How is it that patent protection is so strongly on the WTO agenda but labor mobility—an issue of near infinitely more importance for human well-being and much more naturally a ‘trade’ issue—is not?

The GATS Mode-4 as a window of opportunity

Given acrimonious controversies and powerful debates surrounding the issue of permanent migration, the GATS Mode-4 should be viewed as a great advantage for both labor-sending and -receiving countries. The temporariness of migration saves the host country government the costs of providing social safety nets to foreign workers. Since foreign workers need not be fully integrated into the host country, presumably potential sociocultural tensions would be relatively lower as well than would be the case under permanent migration. The temporary nature of foreign labor movement also allows the host country to adjust its short-term migrant employment contracts to its domestic employment conditions and officially restrict access to welfare state benefits.

Mode-4 should also be advantageous for labor-sending countries, as remittances are usually much larger for migrants who intend to return home. As migrants' families stay at home, there is a greater chance that the migrants themselves will return home. As explained before, migrants may also return home for other reasons, such as: (1) they may have made their initial decision to emigrate on the basis of erroneous information; (2) return migration may also have been planned as part of an optimal life-cycle relocation sequence; and (3) when they can freely choose their location and length of stay abroad, some migrants may rationally choose to return after a temporary emigration. Moreover, as migrants return home, it is less of a brain-drain and more of a brain-gain for developing countries.[17]

But as it stands now, the GATS Mode-4 falls short of providing a systematic, rule-based multilateral platform to promote temporary cross-border labor mobility. Moreover, its WTO-mandated jurisdiction covers a very small share of global service trade and that of cross-border labor mobility. Estimates of the economic size of Mode-4 is very modest, and ranges between 1 and 2 percent of the total two-way trade in services (Karsenty, 2000). Due to a lack of reliable and comparable international trade statistics, and also because of complexities involved in separating values added through Mode-4 from the other modes of services trade under the GATS, estimates of Mode-4 values have largely been approximate. An OECD (2003) study, for example, estimated the value at around $30 billion, while an IOM (2003) study, which used remittance as a proxy to measure global Mode-4 trade flows showed the amount at $72.3 billion in 2001 (Kemekliene, 2007, 7). Still, over the years, the mode has succeeded in generating so much debate that it remains the most politicized and publicly debated mode of services stipulated by the GATS. Some of these criticisms and challenges are elaborated below.

Conceptual challenges and operational ambiguities

First of all, the GATS Mode-4 faces an uphill conceptual challenge. Surprisingly, one of the most profound conceptual challenges to the mode is launched by one of the staunchest enthusiasts of cross-border labor mobility—namely Pritchett. In his book *Let Their People Come*, Pritchett (2006, 114–120) argues that the very same principles of the WTO that make it a powerful institutional mechanism for the liberalization of goods trade may not work for cross-border labor mobility, as none of the three fundamental principles of the WTO—the MFN treatment, tariffs on prices not quantities, and reciprocity of trade—can be successfully applied to MODE-4 negotiations. Under the MFN principle if a country grants a concession to reduce tariffs, this will create a downward dynamic of restrictions for other members of the WTO, but it may not work similarly when it comes to labor mobility.

Pritchett argues that an agreement which may be reached bilaterally about the movement of X persons of Mexicans to the US cannot be extended automatically to X persons of another nationality. Moreover, while equal treatment of equivalent goods irrespective of national origin may be perceived as 'fair,' the same may not be true in respect of natural persons. Every country has laws that treat different people differently, and also, people feel differently about people on the basis of cultural heritage, ethnicity, language, and historical background. On top of all that comes security concerns in the post-September 11 world.[18]

The second basic principle of the WTO—prices not quantities—would be hard as well for services trade of any kind, specifically for Mode-4, because every country reserves the right to determine the numbers of persons crossing its borders. Pritchett argues that Mode-4 implies agreements more about quantities, not prices, and administrative control of the process. Mode-4 also does not bode well for the third basic principle of the WTO—reciprocity—as it involves giving up access to national markets in one product in order to gain market access in another product. Pritchett argues that such a reciprocity will be difficult to establish in respect of the mobility of unskilled labor—labor surplus-developing countries may not have something to offer in exchange for exporting labor to developed countries. As none of the traditional WTO principles applies to Mode-4, Pritchett concludes that Mode-4 has little chance of being politically feasible in OECD countries.

Pritchett's apparently convincing arguments, however, should be taken with a grain of salt. The GATT itself threw away the principle of prices not quantities, as well as the MFN principle in the 1950s and 1960s. In the 1950s, the erstwhile GATT granted what is called Special and Differential Treatment (SDT) provisions which allowed developed countries to grant certain flexibilities in respect of the principles of reciprocity and the MFN in trading with developing nations in order to compensate for their unequal economic status and to encourage their greater participation in the evolving international trading system. Over the course of the past five decades numerous schemes of the Generalized Systems of Preferences (GSP) evolved through using the SDT provisions (Dowlah, 2011b; Michalopoulas, 2000). Similarly, in the early 1960s, the GATT adopted what is known as the Short Term Arrangement (STA) for quantitative restrictions on international trade in textiles and clothing (on the basis of quantity, not on the basis of prices), which later turned into a systemic discriminatory regime of the Multi-Fiber Arrangement (MFA) which lasted for more than four decades, until 2009. If the GATT could make such exceptions for such a long period of time for textiles and clothing trade in order to benefit the developed countries, certainly the WTO can make similar exceptions in respect of Mode-4 to benefit the less developed countries.

Moreover, Pritchett's argument that labor surplus-developing countries may not have something to offer in exchange for exporting labor to the developed countries may not hold water either. As explained below, the developing countries may well be able to offer something to the developed countries in cross-modal negotiations. For example, they may open up other services sectors, such as telecommunications and entertainment sectors, for the developed countries in exchange for concessions in respect of Mode-4.

Second, Mode-4 is loaded with definitional and operational ambiguities. The Annex on the Movement of Natural Persons Supplying Services (Mode-4) identifies the following four main categories of the temporary movement of natural persons: (1) Intra-corporate transferees (ICTs), such as managers, specialists, trainees; (2) Business visitors (BV)s and services sales persons, such as foreign service providers entering another member's territory for the purpose of setting up a commercial concern (exploring the possibility of making a FDI for their company), or negotiating a sale of services; (3) Contractual service suppliers (CSSs), such as service providers who enter another WTO member's territory on a contract to provide a service to a firm in the destination country; (4) independent professionals (IPs), such as self-employed professionals and workers who enter another member's territory for the purpose of temporarily supplying a service.

The framers of Mode-4, however, left the length of employment that would be considered temporary open to the discretion and interpretation of individual WTO members. As a result, as mentioned above, some countries grant 90-day visas for temporary entry of ordinary service providers, while allowing up to five years for certain intra-corporate transfers. Moreover, immigration systems in most countries do not separate out migration in terms of service or non-service activities, and visa categories for trade do not make a distinction as to whether they are commercial or whether they involve trade for GATS purposes. Complexities also arise with the employment of independent professionals. Although Mode-4 does not cover natural persons seeking access to the receiving country's employment market, the movement of independent professionals, under which service providers seek employment in a foreign country on a temporary basis, may be open to interpretation. Kemekliene (2007), for example, points out that Mode-4 liberalization may be intertwined with the current debates on EU enlargement and increased labor mobility from the new member states in the EU countries.

The Mode-4 framework also remains ambiguous in respect of the question whether it covers natural persons employed only by a service supplier foreign firm, or those employed by host country firms as well. As the GATS left it open to member countries' discretion to determine what skill levels would be covered for temporary labor movement across borders, it allows labor-receiving countries to be more selective and gear their policies to meet specific shortages, encouraging migration of skilled labor, and so on. The GATS agreement is also unclear on how to separate out services of foreign workers when it involves more than one mode of delivery of services. As mentioned above, it is plausible that the same natural person provides a service as a commercial presence (Mode-3) and as a temporary service by a natural person (Mode-4) at the same time.

Lack of commitments of WTO members

Third, Mode-4 has so far been weighed down by lack of commitment and openness. The GATS negotiations, including that of Mode-4, involve a request and offer system under which WTO members put forward requests for the liberalization of trade in services from other members and make their own offers of such liberalization. Interestingly, the offers submitted to the WTO are circulated to all member states, but the requests are kept confidential. The GATS also allows members to decide on a case-by-case basis in which service sectors (or subsectors) and to which modes of service supply they would like to make commitments—there is no obligation on the part of a WTO member to schedule any particular service sector for commitments.

The commitments made by the WTO members for liberalizing Mode-4 so far suggest that: (1) they are very limited compared to other modes of service supply; (2) most of the commitments have been horizontal rather than sectoral in nature, that is, they are applicable to all sectors of a country's schedule of commitments; (3) exceptions made to senior and skilled intra-corporate executives and transferees, and often linked to Mode-3, such as foreign direct investment; (4) most of the commitments do not cover low-skilled persons or services from developing countries; and (5) no significant difference exists between the commitments scheduled by the developed and developing countries. Apparently, most countries are unwilling to make significant commitments, as a commitment once made remains a binding obligation (Francois and Hoekman, 2010; Chaudhuri *et al.*, 2004; Matoo *et al.*, 2008).

The commitments made so far to the WTO also reveal that for many developing countries the coverage of specific commitments was well below 50 percent of which they 'locked in' on a unilateral basis prior to joining the WTO,[19] and not much progress has been made since the GATS came into force in 1995 (WTO, 2005; Adlung and Roy, 2005). In a study of 93 member countries, Borchet and colleagues (2010) found that the 'bound' commitments were 2.3 times more restrictive than currently applied policies, which meant that these countries could more than double their restrictiveness without violating their commitments to the WTO. Second, sectoral commitments of member countries varied widely—while uniformly high commitments were made for tourism and related services (almost 70 percent in both developed and developing countries), public services (such as education, health, transport, postal and basic telecom) were subject to least commitments. Interestingly the most restrictive sectors, which are also potentially most beneficial, had been foreign direct investment (FDI) (Mode-3) and the movement of individual service providers (Mode-4), and between these two, Mode-4 remained the least open (Hoekman and Mattoo, 2011).

While Mode-4 remains the least liberalized among the four modes of the GATS, commitments of the EU (from the labor-receiving end) and the LDCs (from the labor-sending end) provide some insights into the current state of restrictions. The EU's commitments show that it emphasizes that CSSs and IPs must possess a university degree or technical qualification demonstrating knowledge at the equivalent level and at least three years' experience in the sector for the CSS and six years in the sector for the IP. In the EU's sector-specific commitments, the main scheduled limitations include economic needs tests, quantitative limits on foreign employment, training of local staff, wage parity conditions, domestic labor market conditions, and residency requirements.[20] LDCs, on the other hand, emphasize liberalization in most of the sectors including professional services, but request inclusion of job categories beyond highly skilled providers, and inclusion of diplomas, university degrees, and demonstrated experience as substitutable options (Katengekwa, 2006).

While any service provider from a developing country may gain free access to developed countries' service markets, the actual level of market access via Mode-4, however, depends on a national schedule of commitments of the host country, and service providers have to be pre-employed by the host country's industries and screened by the host country's government before they come to deliver services. Thus, in all matters related to length of stay, the level of skills, and the nature of contract for the temporary service providers, host countries enjoy greater latitude. Moreover, Mode-4 entries are also subject to: (1) visa formalities, which are controlled by immigration and labor market policies, not by international trade; (2) prohibitions and quotas—the so-called economic needs tests, which require the recruiting and retaining of sufficient national workers prior to filing work permit or visa applications; (3) wage-parity conditions—which require that wages paid to foreign workers be similar to wages paid to national workers; (4) discriminatory treatment, such as residency or citizenship requirements, social security tax payments, and preferences to domestic workers; and finally (5) non-recognition of professional qualifications of foreigners and burdensome licensing requirements in host countries.

Lack of progress in WTO negotiations

If one thing has become clear in recent years about multilateral negotiations under the WTO, it must be that the so-called Green Room process has outlived its effectiveness. During the period of the GATT (1947–1994), the Green Room process helped major interest groups build consensus informally, instead of reaching a decision in open platform. In recent years, under the WTO, with its enlarged membership and increasingly vocal stances of the developing countries, the Green Room practice has increasingly been criticized for favoring representation from large and high-income WTO members and undermining the interests of low-income countries. Such apprehensions have underpinned several setbacks/breakdowns in WTO negotiations in recent years as reflected in the fiasco of the Seattle Ministerial in 1999 and deadlock at the Cancun Ministerial in 2003, and repeatedly stalled negotiations under the ongoing Doha Round (Jones, 2009).

The Green Room process may not lead to any meaningful negotiation for the liberalization of Mode-4 either, simply because of the fact that Mode-4 negotiation is essentially handicapped by the traditional mercantilist paradigm of WTO which relies on reciprocal exchanges of concessions. Pritchett (2006) is quite right in this regard: labor-surplus developing countries have little to offer to powerful interests in labor-receiving developed countries in the way of reciprocity for liberalizing cross-border labor mobility. The absence of homogeneous products—which could be compared across countries—also stands in the way.

Goods may be more widely accepted with different national origins, but the case is not the same when it comes to service by natural persons abroad.

Moreover, with the inclusion of the services trade, WTO negotiations have become more complex compared with the GATT period, when cross-border trade was limited to manufacturers, and negotiations focused primarily on tariff concessions. The GATS, on the other hand, involves three additional modes of negotiations—consumer movements, factor flows (capital and labor), and the treatment of products (services) and/or their suppliers. Consequently, technical, economic, political, and legal frictions involved in such trades render service negotiations more complicated, time-consuming, and resource-intensive (Adlung, 2009). In addition, service barriers tend to be much higher than those for trade in goods in both high-income and low-income countries, and emerging markets demonstrate substantially higher barriers in service trade than in OECD countries (Borchert *et al.*, 2010).

Another problem with the GATS negotiation has been that the focus of the Uruguay Round was on creating an architecture of the GATS, not so much on actually opening up the services trade. The actual opening up of the services trade was left to WTO members—they were expected to make greater GATS commitments in successive rounds of negotiations in order to achieve progressively higher levels of liberalization. The Uruguay Round also mandated negotiations at the bilateral or multilateral levels to increase the general level of specific commitments undertaken by members. Subsequently, the GATS also expanded its mandate by asking members to commit themselves to negotiate in four rule-making areas—domestic regulation, emergency safeguards, government procurement, and subsidies—which were not concluded in the Uruguay Round.

The depth and breadth of the evolving GATS regime prompted some scholars to observe that the current WTO framework takes precedence over trade-related domestic policies and economics of contracting parties, reflecting a qualitative shift in the normative underpinnings of the evolving world order. While the GATT focused on the limited cross-border exchange of manufactures through bilateral state-to-state negotiations, the WTO advances and consolidates commercial law (*lex mercantoria*) defining the global governance increasingly in terms of the logic of market access, relegating states' prime role essentially to the provision of an appropriate regulatory framework for market access (Higgott and Weber, 2005). Under this evolving framework, the GATS aims to achieve the progressive commercialization of many public services which were previously solely in the domain of nation-states. The conflict between the trade of tangible goods under the GATT and the trade of services under the GATS also plays out in the bifurcated policy or conflict between what Matsushita (2004, 87) describes as the right to "maintain restriction under the GATS and the right to liberalize under the GATT 1994."

Lack of progress under the Doha Development Round

The Doha Development Round (DDR), a new round of multilateral services negotiations, launched in November 2001 by the Fourth WTO Ministerial held in Doha (Qatar), provided a mandate for continued negotiations for widening and deepening the current trading conditions in services. The DDR mandate, however, explicitly maintained that the negotiations must respect a member's right to regulate according to its national policy objectives and decide on which sectors and to what extent it is ready to commit to market access under the GATS. Earlier, the Singapore Ministerial, held in 1996 immediately after the successful conclusion of the Uruguay Round, introduced what is known as the 'Four Singapore Issues'—trade and investment, trade and competition policy, transparency in government procurement, and trade facilitation. The second WTO Ministerial, held in Geneva in 1998, was devoted to the commemoration of the fiftieth anniversary of the GATT, but it managed to adopt what is called the Declaration on Global Electronic Commerce.

After the Seattle Ministerial ended in fiasco in 1999, in 2001 at the Doha Ministerial, developed countries sought to include the Singapore Issues in the DDR. As the developing countries opposed such inclusion, the issue of inclusion of the Singapore Issues in the DDR was postponed until the next WTO Ministerial held in Cancun (Mexico) in 2003, when the differences over the inclusion of the Singapore Issues resulted in the collapse of the Cancun Ministerial. The next WTO Ministerial, held in Hong Kong in 2005, however, succeeded in narrowing down disagreements on some of the contentious issues.

A major breakthrough for the less developed countries, especially for the LDCs, came at the eighth WTO Ministerial held in Geneva in 2011. The Ministerial succeeded in adopting a waiver to WTO members to deviate from the MFN obligations of non-discrimination in order to provide preferential treatment to services and service suppliers from the LDCs. Apparently, the LDCs stand to gain from such preferential treatment as it will allow the developed countries to grant preferential treatment to the LDCs, over other developing countries, to increase their import of services, including Mode-4 services in which the LDCs have special export interests.

In order to promote expeditious and effective operationalization of the LDC services waiver, the next WTO Ministerial, held in Bali (Indonesia) in 2013, asked the LDCs to submit a collective request identifying the sectors and modes of supply of particular export interest, and initiated steps for accelerating the process of securing meaningful preferences for LDCs' services and service suppliers. The LDCs, however, must understand that potential gains from such a 'services waiver' may significantly hinge on their own capabilities. The special and differential treatment (SDT) provisions of the GATT, the 'manufactures waiver' adopted by the Dillion Round in 1961, opened up similar opportunities in respect of manufacturers' exports from developing countries. The experience with various schemes of the Generalized Systems of Preferences (GSP), which sprang up in many developed countries to provide such SDT facilities, had been less than reassuring (Dowlah, 2011b; Ozden and Reinhardt, 2002).

Built-in problems with WTO negotiations

As the discussion above indicates, apart from the LDC waiver, no meaningful success has been achieved in respect of the GATS or Mode-4 in WTO negotiations thus far. Some of the major problems that thwart progress in WTO negotiations may be enumerated as follows. First of all, any negotiation under the WTO remains perpetually hostage to its built-in structural problem: 'Nothing is agreed until everything is agreed.' Such a principle could be manageable under the GATT, which was basically a club of developed countries, but it has become increasingly unwieldy for the WTO, which currently boasts 159 members. Such an increase in the number and diversity of the WTO membership has complicated the definition of 'common ground' at any particular stage of a negotiating process. Pushing too hard in areas of active interest thus risks triggering highly inconvenient counter-requests (Magdeleine and Maurer, 2008).

Second, the traditional Green Room process of decision making, as explained above, has been drawing increasing criticism from developing country groups for lack of proper and meaningful representation of stakes of all parties in the WTO negotiation. Third, any negotiation in services trade is also constrained by the fact that developing countries demand greater openness in respect to agriculture and non-agricultural market access (NAMA) prior to services issues in which developed countries have greater exports interests. In addition, while developed countries are seeking further reductions of continuing high industrial tariffs in the developing world, especially in countries like Brazil, India, and China, developing countries are trying to tie their cuts in industrial tariffs to reductions in agricultural tariffs and subsidies (Fergusson, 2011).

When it comes to Mode-4 specifically, it is becoming increasingly clear that despite apparent convergence of economic interests of the labor-sending and -receiving countries, and despite the Mode seeming to provide a credible window of opportunity for temporary cross-border labor mobility, WTO negotiations under the Doha Round have thus far failed to make any progress in this regard. Economics tells us that productive factors move, when they are permitted to do so, from nations where they are abundant (low productivity) to nations where they are scarce (high productivity), but cross-border mobility of workers has so far largely failed to follow the economic logic of factor movement.

A major obstacle for negotiation in Mode-4 stems from lack of reciprocity—that the developing countries do not have much to reciprocate for such trade with the developed countries. Obviously, one plausible way to address the problem would be to expand the 'service waiver,' granted to the LDCs in 2011, to include all labor-sending developing countries under programs like the GSP schemes, under which developed countries grant preferential treatment to many developing countries, and not only to the LDCs. Second, feasible schemes could be developed for broad-based exchange of concessions by exploiting competitive advantages across sectors and modes of services. As Mattoo and Olarreaga (2001) explain, sectoral comparative advantage can be exploited by improving access to capital from the developed countries in exchange for individual service providers from the developing countries, or trading goods in exchange for trading services, or promoting modal comparative advantage, the developing countries obtaining greater labor movement in exchange for allowing greater commercial presence for foreign service providers.

Such a strategy would presumably enable the developing countries to grant concessions, for example, in banking and telecom sectors in exchange for concessions in Mode-4, or awarding service contracts to Western companies in exchange for jobs for software engineers. Apparently, so far such proposals also have not worked well. Some developing countries found this exchange of service sector contracts for gaining jobs for some skilled people less equitable for their populations. The developed countries also found such cross-sectoral and cross-modal exchange of concessions less appealing (Mattoo *et al.*, 2008). After all, if liberalization in goods and other services proves too difficult politically to achieve, only then will the benefits of formally liberalizing the international labor flow be worth contemplating (Hanson, 2006).

Current trends in the temporary movement of labor

Bilateral labor mobility

Interestingly, cross-border labor mobility is on the rise in recent decades, despite lackluster progress of negotiations under the WTO. Apparently, greater movement of labor across borders is being propelled by increasing pressures from multinational corporations, and the demand for both skilled and low-skilled workers in many developed countries. As Table 4.11 indicates, the annual flow of temporary workers' migration increased from 2.2 million in 2005 to 2.5 million in 2008 in OECD countries. In subsequent years, during 2009 to 2011, however, the annual flow of temporary workers to the OECD came down to about 2.0 million, coinciding with the global economic crisis. Immigration authorities in OECD countries place temporary workers into four broad categories—trainees, working holiday makers, seasonal workers, and intra-corporate workers. As Table 4.11 indicates, the single largest category of temporary workers during the entire period from 2005 to 2011 has consistently been seasonal workers. Most of these unskilled workers—who comprised 25 percent of all temporary workers—were employed in agriculture. The second largest category was the working holiday makers, about 20 percent of all temporary workers, who enter under youth mobility/summer jobs programs that may last for up to one year.

Table 4.11 also shows a small number of temporary work permits under the category of intra-company transfers—which include services like training, information technology, accounting services, installation of equipment, and so on. Their share among all temporary workers ranged between 5 to 6 percent, although the actual share would be much higher if all intra-corporate transfers are categorized as temporary transfers. In some OECD countries some intra-corporate transfers—those who are transferred on long-term assignments—are

Table 4.11 Temporary worker migration in OECD countries, 2005 to 2011 (in thousands)

Category	*2005*	*2006*	*2007*	*2008*	*2009*	*2010*	*2011*
Trainees	106	129	164	146	114	105	114
Working holiday makers	312	335	397	431	423	419	413
Seasonal workers	605	578	571	577	521	507	358
Intra-corporate transfers	84	104	118	117	106	124	127
Canada	6.3	7.8	8.6	9.9	9.7	13.6	13.5
Germany	3.5	4.8	5.4	5.7	4.4	5.9	7.1
Japan	4.2	5.6	7.2	7.3	5.2	5.8	5.3
Spain	1.2	1.0	1.4	1.3	0.9	0.7	0.8
UK	22.4	29.7	33.1	36.1	29.1	17.5	21.0
USA	65.5	72.6	84.5	84.1	64.7	74.7	70.7
Other temporary workers	1,093	1,330	1,286	1,235	929	914	950
All categories (total)	2,200	2,475	2,536	2,507	2,092	2,069	1,963

Source: Compiled from OECD (2011, 2013).

granted permits which are indefinitely renewable and often categorized as permanent migration. The recorded number of intra-corporate transfers also shows an increase in recent years—from 84,000 in 2005 to 127,000 in 2011—by more than 50 percent in six years. The bulk of these temporary migrations, however, took place in two OECD countries—the UK and the US—but their share seems to have fallen in recent years. As Table 4.11 indicates, while the US had a share of 78 percent in temporary migrations in 2005, this share fell to 56 percent in 2011; during the same period, the share of the UK fell from 27 percent to 16.5 percent.

Moreover, the immigration category, 'Other temporary workers,' lumps together many professionals like doctors, software engineers, and other tertiary educated skilled migrants. Lack of disaggregated data in this category makes it hard to predict the actual level of Mode-4 services being rendered across developed countries. Available data from the UK for the period of 1995 to 2000 indicate that the number of temporary permits granted in services increased by 50 percent during this period, and most permits were issued in healthcare, computers, and business and financial services. Exactly how many of these temporary work permits would belong to Mode-4 is not easy to determine, but it seems clear that Mode-4 entries may be especially important for trade in health services as well as other professional services, such as consultancy, IT, and other related services (Kemekliene, 2007).

In 2011, the US issued approximately 460,000 temporary work permits,[21] of which 15.3 percent went to intra-company transfers, 12 percent went to seasonal workers, 21 percent went to working holiday makers, and the rest, 51 percent, was categorized as 'other temporary workers.' The intra-corporate visa, known as the L1 visa, is limited to managers, executives, and specialists. Such visas are exempt from economic needs tests and they are granted three years of stay. Like other OECD countries, in the US also many professionals like doctors and engineers are lumped together under the category of 'Other temporary workers.' It is thus hard to determine the actual number of Mode-4 entries.

Ideally, immigrants who enter the US under H-1B visas may be considered as Mode-4 temporary service providers. The program was created in 1990 to enable US employers to hire temporary foreign workers in specialty occupations, and highly trained foreign professionals who enter the US under the program are granted temporary work permits for an initial stay of three years. Although the original law capped the number of H-1B visas at 65,000 per fiscal year, available records suggest that the cap was increased to 115,000 during the 1997 to 2001 period, then to 195,000 during the 2002 to 2003 period, but was reduced to 85,000 during the 2005 to 2009 period, including 20,000 to whom the cap did not apply as they had Masters degrees or higher education from the US institutions.

A GAO (2011) report indicates that petitions for H-IB workers' visas exceeded the cap in all but three years during the 2000 to 2009 period, when over 94 percent of submitted petitions were approved. In 2009, of the top 10 H-IB hiring employers, six had headquarters in India, and during the 2000 to 2009 period, 64 percent of all H-IB visas were granted to persons originating from four countries—India, China, Canada, and the Philippines—India being the largest recipient. The US H-IB visas of the decade show the following occupational composition: systems analysis and programming (42 percent), college/university education (7 percent), accountants and auditors (4 percent), electrical engineers and electronics (4 percent), other computer-related professionals (4 percent), physicians/surgeons (3 percent), biological sciences (2 percent), and all others (35 percent). Some scholars, however, believe that the US H-1B visa program has worked less as a temporary migration scheme than as a selective permanent migration scheme, as such visas tacitly open the door for permanent migration on a selective basis (Lowell, 2000).

Obviously, movements of professionals across borders, especially from the South to the North, have been rising sharply in recent years. Much of these movements are, however, engineered by immigration policies in developed countries which are increasingly encouraging the selective migration of skilled labor,[22] which has prompted some scholars to say, *Give Us Your Best and Brightest* (Kapur and McHale, 2005), and *Let their People Come* (Pritchett, 2006). As the discussion above indicates, the primary beneficiaries of such selective migration are middle-income developing countries like India, China, and the Philippines—not low-income developing countries or LDCs. Middle-income developing countries are also among the top recipients of workers' remittances, indicating that most of the benefits of global labor mobility—in terms of remittances—are accruing to those countries. Unless the movement of unskilled and semi-skilled workers is given special consideration along with the persons of professional qualifications, low-income developing countries, especially the LDCs, will have little to gain from global labor mobility.

Multilateral labor mobility

Recent studies indicate that cross-border temporary labor mobility is also on the rise among countries that enjoy geographic proximity or which are at similar levels of economic development under the auspices of regional trade agreements (RTAs). Countries belonging to the RTAs impose lower barriers to trade within the group than to trade with non-member nations. According to UNCTAD (2014, 86), the WTO had been notified of some 585 RTAs by 2014, of which 379 were in force, about 200 were South–South agreements, but a large proportion of the RTAs include either the EU or the US as a partner, and both have come to be identified as the two main 'hubs' in the pattern of RTAs, with their various partner countries being the 'spokes.'

The RTAs are viewed as 'WTO plus' if they are more stringent than provisions already covered by the multilateral trade regime, or 'WTO extra' if they deal with provisions that go beyond current multilateral trade agreements. Several preferential trading blocs, such as the European Union (EU), the European Free Trade Agreement (EFTA), and the European Economic Area (EEA), and the North American Free Trade Agreement (NAFTA) may be considered as 'WTO extra' when it comes to temporary labor mobility across borders. In addition, cross-border labor mobility appears to be on the rise in these RTAs,[23] and with the Doha Round's progress being uncertain, such RTAs provide a credible alternative vehicle, at least as an interim measure, for the further liberalization of Mode-4 (Stephenson and Hufbauer, 2010; Baldwin and Freund, 2010; Dowlah, 2011b).

Among the leading RTAs around the world, presumably the NAFTA provides a robust example for cross-border labor mobility.[24] The NAFTA came into force in 1994, superseding the existing Canada–US Free Trade Area Agreement (Canada–US FTA) reached earlier in 1988, with the aim of creating a free trade zone comprising all three North American countries: Canada, Mexico, and the US. Major objectives of NAFTA included the elimination of barriers to trade in goods and services, to promote conditions of fair competition, improve investment opportunities, and protect intellectual property rights. Facilitation of cross-border labor mobility, however, never featured as a major goal of the RTA. From the very beginning, NAFTA thus confronted twin problems: a concurrent increase in free trade and border control—while one opens the border for trade, the other shuts it to immigration (Gallegos, 2004). As a result, NAFTA has been criticized for seeking to tear down barriers to capital mobility, while tightening border barriers for workers, especially Mexican workers, so that factory owners are provided with unhindered access to cheap Mexican labor (Fernandez-Kelley and Massey, 2007).[25]

Despite such limitations, the NAFTA contains a provision called 'Temporary Movement of Business Persons,' which facilitates considerable temporary movement of businesspeople involved in goods or services trade or in investment activities across the borders of Canada, Mexico, and the US. A cornerstone of NAFTA's provision for services trade is provided by the TN non-immigrant visa, which permits qualified Canadian and Mexican citizens to seek temporary entry into the US to engage in business activities at a professional level. The TN visas are granted to traders and investors, business visitors, ICTs, and professionals, which include accountants, engineers, lawyers, pharmacists, scientists, and teachers. The TN visas have been uncapped for Canadians since the beginning of the NAFTA in 1994 and for Mexicans since 2004.

Upon demonstrating proof of a job offer, Canadian and Mexican nationals can obtain the TN visa which permits employment for one year with unlimited renewals.[26] There is no limit to the number of times a Mexican or Canadian citizen can be granted TN status, provided that they remain a temporary non-immigrant. During the 1996 to 2003 period, 572,992 TN visas were issued for Canadian citizens, while the number of such visas for Mexicans stood at 12,449. In recent years, TN visas issued by the US were as follows: 8,476 in 2008; 7,327 in 2009; 7,090 in 2010; 7,398 in 2011; and 7,165 in 2012.[27] NAFTA also emphasizes the development of mutually acceptable standards and criteria for the licensing and certification of professional service suppliers based on factors such as educational background, qualifying examinations, and experience, and specifies 62 such professions.

Besides the TN Visa, and outside the scope of NAFTA, the US also grants Treaty Trader (E-1) and Treaty Investor (E-2) visas for citizens of countries with which it maintains treaties of commerce and navigation. Such visas may be a non-immigrant visa for temporary stay, or an immigrant visa for permanent residence, but candidates must be engaged in substantial trade, including trade in services or technology, in qualifying activities, such as international banking, tourism, and so on, principally between the US and the treaty country; or develop and direct the operations of an enterprise in which a person has invested a substantial amount of capital. In 2012, the US issued 45,110 such visas.[28]

The European Union RTAs

While NAFTA focuses mainly on the mobility of capital in the region, albeit while restricting worker mobility and granting limited temporary mobility of labor, the EU, being a flagship example of economic union, on the other hand, guarantees total labor mobility among its 27 member countries, of course, with a provision that newest members must wait for 10 years. It has brought Mode-4 within the scope of its RTAs. The European Community (EC) has, however, negotiated relatively few RTAs with developing countries that cover services, but it has signed several association agreements with Mediterranean countries, with Chile and Mexico, and an Economic Partnership Agreement (EPA) with the countries of the Caribbean Community (CARICOM) and the Dominican Republic (the CARIFORUM grouping).

While there are no in-depth service provisions in the agreements with Mediterranean countries and Mexico, the EU-RTA with Chile incorporates an article on the 'Movement of Natural Persons,' as well as an annex which specifies 33 categories of professional service providers that the EU will accept from Chile without numerical limit for a period of three months, subject to the 'necessary academic qualification and experience.' The CARIFORUM-EU EPA also follows a similar structure, but it has expanded categories of workers beyond Mode-4 to include CSSs, IPs, and graduate trainees. Under the CARIFORUM-EPA, the EC has also committed to accept 29 categories of professional service providers without numerical limit, provided that these professionals have a university degree and at least three years' experience.

Canada also has negotiated several free trade agreements (FTAs) providing increased access not only for professionals, but also for semi-skilled foreign workers. The Canada–Chile FTA, signed in 1997, not only covers investors, traders, BVs, ICTs, and other professionals, but it also places no limits of stay on 72 of these categories. Canadian FTAs with Colombia and Peru, signed in 2008 and 2009 respectively, cover all professional categories and impose no numerical limits and no specified length of stay. These FTAs also recognize 50 categories of technicians—such as mechanics, construction inspectors, food and beverage supervisors, and chefs, who are admitted without any specified length of stay.

RTAs of other regions

Similarly, the Japanese RTAs with Mexico and Chile provide access to traders, investors, BVs, ICTs, and IPs, and with Indonesia and the Philippines provide access to nurses and care workers. Australia and New Zealand have also signed a joint RTA with a 10-member ASEAN group in 2008 covering four usual categories, plus an additional category of installers (by New Zealand). Australia and New Zealand allow the longest stay of ICTs (three to four years), and one year for IPs and CSSs. The New Zealand–China agreement specifies five categories of labor: investors, BVs, ICTs, CSSs, and a new category, installers. The CSS category includes artisans with Chinese cultural characteristics, Mandarin teachers, and Chinese medicine specialists. New Zealand allows entry of designated professionals from China for up to three years. The Australia–Chile RTA (2009) permits temporary labor mobility to the usual four categories.

Leading RTAs thus provide a credible alternative, at least as an interim measure, to promote greater liberalization of cross-border labor mobility.[29] Most of the developed countries, however, focus largely on professional service providers (or a tertiary educated skilled labor force), although some countries have granted unlimited access or long-term visas to relatively less educated technicians, contractual service suppliers, independent professionals, and even to graduate trainees, nurses, and care givers. Second, it appears that the countries which face considerable labor shortages and pressure from domestic private sectors are more likely to provide greater access to foreign workers. Third, in granting greater access or forming RTAs, geographical and cultural proximity, strong similarities in GDPs, and large differences in factor endowments seem to play key roles. For developing countries, obviously, the major interest in promoting greater labor mobility resides in the IP and CSS categories, and greater flexibility in these categories would allow most developing countries to gain greater benefits from temporary labor exports.

Conclusions

The available literature suggests that a basic convergence of economic interests appears to be emerging between labor-scarce developed countries and labor-surplus developing countries for more robust cross-border labor mobility in the contemporary world. With remittances emerging as a formidable source of external finance, labor-sending developing countries have a significant interest in boosting labor exports. The developed countries also have a considerable interest in the greater utilization of foreign labor, as their populations are aging, and many of their service sector jobs are becoming less appealing to the domestic labor force. The developed countries' overwhelming emphasis on tertiary educated migrants, however, appears to be causing a significant brain-drain—the net transfer of human capital and scarce resources away from developing countries. The GATS Mode-4 thus provides a unique window of opportunity for both sides to reap the benefits of greater labor mobility without being burdened by the usual baggage associated with permanent migration. As labor must return after the contract—as opposed to permanent or other forms of migration, which are generally plagued with politically sensitive and economically significant controversial affects—Mode-4 may be viewed as a great compromise for the liberalization of temporary cross-border labor mobility.

As the potential of the current Doha Round to achieve considerable success in respect of cross-border labor mobility is out of the question, the RTAs seem to be a logical path to follow at least as an interim measure to promote greater liberalization of the temporary movement of natural persons across borders. The examples set by some leading RTAs, such as the NAFTA and Canadian FTAs, could well be emulated by other RTAs around the world for liberalizing cross-border mobility among countries having geographical and cultural proximity, strong similarities in GDPs, and major differences in factor endowments. At the same time, efforts should be directed at culminating the ongoing processes to establish a multilateral platform under the WTO for systematic and rule-based global labor mobility as envisaged by GATS Mode-4.

Notes

1 According to World Development Indicators (World Bank, 2009a, 2009b), during the 1977 to 2007 period, the service sector's value added increased from 58 percent to 74 percent in high-income OECD countries, from 40 percent to 59 percent in middle- and low-income countries, and from 55 percent to 70 percent across the world. See Table 1 in Francois and Hoekman (2010).

2 This is, however, the highest share of migrants in the world population in decades. The share of migrants in the world population was 2.3 percent in 1965, 2.1 percent in

1975, 2.2 percent in 1985, and 2.9 percent in 1995 and 2005. See Table 2.1 in Martin (2009).

3 The numbers are based on UNDESA (2013), according to which international migration stock stood at 174.5 million in 2000. Most UN publications also put the stock of international migrants in 1960 at 75 million. Czaika and Hass (2013), on the other hand, put the number at 167 million for 2000, and 93 million for 1960.

4 The rest are broadly considered as political and environmental refugees. In 2013, the number of such refugees in the world was estimated at 15.7 million, about 7 percent of all international migrants (OECD-UNDESA, 2013).

5 In 2012, for example, remittance inflows to oil-exporting Kuwait, Saudi Arabia, and Qatar were $8 million, $246 million, and $803 million, respectively, but remittance outflows were $16 billion, $29 billion, and $11 billion, respectively. See the World Bank's Migration Database (migration remittance outflows) at: www.worldbank.org/migration (accessed June 10, 2014).

6 These estimates are based on the official transfer of remittances. The actual inflows of remittances to many developing countries would be about 50 percent higher with the inclusion of unofficially channeled remittances. For more details see World Bank (2010a).

7 The term ODA generally refers to contributions of donor government agencies to developing countries and to multilateral institutions. The IMF defines ODA as:

> Flows of official financing administered with the promotion of the economic development and welfare of developing countries as the main objective, and which are concessional in character with a grant element of at least 25 percent (using a fixed 10 percent rate of discount).

The term FDI, on the other hand, implies a "cross-border investment by a resident entity in one economy with the objective of obtaining a lasting interest in an enterprise resident in another economy," and a foreign investor must own at least 10 percent or more of the voting stock or ordinary shares of the investee company to be deemed FDI. See www.oecd-ilibrary.org/sites/factbook-2013-en/04/02/.../index.html?

8 Being the dominant school of thought in recent years, this strand of thought has numerous contributors, including Korovilas (1999); Guiliano and Ruiz-Arranz (2005); Lopez-Cordovo and Olmedo (2006); Massey *et al.* (1993); Ratha and Shaw (2007); Haas (2005).

9 The observation by Ratha (2007) that a 10 percent increase in remittances leads to a decline in poverty by 3.5 percent should also indicate that it will take at best 20 years for a country to be totally poverty-free if it can maintain 10 percent annual growth in remittances.

10 Based on the World Bank Migration Database (accessed July 11, 2014). Table 4.9 shows the number of tertiary educated migrants for the year 2000, the latest year for which such data are available with the database.

11 See Massey *et al.* (1993) for an excellent summary of earlier theories, and see Kurekova (2011) for summaries of more recent theories.

12 The flip-side of this trend, however, is that while skilled migrants typically earn more, and so may be expected to remit more, they are also likely to spend more time abroad and to reunite with their close family in the host country, which, in turn, may contribute to a smaller propensity to remit (Docquier and Marfouk, 2004).

13 A glaring example of technology diffusion would be the Indian IT industry. Some Indian information technology workers, who worked in Silicon Valley with temporary visas, returned to India, boosting Indian IT exports from $150 million in 1990 to $69 billion in 2011. According to the Indian National Association of Software and Services Companies (NASSCOM), the Indian IT industry, one of the largest employers in the country, has increased its share in global outsourcing to 58 percent in the fiscal

year 2012, when it added 230,000 jobs. See www.nasscom.in/indian-itbpo-sector-revenue-estimated-cross-usd-100-billion-mark accessed on July 10, 2014. See also World Bank (2009b).

14 The economic effects of such demographic transition are projected to be enormous as well—with significantly higher expenditures devoted to health, long-term care, housing, and energy, Western Europe's share in overall savings and investment is projected to decline significantly in the future (World Bank, 2010a, 5).

15 As mentioned above, in 2013, over 51 percent of all international migrants lived in 10 countries—the largest number—46 million (20 percent of the global total) lived in the US, followed by the Russian Federation (11 million), Germany (10 million), Saudi Arabia (nine million), and the United Arab Emirates and the United Kingdom (eight million each).

16 Demand for unskilled labor, especially for those jobs that cannot be outsourced, will be there, but not much growth is expected from such workers. At the same time, some observers challenge the notion that advanced countries, especially European nations, will require immigrant labor due to demographic aging. They argue that the EU countries may be able to mobilize substantial internal migration or draw from the aging population to fill their migration needs. See Dowlah (2012, 2014).

17 The possibility of 'overstaying,' however, cannot be ruled out, as it is a common concern for any type of immigration. Studies suggest that nearly half of illegal immigration originates from legal entries as tourists (Gimpel and Edward, 1999). For enforcement difficulties with GATS Mode-4, some propose the posting of a bond as a solution, and for the brain-drain issue, some propose an appropriate tax and/or compulsory service policies (Hatcher, 2003).

18 Pritchett (2006, 117) gives an interesting example:

> Imagine the announcement that an Iranian firm had won the service contract to clean every Motel 6 (now a French-owned chain) in the United States, and hence 50,000 persons of this Iranian firm's choosing would be branching out to every major city of the United States.

19 In addition, WTO members were expected to submit a revised commitment under the Doha Development Agenda (DDA) by July 2006, but apparently no such schedule was submitted due to uncertainties with the Doha Round negotiations.

20 The EU's commitments for CSS and IP are also subject to numerical ceilings, except in Denmark, the Netherlands, Sweden, and the UK. However, in Poland IPs and in Italy CSSs are not subject to numerical ceilings. Furthermore, the economic needs tests do not apply to IPs and BVs. For more details, see Adlung and Roy (2005); Kemekliene (2007).

21 Under temporary migration, the US immigration reports also categorized another 447,000 international students under this category. All international students, however, may not have temporary work permits. Thus, international students are excluded from the numbers of temporary workers. The numbers are taken from www.oecd.org/migration/imo (accessed June 18, 2014).

22 See, for example, OECD (2013), which provides a detailed description of how each of the OECD countries has been reshaping its immigration policies in recent years to promote selective immigration.

23 It is notable that the case is not the same with preferential trading agreements among geographically distant members with differing levels of development, such as the Asia Pacific Economic Cooperation (APEC). Labor mobility tends to increase among RTAs, as member countries enjoy geographic proximity and more or less similar levels of economic development.

24 The discussion on leading RTA provisions on labor mobility across borders is primarily based on Stephenson and Hufbauer (2010, 29–68), and Dowlah (2011b). For more details, see also Martin (2009); O'Rourke (2009); Medina and Sobel (2009).

25 Mexican President Salinas de Gortari made this point more unambiguous: "the whole point of NAFTA for Mexico is to be able to export goods and not people. That means creating jobs in Mexico" (cited in Fernandez-Kelley and Massey, 2007, 105).
26 The TN visas, however, do not grant equal treatment to the Canadians and the Mexicans. Canadians are exempt from most guest worker visa regulations, including the need for the employing sponsor to obtain prior approval to hire someone from abroad. Canadian citizens can present documents and credentials to immigration officials at the port of entry. Mexicans, on the other hand, must have an employer submit petitions and the Labor Condition Attestation (a document signed by the employer saying that the wages and working conditions will be the same as for Americans, among other things).
27 See the US State Department website at: www.state.gov (accessed September 12, 2013).
28 Based on the US State Department website at: www.state.gov (accessed September 12, 2013).
29 The RTAs, however, are often criticized for diverting trade away from the most efficient global producers to regional partners, and reducing the potential for future multilateral liberalization. At the same time, given the concerns of multiculturalism, researchers tend to agree that real resource gains would be possible if countries forming RTAs integrate their labor markets, regulatory frameworks, harmonize standards, and cooperate extensively on trade facilitation (Baldwin and Freund, 2010).

References

Adams, R. (2003). International migration, remittances, and brain drain; A study of 24 labor-exporting countries. World Bank Research Working Paper No. 3069, Washington, DC.

Adams, R. (2005). Remittances, household expenditure and investment in Guatemala. World Bank Research Working Paper No. 3532, Washington, DC.

Adams, R. and Page, J. (2004). Do international migration and remittances reduce poverty in developing countries? World Bank Policy Research Working Paper No. 3179, Washington, DC.

Adelman, I. and Taylor, J. (1990). Is structural adjustment with a human face possible? The case of Mexico. *Journal of Development Studies*, 26(3), 387–407.

Adlung, R. (2009). Services liberalization from a WTO/GATS perspective: In search of volunteers. Staff Working Paper ERSD-2009–05, WTO Economic Research and Statistics Division. Geneva: World Trade Organization.

Adlung, R. and Roy, M. (2005). Turning hills into mountains? Current commitments under the GATS and prospect for change. WTO Staff Working Paper ERSD-2005–01. Geneva: World Trade Organization.

Agunias, D. and Newland, K. (2007). Circular migration and development: Trends, policy routes, and ways forward. *MPI Policy Brief*, April. Migration Policy Institute. Washington, DC: World Bank.

Amuedo-Dorantes, C. and Pozo, S. (2004). Workers' remittances and the real exchange rate: A paradox of gifts. *World Development*, 32(8), 1407–1417.

Anderson, K. and Winters, A. (2008). The challenge of reducing international trade and migration barriers. World Bank Policy Research Working Paper No. 4598. Washington, DC: World Bank.

Baldwin, R. and Freund, C. (2010). Preferential trade agreements and multilateral liberalization. In O. Cattaneo *et al.* (eds), *International Trade in Services: New trends and opportunities for developing countries* (pp. 121–141). Washington, DC: World Bank.

Bettin, G., Presbitero, A., and Spatafora, N. (2014). Remittances and vulnerability in developing countries. World Bank Policy Research Paper No. 6812. Washington, DC: World Bank.

Bhagwati, J. (1976). The international brain drain and taxation. A survey of the issues. In J. Baghwati (ed.), *The Brain Drain and Taxation II: Theory and empirical Analysis.* Amsterdam: North-Holland.

Biene, M., Docquier, F., and Rapoport, H. (2001). Brain drain and economic growth: Theory and evidence. *Journal of Development Economics*, 64 (1), 275–289.

Birks, J. and Sinclair, A. (1980). *International Migration and Development in the Arab Region.* Geneva: International Labor Organization.

Bollard, A., McKenzie, D., Morten, M., and Rapoport, H. (2011). Remittances and the brain drain revisited: The microdata show that more educated migrants remit more. *World Bank Economic Review*, 25(1), 132–156.

Borchet, I., Gootiz, A. and Mattoo, A. (2010). *Restrictions on Services Trade and FDI in Developing Countries.* Washington, DC: World Bank.

Borjas, G. and Bratsberg, B. (1996). Who leaves? The outmigration of the foreign born. *Review of Economics and Statistics*, 78(1), 165–176.

Bradford, S. and Lawrence, R. (2004). *Has Globalization Gone Far Enough? The costs of fragmented markets.* Washington, DC: Institute of International Economics.

Bretell, C. and Hollifield, J. (2008). *Migration Theory: Talking across disciplines* (2nd edn). New York: Routledge.

Brochmann, G. and Hammer, T. (eds). (1999). *Mechanisms of Immigration Control.* Oxford: Berg.

Brown, S. (2006). Can remittances spur development? A critical survey. *International Studies Review*, 8(1), 55–75.

Caglar, O., Rapoport, H., and Schiff, M. (2011). Five questions on international migration and development. *The World Bank Economic Review*, 25(1), 1–12.

Carrington, W. and Detragiache, E. (1998). How big is the brain drain? IMF Working Paper No. 98/102. Washington, DC: International Monetary Fund.

Castles, S. and Miller, M. (2009). *The Age of Migration: International population movements in the modern world* (4th edn). Basingstoke: Palgrave Macmillan.

Cattaneo, O., Engman, M., Saez, S., and Stern, R. (eds). (2010). *International Trade in Services: New trends and opportunities for developing countries.* Washington, DC: World Bank.

Chami, R., Fullenkamp, C., and Jahjah, S. (2003). Are immigrant remittance flows a source of capital for development? IMF Working Paper No. 03/89. Washington, DC: International Monetary Fund.

Chami, R., Fullenkamp, C., and Jahjah, S. (2008). Macroeconomic consequences of remittances. IMF Occasional Paper No. 259. Washington, DC: International Monetary Fund.

Chaudhuri, S., Mattoo, A., and Self, R. (2004). Moving people to deliver services: How can the WTO help? World Bank Policy Research Working Paper No. 3238. Washington, DC: World Bank.

Clemens, M.A. and McKenzie, D. (2014). Why don't remittances appear to affect growth? World Bank Policy Research Working Paper No. 6956. Washington, DC: World Bank.

Cline, W. (2004). *Trade Policy and Global Poverty.* Washington, DC: Center for Global Development.

Cox-Edwards, A. and Ureta, M. (2003). International migration, remittances and schooling: Evidence from El Salvaor. *Journal of Development Economics*, 72(2), 429–461.

Czaika, M. and Hass, H. (2013). The globalization of migration: Has the world really become more migratory? DEMIG Working Paper No. 68, April. International Migration Institute, University of Oxford.

D'Costa, A. (2008). The international mobility of technical talent: Trends and development implications. In A. Solimano (ed.), *The International Mobility of Talent: Types, causes and development impacts.* Oxford: Oxford University Press.

Das, A. and Serieux, J. (2010). Remittances and reverse flows in developing countries. IDEAs Working Paper Series, No. 02/2010. Washington, DC: Center for Global Development.

Djajic, S. and Milbourne, R. (2002). A general equilibrium model of guest workers migration: The source country perspective. *Journal of International Economics*, 25(3–4), 335–351.

Docquier, F. and Marfouk, A. (2004). Measuring the international mobility of skilled workers (1900–2000): Release 1.0. Policy Research Working Paper Series, No. 3381. Washington, DC: World Bank.

Docquier, F. and Rapoport, H. (2009). Skilled migration: The perspective of developing countries. In J. Bhagwati and G. Hanson (eds), *Skilled Immigration Today: Prospects, problems, and policies* (pp. 247–284). Oxford and New York: Oxford University Press.

Dos Santos, M. and Postel-Vinay, F. (2003). Migration as a source of growth: The perspective of a developing country. *Journal of Population Economics*, 16(1), 161–175.

Dos Santos, M. and Postel-Vinay, F. (2004). The impact of temporary migration on human capital accumulation and economic development. *Business Economics Review*, 47(1), 77–88.

Dowlah, C. (2011a). Workers' remittances and national economic development: Contemporary trends and macroeconomic policy options. In M. Quddus and M. Rashid (eds), *Bangladesh Economy in the 21st Century* (pp. 195–220). Dhaka: University Press.

Dowlah, C. (2011b). Trade preferences and economic growth: An assessment of the US GSP schemes in the context of least developed countries. In L. YongShik *et al.* (eds), *Law and Development Perspective on International Trade Law* (pp. 334–355). New York: Cambridge University Press.

Dowlah, C. (2012). Can WTO-GATS Mode 4 spur greater labor mobility from the LDCs? *Law and Development Review*, 5(2), 56–82.

Dowlah, C. (2014). Cross-border labor mobility—A critical assessment of WTO's GATS Mode 4 vis-à-vis regional trade agreements. *Journal of International Trade Law and Policy*, 13(1), 2–18.

Durand, J., Porrado E., and Massey, D. (1996). Migradollars and development: A reconsideration of Mexican case. *International Migration Review*, 30(2), 423–444.

Duryea, S., Lopez-Cordova, E., and Olmedo, A. (2005). *Migrant Remittances and Infant Mortality: Evidence from Mexico.* Washington, DC: Inter-American Development Bank.

Dustmann, C. (1996). Return migration: The European experience. *Economic Policy: A European Forum*, 11(22), 213–250.

Dustmann, C. and Kirchkamp, O. (2002). The optimal migration duration and activity choice after re-migration. *Journal of Development Economics*, 67(2), 351–372.

Dustmann, C. and Glitz, A. (2005). Immigration, jobs and wages: Theory, evidence and opinion. Center for Research and Analysis of Migration, CEPR, London.

Faini, R. (2007). Remittances and the brain drain: Do more skilled migrants remit more? *World Bank Economic Review*, 21(2), 177–191.

Faist, T. (2000). *The Volumes and Dynamics of International Migration and Transnational Social Spaces.* Oxford: Oxford University Press.

Fergusson, I.F. (2011). The World Trade Organization: The Non-agricultural Market Access (NAMA) negotiations. Congressional Research Service, 7–5700. RL33634. Washington, DC: US Congressional Research Service.

Fernandez-Kelly, P. and Massey, D. (2007). Borders for whom? The role of NAFTA in Mexico–U.S. migration. *Annals of the American Academy of Political and Social Sciences*, 610(1), 98–118.

Francois, J. and Hoekman, B. (2010). Services trade and policy. *Journal of Economic Literature*, 48(3), 642–692.

Gallegos, G. (2004). Border matters: Redefining the national interest in U.S.–Mexico immigration and trade policy. *California Law Review*, 92(6), 1729–1778.

GAO (United States Government Accountability Office). (2011). H-IB Visa Program: Reforms are needed to minimize the risks and cost of current program. GAO report to Congressional Committee, GAO-11–26, January. Washington, DC.

Gibson, J. and McKenzie, D. (2010). The economic consequences of 'brain drain' of the best and the brightest: Macroeconomic consequences from five countries. World Bank Development Research Group, Paper No. 5394. Washington, DC: World Bank.

Gilles, S. (1997). *Dual Labor Markets: A macroeconomic perspective.* Cambridge, MA: MIT Press.

Gimpel, J. and Edward, J. (1999). *The Congressional Politics of Immigration Reform.* Boston, MA: Allyn & Bacon.

Giuliano, P. and Ruiz-Arranz, M. (2005). Remittances, financial development and growth. IMF Occasional Research Paper. Washington, DC: International Monetary Fund.

Gootiz, B. and Mattoo, A. (2009). Services in Doha: What's on the table? *Journal of World Trade*, 43(5), 1013–1030.

Greenway, D. and Nelson, D. (2006). The distinct political economies of trade and migration policy through the window of endogenous policy models. In F. Foders and R. Langhammer (eds), *Labor Mobility and the World Economy.* Berlin: Springer Verlag.

Haas, De Hein. (2005). International migration, remittances and development: Myths and facts. *Third World Quarterly*, 26(8), 1269–1284.

Hamilton, B. and Whalley, J. (1984). Efficiency and distributional implications of global restrictions on labor mobility. *Journal of Development Economics*, 14(1–2), 61–75.

Hanson, G. (2006). Illegal migration from Mexico to the United States. NBER Working Paper, March. Washington, DC: National Bureau of Economics Research.

Hanson, G. and Woodruff, C. (2003). Emigration and educational attainment in Mexico. Child Migration Research Network, April.

Hatcher, M. (2003). Draft model schedule for Mode 4: A proposal. In A. Mattoo and A. Carzaniga (eds), *Moving People to Deliver Services.* Washington, DC: World Bank.

Hatton, T. (2007). Should we have a WTO for international migration? *Economic Policy*, 22(50), 339–383.

Hendricks, L. (2002). How important is human capital for development? Evidence from immigrant earnings. *American Economic Review*, 92(1), 198–219.

Higgott, R. and Weber, H. (2005). GATS in context: Development, an evolving lax mercatoria and the Doha Agenda. *Review of International Political Economy*, 12(3), 434–455.

Hoekman, B. (2011). The WTO and the Doha Round: Walking on two legs. *Economic Premise*, No. 68, October. Available online at: www.worldbank.org/economic promise.

Hoekman, B. and Kostecki, M. (2001). *The Political Economy of the World Trading System: From GATT to WTO.* New York: Oxford University Press.

Hoekman, B. and Mattoo, A. (2011). Services trade liberalization and regulatory reform: Reinvigorating international cooperation. World Bank Policy Research Working Paper No. 5517. Washington, DC: World Bank.

Hoekman, B., Mattoo, A., and English, A. (2002). *Development, Trade, and the WTO: A handbook.* Washington, DC: World Bank.

Hughes, G. and McCormick, B. (1994). Did migration in the 1980s narrow the North–South divide? *Economica*, 61(244), 509–527.

Hugo, G. (1998). Village community ties, village norms, and ethnic and social networks: A review of evidence from the Third World. In G. DeJong and R. Gardner (eds), *Migration Decision Making: Multidisciplinary approaches to microlevel studies in developed and developing countries.* New York: Pergamon Press.

IMF (International Monetary Fund). 2007. *IMF Balance of Payments Statistics, 2007.* Washington, DC.

IMF (International Monetary Fund). (2008). *Globalization: A brief overview*, May. Washington, DC: International Monetary Fund.

IOM (International Organization of Migration). (2003). *World Migration Report 2003. Managing migration—Challenges and responses for people on the move.* Geneva: International Organization of Migration.

IOM (International Organization of Migration). (2009). *Migration, Environment and Climate Change: Assessing the evidence.* Geneva: International Organization of Migration.

ITC (International Trade Center). (2014). Trade in services strategy 2013–15: Services sector export competitiveness roadmap. Available online at: www.intracen.org/news/ITC-talking-points-on-trade-in-services/#sthash.0pToCxqD.dpuf.

Jones, K. (2009). *The WTO Green Room, Coalitions, and the Problem of Representation.* Oxford Scholarship Online. Oxford University Press. Available online at: www.oxfordscholarship.com/view/10.1093/acprof:oso/9780195378825.001.0001/acprof-9780195378825-chapter-4.

Jones, R. (1998). The renewed role of remittances in the new world order. *Economic Geography*, 74(1), 1–17.

Kapur, D. and McHale, J. (2003). Migration's new payoff. *Foreign Policy*, 39(139), 48–57.

Kapur, D. and McHale, J. (2005). *Give Us Your Best and Brightest.* Washington, DC: Center for Global Development.

Karsenty, G. (2000). Just how big are the stakes? An assessment of trade in services by mode of supply. In P. Sauve and R. Stern (eds), *GATS 2000: New directions in services trade liberalization.* Washington, DC: Brookings Institution Press and Harvard University.

Katengekwa, J. (2006). Extension of Mode 4 commitments to include unskilled workers in the WTO. A win–win situation, especially for the LDCs. Paper presented to the OECD Development Center Panel on Migration and Development, Geneva, September 25–26, 2006. Available online at: www.wto.org/english/tratop_e/serv_e/movement.

Keely, C. and Tran, B. (1989). Remittances from labor migration: Evaluations, performance, and implications. *International Migration Review*, 23(3), 500–525.

Kemekliene, G. (2007). Magnitude and possible consequences of labor migration under GATS. Paper presented at the Global Labor University Conference, April 1–3. University of the Witwatersrand, Johannesburg, South Africa. Available online at: www.global-labour-university.org/fileadmin/Papers_Wits_conference_2007/Group_B1/kemekliene_paper.pdf.

Korovilas, J. (1998). The Albanian economy in transition: The role of remittances and pyramid investment schemes. *Post-Communist Economies*, 11(3), 399–415.

Kurekova, L. (2011). Theories of migration: Conceptual review and empirical testing in the context of the EU East–West flows. Presented at the Interdisciplinary Conference on Migration, Economic Change, Social Challenge, April 6–9. University College London. Available online at: www.cadmus.eui.eu/bitstream/handle/1814/14049/CARIM_ASN_2010_44.pdf?

Lewis, A. (1954). Economic development with unlimited supplies of labor. *The Manchester School of Economics and Social Studies*, 22(2), 139–191.

Liepziger, D. (2008). 'Brain drain' and the global mobility of high-skilled talent. PREM Notes, No. 46267, September. Washington, DC: World Bank.

Lopez-Cordova, E. and Olmedo, A. (2006). International remittances and development: Existing evidence, policies and recommendations. Occasional Paper No. 41. Washington, DC: Inter-American Development Bank.

Lowell, L. (2000). H-1B temporary workers: Estimating the population. Working Paper No. 12, Center for Comparative Immigration Studies, University of California, San Diego.

Lowell, L. (2007). Trends in international migration flows and stocks, 1975–2005. OECD Social, Employment and Migration Working Papers. DELSA/ELSA/WD/SEM. Paris: Organization of Economic Cooperation and Development.

Lowell, L. and Findlay, A. (2002). *Migration of Highly Skilled Persons from Developing Countries: Impact and policy responses.* Project Report for the ILO and DFID. Geneva: International Labor Organization.

Lucas, R. (1990). Why doesn't capital flow from rich to poor countries? *American Economic Review*, 80(2), 92–96.

Magdeleine, J. and Maurer, A. (2008). Measuring GATS Mode 4 trade flows. Staff Working Paper ERSD-2008–05, WTO Economic Research and Statistics Division. Geneva: World Trade Organization.

Markusen, J. (1983). Factor movements and commodity trade as complements. *Journal of International Economics*, 14(3–4), 341–356.

Martin, P. (2009). Sustainable labor migration policies in globalized world. In A. Sobel (ed.), *Challenge of Globalization: Immigration, social welfare, global governance* (pp. 18–42). London: Routledge.

Massey, D. and Parrado, E. (1994). Migradollars: The remittances and savings of Mexican migrants to the United States. *Population Research and Policy Review*, 13(1), 3–30.

Massey, D., Arango, J., Hugo, G., Kouaouci, A., Pellegrino, A., and Taylor, J. (1993). Theories of international migration: A review and appraisal. *Population and Development Review*, 19(3), 431–466.

Matsushita, M., Schoenbaum, T., and Mavriodis, P. (2004). *The World Trade Organization: Law, practice, and policy.* Oxford: Oxford University Press.

Mattoo, A. and Olarreaga, M. (2001). Reciprocity across modes of supply in the World Trade Organization: A negotiating formula. World Bank Development Research Group and CEPR, London.

Mattoo, A., Stern, R., and Zanini, G. (eds). (2008). *Handbook of International Trade in Services.* Oxford and New York: Oxford University Press.

McCormick, B. and Wahba, J. (2001). Overseas work experience, savings and entrepreneurship among return migrants to LDCs. *Scottish Journal of Political Economy*, 42(2), 164–178.

McKenzie, D. and Rapoport, H. (2007). Network effects and the dynamics of migration and inequality: Theory and evidence from Mexico. *Journal of Development Economics*, 84(1), 1–24.

Medina, M. and Sobel, A. (2009). Economic versus identity: Mass and elite attitudes toward trade, migration, and outsourcing. In A.C. Sobel (ed.), *Challenge of Globalization—Immigration, social welfare, global governance* (pp. 100–126). London: Routledge.

Michalopoulas, C. (2000). The role of special and differential treatment for developing countries in GATT and the World Trade Organization. World Bank Working Paper Series. Washington, DC: World Bank.

Mitsilegas, V. (2012). Immigration control in an era of globalization: Deflecting foreigners, weakening citizens, strengthening the state. *Indiana Journal of Global Legal Studies*, 19(1), 3–19.

Moses, J. and Latnes, B. (2004). The economic costs to international labor restrictions: Revisiting the empirical discussion. *World Development*, 32(10), 1609–1626.

Mountford, A. (1997). Can a brain drain be good for growth in the source economy? *Journal of Development Economics*, 53(2), 287–303.

Mundell, R.A. (1957). International trade and factor mobility. *American Economic Review*, 47(3), 321–335.

Nakosteen, R.A. and Zimmer, M. (1980). Migration and income: The question of self-selection. *Southern Economic Journal*, 46(3), 840–851.

NASSCOM (National Association of Software and Services Companies). Indian IT-BPO Industry. (2009). NASSCOM analysis. Available online at: http://nasscom.in/upload/5216/IT_Industry_Factsheet-Mar_2009.pdf.

Newland, K. (2011). *Migration and Development Policy: What have we learned?* Washington, DC: Migration Policy Institute.

Nielson, J. (2003). Labor mobility in regional trade agreements. In A. Mattoo and A. Carzaniga (eds), *Moving People to Deliver Services* (pp. 93–112). New York: Oxford University Press.

O'Neill, A. (2001). Emigrant remittances: Policies to increase inflows and maximize benefits. *Indiana Journal of Global Legal Studies*, 9(1), 345–360.

O'Rourke, K. (2009). The era of free migration: Lessons for today. In A. Sobel (ed.), *Challenge of Globalization: Immigration, social welfare, global governance* (pp. 58–77). London: Routledge.

O'Rourke, K. and Sinnott, R. (2009). The determinants of individual attitudes towards immigration. *European Journal of Political Economy*, 22(4), 838–861.

OECD (Organization of Economic Cooperation and Development). (2002). *Service Providers on the Move: Labor mobility and the WTO General Agreement on Trade and Services.* Paris: OECD.

OECD (Organization of Economic Cooperation and Development). (2003). *Service Providers on the Move: The economic impact of Mode 4, Working Party of the Trade Committee.* Paris: OECD.

OECD (Organization of Economic Cooperation and Development). (2011). *International Migration Outlook 2011.* Paris: OECD.

OECD (Organization of Economic Cooperation and Development). (2013). *International Migration Outlook 2013.* Paris: OECD.

OECD-UNDESA. (2013). *World Migration in Figures*, October. New York: United Nations Department of Economic and Social Affairs.

Ozden, C. and Reinhardt, E. (2002). *The Perversity of Preferences: The generalized system of preferences and developing country trade policies, 1976–2000.* World Bank Development Research Group. Washington, DC: World Bank.

Ozden, C., Rapoport, H., and Schiff, M. (2011). Five questions on international migration and development. *World Bank Economic Review*, 25(1), 1–12.

Page, J. and Plaza, S. (2006). Migration remittances and development: A review of global evidence. *Journal of African Economies*, 15(2), 245–336.

Piore, M. (1979). *Birds of Passage: Migrant labor in industrial societies.* Cambridge: Cambridge University Press.

Population Council. (2005). Report of the Global Commission on International Migration. *Population and Development Review*, 31(4), 787–798.

Pradhan, G., Upadhyay, M., and Upadhyaya, K. (2008). Remittances and economic growth in developing countries. *The European Journal of Development Research*, 20(3), 497–506.

Pritchett, L. (2006). *Let their People Come: Breaking the gridlock on international labor mobility.* Washington, DC: Center for Global Development.

Ranis, G. and and Fei, J. (1961). A theory of economic development. *American Economic Review*, 51(4), 533–565.

Ratha, D. (2007). *Leveraging Remittances for Development.* Migration Policy Institute. Washington, DC: World Bank.

Ratha, D. and Shaw, W. (2007). South–South migration. World Bank Working Paper No. 102. Washington, DC: World Bank.

Reich, M., Gordon, D., and Edwards, R. (1973). Dual labor markets: A theory of labor market segmentation. *American Economic Review*, 63(2), 359–365.

Reichlin, P. and Rustichini, A. (1998). Diverging patterns with endogenous labor migration. *Journal of Economic Dynamics and Control*, 22(5), 703–728.

Rodrik, D. (1997). *Has Globalization Gone Too Far?* Washington, DC: Institute of International Economics.

Rodrik, D. (2002). Final remarks. In T. Boeri, G. Hanson, and B. McCormick (eds), *Immigration Policy and the Welfare System* (pp. 314–317). Oxford: Oxford University Press.

Schiff, M. (1994). How trade, aid and remittances affect international migration. IMF Policy Research Working Paper No. 1376. Washington, DC: IMF.

Schiff, M. (2005). Brain gain: Claims about its size and impact on welfare and growth are greatly exaggerated. World Bank and IZA Discussion Paper No. 1599, May. Washington, DC:World Bank.

Silver, B. (2003). *Forces of Labor Workers' Movements and Globalization since 1870.* Cambridge: Cambridge University Press.

Sjaastad, L.A. (1962). The costs and returns of human migration. *Journal of Political Economy*, 70(5), 80–93.

Stahl, C. (1982). Labor emigration and economic development. *International Migration Review*, 16(4), 869–899.

Stahl, C. (1992). International labor migration and international development. ILO International Migration Working Paper. Geneva: International Migration Organization.

Stark, O., Helmenstein, C., and Prskawetz, A. (1997). A brain gain with a brain drain. *ECOLET*, 55(2), 227–234.

Stark, O. and Bloom, D. (1985). The new economics of migration. *American Economic Review*, 75(1), 191–196.

Stephenson, S. and Hufbauer, G. (2010). Increasing labor mobility: The options for developing countries. In O. Cattaneo *et al.* (eds), *International Trade in Services: New trends and opportunities for developing countries* (pp. 29–68). Washington, DC: World Bank.

Taylor, J., Massey, D., Arango, J., Hugo, G., Kouaouci, A., and Pellegrino, A. (1996). International migration and national development. *Population Index*, 62(3), 181–212.

Tinsabadh, C. (1989). Maximizing development benefits from labor migration: Thailand. In R. Amjad (ed.), *To the Gulf and Back: Studies on the economic impact of Asian labor migration* (pp. 304–343). Geneva: International Labor Organization.

Todaro, M. (1969). A model of labor migration and urban unemployment in less developed countries. *American Economic Review*, 59(1), 139–148.

UN (United Nations). (2002). *International Migration Report 2002*. UN Population Division. New York: United Nations.

UN (United Nations). (2008). *International Migration and Development: Report of the Secretary General*. Report No. A/63/265. New York: United Nations.

UNCTAD (United Nations Conference on Trade and Development). (2003). *Increasing the Participation of Developing Countries through Liberalization of Market Access in GATS Mode 4 for Movement of Natural Persons Supplying Services*. Geneva: UNCTAD/TD/B/COM.1/EM.22/2/2003.

UNCTAD (United Nations Conference on Trade and Development). (2005). *Trade in Services and Development Implications*. Geneva: UNCTAD/TD/B/COM.1/71/2005.

UNCTAD (United Nations Conference on Trade and Development). (2009). *Contribution of Migrants to Development: Trade, investment and development linkages*. Geneva: UNCTAD/DITC/TNCD/2009/2.

UNCTAD (United Nations Conference on Trade and Development). (2013). *World Investment Report 2013: Global value chains: Investment and trade for development*. New York and Geneva: United Nations Publications.

UNCTAD (United Nations Conference on Trade and Development). (2014). *Trade and Development Report, 2014*. New York and Geneva: United Nations Publications.

UNDESA (United Nations Department of Economic and Social Affairs). (2013a). *International Migration Report, 2013*. UNDESA-Population Division. New York: United Nations.

UNDESA (United Nations Department of Economic and Social Affairs). (2013b). *Trends in International Migration Stock. The 2013 revision of migrants by destination and origin*. UN Database, POP/DB/MIG/Stock/Rev.2013/Origin. UNDESA Population Division. New York: United Nations.

UNDP (United Nations Development Program). (2011). *Towards Human Resilience: Sustaining MDG progress in an age of economic uncertainty*. New York: United Nations.

UNFPA (United Nations Population Fund). (2014). *State of World Population 2014*. New York: United Nations.

Wallerstein, I. (1979). *The Capitalist World Economy*. Cambridge: Cambridge University Press.

Walmsley, T. and Winters, A. (2005). Relaxing the restrictions on the temporary movement of natural persons: A simulation analysis. *Journal of Economic Integration*, 20(4), 688–726.

Walmsley, T., Winters, L., Parsons, C., and Ahmed, S. (2005). GATS Mode 4: How trade in services can help developing countries. Quantifying the international bilateral movements of migrants. Briefing No. 4. Development Research Center, November.

Whalley, J. (1985). *Trade Liberalization among Major World Trading Areas*. Cambridge, MA: MIT Press.

Winters, A. and Mattoo, A. (2011). *Unfinished Business? The WTO's Doha Agenda*. Washington, DC: World Bank.

Winters, A., Walmsley, T., Wang, Z., and Grynberg, R. (2003). Liberalizing temporary movement of persons: An agenda for the development round. *World Economy*, 26(8), 1137–1161.

World Bank. (2003). *Global Economic Prospects: Realizing the development promises of the Doha Round.* Washington, DC: World Bank.

World Bank. (2005). *Global Economic Prospects: Trade, regionalism, and development.* Washington, DC: World Bank.

World Bank. (2006). *Global Economic Prospects, 2006: Economic implications of remittances and migration.* Washington, DC: World Bank.

World Bank. (2008). *Migration and Remittances Factbook, 2008.* Washington, DC: World Bank.

World Bank. (2009a). *World Development Indicators Database, 2009.* Washington, DC: World Bank.

World Bank. (2009b).The service revolution in South Asia. PREM, South Asia Region, June. Washington, DC: World Bank.

World Bank. (2010a). *Labor Migration from North Africa.* Volume 1, *Main Report. Middle East and North Africa Region.* Washington, DC: World Bank.

World Bank. (2010b). *Outlook for Remittances Flows 2011–12, Migration and Development Brief 13.* Migration and Remittances Unit. Washington, DC: World Bank.

World Bank. (2011a). *Migration and Remittances Factbook, 2011.* Washington, DC: World Bank.

World Bank. (2011b). *Outlook for Remittance Flows 2011–14.* Migration and Development Brief No. 17. Washington, DC: World Bank.

WTO (World Trade Organization). (2004). *World Trade Report: Exploring the linkage between the domestic policy environment and international trade.* Geneva: WTO.

WTO (World Trade Organization). (2005). WTO Staff Working Paper ERSD-2005–01. www.wto.org/english/tratop_e/serv_e/sym_april05_e/cossy_e.ppt–2005–05–13.

WTO (World Trade Organization). (2009). *International Trade Statistic 2009.* Geneva: WTO.

WTO (World Trade Organization). (2011). *World Trade Report 2011.* Geneva: WTO.

WTO (World Trade Organization). (2012). WTO ministers adopt waiver to permit preferential treatment of LDC service suppliers. Available online at: http://wto.org/english/news_e/news11_e/serv_17dec11_e.htm (accessed February 27, 2014).

WTO (World Trade Organization). (2014). *Annual Report 2014.* Geneva: WTO.

5 Concluding remarks

Introduction

The international trading system has never been more liberalized, more globalized, and less discriminatory than it is today. Much of the credit for such a phenomenal achievement may presumably be attributed to the multilateral trading system that evolved under the auspices of the General Agreement on Tariff and Trade (GATT) during the 1947 to 1994 period, and its successor, the World Trade Organization (WTO), since 1995. Even in the sixteenth through the eighteenth centuries, international trade was dominated by mercantilist regimes, characterized by archaic policies of protections, economic nationalism, and self-sufficiency. Mercantilist trading regimes flourished principally through the acquisition of colonies, which brought unprecedented prosperity for many European colonial powers at the expense of the rest of the world. In the nineteenth century the world began to witness a movement toward more liberal trade regimes, but experienced formidable setbacks in the 1870s and 1930s. It is since World War II that the world has been witnessing a sustained drive toward a more liberalized and more globalized international trading system under the GATT-WTO trade regimes.

The GATT, however, concentrated primarily on manufactures—especially on products of exports interests to the developed countries. Successive rounds of GATT negotiations succeeded in bringing down tariff barriers significantly for global trade in manufactures. But trade in textiles and clothing (T&C)—a manufacturing activity in which the developing countries had exports interests—experienced movement in the opposite direction. The sector was systematically subjected to widespread protectionist measures in developed countries ostensibly to limit exports from developing countries. Similarly, the agricultural sector, in which developing countries had dominant exports interests, remained almost completely outside multilateral trade rules and disciplines, and was subjected to massive domestic supports, export subsidies as well as other protectionist measures in developed countries.

It was the WTO, the successor of the GATT, which for the first time in world history brought all international trade sectors—agriculture, manufacturing, and services—into strengthened GATT disciplines and principles in 1995. The WTO also emerged as the most powerful regulatory and watchdog agency unparalleled in world history. The WTO, however, does not guarantee unfettered free trade—it rather provides a platform for multilateral trade negotiations (MTNs), where members exchange liberalization commitments, and the outcome of such negotiations depends largely on member countries' market power and negotiation capabilities.

Agriculture

Bringing the agricultural sector into the strengthened GATT discipline has been one of the hallmark achievements of the Uruguay Round (1986–1994)—the last round of MTNs under the GATT. Prior to that, in the absence of international rules and disciplines, and also because of the sensitive character of agriculture and food, both the developed and developing countries adopted elaborate protectionist measures in order to shelter their agriculture from international competition. Ironically, while developed countries provided massive doses of domestic supports to their farmers, developing countries taxed their farmers. The Uruguay Round Agreement on Agriculture (URAA) granted a 10-year transition period for the liberalization of the sector by 2005. With the implementation of the agreement, non-tariff barriers in agriculture were transformed into tariffication, domestic supports and trade distorting subsidies were reduced significantly, and overall support measures in the sector were made more transparent than before. At the same time, international trade in agriculture has expanded substantially since the mid-1990s, reflecting increased globalization, integration of new participants in world markets, and considerable liberalization of global agricultural markets. The share of developing countries in global production and exports of agricultural goods, including processed products, is now on the rise.

The agricultural sector, however, still remains far from full-scale liberalization—much of the sector is still sheltered by protectionist measures, such as producer supports, export subsidies, commodity supports, high bound tariffs, tariff peaks, tariff rate quotas, tariff escalations, and so on. Even applied MFN tariffs in agriculture are still three times higher compared with those in the manufacturing sector. Considerable ambiguities still remain with regard to indispensable characteristics of the Green box, Amber box, and Blue box measures. Moreover, domestic supports to agriculture in the powerhouses of agriculture—the EU and the US—are still around one-fifth of farmers' income, which raises question about the compliance of these countries with WTO commitments. The cost of such widespread protections in agricultural trade has been staggering in terms of lost income and welfare to the developing countries as well as to the world economy.

Projected welfare benefits of the further liberalization of agriculture for the world economy is believed to be the largest among all sectors of international trade, as the manufacturing sector has already been liberalized to a great extent, and liberalization of the service sector is possible only to a certain extent. Developing countries would benefit from further tariff reforms in agriculture, as it would enhance their market access to developed country markets. With the removal of subsidies in the developed countries, terms of trade for the developing countries would be worsened as prices of currently subsidized exports would rise, but, in the end, expected benefits would far outweigh costs for the developing countries from the further liberalization of agricultural trade, especially in terms of the employment of unskilled labor, income of their farmers, and an increased share in global exports.

The developing countries thus have a major stake in the further liberalization of the agricultural sector. Any future WTO negotiations on domestic support reduction should focus on closing the built-in loopholes of the URAA—by making domestic support reductions both product and non-product specific, targeting commodities in which domestic subsidies are highly concentrated in the developed countries, adopting a more effective base period for the AMS calculation and making such calculations adjustable to inflation and exchange rates, and further specifying essential characteristics of agricultural policies attributable to various support boxes. Developing countries should also focus on reforming their own economies—as reaping greater benefits from a liberalized agriculture would substantially hinge on the extent to which they liberalize their own economies.

Textiles and clothing

One of the crowning achievements of the Uruguay Round Agreement was full integration of the T&C sector into the strengthened GATT discipline through a 10-year transition period under the Agreement on Textiles and Clothing (ATC). Similarly, bringing a determined end to the 40-year streak of the discriminatory and protectionist MFA regimes, through the full and faithful implementation of the ATC without any extension, has been a historic achievement of the WTO. As a result, international trade in the T&C sector is now as free as any other manufacturing sector in the world. The tides unleashed by the liberalization has been sweeping the world since the very beginning of the phasing out of the MFA regimes. Developing countries, demonstrating their natural competitive advantage in this labor-intensive sector, emerged as the leading exporters of T&C products by the mid-1990s, and the trend continues. While hitherto dominant developed countries lost their shares in global exports and experienced massive unemployment, in the developing countries production, exports, and employment in the sector are on the rise. At the same time, the global market is now more competitive than ever before, T&C prices fell sharply, production soared, and consumers are better off across the world. The principle of comparative advantage that underpins mutually beneficial international trade on the basis of lower opportunity costs stands fully vindicated once again.

Although predictions of many doomsayers did not come true, the experience over the course of the past two decades, since the beginning of integration of the T&C sector into the GATT discipline, does indicate that all developing county T&C exporters did not do equally well—rising tides did not raise all boats. While some developing countries, especially Asia, succeeded in increasing their

T&C exports without preferential market access, others with preferential access, especially in Latin America and Africa, experienced a decline in their exports. This experience demonstrates that factors like the availability of low-cost labor, proximity to buyers' markets, dependence on assembly-type production systems, preferential rules of origin that prohibit the use of competitive inputs, and so on may not guarantee success in an environment of fiercely competitive and fully liberalized international trading systems in the T&C sector. The experience with the liberalization of the sector also indicates that developing countries that are well positioned to reap the benefits of a liberalized trading system are those which are capable of supplementing low-wage labor with better backward linkages, reduce value additions from imports, improve turn-over time, integrate advanced technology in the production processes, and move into higher value-added products through global value chains.

Some LDCs, however, appear to be doing exceedingly well by utilizing preferential or duty-free access to developed country markets. These countries may face very serious erosion of preference margins, and such margins may even disappear if the Doha Round negotiations on NAMA tariff reductions materialize. Many of these countries also depend on an assembly-type production system and significantly high levels of imported materials, which inevitably lead to smaller value addition to their GDPs. These countries need to develop backward linkages to reduce their dependence on imports, and move to higher value-addition products in order to be competitive in the preference-eroded or preference-free trade regimes in the future. The experience of Sub-Saharan countries, which all but lost their T&C sectors with the phasing out of quota restrictions, does provide useful lessons as well. Foreign investors rushed into these countries to take advantage of unused or underused quotas, but then pulled out their investments when quota hopping became unnecessary. Obviously, the interests of host countries played little role in the investment decisions of some foreign investors.

It is also clear that despite unprecedented liberalization, average tariffs in the T&C sector are still much higher than average tariffs in other manufacturing sectors, and the sector still faces numerous tariff peaks and tariff escalations. Moreover, this sector also faces significant non-tariff barriers, such as non-harmonized rules of origin, non-universalized customs and documentation formalities, non-uniform classification practices with respect to many products, and other social and environmental requirements. At the same time, the global value chain in this sector remains under firm control of oligarchic multinational businesses, whose efforts to squeeze the profits of developing country apparel exporters often result in poorer working conditions for T&C workers. Developing countries thus have high stakes in WTO negotiations in the T&C sector in the future.

Cross-border labor mobility

Currently, only about 3.2 percent of the world population is considered a migrant population, and global labor mobility—no matter whether permanent or temporary—remains a highly contentious and politically sensitive issue all over the world. The world population is projected to increase to 8.1 billion by 2025, and to 9.6 billion by 2050, from the current level of 7.2 billion. Almost all the additional people are expected to enlarge the population of the developing countries, which is projected to rise from 5.9 billion in 2013 to 8.2 billion in 2050. At the same time, the population of the developed part of the world is expected to age and decline. Such a dramatic transformation in demographics around the world is very likely to result in a much higher demand and supply of cross-border labor mobility in both the short and long term.

Available literature suggests a basic convergence of economic interests between the developed (labor-scarce) and the developing (labor-surplus) countries for greater cross-border labor mobility. With remittances emerging as a formidable source of external finance, labor-surplus developing countries do have a significant interest in boosting labor exports. Developed countries also have a considerable interest in the greater utilization of foreign labor as their populations are aging, and many of their service sector jobs are becoming less appealing to a domestic labor force.

At the same time, labor is not a value-neutral commodity—people tend to accept foreign-made goods more easily and comfortably than foreign nationals delivering a service or living in their midst. Although the China Wall and the Egyptian pyramids were not built without migrant labor, labor migration entails contentious social, cultural, and political debates in both the developed and developing countries. Labor-sending developing countries are also becoming increasingly concerned by what is called the brain-drain—the net transfer of human capital and scare resources from low-income countries to the developed countries as their tertiary educated skilled workers migrate. Although some literature sheds light on the beneficial effects to labor-sending countries in the form of counter-flows of remittances, incentives to accumulate human capital, investments, trade relations, knowledge and technology transfers, and innovations, the balance between the brain-drain and brain-gain remains a highly perplexing and controversial issue.

Coming into such a backdrop, the GATS Mode-4—the temporary movement of natural persons across borders as service suppliers—should be seen as a unique window of opportunity for both sides to reap the benefits of greater labor mobility without being burdened by the usual baggage associated with permanent migration. As labor must return after the contract—as opposed to permanent or other forms of migration, which are generally plagued with politically sensitive and economically significant controversial affects—GATS Mode-4 may also be viewed as a great compromise for the liberalization of temporary cross-border labor mobility.

Although not much progress has been made under the current Doha Round in respect of GATS Mode-4, available evidence suggests that there has been a considerable increase in the temporary movement of professionals across borders—both on a bilateral and multilateral basis. The bilateral flows have largely been engineered by immigration policies in certain developed countries, and multilateral flows have been taking place under the auspices of various regional trade agreements (RTAs). With the Doha Round clinically dead, the examples provided by RTAs may be deemed building blocks to promote greater liberalization of the temporary movement of natural persons across borders. In particular, the examples set by some of the leading RTAs, such as NAFTA and Canadian FTAs, can serve as models for the liberalization of cross-border mobility among countries having geographical and cultural proximity, strong similarities in GDPs, and major differences in factor endowments.

Available economic research seems to be upbeat about the potential benefits of the greater liberalization of cross-border labor mobility. Political support is also being mounted all over the world, as indicated by the robust programs offered by several RTAs. The only downside is that developed countries are deliberately skewing their immigration policies to encourage the selective migration of skilled labor, while developing countries would benefit the most from the migration of their unskilled labor. That makes it imperative for the WTO to develop a fully functional multilateral platform for systematic and rule-based global labor mobility under GATS Mode-4.

Conclusions

In sum, the world has been witnessing a sustained development toward a more liberalized and more globalized international trading system since the end of World War II. Much of the credits for the scale, depth, and magnitude of liberalization and globalization may be attributed to the multilateral trading system that evolved under the auspices of the GATT and its successor, the WTO. While the GATT focused mainly on the manufacturing sector and thus on the exports interests of the developed countries, the WTO that replaced it in the mid-1990s made a far-reaching difference by embracing all international trade sectors—agriculture, manufacturing, as well as services. The WTO also comes with strengthened multilateral trade disciplines and principles, along with stronger regulatory and watchdog powers unparalleled in world history.

Such a comprehensive and all-encompassing mandate and scope of the WTO raises the stakes for all countries in multilateral trade negotiations and agreements, but it does so more strikingly for the less developed countries. The reasons are quite obvious. First, the WTO, despite its enormous outreach and sharper teeth, by itself does not guarantee unfettered free trade—it rather provides a global platform for multilateral trade negotiations, where the bargaining and negotiation outcome largely depends on member countries' global market power. Second, the less developed countries have a huge stake in the evolving multilateral trading system under the WTO also because of the fact that all three trading sectors in which they enjoy a competitive advantage—agriculture, textiles and clothing, and cross-border labor mobility—still remain less liberalized than the sectors in which developed countries have exports interests.

Finally, in this increasingly globalized and integrated world economy, survival and economic growth of the less developed countries will depend not only on success in international trade, but also squarely on securing beneficial deals in multilateral trade agreements under the WTO. Developing countries must strengthen their capabilities for articulating their positions and making well-organized representations to the WTO negotiations. At the same time, the WTO itself must also undertake fundamental reforms, especially in respect of its decision-making processes, to ensure greater accommodation of the interests of the less developed countries and more transparent multilateral trade negotiations in the future.

Index

Page numbers in *italics* denote tables, those in **bold** denote figures.

For Product Safety Concerns and Information please contact our EU representative GPSR@taylorandfrancis.com Taylor & Francis Verlag GmbH, Kaufingerstraße 24, 80331 München, Germany